MASTERING SPANISH

LAUREL H. TURK
DePauw University

AURELIO M. ESPINOSA, JR.
Stanford University

D. C. HEATH AND COMPANY
Lexington, Massachusetts   Toronto   London

SECOND EDITION

MASTERING

SPANISH

International Standard Book Number: 0-669-94425-4

Library of Congress Catalog Card Number: 74-4733

PREFACE

Mastering Spanish, Second Edition, is a second-year college program. It is designed to further the development of the language through review of the fundamentals of Spanish structure, to emphasize oral and reading comprehension, and to provide opportunity for self-expression in speaking and writing. Students who have completed one year of college Spanish or its equivalent in secondary school will find additional material which is essential for a good command of the language.

To fulfill these aims, the text consists of three *Repasos,* twelve regular lessons, *Lecturas,* an art section, a section on Spanish letter writing, five appendices, and end vocabularies. The maps and illustrations provide the basis for a great variety of topics which supplement the material on the cultural background of the Spanish-American countries. Throughout the text, emphasis is placed on the acquisition of a practical vocabulary and on the active use of the language. The dialogues, which introduce the *Repasos* and regular lessons, deal with situations from daily life and are within the experience of present-day students.

Mastering Spanish is a continuation of Turk and Espinosa, *Foundation Course in Spanish, Third Edition,* Heath, 1974. However, it is written so that it may be used as a logical extension of most basic, first-year programs. It provides ample material for a one-semester course which meets four times per week. In a course meeting three days per week, some of the exercises and/or *Lecturas* may be omitted without detriment to the over-all effectiveness of the text. If it is used in conjunction with other reading material in addition to the *Lecturas,* it may be necessary to carry over a few lessons into the second semester or even to spread them through the whole year.

The three *Repasos* are devoted largely to a review of all the simple and compound indicative tenses and of formal singular and plural and familiar singular command forms of the verb. This stress on verb forms is recognized as a necessity if the student is to gain complete mastery of the language. Each of the three reviews consists of a dialogue, with a section of oral exercises, a section on pronunciation, a verb review including varied drill exercises, and finally, a vocabulary list, which includes a few individual words and all the idiomatic phrases and expressions used in the dialogue and other parts of the lesson. In addition to the specific focus on developing a firm command of the verb forms, the *Repasos* contain strategies to facilitate and to reinforce comprehension and speaking. In *Repaso primero* the second part of the section of oral exercises consists of a series of questions in Spanish based on the dialogue, followed by others which represent an application of the dialogue. In *Repaso dos* the second part contains a list of words and expressions to be substituted in the dialogue or used in a new dialogue based on the model; this list alternates from one lesson to the next with two sets of initial exchanges for use in preparing an original dialogue. The entire verb review contained in these three lessons may be taken up before *Lección primera*, or certain sections may be assigned in conjunction with the regular lessons.

The twelve regular lessons contain: (1) a practical dialogue, with a section of oral exercises; (2) a section on pronunciation and intonation (through *Lección nueve*); (3) *Notas gramaticales*, with *Ejercicios* placed after the explanation of grammatical points; (4) a *Resumen*, which offers additional oral drills and short English sentences to be expressed in Spanish, and which summarizes the major points taken up in the lesson; and (5) a summary list of new words and expressions. A reading selection (*Lectura*) follows each lesson.

Throughout the text the headings as well as the directions are given in Spanish. In the *Pronunciación* and *Notas gramaticales* sections, however, the explanations are given in English to ensure comprehension. Additional grammatical terms and expressions for use in the classroom and laboratory are listed in Appendix B.

The pronunciation material constitutes a basic and effective survey of Spanish phonology. This section is included through *Lección nueve* to ensure that the student will continue to apply the principles involved in good Spanish pronunciation.

The *Notas gramaticales* give a systematic, logical, and pragmatic review of the fundamentals of Spanish structure. They are advanced in scope and include points frequently omitted in other texts. However, they retain their basic nature and emphasize general practice rather than exceptions. An important feature of the *Notas gramaticales* is that each major structure is immediately followed by appropriate and adequate drills. Wherever feasible, these exercises are devised so that they may be done orally by the student. The device of placing the exercises immediately after the grammatical summary enables the student to center his attention on the particular point under discussion and to review a maximum number of points in a relatively short time. This method of presentation also permits an easy division of each lesson into assignments. The sentences in the exercises are purposely kept short to encourage rapid drill work. The vocabulary of the drills is most often limited to words of high frequency, permitting the student to focus on the structure under consideration.

The *Lecturas* present reading and conversational material which is topically related to the dialogue of each lesson. The content of these narratives should be of interest to college students of today and at the same time should serve to widen their active vocabularies in Spanish. The meanings of certain new words, of idiomatic expressions not previously introduced, and of a limited number of difficult phrases or expressions are given in footnotes. The *Lecturas* are followed by exercises in which stress is again placed on developing expression and fostering the student's ability to use Spanish.

The sixteen-page section in full color on painting in Spanish America and the accompanying essay are a special feature of the book. (Spanish art is featured in *Foundation Course in Spanish*). Black and white illustrations supplement the information included in the *Lecturas*. All illustrations may serve as topical bases for oral and written expression.

For those who may wish to carry on social or commercial correspondence in Spanish, some commonly used phrases and formulas are given in the special section on letter writing, called *Cartas españolas*.

Appendix A contains a summary of Spanish pronunciation, with an explanation of terms used; Appendix B includes lists of expressions used in the classroom and the laboratory, grammatical terms, punctuation marks, and the abbreviations and signs used in the text; Appendix C gives the cardinal and ordinal numerals, the days of the week, the months of the year, the seasons, dates, and ways to express the time of day; Appendix D contains the regular verb paradigms and complete lists of verbs with various types of irregularity used in the text, as well as a few additional verbs which may be encountered in later study of Spanish; and Appendix E includes lists of verbs which are followed immediately by an infinitive without a preposition, verbs which require certain prepositions before an infinitive, and verbs used in the text whose meanings change when used reflexively.

The Spanish–English vocabulary is intended to be complete with the exception of a few proper and geographical names which are either identical in Spanish and English or whose meaning is clear, a few past participles used as adjectives when the infinitive is given, some of the titles of literary and artistic works mentioned in the *Lecturas*, the Spanish examples translated in the *Cartas españolas* section, and a few diminutives given in *Lección diez*. Idioms are listed under the most important word in the phrase, and, in most cases, cross listings are given. Irregular plural forms of nouns and adjectives are included only for those forms which are used in the plural in the text. The English–Spanish vocabulary contains only the English words used in the English–Spanish exercises.

In this edition of *Mastering Spanish*, three *Repasos* replace the former four preliminary lessons. The dialogues have been revised and reorganized and the content changed in some of them. The section of oral exercises in each lesson has been expanded to provide more oral practice for the student, particularly in preparing original dialogues and conversations. The pronunciation section, expanded through *Lección nueve* in order to include in *Lección ocho* items on intonation previously contained in one of the preliminary lessons, remains essentially unchanged. An effort has been made to clarify a few of the more difficult matters taken up in the *Notas gramaticales*. The drill exercises, both oral and written, remain essentially the same as in the first edition, although some of the English-to-Spanish sentences have been eliminated. The summary list of words and expressions included at the end of each lesson should serve as a valuable review for students and should avoid much vocabulary thumbing. Twelve relatively short *Lecturas* replace the six longer ones of the earlier edition. As stated earlier, the content of each is closely related to that of the previous lesson dialogue. The section on letter writing has been expanded in this edition.

The *Workbook* has been completely revised. The exercises, which have been rewritten, differ from those in the text, including the ones for the *Lecturas*. Thus, the book offers a wide variety of additional drills on all the major structures. A feature of the new edition of the *Workbook* is the inclusion of five comprehensive tests, each of which covers a unit of three lessons.

As an aid to the teacher and student, an innovative tape program accompanies the text, covering the dialogues, most of the oral exercises, and the *Lecturas*. A comprehension exercise, based on each *Lectura,* has been included in the tape for each regular lesson and for the comprehensive tests; space is provided in the *Workbook* for the student's responses. The exercise consists of true-false statements, sentences to be completed in Spanish, questions to be answered in complete Spanish sentences, etc. The teacher who does not use the *Workbook* may want to duplicate, for students who listen to the tapes, the sections in the *Workbook* provided for these exercises.

In the preparation of this edition the authors wish to express their deep appreciation for the valuable suggestions and constructive criticism offered by colleagues who have used the earlier edition, and by Mario E. Hurtado, Project Editor, of the Modern Language Department of D. C. Heath and Company.

L.H.T.
A.M.E., Jr.

CONTENTS

x

MAPS

ADDITIONAL MATERIALS:

Workbook and Testing Program

Tapes
  Number of reels: 8 7" double track
  Speed   3 3/4 ips
  Running time: 8 hours (approximately)
  Also available in 8 cassettes

MASTERING SPANISH

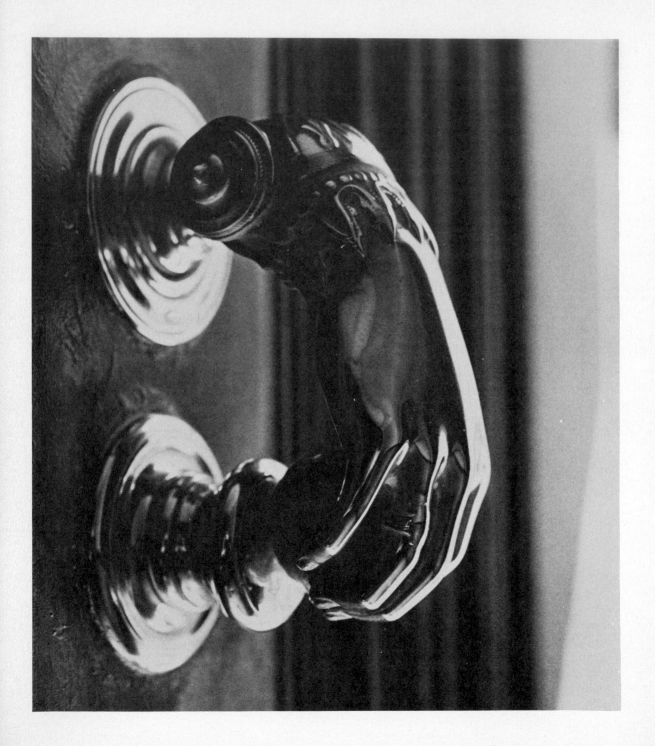

REPASO PRIMERO

Presente de indicativo de los verbos regulares.   Verbos que tienen
formas irregulares en el presente de indicativo.   Verbos que cambian
la vocal radical en el presente de indicativo.   Formas de mandato
correspondientes a «usted, ustedes».   Formas de mandato
correspondientes a «tú»

En el Departamento de Español

(*Carlos habla con la secretaria del Departamento de Español.*)

Carlos.	Buenos días, señorita Flores. ¿Puede decirme si el profesor Valdés está en su oficina?
Srta. Flores.	Creo que sí, Carlos. Siéntese usted, por favor. Voy a ver si puede recibirle. (*Al poco tiempo entra el señor Valdés.*)
Sr. Valdés.	¡Hola, Carlos! ¿Me busca usted?
Carlos.	Sí, señor. Quiero saber si me permite usted asistir a su clase de español este semestre.
Sr. Valdés.	¡Cómo no! Con mucho gusto. ¿Prefiere usted la sección de las nueve o la de las doce?
Carlos.	Mi novia va a estar en la sección de las nueve . . .
Sr. Valdés.	En ese caso le conviene la sección de las doce, ¿verdad? (*Se dirige a la secretaria.*) Traiga las listas de las clases, señorita Flores.
Srta. Flores.	Aquí las tiene usted. Hay más de veinte estudiantes en la sección de las doce y unos trece en la de las nueve.
Sr. Valdés.	A ver si puedo admitirle en la sección de las doce. Cuente los nombres otra vez.
Srta. Flores.	Hay veinte y seis en la sección de las doce y trece en la otra.
Sr. Valdés.	(*Con ironía.*) Bueno, Carlos, ¿qué le vamos a hacer? Haga el favor de añadir su nombre a la lista de la sección de las nueve.
Carlos.	¡Caramba! ¡Qué suerte tengo! Muchas gracias, señor Valdés.

1

A. Aprendan el diálogo de memoria (*Memorize the dialogue*) para poder repetirlo con el profesor (la profesora) o con algunos de sus compañeros.

B. Para contestar en español en oraciones (*sentences*) completas:

Preguntas sobre el diálogo

1. ¿Cómo se llama la secretaria del Departamento de Español?   2. ¿Qué le pregunta Carlos a la señorita Flores?   3. ¿Qué contesta la señorita Flores?   4. ¿Qué quiere saber Carlos?   5. ¿Cuál de las dos secciones prefiere Carlos?   6. ¿Por qué quiere estar en esa sección?   7. ¿Cuántos estudiantes hay en la sección de las nueve?   8. ¿Qué decide hacer el profesor Valdés?

Aplicación del diálogo

1. ¿Cómo está usted?   2. ¿Cómo se llama el profesor (la profesora) de esta clase?   3. ¿A qué hora empieza esta clase?   4. ¿Cuántos estudiantes hay en esta clase?   5. ¿Qué estudiamos en esta clase?   6. Si usted llega tarde, ¿le permite entrar el profesor?

Pronunciación

American-Spanish pronunciation. The differences in pronunciation between American Spanish and Castilian or Peninsular Spanish are matters of some concern to teachers and students of Spanish. Since Spanish is spoken in so many different areas, it is only natural that there should be differences from country to country. In general, however, the pronunciation of educated persons differs only in two important respects:

a. In American Spanish (and also in southern Spain), **c** before **e** or **i**, and **z**, are not pronounced as interdental *th* (as in northern and central Spain) but as a dental **s**,[1] not unlike the English *s* in *sent*.

b. In some parts of Spain and quite generally in Spanish America, **ll** (pronounced somewhat like *lli* in *million* in other parts of Spain) is pronounced as the *y* sound in *yes*, with somewhat stronger friction than in English *y*.

In both cases the two variants are accepted as standard forms of pronunciation. Because of the geographic situation of our country in the Western Hemisphere, it seems natural to use the so-called American-Spanish pronunciation of these sounds in this book.

[1] A few basic phonetic terms will be introduced in this text to allow for greater accuracy in the description of Spanish speech sounds. For a definition of the terms used, see Appendix A, pages 292–294.

Certain other traits of American Spanish (and of some parts of Spain) are considered popular or regional and are generally avoided by educated persons. Some of these are: aspiration of s final in the word or syllable, that is, to pronounce s in such circumstances as English h: **ehtoh campoh** for **estos campos;** confusion of l and r when final in the word or syllable: **comel** for **comer;** pronunciation of y (and ll) as English z in *azure;* retention of aspirate h, as in Old Spanish: **jumo** for **humo** (with silent h); pronunciation of Spanish j and g before e or i as English h. All these forms should be carefully avoided.

Review the sounds of **c** before **e** or **i,** of **s,** and of **y** (Appendix A, pages 296–298) and pronounce after your teacher:

1. difícil	hacer	necesitar	oficina	lección
2. almorzar	empezar	comienza	razón	conduzco *to drive, conduct*
3. caballo	ellos	hallar *to find*	llegar	llover
4. ayer	leyendo	yo	y ella	y usted
5. semestre	asistir	vender	humo *smoke*	jamón

"s"

To help you understand and use Spanish more readily, you will need to review some of the verbs and expressions used earlier in your study of the language.

Para repasar
(*For review*)

I. Repaso de las formas del presente de indicativo de los verbos regulares

In Appendix D, page 314, review the forms of the present indicative tense of regular verbs. Some common verbs are:

comprar   *to buy*
esperar   *to wait (for), hope*
hablar   *to speak, talk*
llevar   *to take, carry*

mirar   *to look (at)*
necesitar   *to need*
tomar   *to take, drink, eat*
trabajar   *to work*

aprender (a + *inf.*)   *to learn*
  (*to + inf.*)
comer   *to eat*

comprender   *to understand*
vender   *to sell*

abrir   *to open*
escribir   *to write*

permitir   *to permit, allow*
vivir   *to live*

a. Repitan la frase; luego, al oír un sujeto nuevo, substitúyanlo en la frase, cambiando la forma del verbo cuando sea necesario:

1. *Los estudiantes* toman café.
   (*Yo, Jorge y yo, Tú, Usted, Ustedes, Ana y María*)
2. *José* aprende a hablar español.
   (*José y yo, Yo, Ustedes, Tú, Ramón y Luis, Ella*)
3. ¿Abres *tú* las ventanas?
   (*ustedes, yo, Carolina, los muchachos, tú y yo, él*)

b. Para contestar afirmativamente[1] en español:

1. ¿Hablan ustedes español?
2. ¿Espera Elena el autobús?
3. ¿Necesitan ellos más tiempo?
4. ¿Compran ustedes muchas cosas?
5. ¿Aprenden ustedes a hablar bien?
6. ¿Come Luisa a las seis?
7. ¿Abren ustedes la puerta a veces?
8. ¿Escribo yo en la pizarra?

c. Para contestar negativamente[1] en español:

1. ¿Compras papel en la biblioteca?
2. ¿Espera Ricardo a Marta?
3. ¿Comes temprano todas las noches?
4. ¿Comen ustedes con Bárbara?
5. ¿Escriben ustedes el diálogo?
6. ¿Escribo yo una composición?

II. Algunos verbos que tienen formas irregulares en el presente de indicativo

Some common verbs with irregular forms in the present indicative are:

decir	*to say, tell*	**digo**	**dices**	**dice**	decimos	decís	**dicen**
estar	*to be*	**estoy**	**estás**	**está**	estamos	estáis	**están**
haber	*to have* (aux.)	**he**	**has**	**ha**	**hemos**	habéis	**han**
ir	*to go*	**voy**	**vas**	**va**	**vamos**	vais	**van**
oír	*to hear*	**oigo**	**oyes**	**oye**	**oímos**	oís	**oyen**
poder	*to be able, can*	**puedo**	**puedes**	**puede**	podemos		
		podéis	**pueden**				

---

[1] Adverbs of manner are often formed by adding **-mente** to the feminine singular of adjectives.

querer *to wish, want*   **quiero quieres quiere** queremos
                         queréis **quieren**
ser *to be*   **soy eres es somos sois son**
tener *to have, possess*   **tengo tienes tiene** tenemos tenéis
                         tienen
venir *to come*   **vengo vienes viene** venimos venís
                         vienen

A number of irregular verbs have regular forms in the present indicative
tense, except in the first person singular: **caer**, *to fall* (**caigo**); **dar**, *to give*
(**doy**); **hacer**, *to do, make* (**hago**); **poner**, *to put, place* (**pongo**); **saber**, *to
know* (a fact) (**sé**); **salir**, *to go out, leave* (**salgo**); **traer**, *to bring* (**traigo**);
valer, *to be worth* (**valgo**); **ver**, *to see* (**veo**). Also irregular only in the first
person singular are **conducir**, *to drive, conduct* (**conduzco**); **conocer**, *to
know* (a person) (**conozco**); **escoger**, *to choose* (**escojo**).

See Appendix D, page 326, for accented forms in the present indicative tense of **enviar**, *to send*, and **continuar**, *to continue*, and for forms
of verbs ending in **-uir**: **huir**, *to flee*.

a. Repitan la frase; luego, repítanla otra vez, cambiando el sujeto y el
verbo al plural.

MODELOS: Yo puedo ir.   Yo puedo ir.
                                     Nosotros podemos ir.

          ¿Tiene usted mucho   ¿Tiene usted mucho tiempo?
            tiempo?   ¿Tienen ustedes mucho tiempo?

                     often
1. Yo doy paseos a menudo.   7. ¿Ve usted a Margarita?
2. ¿Qué quiere usted hacer?   8. Yo los pongo en el coche.
3. ¿Conoce ella a mi tío?   9. ¿Puede él esperar aquí?
4. Él tiene mucha suerte.   10. ¿Le envía usted algo a Inés?
5. Yo les traigo regalos a veces.   11. Mi hermana oye la música.
6. ¿Dónde está ella ahora?   12. Yo escojo muchas cosas.

b. Lean en español, supliendo (*supplying*) la forma correcta del verbo
entre paréntesis en el presente de indicativo:

1. (decir) ¿Qué le _____ tú a Juan? —Yo no le _____ nada.   2. (estar)
                                                  near
¿Dónde _____ yo ahora? —Usted _____ cerca de la mesa.   3. (poder)
¿_____ ustedes esperar unos minutos? —Sí, _____ esperar un rato.

4. (hacer) ¿Qué _____ usted esta tarde? —No _____ nada.   5. (ver) ¿_____ ustedes estos mapas? —Sí, los _____ bien.   6. (saber) ¿_____ usted si mi novia está en la clase? —No, no _____ si ella está en la clase.   7. (conocer) ¿_____ tú a mi tía? —Sí, la _____ muy bien.   8. (salir) ¿_____ yo de casa temprano? —Sí, usted _____ a las siete y media.   9. (ir) ¿_____ usted a asistir a esta clase? —Sí, _____ a asistir a esta clase este semestre.   10. (venir) ¿Quién _____ a ayudar a Pablo? —Yo _____ a ayudarle esta noche.   11. (ser) ¿_____ tú estudiante? —Sí, _____ estudiante de esta universidad.   12. (continuar) ¿_____ ustedes leyendo la novela? —Sí, _____ leyendo varias páginas cada día.

c. Para expresar en español:

1. I leave at a quarter after eight.   2. I don't know whether John is coming.   3. I see many cars in the street.   4. I go to the library.   5. I choose several books.   6. I put the books on the table.   7. We hear the music.   8. We bring records to class.   9. We are lucky.   10. Do you (*fam. sing.*) want to attend this class?   11. Do you (*fam. sing.*) say that the secretary is in the office?   12. Do you (*pl.*) say that you can wait a few minutes?

III. Verbos que cambian la vocal radical (*Stem-changing verbs*)

Some verbs of Class I are:

almorzar (ue)   *to take (eat) lunch*
cerrar (ie)   *to close*
comenzar (ie)   *to commence, begin*
contar (ue)   *to count; to tell*
despertar (ie)   *to awaken; wake up*
devolver (ue)   *to return, give back*

empezar (ie)   *to begin*
encontrar (ue)   *to encounter, find*
jugar (ue)   *to play* (a game)
pensar (ie)   *to think:* + inf. *to intend*
perder (ie)   *to lose, miss*
recordar (ue)   *to recall, remember*
sentarse (ie)   *to sit down*
volver (ue)   *to return, come back*

cerrar: **cierro   cierras   cierra**   cerramos   cerráis   **cierran**
volver: **vuelvo   vuelves   vuelve**   volvemos   volvéis   **vuelven**
jugar: **juego   juegas   juega**   jugamos   jugáis   **juegan**

Some Class II verbs are:

divertirse (ie, i) *to have a good*   sentir (ie, i) *to feel, regret, be*
  time, amuse oneself   *sorry*
preferir (ie, i) *to prefer*   dormir (ue, u) *to sleep*

sentir: **siento sientes siente** sentimos sentís **sienten**
dormir: **duermo duermes duerme** dormimos dormís **duermen**

Some Class III verbs are: *(e changes to i)*

conseguir[1] (i, i) *to get, obtain*   seguir[1] (i, i) *to follow, continue*
pedir (i, i) *to ask (for), request*   servir (i, i) *to serve*
reír (i, i) *to laugh*   vestirse (i, i) *to dress oneself,*
repetir (i, i) *to repeat*   *get dressed*

pedir: **pido pides pide** pedimos pedís **piden**
reír: **río ríes ríe** reímos reís **ríen**

a. Repitan la frase; luego, al oír un sujeto nuevo, substitúyanlo en la frase, cambiando la forma del verbo cuando sea necesario:

1. *Jaime* empieza a leer el diálogo.
   (*Yo, Vicente y yo, Ellos, Tú, Enrique, Usted y él*)
2. *Nuestros amigos* lo sienten mucho.
   (*Mi hermana, Tú, Yo, Dorotea y yo, Mis tíos, Usted*)
3. ¿Juegan *ustedes* al fútbol?
   (*usted, tú, Ramón y Luis, nosotros, yo, tu hermano*)
4. ¿Cuánto tiempo duerme *Juanita*?
   (*tú, yo, ustedes, tu hermanito, él y yo, los niños*)
5. ¿Le pide *usted* a Clara un favor?
   (*Isabel, tú, yo, ellos, ustedes, nosotros*)

b. Para expresar en español:

1. I close the door.   2. Paul begins to talk in Spanish.   3. Do you (*pl.*)
intend to see the film?   4. Mary and I return at a quarter after five.

---

[1] See Appendix D, pages 323–325, for the first person singular present indicative of verbs with changes in spelling, including those ending in -**guir**: **conseguir** (**consigo**), **seguir** (**sigo**).

5. The boys have a good time, don't they?   6. I ask for books in the
library.   7. Do you (*fam. sing.*) sleep seven hours each night?   8. I
always repeat the words.   9. Many students continue studying until
midnight.   10. My mother serves coffee or chocolate.

IV. Formas de mandato correspondientes a «usted, ustedes»

Infinitive	Stem	Singular	Plural
tomar	tom-	tome Ud.[1]	tomen Uds.[1]
comer	com-	coma Ud.	coman Uds.
abrir	abr-	abra Ud.	abran Uds.
traer	**traig-**	**traiga** Ud.	**traigan** Uds.
cerrar (ie)	**cierr-**	**cierre** Ud.	**cierren** Uds.
volver (ue)	**vuelv-**	**vuelva** Ud.	**vuelvan** Uds.
pedir (i)	**pid-**	**pida** Ud.	**pidan** Uds.
seguir (i)	**sig-**	**siga** Ud.	**sigan** Uds.

In Spanish, the stem for the formal command of all verbs, except the five
which follow, is that of the first person singular present indicative. (In
reality, the formal command forms are those of the third person singular
and plural of the present subjunctive tense, which will be discussed
later.) **Usted (Ud.)** and **ustedes (Uds.)** are usually expressed with the
verb and are placed after it; in a series of commands, however, it is not
necessary to repeat **usted** or **ustedes** with each verb:

Infinitive	1st Sing. Pres. Ind.	Singular Command	Plural Command
dar	**doy**	**dé** Ud.	**den** Uds.
estar	**estoy**	**esté** Ud.	**estén** Uds.
ir	**voy**	**vaya** Ud.	**vayan** Uds.
saber	**sé**	**sepa** Ud.	**sepan** Uds.
ser	**soy**	**sea** Ud.	**sean** Uds.

Remember that certain verbs ending in **-car, -gar, -zar** change **c** to **qu,**
g to **gu,** and **z** to **c** before the endings **-e (-é), -en: busque(n) Ud(s).,**

---

[1] In writing, **usted** and **ustedes** may be abbreviated to **Ud.** and **Uds.,** or **Vd.** and **Vds.**

llegue(n) Ud(s)., empiece(n) Ud(s). Some infinitives of these types are:

acercarse *to approach*
almorzar (ue) *to eat lunch*
buscar *to look for*
comenzar (ie) *to commence*
empezar (ie) *to begin*
entregar *to hand* (*over*)

jugar (ue) *to play* (a game)
llegar *to arrive*
pagar *to pay* (*for*)
practicar *to practice*
sacar *to take* (*out*)
tocar *to play* (music)

a. Repitan la frase; luego, repítanla otra vez, cambiando el mandato al plural:

1. Pase Ud., por favor. 2. Espere Ud. unos minutos. 3. Aprenda Ud. el diálogo. 4. Escriba Ud. la composición. 5. Siéntese[1] Ud. ahora. 6. No le[1] permita Ud. entrar. 7. No siga Ud. cantando. 8. Tráigales Ud. refrescos. 9. Empiece Ud. a leer. 10. No juegue Ud. aquí.

b. Lean la frase en español; luego, cámbienla a la forma de mandato correspondiente a **Ud.**, según los modelos.

MODELOS: Juan abre la puerta.   Juan, abra Ud. la puerta.
          Juan no cierra el libro.   Juan, no cierre Ud. el libro.

1. Roberto entra en el cuarto. 2. Ricardo trae las listas. 3. Jaime busca un regalo. 4. Ana cuenta los nombres. 5. Carlos no llega tarde. 6. Luisa no empieza a cantar. 7. José no sigue leyendo en inglés. 8. Miguel va al cine. 9. Elena está en casa a las diez. 10. Tomás no sale a tomar café. 11. Inés no les pide un favor. 12. Jorge pone los libros sobre la mesa.

c. Para expresar en español de dos maneras (*in two ways*): primero, empleando la forma de mandato correspondiente a **Ud.**, y luego la forma correspondiente a **Uds.**:

1. Open the windows. 2. Learn the dialogue. 3. Repeat the sentence. 4. Return before four o'clock. 5. Don't arrive late. 6. Don't take the photos yet. 7. Don't continue singing tonight. 8. Don't go to the library, please.

[1] For review of the position of object pronouns with respect to verbs used in commands, see Lección dos, page 60.

V. Formas de mandato correspondientes a «tú»

Familiar singular commands are:

Affirmative	Negative	Affirmative	Negative
toma (tú)	no tomes (tú)	**vuelve** (tú)	no **vuelvas** (tú)
come (tú)	no comas (tú)	**pide** (tú)	no **pidas** (tú)
abre (tú)	no abras (tú)	busca (tú)	no **busques** (tú)

The affirmative familiar singular command has the same form as the third person singular of the present indicative in all verbs except the nine which follow. This form is often called the singular imperative. The subject pronoun **tú** is omitted except for emphasis.

The negative familiar singular command is the familiar second person singular of the present subjunctive tense; that is, add -s to the third person singular present subjunctive.

The nine verbs which have irregular familiar singular command forms are:

decir:	**di**	no **digas**	ser:	**sé**	no **seas**
hacer:	**haz**	no **hagas**	tener:	**ten**	no **tengas**
ir:	**ve**	no **vayas**	valer:	**val** (vale)	no **valgas**
poner:	**pon**	no **pongas**	venir:	**ven**	no **vengas**
salir:	**sal**	no **salgas**			

Note these examples of familiar commands of certain reflexive verbs:

levantarse: **levántate** (tú) *get up*	no te **levantes**	*don't get up*
sentarse: **siéntate** (tú) *sit down*	no te **sientes**	*don't sit down*
vestirse: **vístete** (tú) *get dressed*	no te **vistas**	*don't get dressed*
ponerse: **ponte** (tú) *put on*	no te **pongas**	*don't put on*
irse: **vete** (tú) *go away*	no te **vayas**	*don't go away*

a. Lean la frase en español; luego, cámbienla a la forma de mandato correspondiente a **tú**; después, expresen el mandato negativamente:

1. Juan abre la puerta.
2. Ana cierra las ventanas.
3. Dorotea cuenta los nombres ahora.
4. Luis sale despacio.

Students await classes at the University of Los Andes, Bogotá, Colombia.

5. Roberto viene conmigo.   8. Tomás se pone los guantes.
6. Marta se sienta en esa silla.   9. Elena se va pronto.
7. Juanito se viste ahora.   10. Enrique se levanta tarde.

b. Para expresar en español empleando la forma correspondiente a **tú,** primero afirmativa y luego negativamente:[1]

1. Write the composition.   2. Come with the other students.   3. Do that before tomorrow.   4. Return the books today.   5. Leave early.   6. Get up before eight o'clock.   7. Sit down near the table.   8. Put on your hat.

Park in Buenos Aires, Argentina, with modernistic sculpture (made of automobile bumpers) in the foreground.

ENRIQUE ROMANO

[1] When two or more adverbs in **-mente** are used in a series, **-mente** is added only to the last one.

Resumen de palabras y expresiones[1]

a las (seis)   at (six) o'clock
a menudo   often, frequently
a veces   at times
a ver   let's see
admitir   to admit
al poco tiempo   after (in) a short time
antes de *prep.*[2]   before
añadir   to add
aquí las tiene usted   here they are
asistir a   to attend
buenos días   good morning
¡caramba!   gosh! confound it!
cerca de *prep.*   near
¡cómo no!   of course! certainly!
¿cómo se llama . . . ?   what is the name
   of . . . ?
con ironía   ironically
con mucho gusto   gladly, with great
   pleasure
convenir (a)   to be advisable *or*
   suitable (to)
(creer) que sí   (to believe) so
¿cuánto tiempo?   how long (much
   time)?
dar un paseo   to take a walk (stroll)
(Departamento) de Español   Spanish
   (Department)
dirigirse a   to direct oneself to, go
   (turn) to

en casa   at home
esta noche   tonight
haga (Ud.) el favor de + *inf.*   please
   + *verb*
jugar (ue) (a + *obj.*)   to play (*a game*)
la lista   list, roll (*class*)
llegar tarde   to arrive (be) late
¿(no es) verdad?   isn't it? *etc.*
otra vez   again, another time
pase(n) Ud(s).   come in
pensar (ie) + *inf.*   to intend, plan
por favor   please (*at end of request*)
¿qué le vamos a hacer?   we can't do
   anything about it, it can't be helped
¡qué suerte tengo!   how lucky
   (fortunate) I am!
sacar (fotos)   to take (photos)
salir de casa   to leave home
**la sección (de las nueve) o la (de las
   doce)**   the (nine-o'clock) section or
   that (of twelve o'clock)
el semestre   semester
sentirlo (ie, i) mucho   to be very
   sorry
todas las noches   every night
   (evening)
todos los días   every day
unos, -as   some, a few, about
   (*quantity*)

---

[1] The words and expressions used in the dialogue and/or exercises of each lesson are given
for reference. Many of them will be familiar to the student from earlier study of Spanish.
[2] See Appendix B, page 309, for the abbreviations used in this text.

REPASO DOS

El pretérito y el imperfecto de indicativo de los verbos regulares.
Verbos que tienen formas irregulares en el pretérito de indicativo.
Verbos que cambian la vocal radical, Grupos II y III, en el pretérito.
Verbos que tienen formas irregulares en el imperfecto de indicativo

Un día de mala suerte

(Carlos encuentra a un compañero de clase en el vestíbulo de la residencia de estudiantes.)

Juan. ¡Hola, Carlos! No te vi en clase esta mañana. ¿Qué pasó?

Carlos. ¡Un desastre! Tuve que ir al centro porque no encontré en la librería el libro de texto para la clase de español.

Juan. ¿Lo hallaste en el centro?

Carlos. ¡No, Juan! Además, como tengo clases esta tarde, tuve que volver en taxi.

Juan. ¿Dónde almorzaste?

Carlos. Almorcé en el Centro de Estudiantes. Por cierto, pagué ochenta centavos por una hamburguesa malísima.

Juan. Te busqué para invitarte a almorzar conmigo, pero no estabas en tu cuarto.

Carlos. Anoche supe que necesitaba este libro. A propósito, ¿de qué habló el profesor esta mañana?

Juan. De los usos de los tiempos. Como ves, no perdiste nada.

Carlos. ¡Hombre! ¡La parte más difícil de la lección! Bueno, tengo que irme. No quiero llegar tarde a clase. Hasta luego.

15

A. Aprendan el diálogo de memoria para poder repetirlo con el profesor (la profesora) o con uno de sus compañeros.

B. Repasen y estudien las expresiones siguientes para emplear algunas de ellas en el diálogo citado, o para usarlas en un diálogo nuevo basado sobre el modelo:

above-mentioned

---

ayer por la mañana (la tarde)
  yesterday morning (afternoon)
el batido de leche   milk shake
la compañera de clase   classmate (*f.*)
el cuarto de estar   living room, lounge
el emparedado de jamón (queso)
  ham (cheese) sandwich
ir a casa   to go home
ir a casa de (Ana)   to go to (Ann's)
ir a la iglesia   to go to church

ir al centro   to go downtown
ir de compras   to go shopping
ir en autobús (avión, coche, taxi)
  to go by bus (plane, car, taxi)
nada de particular   nothing special
¿qué hay de nuevo?   what's new?
¿qué hiciste?   what did you do?
los usos del imperfecto (pretérito)
  de indicativo   uses of the imperfect
  (preterit) indicative

Pronunciación   **A.** Spanish **b** (and **v**), **d.** Each of these consonants (**b** and **v** are pronounced exactly alike) has two different sounds, a voiced stop sound and a voiced continuant sound.

When initial in a breath-group or when after **m** or **n** (also pronounced **m** in this case), whether within a word or between words, Spanish **b** (or **v**) is a voiced bilabial stop, like English *b* in *boy*, but somewhat weaker. In all other positions, it is a voiced bilabial continuant; the lips do not close completely as in stop **b**, but allow the breath to pass between them through a very narrow passage. When between vowels the articulation is especially weak. Avoid the English *v* sound.

At the beginning of a breath-group or when after **n** or **l**, Spanish **d** is a voiced dental stop, like English *d*, but with the tip of the tongue touching the inner surface of the upper teeth, rather than the ridge above the teeth as in English. In all other cases the tongue drops even lower and the **d** is pronounced as a voiced interdental continuant, like a weak English *th* in *this*. The sound is especially weak in the ending **-ado** and when final in a word before a pause.

Pronounce after your teacher:

1. bueno   caramba   vamos   venir   un vaso

2. saber   muy bien   novia   no volvió   ¿quiere verla?

3. dormir   ¿dónde?   aprender   el día   el dinero

4. cansado   además   verdad   usted   le dice

B. In Appendix A, pages 294–300, review the Division of Words into Syllables, Linking of Words, and Word Stress; then write the last two exchanges of the dialogue on page 15, dividing them into breath-groups and syllables, indicating the linking of sounds between words by means of a linking sign, and underlining the syllables that are stressed.

I. Repaso de las formas del pretérito y del imperfecto de indicativo de los verbos regulares   **Para repasar**

Review in Appendix D, pages 314–315, the forms of the preterit and imperfect indicative tenses of regular verbs.

Repitan la frase; luego, al oír un sujeto nuevo, substitúyanlo en la frase, cambiando la forma del verbo cuando sea necesario:

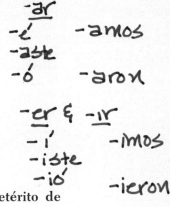

1. *Yo* no esperé a Tomás.
   (*Tú, Ud., Los estudiantes, Elena, Luisa y yo, Uds.*)
2. *Felipe* aprendió bien el diálogo.
   (*José y yo, Yo, Uds., Tú, Ana y Luis, Ella*)
3. *Ellos* miraban el mapa de México.
   (*Ella, Yo, Tú, El profesor, Isabel y yo, Uds.*)
4. *Mis padres* vivían en la Argentina.
   (*El señor Díaz, Yo, Mi hermano y yo, Tú, Uds., Ud.*)

II. Algunos verbos que tienen formas irregulares en el pretérito de indicativo

Some common verbs are:

decir: dije dijiste dijo dijimos dijisteis dijeron
hacer: hice hiciste hizo hicimos hicisteis hicieron
querer: quise quisiste quiso quisimos quisisteis quisieron
venir: vine viniste vino vinimos vinisteis vinieron

walk
andar: anduve anduviste anduvo anduvimos anduvisteis anduvieron

estar:	estuve estuviste estuvo estuvimos estuvisteis estuvieron
poder:	pude pudiste pudo pudimos pudisteis pudieron
poner:	puse pusiste puso pusimos pusisteis pusieron
saber:	supe supiste supo supimos supisteis supieron
tener:	tuve tuviste tuvo tuvimos tuvisteis tuvieron
traer:	traje trajiste trajo trajimos trajisteis trajeron
dar:	di diste dio dimos disteis dieron
ir, ser:	fui fuiste fue fuimos fuisteis fueron
ver:	vi viste vio vimos visteis vieron

In the listed forms note that:

(1) Four verbs have **i**-stems and six have **u**-stems. There are no written accents on any of the forms, and in the first eleven verbs the first person singular ends in **-e** and the third person singular ends in **-o**.
(2) The third person singular of **hacer** is **hizo**; the third person plural ending of **decir** and of **traer** is **-eron**.
(3) **Ir** and **ser** have the same forms.

A few verbs have special meanings in the preterit tense. The preterit of **saber** usually means *learned, found out*: **Anoche supe eso**, *Last night I learned that*; that of **tener** often means *got, received*: **Yo tuve una carta,** *I got (received) a letter*; that of **querer** often means *tried*: **Juan quiso hacer eso pero no pudo,** *John tried to do that but he couldn't*; that of **querer** used negatively often means *refused to, would not*: **Ellos no quisieron esperar,** *They refused to (would not) wait.*

a. Para contestar afirmativamente:

1. ¿Tuviste que ir al centro?
2. ¿Tuvo que ir Carlos también?
3. ¿Hiciste una excursión ayer?
4. ¿Hizo Juan un viaje a México?
5. ¿Diste un paseo con Luisa?
6. ¿Dieron Uds. un paseo ayer?
7. ¿Fuiste de compras con Pablo?
8. ¿Fueron Uds. en taxi?

b. Para contestar negativamente:

1. ¿Estuviste en casa anoche?
2. ¿Trajeron Uds. fotos a clase?

3. ¿Pudiste trabajar mucho
ayer?

4. ¿Vio Carlos un partido de
fútbol?

5. ¿Vinieron Uds. a clase el
sábado?

6. ¿Le dijiste la verdad a
Carolina?

c. Repitan la frase; luego, repítanla otra vez, cambiando la forma del verbo al pretérito de indicativo:

1. Yo no hago nada por la mañana.   2. José y yo no vemos a nadie.
3. María no quiere ir al cine.   4. Los jóvenes no pueden esperar.
5. ¿Adónde vas en autobús?   6. ¿Qué ves en el cuarto de estar?   7. Oigo cantar a alguien.   8. ¿Quién te trae muchos regalos?   9. Mis padres no dicen eso.   10. Pongo los paquetes sobre la mesa.   11. Mi madre tiene que volver en taxi.   12. Él no sabe nada de particular.

d. Para expresar en español:

1. Mr. Díaz, what did you do yesterday afternoon?   2. Johnny, where did you (*fam. sing.*) go this morning?   3. Did you (*pl.*) bring the magazines to class?   4. I couldn't find my textbook last night.   5. Charles came to work at ten o'clock.   6. When did you (*fam. sing.*) find out that Paul went to New York?   7. I know that he made the trip by plane.
8. John said that he encountered (**a**) Mary downtown.

III. Otros tipos de verbos que tienen formas irregulares en el pretérito de indicativo

1. Certain **-ar** verbs which have changes in the formal commands (see Repaso primero, pages 8–9) have similar changes in the first person singular preterit:

buscar:	**busqué** buscaste buscó, *etc.*	
llegar:	**llegué** llegaste llegó, *etc.*	
empezar (ie):	**empecé** empezaste empezó, *etc.*	

2. Certain verbs ending in **-er** and **-ir** preceded by a vowel replace unaccented **i** by **y** in the third person singular and plural of the preterit. Accents must be written on the other four forms. **Caer**, *to fall,* and **leer**, *to read,* have the same changes as **creer**, *to believe,* and **oír**, *to hear:*

creer: creí **creíste creyó creímos creísteis creyeron**
oír: oí oíste **oyó** oímos oísteis **oyeron**

3. Verbs ending in **-ducir** and **-uir** (except **-guir**) have irregular forms in
the preterit and also in the present indicative. In Appendix D, review
the forms of the models **conducir,** page 325, and **huir,** page 326.

a. Escriban cada frase, cambiando la forma del verbo al pretérito de
indicativo; luego, lean la frase nueva en voz alta (*aloud*):

1. Yo no almuerzo hasta la una.   2. Llego tarde al partido.   3. Me
acerco rápidamente al estadio.   4. Pago tres dólares por mi billete.
5. Le entrego el dinero al empleado.   6. Entro y busco un asiento.
7. Empiezo a sacar fotos de los jugadores.   8. Saco ocho o diez fotos.

9. Por la mañana juego al golf.   10. Por la tarde toco unos discos primero.
11. Después, busco mi libro de español.   12. Por fin comienzo a estudiar.
13. Leo bien toda la lección.   14. Practico el diálogo varias veces.
15. A las cinco conduzco mi coche a casa de Ramón.

b. Repitan la frase; luego, repítanla otra vez, cambiando la forma del
verbo[1] al pretérito de indicativo:

1. Ellos empiezan a examinar la lista.   2. Yo cierro las puertas.   3. ¿No
cierras tu libro?   4. ¿No vuelven Uds. a las cinco?   5. Jorge le devuelve
el dinero a su amigo.   6. Ella no recuerda el diálogo.   7. Carlos y yo
lo recordamos muy bien.   8. Ellos pierden el autobús.   9. Carlos
nunca piensa en Juanita.   10. ¿Se sienta Felipe en la sala de clase?

c. Para contestar afirmativamente:

1. ¿Buscaste el libro de texto?
2. ¿Tocaste la guitarra anoche?
3. ¿Jugaste al fútbol el
     sábado?
4. ¿Condujiste el coche al
     centro?
5. ¿Almorzaron Uds. a las doce?
6. ¿Oyeron Uds. la orquesta
     ayer?
7. ¿Creyeron Uds. lo que dijo
     ella?
8. ¿Leyeron Uds. la novela?

[1] All verbs to be changed in this exercise are stem-changing verbs, Class I; remember
that the stem vowel of these verbs does not change in the preterit.

IV. Verbos que cambian la vocal radical, Grupos II y III, en el pretérito

Stem-changing verbs, Class II and Class III, change **e** to **i** and **o** to **u** in the third person singular and plural of the preterit:

	3rd Singular	3rd Plural
sentir:	**sintió**	**sintieron**
dormir:	**durmió**	**durmieron**
pedir:	**pidió**	**pidieron**

a. Repitan la frase; luego, repítanla otra vez, cambiando la forma del verbo al pretérito:

1. Los muchachos se divierten. 2. María se divierte también.
3. Ricardo prefiere ir al Centro de Estudiantes. 4. Ellos prefieren no acompañarle. 5. Mi padre duerme la siesta. 6. Juan consigue un puesto. 7. ¿Le pide Ud. a él alguna cosa? 8. Los niños nunca me piden nada. 9. Mi hermano se viste rápidamente. 10. Mis hermanas se visten despacio. 11. ¿Sigue Ud. por este camino? 12. ¿Repiten ellos el diálogo?

b. Para expresar en español:

1. They sleep well; they slept well. 2. Tom has a good time; he had a good time. 3. Jane asks for the book; she asked for the book. 4. My mother serves coffee; she served coffee. 5. The teacher repeats the question; he repeated the question. 6. Henry continues working there; he continued working there. 7. I do not drive my car downtown; I did not drive my car downtown. 8. I take a nap; we took a nap. 9. I obtained a job; my brother obtained a job also. 10. I ate lunch in the Student Center; Charles ate lunch there also.

V. Verbos que tienen formas irregulares en el imperfecto de indicativo

All verbs in Spanish have regular forms in the imperfect indicative tense except **ir, ser, ver.** Their forms are:

ir:	**iba**	**ibas**	**iba**	**íbamos**	**ibais**	**iban**
ser:	**era**	**eras**	**era**	**éramos**	**erais**	**eran**
ver:	**veía**	**veías**	**veía**	**veíamos**	**veíais**	**veían**

Mayan altar, Tikal, Guatemala.

Mayan sculptured relief,
Palenque, Mexico.

Repitan la frase; luego, repítanla otra vez, cambiando la forma del verbo al imperfecto de indicativo:

1. Yo no sé nada de particular. 2. Carlos siempre tiene suerte. 3. Marta no está en su cuarto. 4. No queremos llegar tarde. 5. Van a la biblioteca todas las noches. 6. Vamos a la iglesia los domingos. 7. Es un día hermoso. 8. Las clases no son grandes. 9. Los vemos todos los días. 10. Yo los veo a menudo.

Resumen de palabras y expresiones

a propósito   by the way
el Centro de Estudiantes   Student Center
la compañera de clase   classmate (*f.*)
el compañero de clase   classmate (*m.*)
el desastre   disaster, catastrophe
dormir (ue, u) la siesta   to take a nap
(estar) en el centro   (to be) downtown
hacer un viaje (una excursión)   to take *or* make a trip (an excursion)
la hamburguesa   hamburger
hasta luego   see you later, until (I'll see you) later

el libro de texto   text, textbook
pensar (ie) en   to think of (about)
por cierto   certainly, in truth, in fact
por fin   finally, at last
por la mañana (la tarde)   in the morning (afternoon)
la residencia de estudiantes   student residence hall (dormitory)
tener que + *inf.*   to have to
el tiempo   tense
toda la (lección)   all the *or* the whole (lesson)
el uso   use

REPASO TRES

El futuro y el condicional de los verbos regulares.   Verbos que tienen
formas irregulares en el futuro y en el condicional.   Los tiempos
compuestos.   Formas del participio presente

La grabadora de Roberto

*(Tomás encuentra a un compañero de clase en el Centro de Estudiantes. Son las
siete menos cuarto de la tarde.)*

Tomás.	Ricardo, ¿dónde has estado? Te llamé por teléfono esta tarde y nadie contestó.
Ricardo.	He estado en el cuarto de Roberto. Su papá le ha regalado una grabadora de cinta portátil.
Tomás.	¿De veras? ¡Qué suerte ha tenido!
Ricardo.	Esta noche pensamos grabar la conferencia del profesor Valdés. ¿Podrás ir con nosotros?
Tomás.	¡Encantado! La conferencia comenzará a las siete y diez, ¿verdad?
Ricardo.	Sí. Para llegar a tiempo habrá que ir a buscar a Roberto en seguida. *(A los pocos minutos están llamando a la puerta del cuarto de Roberto.)*
Roberto.	*(Abriendo la puerta.)* Pasen ustedes. ¿Qué tal, Tomás? No sabía que venías. Me alegro mucho de verte.
Tomás.	¡Hola, Roberto! Me han dicho que tienes una grabadora nueva. Me gustaría verla.
Roberto.	Está allí sobre mi escritorio. *(Dirigiéndose a su compañero de cuarto.)* Jaime, para el tocadiscos, por favor. No se oye nada.
Jaime.	¿Por qué no grabamos una cinta en español?
Ricardo.	No olviden que tenemos que ir a la conferencia del profesor Valdés esta noche.
Jaime.	¡Hombre! Tienes razón. Y queremos llevar la grabadora.
Ricardo.	Pues, ¡apúrense! No tenemos mucho tiempo.

25

A. Aprendan el diálogo de memoria para poder repetirlo con el profesor (la profesora) o con algunos de sus compañeros.

B. Preparen un diálogo original, de unas seis líneas, para recitar en clase, empleando las frases y preguntas siguientes como elemento inicial:[1]

1. **Carlos.**   Tuve que ir al centro esta mañana.
   Roberto.   ¿Fuiste en coche?

2. **Srta. Flores.**   Este joven quiere saber si le permite Ud. asistir a una de sus clases.
   Sr. Valdés.   ¿Cuál de mis clases le interesa?

3. **Juan.**   María, me ha regalado mi padre una grabadora de cinta portátil.
   María.   ¿Por qué no grabamos una cinta en español?

Pronunciación

Intonation. Review the section on intonation in Appendix A, pages 300–302, paying special attention to the remarks on interrogative sentences and exclamations. A few additional observations follow:

a. The intonation pattern used to express special interest in an exclamatory sentence may also be used in questions (especially in those beginning with an interrogative word) and in declarative sentences. The voice rises above the normal tone when the last accented syllable is reached (level 3), and falls below the normal tone in the following syllable (or within the accented syllable, if no unstressed syllable follows). In a declarative sentence this pattern may be used to give special emphasis to any word of the breath-group. Examples:

¿Quién te lo   **Level 3**
ha dicho?   **2**
                          1

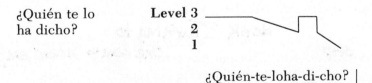

¿Quién-te-loha-di-cho? |

---

[1] Review of dialogues on pages 1 and 15 will be helpful to the student in preparing the new dialogues.

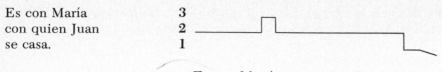

Es con María	3
con quien Juan	2
se casa.	1

Es-con-Ma-rí-a-con-quien-Juan-se-ca-sa |

b. The pattern described in the preceding section is typical of commands and requests. The latter differ in that in requests the intervals between accented and unaccented syllables are less than in commands; furthermore, in requests the entire breath-group is usually uttered on a higher tone. Examples:

	Command	**Request**

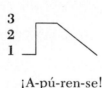

¡Apúrense! 3 2 1

¡A-pú-ren-se!   A-pú-ren-se |

c. If an interrogative sentence consists of two breath-groups, the first group ends below the normal tone. Example:

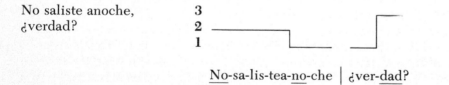

No saliste anoche,	3
¿verdad?	2
	1

No-sa-lis-tea-no-che | ¿ver-dad?

Write the interrogative and exclamatory sentences of the dialogue of this lesson, dividing them into breath-groups and syllables, and outline the intonation patterns.

I. Repaso de las formas del futuro y del condicional de los verbos regulares **Para repasar**

In Appendix D, page 315, review the forms of the future and conditional indicative tenses of regular verbs.

Repitan la frase; luego, al oír un sujeto nuevo, substitúyanlo en la frase, cambiando la forma del verbo cuando sea necesario:

1. *Inés* los llevará a casa.
   (*Yo, Tú, Mis hermanas, Marta y yo, Uds., Mi amiga*)
2. *Mis padres* no venderán el coche.
   (*Mi tío, Ella y yo, Tú, Uds., Yo, Ana*)
3. *Nosotros* asistiremos a la conferencia.
   (*Mis amigos, Ud., Tú, Yo, Tomás, Él y yo*)
4. *Ella* hablaría con otros estudiantes.
   (*Yo, Uds., Nosotros, Tú, José, Ellos*)
5. *Yo* no comería hasta las seis.
   (*Nosotros, Las muchachas, Él, Tú, Uds., Mi padre*)

II. Verbos que tienen formas irregulares en el futuro y en el condicional

Verbs irregular in the future and conditional indicative tenses are:

Infinitive	Future	Conditional
1. haber	habré, -ás, -á, etc.	habría, -ías, -ía, etc.
poder	podré, -ás, -á, etc.	podría, -ías, -ía, etc.
querer	querré, -ás, -á, etc.	querría, -ías, -ía, etc.
saber	sabré, -ás, -á, etc.	sabría, -ías, -ía, etc.
2. poner	pondré, -ás, -á, etc.	pondría, -ías, -ía, etc.
salir	saldré, -ás, -á, etc.	saldría, -ías, -ía, etc.
tener	tendré, -ás, -á, etc.	tendría, -ías, -ía, etc.
valer	valdré, -ás, -á, etc.	valdría, -ías, -ía, etc.
venir	vendré, -ás, -á, etc.	vendría, -ías, -ía, etc.
3. decir	diré, -ás, -á, etc.	diría, -ías, -ía, etc.
hacer	haré, -ás, -á, etc.	haría, -ías, -ía, etc.

The future and conditional tenses have the same stem, and the endings are the same as for regular verbs. Note that the irregularity is in the infinitive stem used: in group (1) the final vowel of the infinitive has been dropped, in (2) the final vowel of the infinitive has been dropped and the letter **d** inserted to facilitate pronunciation, and in (3) contracted stems are used.

a. Formen frases completas empleando las palabras **Carlos dice que** como elemento inicial y cambiando el infinitivo en cursiva (*in italics*) a la forma correcta del futuro:

1. *tener* que trabajar el lunes.
2. *poder* ir a la conferencia.
3. *salir* de casa a las ocho.
4. *hacer* una excursión el domingo.
5. *poner* las cosas en el coche.
6. *haber* mucha gente en el teatro.
7. *haber* que salir a las siete.
8. no *venir* a vernos mañana.
9. no *querer* acompañarnos al cine.
10. *valer* más esperar hasta otro día.

Repitan el ejercicio, empleando las palabras **Carlos dijo que** como elemento inicial y cambiando el infinitivo en cursiva a la forma correcta del condicional.

b. Para expresar en español:

1. Will you (*fam. sing.*) be able to go to the lecture? 2. We shall have to go to pick up Robert at once. 3. We shall leave home at half past seven. 4. It will be necessary to arrive on time. 5. At what time will you (*pl.*) want to return home? 6. Where will you (*pl.*) put the packages? 7. Mary said that she would be able to tape the lecture. 8. Martha and Ann said that they would come a little before eight o'clock. 9. Tom recalled that there would be another lecture tomorrow night. 10. We said that we would not have time (in order) to hear the two lectures.

III. Formación de los tiempos compuestos

The compound tenses are formed by using the appropriate form of the auxiliary verb **haber** with the past participle. In Appendix D, page 317, review the present perfect, pluperfect, preterit perfect, future perfect, and conditional perfect indicative tenses. The following past participles are irregular:

abrir:	**abierto**	*opened*	descubrir:	**descubierto**	*discovered*
decir:	**dicho**	*said*	devolver:	**devuelto**	*given back*
describir:	**descrito**	*described*	envolver:	**envuelto**	*wrapped*

escribir:	**escrito**	*written*	poner:	**puesto**	*put, placed*
hacer:	**hecho**	*done*	romper:	**roto**	*broken*
ir:	**ido**	*gone*	ver:	**visto**	*seen*
morir:	**muerto**	*died*	volver:	**vuelto**	*returned*

Also note the written accent on the following forms: caer, **caído**; creer, **creído**; leer, **leído**; oír, oído; reír, reído; traer, **traído**.

a. Para contestar afirmativamente:

1. ¿Has abierto la puerta?
2. ¿Has escrito la composición para hoy?
3. ¿Has envuelto el paquete?
4. ¿Has puesto la maleta en el coche?
5. ¿Ha roto Juan el vaso?
6. ¿Han dicho Uds. la verdad?
7. ¿Han visto Uds. la película?
8. ¿Habían ido Uds. al cine?
9. ¿Habían devuelto Uds. los libros?
10. ¿Habían oído Uds. la orquesta?

b. Repitan la frase; luego, repítanla dos veces más, cambiando la forma del verbo al pluscuamperfecto (*pluperfect*) y al futuro perfecto de indicativo (y observando la posición del pronombre usado como objeto del verbo):

1. Yo le he devuelto el dinero.   2. Luisa no les ha dicho eso.   3. ¿Han vuelto ellos a casa?   4. ¿Quiénes los han visto? —Nosotros los hemos visto.   5. ¿Adónde has ido?   6. Carlos nos lo ha traído.

c. Lean la frase en español; luego, repítanla cuatro veces, cambiando la forma del verbo al imperfecto, al pretérito, al futuro y al perfecto presente de indicativo:

1. Yo busco a Tomás.   2. Ellos no traen nada.   3. Yo empiezo a leer el diálogo.   4. Él y yo abrimos las ventanas.   5. Marta se pone el sombrero.   6. ¿Vas tú a la conferencia?

d. Para expresar en español:

1. Where have you (*fam. sing.*) been?   2. I have been at (in) the bookstore.   3. Have you (*pl.*) heard the tape?   4. We have not had time (in order) to go to the laboratory.   5. Have you (*fam. sing.*) seen my tape recorder?   6. I had seen it in the classroom.   7. John said that he had returned at a quarter to seven.   8. Helen had not told me that.

IV. Repaso de las formas del participio presente

Review the forms of the present participle in Appendix D, page 314. Some verbs which have irregular present participles are:

caer:	**cayendo**	*falling*		oír:	**oyendo**	*hearing*
creer:	**creyendo**	*believing*		poder:	**pudiendo**	*being able*
decir:	**diciendo**	*saying, telling*		traer:	**trayendo**	*bringing*
ir:	**yendo**	*going*		venir:	**viniendo**	*coming*
leer:	**leyendo**	*reading*				

In stem-changing verbs, Class II and Class III, the stem vowel **e** becomes **i** and **o** becomes **u** in the present participle. Examples:

sentir:	**sintiendo**	*feeling*	dormir:	**durmiendo**	*sleeping*
pedir:	**pidiendo**	*asking*			

Repitan la frase; luego, repítanla otra vez, substituyendo el verbo con la forma correcta del presente de indicativo del verbo **estar** seguida del (*followed by the*) participio presente:

1. Mi padre lee el periódico.   2. Nosotros miramos el mapa.   3. Roberto aprende la lección.   4. María escribe una carta.   5. Los estudiantes oyen los discos.   6. Mi mamá duerme la siesta.   7. Carlos trae unas flores para Juanita.   8. Juan come con sus amigos.

Boating in Chapultepec
Park, Mexico City.

Resumen de palabras y expresiones

a los pocos minutos   after (in) a few minutes
a tiempo   on time
alegrarse (mucho) de   to be (very) glad to
apurarse   to hurry (up)
buscar a uno   to come (go) for one, pick one up
la **cinta**   tape
el **compañero de cuarto**   roommate (*m.*)
la **conferencia**   lecture; conference
de la tarde   p.m., in the afternoon
de veras   really, truly
en seguida   at once, immediately
¡encantado, -a!   (I'll be) delighted (to)!
el **escritorio**   desk, writing desk
la **grabadora (de cinta)**   tape recorder

grabar   to tape, record
habrá que + *inf.*   it will be necessary to
llamar por teléfono   to telephone, call by telephone
mañana (por la noche)   tomorrow (night, evening)
me gustaría (ver)   I should like (to see)
mucho tiempo   long, a long time
no se oye nada   one cannot hear anything, nothing is heard
parar *trans.*   to stop
portátil   portable
¿qué tal?   how are you? how goes it?
regalar   to give (*as a gift*)
tener razón   to be right
tener tiempo para + *inf.*   to have time to
valer más   to be better

LECCIÓN PRIMERA

Usos de «estar» y «ser».   La construcción reflexiva para expresar el sujeto indefinido y para expresar la voz pasiva.   La «a» personal. «Conocer» y «saber»

un desconocido = stranger
el extranjero = overseas, abroad, or other countries
extrano
raro = strange   *forastero = outsider*

Un nuevo[1] estudiante extranjero   *foreign*

(Carlos habla con Pablo en la sala de clase antes de la llegada del profesor. Es la una y cinco de la tarde.)

Carlos.	¡Hombre! ¿Dónde has estado? ¡Creía que estabas enfermo!
Pablo.	He tenido que acompañar a su primera clase a un nuevo estudiante extranjero.
Carlos.	¿Es el joven que está hablando con Dorotea?
Pablo.	Sí, están sentados en la primera fila. ¿No le conoces todavía?
Carlos.	Todavía no. ¿De dónde es?
Pablo.	Es colombiano. Se llama Luis Sierra. Su padre es un médico muy distinguido de Bogotá.
Carlos.	Ya sé quién[2] es. Su padre está casado con una norteamericana que estudió en esta universidad, ¿verdad?
Pablo.	Exactamente. Y ella escribe artículos sobre los problemas sociales y económicos de Colombia.
Carlos.	Se han publicado algunos en el periódico de la universidad, ¿verdad? Son interesantes y están muy bien escritos.
Pablo.	Se dice que Luis es músico y que toca la guitarra maravillosamente.
Carlos.	¡Hombre! En ese caso hay que invitarle a formar parte de nuestra comparsa musical.
Pablo.	Estará en su elemento. Parece ser un joven muy simpático.
Carlos.	Bueno, ya entra el profesor. Me lo presentarás después.
Pablo.	Con mucho gusto. Espérame después de esta clase.

[1] Before a noun **nuevo, –a,** means *new* in the sense of *another, different,* and after the noun, *new, brand-new.*   [2] Note that an accent mark is written on interrogative words when used in indirect questions as well as in direct questions.

35

A. Para contestar en español en oraciones completas:

Preguntas sobre el   1. ¿Dónde se encuentran Carlos y Pablo?   2. ¿Qué ha tenido que hacer
diálogo[1]   Pablo?   3. ¿Quién está hablando con Dorotea?   4. ¿Dónde están
                      sentados Luis y Dorotea?   5. ¿De dónde es Luis?   6. ¿Qué escribe la
                      madre de Luis?   7. ¿Qué dice Carlos de los artículos?   8. ¿Por qué no
                      continúan charlando Carlos y Pablo?

Aplicación del   1. ¿Dónde nos encontramos ahora?   2. ¿A qué hora comienza esta
diálogo   clase?   3. ¿Qué libros ha traído Ud. a clase?   4. ¿En qué fila está
                  sentado (sentada) Ud.?   5. ¿Cuántos estudiantes extranjeros hay en
                  esta universidad?   6. ¿Cuántos estudiantes extranjeros hay en esta
                  clase?   7. ¿De qué países son los estudiantes extranjeros de esta clase?
                  8. ¿Se publican artículos sobre problemas sociales en el periódico de la
                  universidad?

B. Preparen un diálogo original, de unas ocho líneas, para recitar en
clase, empleando las frases y preguntas siguientes como elemento
inicial:

1. **Pablo.**   ¿Qué vamos a hacer esta noche? ¿Ir al cine?
   Carlos.   No; vamos a practicar en casa de Dorotea. ¿Por qué no
                 invitas a tu amigo Luis?

2. **Carlos.**   ¿Qué cursos piensa tomar tu amigo Luis?
   Pablo.   No está seguro todavía. Le interesan las matemáticas, las
                 ciencias políticas, la ecología . . .

Pronunciación

A. Diphthongs. Review in Appendix A, page 298, the sounds of the
diphthongs. A diphthong is a sequence of two vowels pronounced in
one syllable. As the first element of a diphthong, unstressed **i** is pronounced like a weak English *y* in *yes*, and unstressed **u** is pronounced
like *w* in *wet*. As the second element of a diphthong, unstressed **i** and **u**
are glide sounds in the reverse direction: they start from the position
of the preceding vowel and end in the position of Spanish **i** and **u**,
respectively.

Remember that two adjacent strong vowels within a word do not
combine in a single syllable, but form two separate syllables: **ve-o.**
Likewise, when a weak vowel adjacent to a strong vowel has a written

[1] Memorization of all or part of the dialogue in this lesson and hereafter is optional.

accent, it retains its syllabic value and forms a separate syllable: **dí-a.**
An accent on a strong vowel merely indicates stress: **des-pués.**

Pronounce after your teacher:

1. estudiar   secretaria   alguien   comienza   cuando
     cuaderno   nueve   puede   muy   Luis

2. traigo   vais   habéis   seis   oigo
     soy   autor   la universidad   Europa   ¿ve usted?
     ¿lo usamos?   ¿jugó usted?   europeo   autobús   lo humano
     leo   paseo   todavía   librería   señor Díaz
     oímos   país   aprendió   adiós   también

B. Review Linking in Appendix A, pages 299–300, and pronounce as one breath-group:

¿Qué va a hacer?   ¿Y usted?   Ella está enferma.
Tu amigo Luis.   Él no ha vuelto.   Se habla español.
Me interesa el curso.   Está en su elemento.   En esta universidad.
Es la una y cinco.   ¿Diste un paseo?   Después de esta clase.

Notas gramaticales

I. Usos de «estar» y «ser»

A. Estar is used:

1. To express location (*i.e.*, to indicate where the subject is), whether temporary or permanent:

> **Ellos están en casa.** They are at home.
> **¿Dónde ha estado ella?** Where has she been?
> **Monterrey está en México.** Monterrey is in Mexico.

2. With an adjective to indicate the state or condition of the subject when the state or condition is relatively temporary, accidental, or variable:

> **¿Está caliente[1] el café?** Is the coffee hot?
> **Ellos han estado muy tristes.** They have been very sad.
> **(Yo) creía que estabas enfermo.** I thought (that) you were ill.

[1] Remember that in a question a predicate adjective normally follows the verb immediately.

3. With the present participle to stress that an action is (was, has been, etc.) in progress at a given moment:[1]

Pablo está hablando con Dorotea.   Paul is talking with Dorothy.
¿Qué estás haciendo ahora?   What are you doing now?
Él estaba leyendo el periódico.   He was reading the newspaper.
He estado trabajando toda la tarde.   I have been working all afternoon.

4. With the past participle to describe a state or condition resulting from a previous action (in this construction the past participle, which is used as an adjective rather than as a verb, agrees with the subject in gender and number):

Están sentados en la primera fila.   They are seated in the first row.
Los artículos están muy bien escritos.   The articles are very well written.
La ventana ya estaba cerrada.   The window was already closed.

NOTE: Certain verbs, like encontrarse, hallarse, verse, quedar(se), are often substituted for estar:

[handwritten: find oneself   to be seen to remain]

¿Dónde nos encontramos ahora?   Where are we now?
La puerta ya se encontraba (se hallaba) cerrada.   The door was already closed.
Ella quedó sorprendida al saber eso.   She was surprised upon knowing (to know) that.

B. Ser is used:

1. To establish an identity between the subject and a noun or pronoun, and, less commonly, with adverbs, infinitives, or clauses used as nouns:

Él es músico y ella es escritora.   He is a musician and she is a writer.
Soy yo; es ella.   It is I; it is she.
Aquí es donde viven.   Here is where they live.
Ver es creer.   Seeing is believing.
Lo malo es que él no ha vuelto.   What is bad is that he has not returned.

[1] The progressive forms of **ir, salir, venir** are rarely used.

2. With an adjective to express an essential quality or characteristic of the subject that is relatively permanent; this includes adjectives of color, size, shape, nationality, and the like, and those adjectives which describe personal qualities, including the adjectives **joven, viejo, rico, pobre, feliz:**

estar contento o ser feliz (has to be this way)

Luis es colombiano.   Louis is a Colombian.
Los artículos son interesantes.   The articles are interesting.
Estas casas son grandes (blancas).   These houses are large (white).
No somos viejos (jóvenes).   We are not old (young).
Aquel hombre no es rico (pobre).   That man is not rich (poor).

3. With the preposition **de** to show origin, possession, or material, and with the preposition **para** to indicate for whom or for what a thing is intended:

¿De dónde es Luis?   Where is Louis from?
¿Es de Roberto este cuaderno?   Is this notebook Robert's?
Estos relojes son de oro.   These watches are (of) gold.
¿Para quién es la revista?   For whom is the magazine?

4. In impersonal expressions:

Es necesario (mejor) esperar un rato.   It is necessary (better) to wait a while.
No es fácil recordar eso.   It is not easy to remember that.

5. To express time of day:

¿Qué hora es?   What time is it?
Es la una y media.   It is half past one.
Son las diez en punto.   It is ten o'clock sharp.

NOTE: The verb is always plural in expressing time of day, except when followed by **la una,** *one o'clock.*

6. With the past participle to express the passive voice:

El vestido fue hecho por Ana.   The dress was made by Ann.
Ella es estimada de todos.   She is esteemed by all.
Los niños fueron vistos allí.   The children were seen there.

In expressing the passive voice (*i.e.*, when the subject of the verb is acted upon by a person or thing) by means of **ser** and the past participle, the latter agrees with the subject in gender and number. The agent *by* is usually expressed by **por; de** is used, however, when the action represents a mental or emotional act (second example).

When a person receives the action of the verb (second and third examples), the third person plural active construction is replacing the passive construction, particularly in modern usage:

> **Todos la estiman.**   All esteem her (She is esteemed by all).
> **Vieron a los niños allí.**   They saw the children (The children were seen) there.

C. Ser and estar with certain adjectives

The meaning of some adjectives varies according to whether they are used with **ser** or **estar**. In general, **ser** indicates the normal or natural quality of the adjective, while **estar** indicates a temporary or subjective idea, often with the value of *look, feel, taste*, etc. A few examples which show the contrasts are:

With ser	With estar
Ana es buena. Ann is good. (*By nature*)	**Ana está buena.** Ann is well. (*In good health*)
José es malo. Joe is bad. (*By nature*)	**José está malo.** Joe is ill. (*In poor health*)
Él es enfermo. He is sickly. (*An invalid*)	**Él está enfermo.** He is sick. (*Temporary condition*)
Ella es bonita. She is pretty. (*Naturally pretty*)	**¡Qué bonita está ella hoy!** How pretty she is (looks) today! (*Appearance*)
La nieve es fría. Snow is cold. (*By nature*)	**El agua está fría.** The water is cold. (*Changeable, temporary condition*)
Dorotea es lista. Dorothy is clever. (*By nature*)	**Dorotea está lista.** Dorothy is ready. (*Temporary condition*)
Marta es joven. Martha is young. (*Age regarded as characteristic*)	**Marta está joven hoy.** Martha is (looks) young today. (*Appearance*)
¿Es casado o soltero? Is he married (a married man) or single (a bachelor)?	**Está casado con una norteamericana.** He is married to an American woman.

NOTE: In the last example, **casado** is considered a noun when used with ser and an adjective, representing the result of an action (marriage), when used with **estar.**

A. Para contestar afirmativamente, según el modelo.   *Ejercicios*

MODELO: ¿Qué es ella? ¿Escritora?   Sí, ella es escritora.

1. ¿Qué es el padre de Luis? ¿Profesor?
2. ¿Dónde vive Carlos? ¿Allí?
3. ¿Cómo son los artículos? ¿Largos?
4. ¿Cómo son las guitarras? ¿Nuevas?
5. ¿De dónde es aquel estudiante? ¿De Colombia?
6. ¿Qué fue difícil hacer? ¿Aprender el diálogo?
7. ¿Qué hora era cuando llegó ella? ¿Eran las doce?
8. ¿Para quién era el regalo? ¿Para Dorotea?

B. Para contestar negativamente.

MODELO: ¿Está frío el café? (caliente)   No, el café está caliente.

1. ¿Está abierta la ventana? (cerrada)
2. ¿Ha estado Pablo en Venezuela? (México)
3. ¿Estarán Uds. listos a la una? (a las dos)
4. ¿Están mal escritas las composiciones? (bien escritas)
5. ¿Has estado escuchando discos? (estudiando la lección)
6. ¿Estaba contenta la muchacha? (triste)
7. ¿Estuvo Carlos en el Perú dos semanas? (un mes)
8. ¿Todavía está muy enferma tu prima? (mucho mejor)

C. Después de escuchar los dos grupos de palabras, combínenlos en una sola oración *by means of* por medio de la forma correcta de **ser** o **estar** en el presente de indicativo:

1. Nuestros amigos *son* jóvenes.   2. Esta revista *es* para Roberto.   3. Mi tío no *está* listo todavía.   4. Uds. y yo *estamos* hablando en español.   5. Yo sé que *es* necesario practicar.   6. Luis Sierra *es* de Colombia.   7. El joven *es* muy simpático.   8. Esta agua no *está* muy fría.   9. Aquella casa nueva *es* de piedra. *stone*   10. La hermana de Juan *está* muy enferma hoy.

D. Para completar con la forma correcta de **estar** o **ser** en el presente de indicativo, menos [except] en 17 y 18:

1. ¿Qué _es_ el tío de Juan? ¿ _Es_ médico?   2. Enrique _es_ de la Argentina; _es_ argentino.   3. Lima, que _está_ una ciudad grande, _está_ en el Perú.   4. Aunque aquella señora _es_ rica, nunca _está_ contenta.   5. ¿Qué hora _es_ ? —Creo que _son_ las cinco y media.   6. Los Andes, que _son_ montañas muy altas, siempre _están_ cubiertos de nieve.   7. La novia de Carlos _es_ rubia; [blonde] se dice que _es_ muy simpática.   8. El profesor Valdés no _está_ en su oficina hoy porque _está_ enfermo.   9. ¿Cómo _eres_ tú? ¿ _Estás_ muy cansado?   10. No _es_ difícil aprender el diálogo porque _es_ bastante corto.   11. ¿Cuál _es,_ la fecha de hoy? Y, ¿ _es_ martes o miércoles?   12. ¿Qué _estas_ haciendo tú en este momento? —Yo _estoy_ escuchando una cinta.   13. _es_ mejor decir que nosotros no _somos_ ni ricos ni pobres.   14. ¿Para quién _son_ estas cartas que _están_ escritas en portugués?   15. Aquellos niños que _están_ sentados en el patio _son_ muy corteses. [polite]   16. Hoy _es_ un día muy hermoso; por eso mi mamá _está_ trabajando en su jardín.   17. Las ventanas _están_ (*pres.*) abiertas. ¿Por quién _estuvieron_ (*pret.*) abiertas?   18. Este edificio _estuvo_ (*pret.*) construido por el señor Gómez. _Esta_ (*pres.*) bien construido.

II. La construcción reflexiva para expresar el sujeto indefinido *one, they, you, we, people*, y para expresar la voz pasiva

A. To express an indefinite subject, corresponding to English *one, people, we, you* (indefinite), Spanish uses **se** with the third person singular of the verb:

> **Se dice que él es médico.**   They say (People say, One says, We say, It is said) that he is a doctor.
> **No se puede entrar.**   One (People, You) cannot enter.
> **Se trabaja mucho aquí.**   One works (People, You work) hard here.

With a reflexive verb, and occasionally with other verbs, **uno** is used:

> **Uno se levanta tarde los domingos.**   One gets up late on Sundays.
> **No se (Uno no) puede hacer eso.**   One cannot do that (That cannot be done).

As in English, the third person plural may be used to indicate an indefinite subject:

Dicen que él saldrá pronto.   They say (It is said) that he will leave soon.

B. If the subject of a passive sentence is a thing and the doer of the action is not expressed, se is used to substitute for the passive voice. In this case the verb is in the third person singular or plural, depending on whether the subject is singular or plural. The reflexive verb normally precedes the subject in this construction:

Allí se habla español.   Spanish is spoken there.
Se cierran las tiendas a las cinco.   The stores are closed at five o'clock.
Se escribieron los artículos ayer.   The articles were written yesterday.
Se han publicado algunos en el periódico.   Some have been published in the newspaper.

When the subject is singular, as in **Allí se habla español,** the construction may be considered as an indefinite subject or as a passive sentence: *People (They) speak Spanish there,* or *Spanish is spoken there.*

Ejercicios

A. Después de escuchar cada frase, repitan la frase, cambiándola a la construcción reflexiva, según los modelos.

MODELOS: Cierran la puerta a las seis.   Se cierra la puerta a las seis.
           Aquí no compran libros.   Aquí no se compran libros.

1. En el Brasil hablan portugués.   2. Leen libros en la biblioteca.
3. No venden zapatos en la librería.   4. No conocen muy bien la música latinoamericana.   5. Cantan muchas canciones populares.   6. Ven un avión grande en el aeropuerto.   7. Aquí estudian problemas económicos.   8. No abren las oficinas hasta las diez.   9. Escriben muchos artículos buenos para este periódico.   10. Han publicado algunos de ellos.

B. Para expresar en español, usando **se** o **uno** como sujeto indefinido:

1. They say that it is going to rain.   2. How do they do that in Spain?
3. People know that she is in Mexico.   4. We cannot do that easily.
5. One enters through this door.   6. One dresses slowly at times.

III. La «a» personal

When the direct object of the verb is a definite person (or persons) or a personified object, the personal or distinctive **a** (not translated in English) regularly introduces the object, except after **tener:**

> **Encontré a Juanito en el jardín.**   I found Johnny in the garden.
> **Vimos al señor Gómez.**   We saw Mr. Gómez.
> **Temen a la muerte.**   They fear death.   *tener a (always)*
>
> BUT: **Tengo diez primos.**   I have ten cousins.

The personal **a** is also used when the direct object is **quien(es)**, *whom,* **¿quién(es)?** *whom?* or one of the indefinites or negatives[1] **alguien** and **nadie**, and **alguno, -a,** and **ninguno, -a,** when the last two refer to persons:

> **¿Has visto a alguien?**   Have you seen anyone?
> **No he llamado a ninguno de ellos.**   I haven't called any (one) of
>   them.

The distinctive **a** may also be used before a geographical proper name, unless the name is preceded by the definite article, although in current usage **a** is being omitted more and more in such constructions:

> **Visitaron (a) México.**   They visited Mexico.
> **Desean ver el Cuzco.**   They want to see Cuzco.

Because of the flexible word order in Spanish, the distinctive **a** is required occasionally to avoid ambiguity when both the subject and the direct object refer to things:

> **La paz sigue a la guerra.**   Peace follows war.

Ejercicio   Lean en español, supliendo la **a** personal cuando se necesite (*it is needed*):

1. Juan esperó __a__ Bárbara.   2. ¿Han visto Uds. __a__ sus tíos?

---

[1] See Lección cuatro, pages 100–104, for discussion of the indefinites and negatives.

3. ¿ __A__ quién llamaste?   4. Luis conoce bien __a__ Bogotá.
5. Yo conocí __a__ la señora Sierra.   6. No he ayudado __a__ nadie
hoy.   7. Él quería visitar _____ la Argentina.   8. Ana tiene __a__
muchos amigos allí.   9. ¿Acompañó Ud. __a__ alguien ayer?   10. Él
y yo saludamos __a__ la profesora.

IV. «Conocer» y «saber»

Conocer means *to know* in the sense of *to be acquainted with someone,
to know (be familiar with) something, to meet* (for the first time):

> **Yo conozco a la señorita.**   I know the young lady.
> **El profesor conoce bien la ciudad.**   The instructor knows the city
> well.

Saber means *to know* in the sense of *to have knowledge of, know facts;*
followed by an infinitive it means *to know how to, can* (mental ability):

> **Ya sé quién es.**   I already know who he is.
> **Sabíamos que él había llegado.**   We knew that he had arrived.
> **Luis sabe tocar la guitarra.**   Louis knows how to (can) play the
> guitar.

Para leer en español, completando las frases con la forma correcta de   *Ejercicio*
conocer o **saber**:

1. Yo __sé__ que Luis es colombiano.   2. Voy a preguntarle si __conoce__ a
Marta.   3. Nosotros __conocimos__ a Miguel Valdés anoche.   4. ¿__Sabe__ Ud.
dónde vive él?   5. ¿__Sabes__ tú si nuestro profesor __conoce__ bien el arte
mexicano?   6. Los estudiantes __saben__ hablar español.   7. Todo el
mundo __sabe__ que yo no __conozco__ bien el país.   8. Ana no ha __conocido__ a
mi amiga María.

A. Usos de los verbos **estar** y **ser**. Lean en español, supliendo la forma   **Resumen**
correcta del verbo que se necesite:

1. Mi mamá __está__ enferma hoy.   2. Esta comida __está__ (*tastes*)
muy rica.   3. ¿ __Es__ rico su amigo mexicano?   4. ¿Qué __es__
tu padre?   5. Mi hermano quiere __ser__ abogado.   6. Nuestra hermana __está__ contenta.   7. ¿De dónde __eres__ tú?   8. La puerta

~~estuvo~~ *fue* (*pret.*) abierta por mí.   9. La puerta todavía *está* abierta.
10. ¿ *Es* joven tu tía?   11. Yo *he estado* (*pres. perf.*) leyendo el libro.   12. *Son* las nueve y cuarto.

B. Usos de la construcción reflexiva y de la voz pasiva. Para expresar en español:

1. How does one say that in Spanish?
2. People believe that he is from Chile.
3. Books are not sold in this store.

4. One can learn this lesson easily.
5. The letter is written in Spanish.
6. One sits down in order to rest.

7. Caroline made these dresses.
8. The dresses were made by Caroline.
9. The dresses are well made.

10. John closed the door.
11. The door was closed by John.
12. The door is closed now.

Street in Guanajuato, Mexico.

C. Usos de la **a** personal y de los verbos **conocer** y **saber.** Para expresar en español:

1. Whom did you (*fam. sing.*) call?
2. Paul and I saw Louis Morales.
3. Have you (*pl.*) helped Jane today?
4. We know John's parents very well.
5. I know that they left last night.
6. Do you (*pl.*) know anyone in Spain?

Resumen de palabras y expresiones

casado, -a (con) married (to)	**la fila** row
las ciencias políticas political science	**formar parte de** to be a member of, form a part of
colombiano, -a (*also noun*) Colombian	**hay que** + *inf.* one must, it is necessary to
la comparsa group (*of actors, musicians*)	**la llegada** arrival
el curso course	**maravillosamente** marvelously
después de *prep.* after	**las matemáticas** math(ematics)
la ecología ecology	**el músico** musician
en casa de (Dorotea) at (Dorothy's)	**por eso** therefore, for that reason, that's why
en este (ese) momento at this (that) moment	**publicar** to publish
en punto sharp (*time*)	**toda la tarde** all afternoon
estar en su elemento to be in one's element	**todavía no** not yet
estar seguro, -a (de que) to be sure (that)	**todo el mundo** everybody

LECTURA I

Algunos aspectos del sistema educativo en Hispanoamérica

En vista del[1] interés que suscitan[2] los problemas de la educación, será útil examinar algunos aspectos del sistema educativo en los países hispanoamericanos.

A distinción del[3] sistema desarrollado[4] en los Estados Unidos, en Hispanoamérica la administración de la enseñanza[5] de cada país está *establishes* centralizada en un ministerio del gobierno. En este ministerio se fijan los programas de estudio[6] en todos los niveles[7] de la enseñanza, desde la primaria y secundaria hasta[8] la universitaria.

Al terminar la escuela primaria los alumnos que desean prepararse para los cursos universitarios pasan a las escuelas secundarias, llamadas liceos o colegios nacionales en algunos países. Los estudios en estas instituciones duran de cinco a seis años. Al terminarlos satisfactoriamente, los alumnos reciben el título de bachiller,[9] que los capacita para *aspire to* ingresar en[10] una universidad. En México los que aspiran a ingresar en la universidad tienen que asistir durante dos años más a una escuela preparatoria, que equivale, aproximadamente, a un *junior college* en Norteamérica.

La universidad hispanoamericana consta de[11] una serie de facultades (o escuelas, como las llaman en México) y el alumno ingresa directamente en una de ellas. Las principales son las de Medicina, Derecho,[12] Filosofía y Letras,[13] Ciencias Sociales y Políticas, Ciencias Físico-Químicas, Ingeniería, Arquitectura y Pedagogía.

Cada facultad tiene su *regulation* reglamento y plan de estudios, fijados por el

---

[1] **En vista de,** *In view of.*   [2] **suscitan,** *raise, arouse.*   [3] **A distinción de,** *Unlike.*
[4] **desarrollar,** *to develop.*   [5] **enseñanza,** *education, instruction.*   [6] **programas de estudio,** *curricula* (also see **plan de estudios** in fifth paragraph).   [7] **en todos los niveles,** *at all levels.*   [8] **desde . . . hasta,** *from . . . (up) to.*   [9] **título de bachiller,** *bachelor's degree.*   [10] **los capacita para ingresar en,** *qualifies them to enter.*   [11] **consta de,** *consists of.*   [12] **Derecho,** *Law.*   [13] **Letras,** *Letters* (= Literature).

ministerio. Como en el bachillerato, casi ninguna de las asignaturas[1] es de tipo electivo. La extensión del plan de estudios varía de una facultad a otra, pero generalmente exige de cinco a siete años de estudio. Al aprobar[2] los exámenes correspondientes a su facultad, el estudiante recibe el título de licenciado.[3]

Como en Norteamérica, tanto los estudiantes como los educadores[4] están tratando de[5] transformar y modernizar los programas de estudio en todos los niveles y de hacerlos asequibles[6] a sectores más amplios de la población. Y todos—sin omitir los gobiernos de los países hispano-americanos—comprenden también que, además de favorecer las universidades, es necesario aumentar el número de escuelas de artes y oficios[7] y de institutos tecnológicos y científicos si se quiere crear un personal capacitado para competir en el mundo moderno.

Class in phonetics, University of Mexico, Mexico City.

[1] **asignaturas,** *subjects* (of study).   [2] **Al aprobar,** *Upon passing.*   [3] **licenciado,** *licentiate* (holder of a licentiate or master's degree).   [4] **tanto . . . educadores,** *students as well as educators,* or *both students and educators.*   [5] **tratar de,** *to try to.*   [6] **asequibles,** *accessible, available.*   [7] **artes y oficios,** *arts and crafts.*

Elementary school pupil, Ecuador.

Elementary class demonstration of how rain is formed, Quito, Ecuador

Traduzcan al español las frases siguientes, tratando de imitar las cons- **Ejercicio**
trucciones y fraseología del texto:

1. We have been examining certain aspects of the educational system
   of the Hispanic-American countries.
2. It is interesting to learn that the administration of the system is
   centralized in a ministry of education.
3. This ministry determines the curricula of all the educational institutions of the country.
4. Students spend from six to eight years in the primary school and five
   or six more in the secondary school.
5. In some countries the secondary schools are called "liceos" or
   "colegios nacionales."
6. The degree of "bachelor," received when the student finishes the
   secondary school, qualifies him to enter a university.
7. The Spanish-American university consists of a series of schools,
   such as Law, Medicine, and Architecture, and the student enters
   one of them directly.
8. Upon completing the curriculum of one of these schools, the student
   receives the degree of "licentiate."
9. Students as well as educators understand that it is necessary to
   modernize the curricula at all levels.
10. All believe, also, that the educational institutions should make their
    programs available to broader sectors of the population.

NOTE: Students who use the *Workbook* and also listen to the tapes will
find in the tapes a comprehension exercise, based on each Lectura,
which the student is to complete by marking or writing responses in the
Workbook. In classes in which the *Workbook* is not used, the sections
provided for these exercises in the *Workbook* may be duplicated for use
separately.

Student, School of
Mechanical Engineering,
University of Mexico,
Mexico City.

LECCIÓN DOS

Los pronombres personales. Usos de los pronombres personales que
designan el sujeto. Colocación del pronombre como objeto del
verbo. Las formas preposicionales y la construcción redundante.
Los pronombres y verbos reflexivos. Colocación respectiva de dos
pronombres, uno como objeto directo y otro como objeto indirecto.
Repaso de los números cardinales

¿Dónde pasó usted las vacaciones?

(La profesora habla con los estudiantes antes de comenzar la clase de español.)

Srta. Flores.	Esta mañana ustedes han llegado muy temprano. Podemos charlar un poco antes de comenzar la lección.
Carlos.	Señorita Flores, ¿por qué no nos cuenta usted lo que hizo durante el verano?
Srta. Flores.	Pasé el mes de julio en México, estudiando en la Universidad de Guadalajara. Me divertí mucho. Y usted, Carlos, ¿dónde pasó usted las vacaciones?
Carlos.	Las pasé aquí, trabajando en una tienda. No puedo quejarme; me gustó mucho el trabajo.
Srta. Flores.	Me alegro de saber eso. ¿Qué va a hacer con el dinero que ha ganado?
Carlos.	Lo estoy ahorrando para un viaje que pienso hacer el verano que viene.
Srta. Flores.	Se va a hacer rico, Carlos. Y usted, María, ¿qué hizo durante las vacaciones?
María.	Hicimos un viaje muy interesante por el suroeste.
Srta. Flores.	¿Qué sitios visitaron?
María.	Visitamos muchos sitios en los estados de Nuevo México, Arizona y California.
Srta. Flores.	En esos estados muchos ríos, ciudades y montañas tienen nombres españoles, ¿verdad?
María.	¡Ya lo creo! Le habría dado a usted gusto oírme pronunciarlos correctamente.
Srta. Flores.	Bueno, si quieren acercarse y sentarse, podremos comenzar la lección de hoy. Otro día hablaremos más de sus vacaciones.

A. Para contestar en español en oraciones completas:

Preguntas sobre el diálogo

1. ¿Quiénes hablan en este diálogo? 2. ¿Qué le pregunta Carlos a la profesora? 3. ¿Qué hizo la profesora durante el verano? 4. ¿Qué hizo Carlos durante el verano? 5. ¿Qué piensa hacer Carlos con el dinero que ha ganado? 6. ¿Qué hizo María durante las vacaciones? 7. ¿Qué estados visitó María? 8. Según María, ¿qué le habría dado gusto a la profesora?

Aplicación del diálogo

1. ¿Llega el profesor (la profesora) tarde o temprano a la clase de español? 2. Si los estudiantes llegan temprano, ¿qué hacen antes de comenzar la clase? 3. ¿Qué hizo Ud. durante el verano? 4. ¿Qué le gustaría hacer durante las vacaciones de Navidad? 5. ¿Qué estados del suroeste ha visitado Ud.? 6. ¿En qué estados de los Estados Unidos hay ríos y ciudades con nombres españoles? 7. ¿Qué nombres españoles de ciudades norteamericanas recuera Ud.? 8. ¿Por qué tienen esas ciudades nombres españoles?

B. Estudien las expresiones siguientes para emplear algunas de ellas en el diálogo citado, o para usarlas en un diálogo nuevo basado sobre el modelo:

acampar to camp	**practicar el español** to practice
la caminata hike, long walk	Spanish
comprar un coche (una bicicleta)	**quedarse aquí** to stay here
to buy a car (a bicycle)	**seguir (i, i) trabajando** to continue
costar (ue) mucho to cost a	working
great deal	**visitar a mis abuelos** to visit my
la estación de gasolina service	grandparents
(gas) station	**vivir en el Canadá (la Florida)** to
ir de caza to go hunting	live in Canada (Florida)
el lugar de veraneo summer resort	**ya es la hora** the hour is over
pescar to fish	

Pronunciación

A. Spanish **p, t, c (qu, k)**. In pronouncing these consonants, recall that the Spanish sounds are pure stops, not aspirated stops as in English. To avoid the aspiration, or puff of air, that often follows the English sounds ($p^h en$, $t^h en$, $c^h an$), the breath must be held back during the articu-

lation of the sound. The aspiration of the English sound is especially
objectionable before **r** and before unstressed **i** and **u** in diphthongs;
avoid **t**ʰ**iene, t**ʰ**res.** In the case of **t,** remember also that the Spanish sound
is dental; that is, the tip of the tongue touches the back of the upper
teeth, not the ridge above the teeth as in English. Pronounce after your
teacher:

1. patio	pregunta	profesor	mapa	puse
2. tú	admitir	está	tengo	Tomás
3. canto	caso	saco	cuento	busqué
pequeño	aquí	quise	kilómetro	kilogramo
4. tiempo	tiene	quiero	puede	entrego

B. Review the observations on Spanish intonation, Repaso tres, pages
26–27, and Appendix A, pages 300–302, then read in Spanish, noting
carefully the intonation patterns and the division into breath-groups.
Why have certain syllables been underlined?

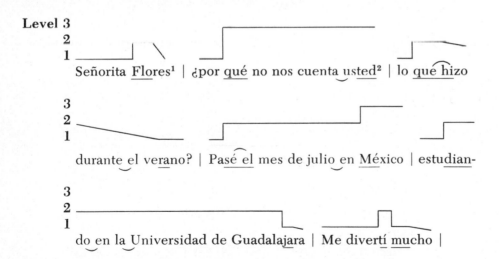

¹ An introductory phrase of this type is treated as a declarative statement, with the voice
rising to the speaker's normal tone on the first accented syllable and falling slightly there-
after; note also that, in direct address, titles such as **señorita, señor, señora** lose their normal
accent and become unstressed words when they precede a proper noun.   ² In an interrogative sentence consisting of two breath-groups and beginning with an interrogative
word (**¿por qué?** in this case), the first group ends above the normal tone.

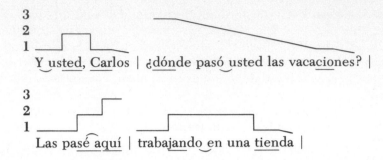

Y usted, Carlos | ¿dónde pasó usted las vacaciones? |

Las pasé aquí | trabajando en una tienda |

Notas gramaticales

I. Los pronombres personales

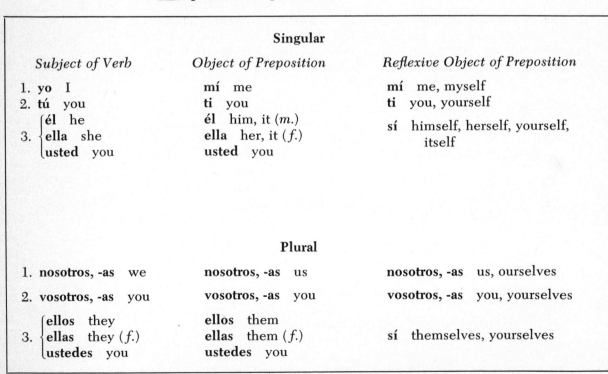

Singular		
Subject of Verb	*Object of Preposition*	*Reflexive Object of Preposition*
1. **yo** I	**mí** me	**mí** me, myself
2. **tú** you	**ti** you	**ti** you, yourself
3. { **él** he / **ella** she / **usted** you	**él** him, it (*m.*) / **ella** her, it (*f.*) / **usted** you	**sí** himself, herself, yourself, itself
Plural		
1. **nosotros, -as** we	**nosotros, -as** us	**nosotros, -as** us, ourselves
2. **vosotros, -as** you	**vosotros, -as** you	**vosotros, -as** you, yourselves
3. { **ellos** they / **ellas** they (*f.*) / **ustedes** you	**ellos** them / **ellas** them (*f.*) / **ustedes** you	**sí** themselves, yourselves

II. Usos de los pronombres personales que designan el sujeto

The subject pronouns, except the formal forms for *you* (**usted** and **ustedes**, which may be abbreviated to **Ud.** and **Uds.**, or **Vd.** and **Vds.**, in writing), are omitted unless needed for clearness or emphasis, or when two are combined as the subject. **Usted** and **ustedes**, which require the third person of the verb in Spanish, are regularly expressed, although excessive repetition should be avoided. The English subjects *it* and *they*, referring to things, are rarely expressed in Spanish, and the impersonal subject *it* is always omitted.

In general, the familiar forms **tú** and **vosotros, -as**, are used when the given name would be used in English (in speaking to children, relatives, or close friends). In most of Spanish America **ustedes** is used for the

Singular

Direct Object of Verb	*Indirect Object of Verb*	*Reflexive Object of Verb*
me me	**me** (to) me	**me** (to) myself
te you	**te** (to) you	**te** (to) yourself
{**le, lo**[1] him		
{**lo** it (*m.*)		
la her, it (*f.*)		{(to) him, it
{**le** you (*m.*)	**le (se)** {(to) her, it	**se** {(to) herself, itself
{**la** you (*f.*)	{(to) you	{(to) yourself
lo it (*neuter*)		

Plural

nos us	**nos** (to) us	**nos** (to) ourselves
os you	**os** (to) you	**os** (to) yourselves
los, les[2] them		
las them (*f.*)	**les (se)** {(to) them	**se** {(to) themselves
{**los, les**[2] you	{(to) you	{(to) yourselves
{**las** you (*f.*)		

[1] In Spanish America **lo** is more frequently used than **le**, meaning *him*.   [2] In Spain the form **les** is often used instead of **los** as direct object referring to masculine persons.

plural of *you*, both familiar and formal (this practice is followed in the dialogues and exercises of this text):

Vamos al café ahora.   We are going (Let's go) to the café now.
Ella lee un libro y él escribe una carta.   She reads a book and he writes a letter.
Él y ella están en la biblioteca.   He and she are in the library.
Ellas son felices.   They (*f.*) are happy.
Usted habla bien el español.   You speak Spanish well.
Tú hablas mejor que él.   You speak better than he.

III. Colocación del pronombre como objeto del verbo

A. All object pronouns (direct, indirect, and reflexive) are regularly placed immediately before the verb, including the auxiliary verb **haber** in the compound tenses (three major exceptions are explained in B, C, D, below):

Nos enviaron una tarjeta.   They sent us a card.
Ella no me llamó anoche.   She didn't call me last night.
Los he visto en la calle.   I have seen them in the street.

B. Object pronouns are placed after, and are attached to, affirmative commands. (In commands the formal **usted(es)** is regularly expressed, but the familiar **tú** is used only for emphasis.) Note that an accent must be written on the stressed syllable of a verb of more than one syllable when a pronoun is added:

Tráigalos usted en seguida.   Bring them at once.
Tómalo (tú), por favor.   Take it, please.

BUT: **Dame el periódico, por favor.**   Give me the newspaper, please.

In negative commands, however, object pronouns precede the verb and are placed between the negative and the verb:

No les escriba usted hoy.   Do not write to them today.
No me digas eso.   Don't tell me that.
No te pongas el vestido nuevo.   Don't put on the new dress.

C. Object pronouns are usually attached to an infinitive:

> **Empecé a leerlo.**   I began to read it.
> **Vamos a sentarnos ahora.**   We are going to (Let's) sit down now.

However, object pronouns may precede conjugated forms of certain verbs and verbal expressions, such as **ir a, haber de, querer, poder, saber,** followed by an infinitive:

> **Lo voy a hacer** or **Voy a hacerlo.**   I am going to do it.
> **Los he de traer** or **He de traerlos.**   I am to bring them.
> **La quieren ver** or **Quieren verla.**   They want to see her (it).
> **Usted se puede sentar** or **Usted puede sentarse.**   You may (can) sit down.
> **Se va a hacer** (or **Va a hacerse**) **rico, Carlos.**   You are going to become rich, Charles.

D. Object pronouns are attached to the present participle, except in the progressive forms of the tenses, in which case they may be attached to the participle or placed before the auxiliary. An accent must be written over the stressed syllable of the participle when a pronoun is attached:

> **Dándome la carta, Juan salió.**   Giving me the letter, John left.
> **Están leyéndola** or **La están leyendo.**   They are reading it.
> **Lo estoy ahorrando** or **Estoy ahorrándolo.**   I am saving it.

A. Repitan cada frase y luego substituyan la frase en cursiva con el   *Ejercicios*
pronombre correspondiente, según el modelo.

MODELO: Carlos ahorró *el dinero.*   Carlos ahorró el dinero.
					Carlos lo ahorró.

1. ¿Dónde pasó Ud. *las vacaciones?*
2. Visitamos *a nuestros abuelos.*
3. Mi hermano compró *la bicicleta.*
4. No he practicado mucho *el español.*
5. ¿No ha hecho Ud. *el trabajo?*
6. No pronuncian bien *los nombres.*

B. Para contestar empleando formas de mandato afirmativas y negativas, substituyendo el substantivo con el pronombre correspondiente.

MODELO: ¿Hago *el trabajo*?   Sí, hágalo Ud. No, no lo haga Ud.

1. ¿Traigo *el disco* ahora?   4. ¿Aprendo *los diálogos*?
2. ¿Compro *las flores*?   5. ¿Cierro *el libro*?
3. ¿Escribo *la composición*?   6. ¿Lavo *el coche* hoy?

C. Después de escuchar cada frase, repítanla dos veces, substituyendo el substantivo con el pronombre correspondiente.

MODELO: Estoy leyendo *el libro*.   Estoy leyéndolo. Lo estoy leyendo.

1. Estoy ahorrando *el dinero*.   4. Yo estaba visitando *a María*.
2. Están trayendo *las sillas*.   5. Uds. no están mirando *el mapa*.
3. Estaban estudiando *la lección*.   6. No estás sirviendo *los refrescos*.

D. Después de escuchar cada frase, repítanla dos veces, substituyendo el substantivo con el pronombre correspondiente.

MODELO: Voy a hacer *el viaje*.   Voy a hacerlo. Lo voy a hacer.

1. ¿Vas a pasar *el verano*   3. No quieren dejar *las guitarras*
   allí?   aquí.
2. Puedo traer *las*   4. No hemos de aprender *la*
   revistas.   *canción*.

IV. Las formas preposicionales y la construcción redundante

A. The prepositional forms are used only as objects of prepositions. They are the same as the subject pronouns, except for **mí** and **ti**:

   Corrían hacia mí.   They were running toward me.
   Charlaré con él (ella).   I shall chat with him (her).

When used with **con**, the forms **mí, ti,** and the reflexive **sí** (see section V, A, page 64) become **conmigo, contigo, consigo,** respectively:

   No van conmigo (contigo).   They aren't going with me (with you).

B. The prepositional phrases **a mí, a ti, a él,** etc., are used in addition to the direct or indirect object pronoun for emphasis:

> **Yo la vi a ella, pero no a Juan.**   I saw <u>her</u>, but not John.
> **A mí me gusta el cuadro.**   <u>I</u> like the picture.

Since the indirect objects **le** and **les** have several meanings, the prepositional forms are often added for clearness. They are added for courtesy when the direct object pronouns meaning *you* (formal) are used:

> **Yo le di a ella las flores.**   I gave her the flowers.
> **Mucho gusto en conocerle(-la) a Ud.**   (I'm very) pleased to meet (know) you.

C. When a noun is expressed as the indirect object of the verb in Spanish, the corresponding indirect object pronoun is normally added. With forms of **gustar,** the prepositional form must be used:

> **Le dimos a Felipe el dinero.**   We gave Philip the money.
> **A Carlos le gusta (Le gusta a Carlos) la casa.**   Charles likes the house.

The prepositional form must also be used when the verb is understood:

> **Les enseñé el reloj a ellos, pero no a ella.**   I showed them the watch, but not her.

The prepositional form would also be used to express a direct object pronoun when the verb is understood: **¿A quién viste? ¿A él?** *Whom did you see? Him?*

Repitan cada frase; luego, substituyan el substantivo con el pronombre correspondiente, según el modelo.   *Ejercicio*

MODELO: Corrieron hasta *la esquina.*   Corrieron hasta la esquina. [corner]
                                            Corrieron hasta ella.

1. Fueron al río con *Ricardo.*   2. Charle Ud. un poco con *Marta.*
3. Estos regalos son para *mis padres.*   4. No hablen Uds. más de *las muchachas.*   5. Los niños corren hacia *la casa.*   6. El coche está enfrente de *ese edificio.*   7. Roberto trabaja en *aquella tienda.*   8. En *esos estados* hay varios parques.

V. Los pronombres y verbos reflexivos

A. Reflexive pronouns, which are used when the subject acts upon itself, may be direct or indirect objects:

Ricardo se sentó.   Richard sat down.
Voy a lavarme la cara.   I'm going to wash my face.
Levántense ustedes.   Get up.
Estamos desayunándonos.   We are eating breakfast.

The pronouns **mí, ti, nosotros, -as, vosotros, -as,** and **sí** (third person singular and plural) may be used reflexively: **para mí,** *for myself*; **para sí,** *for himself, herself, yourself* (formal), *itself, themselves* (*m.* and *f.*), *yourselves*; **Ella se lo llevó consigo,** *She took it with her(self)*.

B. Reflexive verbs are much more frequent in Spanish than in English. A few verbs are always used reflexively in Spanish, while others may also be used as transitive or intransitive verbs, although usually with different meanings. Certain verbs and expressions which are regularly reflexive in Spanish are:

atreverse (a) *to dare* (*to*)	jactarse (de) *to boast* (*of*)
darse cuenta de *to realize*	quejarse (de) *to complain* (*of*)

Many intransitive verbs in English (that is, verbs that cannot take a direct object) are expressed in Spanish by using the reflexive pronoun with a transitive verb. Note the following verbs:

acercar *to bring . . . near*	acercarse (a) *to approach, draw near*
acostar (ue) *to put to bed*	acostarse (ue) *to go to bed*
despertar (ie) *to awaken* (somebody)	despertarse (ie) *to wake up* (*oneself*)
divertir (ie, i) *to amuse*	divertirse (ie, i) *to have a good time*
lavar *to wash* (something)	lavarse *to wash* (*oneself*)
levantar *to raise, lift* (*up*)	levantarse *to get up, rise*
mudar *to change*	mudarse (de) *to change* (one's clothing, lodging, etc.)
sentar (ie) *to seat*	sentarse (ie) *to sit down*

With certain verbs the reflexive translates *to become, get,* or *to be* plus an adjective. A few examples are:

alegrar *to make glad*	alegrarse (de) *to be glad (of, to)*
cansar *to tire (someone)*	cansarse *to become (get) tired*
vestir (i, i) *to dress* (someone)	vestirse (i, i) *to dress (oneself), get dressed*

Other common verbs whose meaning is changed when used reflexively are:

dormir (ue, u) *to sleep*	dormirse (ue, u) *to fall asleep*
hacer *to do, make*	hacerse *to become*
hallar *to find*	hallarse *to be found, be*
llamar *to call*	llamarse *to call oneself, be named*
poner *to put, place*	ponerse *to put on (oneself); (+ adj.) to become*

See Appendix E, pages 333–334, for other verbs of these types.

Repitan cada frase; luego, al oír el sujeto nuevo, cambien la frase según el modelo.   *Ejercicio*

MODELO: *Yo* me dormí en seguida.   Yo me dormí en seguida.
         (*José*)   José se durmió en seguida.

1. *Ana* se puso los guantes.   (*Ana y yo*)
2. *Yo* voy a sentarme cerca de ella.   (*Ricardo*)
3. *La niña* se vistió despacio.   (*Los niños*)
4. *Enrique* se divirtió mucho ayer.   (*Yo*)
5. *Tú* te levantaste tarde hoy.   (*Ud.*)
6. *Jorge* está lavándose las manos.   (*Tú*)
7. *Juan y José* se cansaron de eso.   (*Luis y yo*)
8. *Pablo* se alegró de verlos.   (*Pablo y Carlos*)
9. *Yo* no me atreví a nadar en el río.   (*Nosotros*)
10. *Miguel y yo* nos mudamos de ropa hace media hora.   (*Yo*)
11. *Nosotros* no nos quejamos del profesor.   (*Roberto*)
12. *Tú* no te diste cuenta de eso.   (*Uds.*)

VI. Colocación respectiva de dos pronombres, uno como objeto directo y otro como objeto indirecto

When two object pronouns are used together, the indirect object pronoun always precedes the direct. When both are in the third person, the indirect (**le, les**) becomes **se**. Since **se** may mean *to him, to her, to you* (formal), *to it, to them*, the prepositional forms are often required in addition to **se** for clarity. A reflexive pronoun precedes any other object pronoun.

> **Él nos lo vendió.**   He sold it to us.
> **Lléveselo usted a ellos.**   Take it to them.
> **Ella empezó a leérmela.**   She began to read it to me.
> **No se lo escribas (tú) a ella.**   Don't write it to her.
> **Dándomelos, Pablo salió.**   Giving them to me, Paul left.
> **Luisa se lo puso.**   Louise put it on.

Remember that an accent mark must be written on the stressed syllable of the verb when two object pronouns are attached to an infinitive, an affirmative command form, or present participle.

Ejercicio   Repitan cada frase; luego, substituyan los substantivos en cursiva con los pronombres correspondientes, según los modelos.

MODELOS: Juan le dio *las cosas*   Juan le dio las cosas a Marta.
            a Marta.   Juan se las dio a ella.
        José se lava *la cara.*   José se lava la cara.
                    José se la lava.

1. Le llevé *el dinero a Felipe.*
2. No le escribí *la carta a Luis.*
3. Envíeles Ud. *los libros a sus amigos.*
4. No le vendan Uds. *a Ana el coche.*
5. No quieren traerme *las cosas* hoy.

6. No puedo leerles *el cuento a los niños.*
7. Él está explicándoles *los problemas.*
8. Ellos se están poniendo *los zapatos.*
9. Pónganse Uds. *el abrigo.*
10. No te laves *las manos* todavía.

Para repasar   **VII. Repaso de los números cardinales**

A. Después de repasar los números cardinales y sus usos (*Appendix C, pages* 310–312), lean en español:

1. 18 muchachas.   2. 21 países.   3. 51 universidades.   4. 100 páginas.

5. 116 discos.   6. 200 preguntas.   7. 365 días.   8. 500 casas.   9. 1,000 empleados.   10. 1,000,000 de personas.   11. 5,000,000 de dólares. 12. 150,000 hombres.

B. Repasen el uso de los números para expresar fechas y los nombres de los meses (*Appendix C, page* 312); luego, lean en español:

1. January 1, 1970.   2. May 2, 1972.   3. October 12, 1492.   4. September 29, 1547.   5. July 4, 1775.   6. February 22, 1789.   7. December 10, 1810.   8. November 11, 1812.   9. April 15, 1817. 10. March 31, 1827.   11. June 29, 1903.   12. August 14, 1809.

Resumen

A. Repitan cada frase; luego, substituyan el substantivo en cursiva con el pronombre correspondiente, colocándolo (*placing it*) correctamente:

1. Ellos comenzaron *el trabajo*.   2. Carlos visitó *a su abuelo*.   3. María compró *la bicicleta*.   4. Marta no hizo *los vestidos*.   5. Luis no leyó *las revistas*.   6. Traiga Ud. *las cintas*.   7. Lleven Uds. *sus cuadernos*. 8. Sirvan Uds. *los refrescos*.   9. No despierten Uds. *a Luisa*.   10. No pierdan Uds. *el autobús*.

11. Estamos terminando *las composiciones*.   12. Él y ella están leyendo *la novela*.   13. Mi mamá está visitando *a sus padres*.   14. Estaban practicando *el español*.   15. Vamos a leer *la lección*.   16. Han de llamar *a sus amigos*.   17. No querían lavar *el coche*.   18. Podían aprender *los diálogos*.

B. Repitan cada frase; luego, substituyan los substantivos en cursiva con los pronombres correspondientes:

1. Juan le envió *una tarjeta a Ana*.   2. Léales Ud. *la carta a los niños*. 3. No le vendas *el coche a Pablo*.   4. Ella está poniéndose *el vestido*. 5. Pónganse Uds. *los zapatos*.   6. No te pongas *el sombrero*.   7. Tengo que lavarme *las manos*.   8. Él ya se ha lavado *la cara*.

9. Los niños jugaban en *el parque*.   10. Marta está cerca de *sus padres*. 11. Ellos se quejaron de *las películas*.   12. Están sentados detrás de *su papá*.

"Calandrias" (horse-drawn coaches, often somewhat run-down) await customers in the square in front of the cathedral, Guadalajara, Mexico.

C. Para expresar en español, usando las formas correspondientes a **Ud.** para los mandatos:

1. Martha and he practice with me.
2. He and I work more than they.
3. We saw Barbara; we saw her.
4. I found my gloves; I found them.
5. They took the course; they took it.
6. I bought the cards; I bought them.
7. Write her a letter tomorrow.
8. Take them this magazine, please.
9. Mary likes this picture.
10. Do not give Ann the flowers today.
11. Do not show them (*f.*) to her now.
12. Give it (*m.*) to him, not to us.
13. Jane amused the children; she amused them.
14. Robert's mother awakened him; Robert woke up early.
15. The teacher seated Mary in the first row; Mary sat down there.
16. We did not realize that Richard became a doctor.

Resumen de palabras y expresiones

ahorrar   to save
dar gusto a   to please, give
   pleasure to
detrás de *prep.*   behind
divertirse (ie, i) mucho   to have a very
   good time, amuse oneself very much
enfrente de *prep.*   in front of
haber de + *inf.*   to be (be supposed) to

hace (media hora)   (a half hour) ago
mucho gusto en conocerle (-la) a Ud.
   (I'm very) pleased to meet (know)
   you
un poco   a little, a little while
el (verano) que viene   next
   (summer)
¡ya lo creo!   of course! I should say so!

LECTURA II

La herencia española en el suroeste

Las tierras del suroeste de los Estados Unidos tienen un interés especial: en ellas se hallan en contacto dos grandes culturas, la angloamericana y la hispánica.

Hasta 1810 estas tierras formaban la frontera septentrional[1] del imperio español en América. Pertenecieron a México desde ese año hasta 1848, cuando, por el tratado de Guadalupe Hidalgo, pasaron a los Estados Unidos.

Los españoles exploraron las costas de California y las tierras al norte de México en la primera mitad del siglo XVI. Durante los años 1540–1542 Coronado llegó a la región que hoy se conoce como Kansas y soldados de su expedición descubrieron el Gran Cañón del Río Colorado. En 1598 Juan de Oñate estableció la primera capital de la provincia de Nuevo México en San Juan de los Caballeros, cerca del pueblo indio de San Juan.

Los españoles establecieron misiones y colonias en Arizona y Texas en los siglos XVII y XVIII, y en California en el siglo XVIII. Las actividades misioneras del célebre padre Kino, en Arizona, se realizaron en la última parte del siglo XVII, y las de Fray Junípero Serra, en California, durante los últimos años del siglo siguiente.

La misión y el presidio[2] fueron los instrumentos esenciales utilizados en la colonización española. Se establecían en lugares fértiles y estratégicos y muchos de ellos han dado origen a ciudades hoy populosas y prósperas.

Es importante recordar que tanto la agricultura como la ganadería[3] se desarrollaron en el suroeste después de la llegada de los españoles. Se introdujeron nuevos cultivos[4] y la introducción de los animales domésticos llegó a[5] transformar totalmente la economía de ciertas regiones.

La influencia española en la vida y costumbres de los indios del suroeste fue notable. Además de enseñarles artes y oficios útiles—como

[1] **septentrional,** *northern.*   [2] **presidio,** *garrison of soldiers; fort.*   [3] **ganadería,** *livestock raising.*   [4] **cultivos,** *crops.* (On page 72, line 1, the word means *cultivation.*) [5] **llegó a,** *came to, went so far as to.*

71

la herrería[1] y la carpintería—y nuevos métodos para el cultivo de la tierra, los misioneros propagaban entre ellos la fe cristiana y elementos de la cultura europea.

Lo más notable del suroeste es el vigor con que se han conservado en algunas regiones aspectos de la cultura hispánica. En California, en el norte de Nuevo México y en el sur de Colorado se cantan coplas y romances[2] tradicionales de origen español y circulan refranes, adivinanzas[3] y cuentos populares del mismo origen. En las fiestas religiosas y populares es igualmente clara la influencia española. La arquitectura del suroeste refleja también la influencia del estilo español, combinado en Nuevo México, por ejemplo, con elementos de las culturas indígenas. Como se ha explicado en un libro anterior,[4] muchas palabras españolas han pasado al inglés por el contacto de las dos culturas en el suroeste.

Aunque las tierras del suroeste han atraído siempre inmigrantes de México, la corriente inmigratoria ha aumentado considerablemente durante el siglo actual. La situación desfavorable en que se encuentran muchos de los inmigrantes recientes ha producido problemas graves, que sólo podrán resolverse eliminando obstáculos y preparando el terreno[5] para una más efectiva cooperación y una más fecunda[6] coexistencia de las dos culturas.

Ejercicio   Escriban tres oraciones sobre cada uno de los temas siguientes:

1. Exploraciones de los españoles en los territorios que hoy forman el suroeste de los Estados Unidos.
2. Actividades de misioneros españoles en Arizona y California.
3. Aspectos de la cultura hispánica en el suroeste.

Santa Barbara Mission, Santa Barbara, California (built in 1786, destroyed by earthquake in 1812, and rebuilt in 1815.)

[1] **herrería,** *blacksmithing.*   [2] **coplas y romances,** *popular songs and ballads.*   [3] **adivinanzas,** *riddles.*   [4] Turk and Espinosa, *Foundation Course in Spanish, Third Edition,* Heath, 1974.   [5] **preparando el terreno,** *paving the way.*   [6] **fecunda,** *fruitful.*

LECCIÓN TRES

Usos del pretérito de indicativo.   Usos del imperfecto de indicativo.
Verbos con significados especiales en el pretérito.   La construcción
reflexiva para traducir *each other, one another*.   Observaciones sobre
el uso de algunos verbos

Hablando por teléfono

*(Juan está estudiando; su compañero de cuarto, Miguel, regresa[1] de la
biblioteca.)*

Miguel.	¡Hola, Juan! ¿Qué hay de nuevo?
Juan.	¡Hombre! Acaba de llamarte Carlos.
Miguel.	¿Dejó algún recado?
Juan.	No. Sólo dijo que quería hablar contigo. Me preguntó si yo quería ir al cine con él.
Miguel.	Le llamaré ahora mismo. (*Marca el número en el teléfono.*) 323-1647[2] . . . ¡Qué mala suerte! ¡La línea está ocupada! (*Cuelga el auricular. Al poco rato vuelve a levantar el auricular y marca el número otra vez. Contesta Carlos.*)
Carlos.	¡Bueno![3]
Miguel.	¿Está Carlos? ¿Podría hablar con él?
Carlos.	Habla Carlos. ¿Quién llama?
Miguel.	¡Ah! ¿Eres tú? Aquí habla Miguel.
Carlos.	Hombre, te llamé hace unos minutos para preguntar por el diccionario que te presté.
Miguel.	¿No recuerdas que me lo pediste la semana pasada? Lo busqué pero no pude hallarlo. Creo que lo tiene Luisa. Si quieres, la llamaré.
Carlos.	No, no te preocupes. Ahora recuerdo que ella lo necesitaba para un informe que estaba preparando. Yo la llamaré.
Miguel.	Muy bien. Pues, nos vemos mañana en el partido de fútbol, ¿verdad?
Carlos.	¡Cómo no! Pensamos ir todos. Saluda a Juan de mi parte.
Miguel.	Gracias. Hasta luego, Carlos.

[1] In Spanish America **regresar**, *to return, come back*, is widely used along with **volver**, which
is more common in Spain.   [2] Read: **tres dos tres—uno seis cuatro siete.**   [3] Several
Spanish expressions are used for the telephone greeting *Hello*: **Diga**, or **Dígame** (Spain);
Bueno (Mexico); **Hola** (Argentina); **Aló** (in many other countries).

A. Para contestar en español en oraciones completas:

Preguntas sobre el diálogo

1. ¿Cómo se llaman los estudiantes que hablan en este diálogo? 2. ¿Quién acaba de llamar por teléfono? 3. ¿Qué le había dicho Carlos a Juan? 4. ¿Por qué cuelga Miguel el auricular cuando marca el número de Carlos? 5. ¿Por qué había llamado Carlos a Miguel? 6. Según Miguel, ¿quién tiene ahora el diccionario de Carlos? 7. ¿Qué está preparando Luisa? 8. ¿Dónde se verán Miguel y Carlos?

Aplicación del diálogo

1. ¿Cuáles son algunas expresiones que se emplean en español al contestar el teléfono? 2. ¿Dónde hay un teléfono público cerca de aquí? 3. ¿Tiene Ud. un teléfono en su cuarto? 4. ¿Cuál es el número de teléfono de sus padres? 5. ¿Cuántas veces por semana habla Ud. por teléfono con sus padres? 6. ¿Se necesita un diccionario en esta clase? 7. ¿Cuántos diccionarios tiene Ud.? 8. ¿A cuántos partidos de fútbol ha ido Ud. este semestre?

B. Preparen un diálogo original, de unas ocho líneas, para recitar en clase, empleando las frases y preguntas siguientes como elemento inicial:

1. **Miguel.**   ¿Eres tú, Carlos? Te llamo para preguntarte si te trajeron tus padres el regalo que te habían prometido.

   Carlos.   Sí, Miguel. Y ¡qué sorpresa! No puedes imaginarte lo que me trajeron.

2. **Luis.**   Estamos haciendo planes para una fiesta el sábado por la noche. ¿Podrás venir?

   Dorotea.   ¡Cómo no! Con mucho gusto. ¿Para qué hora me invitas?

Pronunciación

The sounds of **r** and **rr**. Single **r**, except when initial in a word and when after **l**, **n**, or **s**, is a voiced, alveolar, single trill; that is, it is pronounced with a single tap produced by the tip of the tongue against the gums of the upper teeth. The sound is much like *dd* in *eddy* produced rapidly. When initial in a word, when after **l**, **n**, or **s**, and when doubled, the sound is a multiple trill, the tip of the tongue striking the gums in a series of very rapid vibrations. Pronounce after your teacher:

1. comeré   fueron   grabar   haré   eres
   iremos   Carlos   suerte   tres   auricular
   ahora   cuarto   hablar   llamaré   preguntar

2. rato   regalo   Ricardo   honra   guitarra
   alrededor   Enrique   querré   Israel   ferrocarril
   río   erre   carro   correr   recado

3. El perro de San Roque
   no tiene rabo
   porque Ramón Ramírez
   se lo ha cortado.

4. Erre con erre cigarro,
   erre con erre barril,
   rápidos corren los carros
   del ferrocarril.

Notas gramaticales

I. Usos del pretérito de indicativo

The preterit tense, sometimes called the past definite, is a narrative tense. It expresses a single past action or state, the beginning or end of a past action, or a series of acts when viewed as a complete unit in the past, regardless of the length of time involved. Duration is often defined by an adverb or adverbial expression; for example, **nunca** regularly requires the preterit:

¿Dejó algún recado?   Did he leave any message?
Te llamé hace unos minutos.   I called you a few minutes ago.
Pablo hizo tres viajes a México el año pasado.   Paul made three trips to Mexico last year.
Los moros vivieron en España casi ocho siglos.   The Moors lived in Spain almost eight centuries.
Empecé a tocar unos discos.   I began to play some records.
Él nunca creyó lo que le dije.   He never believed what I told him.

II. Usos del imperfecto de indicativo

A. General use of the imperfect tense

The imperfect indicative tense, frequently called the past descriptive, describes past actions, scenes, or conditions which were continuing for an indefinite time in the past. The speaker transfers himself mentally to a point of time in the past and views the action or situation as though it were taking place before him. There is no reference to the beginning or end of the action or situation described:

Era un día frío del mes de febrero. El mar ofrecía un color azul obscuro. La madre y su hijo iban tristes y silenciosos por la playa. Cuando se hallaban a mitad del camino más o menos, vieron a lo lejos dos personas que venían hacia ellos.	It was a cold day in the month of February. The sea was a dark blue color. The mother and her son were going along the beach sad and silent. When they were more or less half way, they saw in the distance two persons who were coming toward them.

B. Specific uses of the imperfect tense

1. To describe what was happening at a certain time:

> **Marta leía (estaba leyendo) y María escribía (estaba escribiendo).** Martha was reading and Mary was writing.

2. To indicate that an action was customary or habitual, or indefinitely repeated, equivalent to English *used to, would,*[1] *was (were) accustomed to* plus an infinitive, and often to *was (were)* plus the present participle:

> **Iban a la iglesia todos los domingos.**   They went (used to go, would go) to church every Sunday.

3. To describe the background or setting in which an action took place or to indicate that an action was in progress when something happened (the preterit indicates what happened under the particular circumstances described):

> **Juan estudiaba cuando yo regresé de la biblioteca.**   John was studying when I returned from the library.
> **Llovía mucho cuando Ana volvió a casa.**   It was raining hard when Ann returned home.

4. To describe a mental, emotional, or physical state in the past; thus, Spanish verbs used for English *believe, know, wish, feel, be able,* etc., are often in the imperfect rather than in the preterit (see section III):

---

[1] Do not confuse *would* meaning a habitual action with *would* used as a conditional: **¿Podría (yo) hablar con él?**   *Could I (Would I be able to) talk with him?* (See Lección seis, page 139.)

Yo creía que estabas enferma.   I believed that you were ill.
Ella quería ir al cine con él.   She wanted to go to the movie with him.

5. To express indirect discourse in the past:

Carlos dijo que quería hablar contigo.   Charles said he wanted to talk with you.
Ana me preguntó si yo podía ir con ella.   Ann asked me if (whether) I could go with her.

6. To express time of day in the past:

¿Qué hora era cuando saliste? —Eran las ocho.   What time was it when you went out? —It was eight o'clock.

III. Verbos con significados (*meanings*) especiales en el pretérito

Certain common verbs, such as **saber, conocer, tener, querer, poder,** often have special meanings when used in the preterit. In general, the imperfect tense indicates existing desire, ability, etc., while the preterit indicates that the act was or was not accomplished. Contrastive examples are:

Sabíamos que Pablo estaba en Chile.   We knew that Paul was in Chile. (*Mental state*)
Supimos anoche que él estaba allí.   We found out (learned) last night that he was there.

Yo conocía[1] bien a Marta.   I knew Martha well.
Yo la conocí el año pasado.   I met her (made her acquaintance) last year.

Tomás quería llamar a Inés.   Tom wanted to call Inez.
Tomás quiso llamarla.   Tom tried to call her.

Ella no quería quedarse en casa.   She didn't want (was not willing) to stay at home.
Ella no quiso quedarse allí.   She refused to (would not) stay there.

---

[1] **Conocer** may be used in all tenses to mean *to recognize.*

Ana tenía una carta cuando la vi.   Ann had a letter when I saw her.
Ana tuvo tres cartas esta mañana.   Ann received (got) three letters
this morning.

Le dije que podía buscar el libro.   I told him that I could look for
the book (*i.e.*, I was able to look, capable of looking, for the book).
Lo busqué pero no pude hallarlo.   I looked for it but couldn't find it
(*i.e.*, I did not succeed in finding it).

Ejercicios   **A.** Repitan cada frase; luego, cambien el tiempo del verbo al pretérito
de indicativo:

1. Miguel regresa de la biblioteca.
2. Habla por teléfono con Carlos.
3. Yo marco el número en el
   teléfono.
4. Ana vuelve a levantar el
   auricular.
5. Carlos quiere hablar con
   Miguel.
6. Luis le pregunta a Ana por un
   buen diccionario.
7. Miguel no puede hallarlo.

8. Carlos no quiere llamar a
   Dorotea.
9. Yo empiezo a preparar el
   informe.
10. El amigo de Juan no hace
    nada.
11. ¿Quiénes te traen regalos?
12. ¿Quién viene contigo?
13. ¿Van Uds. a la fiesta el
    sábado por la noche?
14. Yo busco un regalo para
    Carolina.

B. Repitan cada frase; luego, cambien el tiempo del verbo al imperfecto
de indicativo:

1. Ella quiere charlar un rato contigo.   2. Pablo se preocupa con eso.
3. Dorotea necesita el diccionario de español.   4. Son las diez de la
noche.   5. Pablo y yo no sabemos eso.   6. Vamos a la biblioteca todos
los días.   7. Se encuentran allí a menudo.   8. ¿Puedes hablar con
Ana María a veces?   9. Hay varias personas en la calle.   10. Hacemos
planes para la fiesta.

C. Repitan cada frase; luego, cambien el primer verbo al pretérito y el
segundo al imperfecto de indicativo:

1. Carlos dice que quiere cenar con Miguel.
2. Él me pregunta si yo voy a la biblioteca con él.

3. Cuando marca el número, la línea está ocupada.
4. ¿Ves a la muchacha que piensa tocar los discos?
5. Elena nos escribe que puede visitarnos pronto.
6. Yo veo que hay muchos estudiantes en el teatro.

D. Lean cada frase en español, supliendo la forma correcta del pretérito
o del imperfecto de indicativo de cada infinitivo en cursiva:

1. Juan no *hablar* por teléfono cuando yo *entrar* en su cuarto.
2. Él *estudiar* su lección cuando yo *abrir* la puerta.
3. Juan me *decir* que *querer* enseñarme una composición que había
    escrito.
4. Él me *preguntar* si yo *tener* tiempo para leerla.
5. Al leerla, yo *ver* que *estar* bien escrita y que *ser* muy interesante.
6. Mientras yo *estar* leyéndola, *sonar* el teléfono.
7. Juan *levantar* el auricular y *contestar* en español.
8. Los dos *charlar* unos minutos y luego Juan *colgar* el auricular.
9. Su amigo *querer* saber si Juan *poder* ir al teatro el sábado.
10. Al poco rato yo *mirar* el reloj; *ser* las ocho y yo *tener* que irme en
    seguida.

IV. La construcción reflexiva para traducir *each other, one another*

The plural reflexive pronouns **nos, os, se** may express a mutual or reciprocal action (one subject acting upon another):

> **Nos vemos en el partido de fútbol.**   We'll see (be seeing) each other
>   at the football game.
> **Nos escribíamos a menudo.**   We wrote to each other often.
> **Se saludan todos los días.**   They greet one another every day.

The redundant construction **uno (-a) a otro (-a), el uno al otro, unos a
otros (unas a otras)**, etc., may be added for clarity or emphasis. With
prepositions other than **a**, the redundant form is added regularly:

> **Se burlan uno de otro.**   They make fun of each other (one another).
> **Ellos se gritaron el uno al otro.**   They shouted to each other (one
>   another).

Son hechos uno para otro. (they are made for each other.)

Para contestar afirmativamente en español: *Ejercicio*

1. ¿Se escriben Uds. a menudo?   2. ¿Se verán Uds. mañana?

3. ¿Se miraron ellos tristemente?   5. ¿Se quejaban uno de otro?
4. ¿Van a ayudarse uno a otro?   6. ¿Se saludaron Ana y Pablo?

V. Observaciones sobre el uso de algunos verbos

A. Preguntar and pedir

Preguntar means *to ask* (a question); **preguntar por** means *to ask for* (*about*), *inquire about*:

> **Él me preguntó si yo quería ir.**   He asked me if (whether) I wanted
> to go.
> **Te llamé para preguntar por el libro.**   I called you to ask about the
> book.

Pedir means *to ask* (a favor), *ask for* (something), *to request* (something of someone). Later the use of **pedir**, *to ask* or *request someone to do something*, will be discussed:

> **Le pedí a Miguel el diccionario.**   I asked Michael for the dictionary.
> **Ellas no nos pidieron nada.**   They didn't ask us for anything.

With both these verbs (also with **decir** and a few other verbs), the person of whom something is asked is the indirect object. The neuter pronoun **lo** is used to complete the sentence if a direct object is not expressed:

> **¿Pueden ir también? —Se lo preguntaré (a ellos).**   Can they go too?
> —I shall ask them (*lit.*, ask it of them).
> **¿Le dijo Ud. eso a Felipe? —Sí, se lo dije.**   Did you tell Philip that?
> —Yes, I told him.

B. Tomar, llevar, and other verbs meaning *to take*

Tomar means *to take* in the sense of *to take* (in one's hand), *to take* (meals, food, beverages, etc.):

> **José, toma el libro, por favor.**   Joe, take the book, please.
> **¿Tomas café?**   Do you take (drink) coffee?
> **Tomaron el avión de las dos.**   They took the two-o'clock plane.

Llevar means *to take* (*along*), *carry* (to some place):

>   **Tomás llevó a su novia al baile.**   Tom took his girlfriend to the
>   dance.
>   **Yo tomé la maleta en la mano y la llevé al coche.**   I took the suitcase
>   in my hand and took (carried) it to the car.

Llevarse means *to take* (*carry*) *away* (often *with oneself*):

>   **Ella compró una blusa y se la llevó.**   She bought a blouse and took it
>   with her.

Quitar means *to take away* (*off*), *remove from*; **quitarse** means *to take off*
(from oneself):

>   **Ella quitó el libro de la mesa.**   She took (removed) the book from the
>   table.
>   **Ellos se quitaron los zapatos.**   They took off their shoes.

Sacar means *to take out, take* (photos):

>   **Ella sacó muchas cosas de la bolsa.**   She took many things from her
>   purse.
>   **Yo saqué varias fotos en el parque.**   I took several photos in the park.

A few idiomatic expressions which include other uses of the English
verb *to take* are:

>   **bañarse**   to take a bath, go swimming
>   **dar un paseo (una vuelta)**   to take a walk *or* stroll
>   **desayunarse**   to take (eat) breakfast
>   **despedirse (i, i) (de)**   to take leave (of)   *despedir – to fire (someone)*
>   **dormir (ue, u) la siesta**   to take a nap
>   **hacer un viaje (una excursión)**   to take a trip (excursion)
>   **tardar (mucho) en**   to take (very) long to, be (very) long in, delay
>   (long) in

C. Gustar and querer (a)

The English verb *to like*, usually referring to things, is regularly expressed in Spanish by **gustar**, meaning *to please, be pleasing* (*to*). The

English subject (*I, he, you,* etc.) becomes the indirect object in Spanish, and the English object becomes the subject of the Spanish verb; *e.g.,* instead of *She likes the hat,* turn the sentence into *The hat is pleasing to her:* **Le gusta a ella el sombrero.** This means that normally only the third person singular and plural forms of **gustar** are used. English *it* and *them* are not expressed, and the Spanish subject, when expressed, usually follows the verb:

Me (Nos) gusta la foto.   I (We) like the photo.
¿No le gusta a Ud.?   Don't you like it?
Le gustaban a ella los regalos.   She liked the gifts.

Remember that when a noun is the indirect object of **gustar,** the indirect object pronoun must also be used (see Lección dos, page 63):

A Carlos le gustan (Le gustan a Carlos) los discos.   Charles likes the records.

Querer (a) means *to like, love, feel affection for,* a person:
~use a when followed by person

Queremos mucho a Juanita.   We like Jane very much (We are very fond of Jane).
Felipe y Ana se quieren mucho.   Philip and Ann love each other a great deal.

Ejercicios   **A.** Para contestar afirmativamente en oraciones completas:

1. ¿Cuándo diste un paseo?   ¿Anoche?
2. ¿Cuándo dormiste la siesta?   ¿Ayer por la tarde?
3. ¿Qué autobús tomó Ud.?   ¿El autobús de las dos?
4. ¿Adónde llevó Jorge a María?   ¿Al cine?
5. ¿Cuándo hizo Ud. una excursión?   ¿El sábado?
6. ¿Qué se quitó Ud.?   ¿El abrigo?
7. ¿Quién se bañó esta tarde?   ¿Usted?
8. ¿Quiénes se desayunaron temprano?   ¿Ustedes?
9. ¿Adónde llevaron ellos las cosas?   ¿A casa?
10. ¿Cuál de ellas tardó mucho en llegar?   ¿Luisa?

B. Para contestar negativamente en oraciones completas:

1. ¿A quién le pidió Ud. el diccionario?   ¿A Inés?
2. ¿A quién le preguntó Ud. por el curso?   ¿A Miguel?
3. ¿De quién se despidieron Uds.?   ¿Del profesor Díaz?
4. ¿Dónde sacaron Uds. muchas fotos?   ¿En el parque?
5. ¿A quién quiere Roberto?   ¿A Carolina?
6. ¿Quiénes se quieren mucho?   ¿Marta y Jorge?

A. Lean en español, cambiando cada infinitivo en cursiva a la forma **Resumen**
correcta del pretérito o del imperfecto de indicativo:

1. *Ser* las nueve cuando yo *volver* del aeropuerto.   2. Cuando yo *ver* a
María, la *invitar* a almorzar conmigo.   3. Pablo le *preguntar* a Carolina
si ella *poder* ir al cine con él.   4. Miguel *marcar* el número de María,
pero ella no *estar* en casa.   5. Él *querer* hablar con ella acerca de un
informe que *estar* preparando.   6. Al poco rato él *ir* al café, pero no
poder hallarla.   7. Los estudiantes *charlar* cuando el profesor *entrar*
en la sala de clase.   8. Ellos *saber* que él *ir* a darles un examen.
9. Jorge *andar* despacio por la calle cuando yo le *ver*.   10. Yo le *decir*
que *querer* devolverle su libro de español.

B. Usos del verbo *to take*. Para expresar en español:

1. Thomas took Martha to the dance.   2. Did Paul take the ten-o'clock
bus?   3. Will you (*pl.*) take a trip to Mexico?   4. Why didn't he take a
walk with her?   5. I believe (that) he took a nap.   6. I took several
photos in the park.   7. He took off his hat; he took it off.   8. He took the
watch in his hand.

C. Usos del pronombre reflexivo **se** y de los verbos **gustar** y **querer.**
Para expresar en español:

1. We see each other every day.   2. Raymond and I help each other.
3. They were making fun of each other.   4. Do you visit one another
often?   5. I like this gold watch.   6. Do you (*fam. sing.*) like it?   7. We
like George's guitar.   8. They do not like this picture.   9. Mary likes
to write articles.   10. Do you (*pl.*) like to talk on the telephone?
11. Charles likes Helen very much.   12. I know that the two love each
other.

Statue of Simón Bolívar,
Caracas, Venezuela

Resumen de palabras y expresiones

acabar de + *inf.*   to have just + *p.p.*
acerca de *prep.*   about, concerning
ahora mismo   right now, right away
al poco rato   after a short while
el **auricular**   receiver
el **autobús (de las dos)**   the (two-o'clock)
   bus
¡bueno!   hello! (*telephone*)
colgar (ue)   to hang (up)
de la noche   p.m., in the evening
de mi parte   for me, on my part
el **diccionario**   dictionary
¿está Carlos?   is Charles in (at home)?
habla (Carlos)   this is (Charles),
   (Charles) is speaking
la **línea**   line
los **(las) dos**   the two, both

marcar el número   to dial the number
pensamos ir todos   all of us (we all)
   intend to go
por (el) teléfono   by (on the) telephone
por semana   per (each) week
preocuparse (con, por)   to worry
   (about), be concerned (with, about)
público, -a   public
¡qué mala suerte!   what bad luck!
¡qué sorpresa!   what a surprise!
el **recado**   message
regresar   to return, come back
el **sábado por la noche**   Saturday evening
   (night)
volver (ue) a (levantar)   (to lift *or* take
   up) again

LECTURA III

Una conversación entre estudiantes: la liberación de la mujer

(Luis, un estudiante colombiano, entra en el Centro Universitario, donde encuentra a sus amigos Carlos y Dorotea. Carlos le llama.)

Carlos. ¡Luis! ¡Qué agradable volver a verte! Siéntate aquí con nosotros. ¿No quieres tomar algo?

Luis. ¡Con mucho gusto! He estado en el laboratorio toda la tarde y necesito descansar un poco.

Dorotea. ¿Te vas acostumbrando a[1] la vida en Norteamérica? ¿Qué te ha impresionado más durante tu estancia[2] en los Estados Unidos?

Luis. Pues, en primer lugar,[3] una universidad como ésta, con sus bibliotecas y laboratorios, el sistema de becas[4] y de residencias, los programas deportivos y la abundancia de cursos electivos . . . Nosotros no tenemos los recursos económicos para instituciones de este tipo.

Carlos. ¿Y en segundo lugar?

Luis. Pues, a decir verdad,[5] la libertad de la mujer. Creo que a todo extranjero que visita los Estados Unidos le asombra[6] la posición privilegiada de la mujer norteamericana.

Carlos. Como sabrás,[7] no están satisfechas todavía. ¿Has oído hablar de[8] la liberación de la mujer?

Luis. También en Hispanoamérica hay feministas militantes. Tal vez[9] las necesitemos más que ustedes.

Dorotea. En Hispanoamérica la educación de la mujer es muy conservadora, ¿verdad?

Luis. No es muy liberal, por cierto. Y lo peor es que sólo una minoría muy pequeña se prepara para una carrera universitaria.

Dorotea. Con los grandes cambios que se realizan modernamente en la sociedad, habrá más oportunidades para las generaciones jóvenes, ¿verdad?

[1] **¿Te vas acostumbrando a . . . ?** *Are you gradually becoming accustomed to . . . ?* (For explanation of the use of **ir**, see Lección doce, page 261.) [2] **estancia,** *stay.* [3] **en primer lugar,** *in the first place.* [4] **becas,** *scholarships.* [5] **a decir verdad,** *in truth, really.* [6] **a todo extranjero . . . asombra,** *every foreigner . . . is astonished (amazed) at.* [7] **Como sabrás.** *As you probably know.* (For a discussion of the use of the future tense for conjecture or probability in the present, see Lección seis, page 141.) [8] **¿Has oído hablar de . . . ?** *Have you heard of . . . ?* [9] **Tal vez,** *Perhaps.* (For explanation of the use of the subjunctive after **tal vez,** see Lección diez, pages 220–221.)

Luis. Indudablemente. Las costumbres y formas de vida van cambiando rápidamente. Las jóvenes estudian y viajan más y aprenden a trabajar; en general, están al tanto de[1] lo que pasa en los demás países del mundo.

Dorotea. Pues, eso es lo que deseamos. La mujer feminista está convencida de que para cumplir sus deberes como es debido,[2] necesita cultura completa e independencia.

Luis. Siempre ha habido, por supuesto,[3] mujeres excepcionales en Hispanoamérica. ¿Quién no se acuerda de Gabriela Mistral, la poetisa chilena que ganó el Premio Nobel de Literatura?

Carlos. Uno de los problemas más críticos parece ser la situación de la mujer casada. Para una buena feminista es un insulto el refrán que dice: «La mujer casada, la pierna quebrada, y en casa.»[4]

Luis. Eso ha pasado a la historia;[5] pero es cierto que el hogar[6] es el centro de la vida de la mujer hispana. Es que se trata de[7] dos formas de vida muy distintas. En Hispanoamérica la mayoría de[8] las mujeres casadas no fuman ni conducen sus automóviles; pero no envidian a la mujer norteamericana que cuida de los niños y de su jardín, cocina[9] y hasta limpia la casa cuando es necesario, además de dedicarse a[10] las más diversas profesiones, compitiendo con el hombre.

Dorotea. Es que en la casa hispana hay sirvientes para ocuparse de[11] todo.

Carlos Y no olvidemos que aquí la electricidad coopera en[12] las labores domésticas, para limpiar las alfombras, lavar la ropa, fregar los platos,[13] exprimir las naranjas ... Todo se hace mecánicamente, con un grado mínimo de energía, sin estropear[14] las manos ni romper las uñas.

Luis.` Bueno, no discutamos más. Es claro que las reformas deseadas no son las mismas en todas partes.[15]

Carlos. Pero todos deseamos[16] que las mujeres alcancen la plenitud de su vida, es decir,[17] que tengan los mismos derechos y los mismos deberes que[18] los hombres.

Dorotea. Y también, que puedan intervenir en el gobierno de los pueblos, en perfecta colaboración con los hombres, para procurar la felicidad y bienestar de todos.

---

[1] **están al tanto de,** *they are aware of (informed of).*   [2] **para cumplir ... debido,** *to fulfil her duties as is only right.*   [3] **Siempre ... supuesto,** *There have always been, of course.* [4] **La mujer ... casa,** *Woman's place is in the home (The married woman [should have] a broken leg and [remain] at home).*   [5] **Eso ha pasado a la historia,** *That has become a thing of the past.*   [6] **hogar,** *home.*   [7] **Es que se trata de,** *The fact is that it is a question of.*   [8] **la mayoría de,** *most.*   [9] **cocina,** *cooks.*   [10] **además de dedicarse a,** *in addition to devoting herself to.*   [11] **para ocuparse de,** *to take care of.*   [12] **coopera en,** *takes part in.*   [13] **fregar los platos,** *to wash the dishes.*   [14] **sin estropear,** *without ruining.*   [15] **en todas partes,** *everywhere.*   [16] **todos deseamos,** *we all (all of us) desire.* [17] **es decir,** *that is (to say).*   [18] **los mismos ... que,** *the same ... as.*

Hard work is part of the daily life of the Indian women of Chichicastenango, Guatemala

Escriban un breve resumen, de unas ciento cincuenta palabras, de **Ejercicio**
«Una conversación entre estudiantes: la liberación de la mujer.»

LECCIÓN CUATRO

**Usos del artículo definido. Usos del artículo indefinido. El género
y el número de los substantivos. Usos de las palabras indefinidas
y negativas**

El almuerzo entre amigas

*(Elena se encuentra en el apartamento de Luisa. Están discutiendo los
planes para la próxima reunión del Club Español.)*

Elena. ¡Hemos tenido mucha suerte! El profesor Navarro acepta nuestra
invitación.

Luisa. ¿Hablará sobre la poesía contemporánea?

Elena. Sí, y como él también es poeta, dice que tendrá mucho gusto en leer
algunos poemas suyos.

Luisa. ¡Magnífico! La profesora Valdés dará la bienvenida a todos y luego
presentará al conferenciante.

Elena. *(Mirando su reloj de pulsera.)* Pero, ¿sabes que ya son las doce y
media? Si no me doy prisa, voy a llegar tarde para el almuerzo en la
residencia.

Luisa. ¿Por qué no te quedas a almorzar conmigo? Veré si queda algo en la
nevera . . . *(Abre la nevera.)* Hay leche, queso, jamón, lechuga y
tomates.

Elena. Nunca tomo mucho al mediodía. Si me permites ayudarte, me
quedaré.

Luisa. Bueno; puedes poner la mesa mientras yo preparo unos emparedados
y caliento una lata de sopa.

Elena. No te molestes tanto. Yo me conformo con cualquier cosa.

Luisa. No es ninguna molestia. ¿Tomas café o té?

Elena. Café, por favor, con un poco de leche y azúcar. Yo lo prepararé.

Luisa. *(Al poco rato.)* Bueno, no es ningún banquete, pero estarás[1] muerta
de hambre.

Elena. Como dice el refrán español, «A buen hambre[2] no hay pan duro, ni
falta salsa a ninguno[3]».

---

[1] **estarás,** *you must be (probably are).* (See footnote 7, page 89.)   [2] **A buen hambre,**
When hunger is great. Apocopated feminine forms of adjectives, such as **buen, mal, primer,
tercer, postrer, algún,** and **ningún,** although frequent in Golden Age Spanish, are no longer
considered standard forms. They are still found in proverbs, fixed phrases, and rural
speech.   [3] **ni . . . ninguno,** *nor is anyone in need of sauce.* Compare the English, "Hunger is the best sauce."

A. Para contestar en español en oraciones completas:

Preguntas sobre el diálogo

1. ¿Dónde se encuentra Elena?   2. ¿Qué están discutiendo las dos amigas?   3. ¿Por qué dice Elena que han tenido mucha suerte? 4. ¿Sobre qué hablará el profesor Navarro?   5. ¿Quién presentará al conferenciante?   6. ¿Se queda a almorzar Elena con Luisa?   7. ¿Qué hay en la nevera?   8. ¿Qué prepara Luisa para el almuerzo?

Aplicación del diálogo

1. ¿Hay un Club Español en esta universidad?   2. ¿Asisten muchos estudiantes a las reuniones del Club Español?   3. ¿Son interesantes las reuniones del Club Español?   4. ¿Vive Ud. en una residencia de estudiantes o en un apartamento?   5. ¿Por qué les gusta a algunos estudiantes vivir en un apartamento?   6. ¿Le gustan a Ud. las comidas en las residencias de estudiantes?   7. ¿A qué hora toma Ud. el almuerzo generalmente?   8. ¿De qué refrán español se acuerda Ud.?

B. Estudien las palabras siguientes para emplear algunas de ellas en el diálogo citado o para usarlas en un diálogo nuevo basado sobre el modelo:

la bandeja tray	**la mayonesa** mayonnaise
la botella bottle	**el postre** dessert
la cafetera coffeepot	**la sartén** (*pl.* **sartenes**) frying pan
la cafetera eléctrica electric percolator	**la servilleta** napkin
la ensalada salad	**el tocino** bacon
el flan custard	**la tortilla** omelet (*Spain*); corn pancake (*Mexico*)

Pronunciación

Review the observations on Spanish intonation (Repaso tres, pp. 26–27, and Lección dos, pp. 57–58); then write the first three exchanges of the dialogue of this lesson, dividing them into breath-groups and syllables, and outline the intonation patterns. Read the exchanges, paying close attention to the intonation patterns.

Notas gramaticales

I. Usos del artículo definido

The definite article **el** (*pl.* **los**) or **la** (*pl.* **las**) is used in Spanish, as in English, to denote a specific noun. In addition, the definite article in

Spanish has a number of other important functions. A few of the special uses in Spanish are:

1. With abstract nouns and with nouns used in a general sense, indicating a whole class:

> ¿Quién no admira la belleza? Who doesn't admire beauty?
> ¿Hablará sobre la poesía contemporánea? Will he talk about contemporary poetry?
> Me gusta mucho el arte mexicano. I like Mexican art very much.

2. With titles (except before **don, doña, san, santo, santa**) when speaking about, but not directly to, a person:

> El profesor Navarro acepta nuestra invitación. Professor Navarro accepts our invitation.

> BUT: Buenos días, señora Valdés. Good morning, Mrs. Valdés.
> Don Carlos López dio una conferencia. Don Carlos López gave a lecture.

3. With days of the week and seasons of the year, except after **ser**, and with dates, meals, hours of the day, and modified expressions of time:

> Vendrán el sábado. They will come (on) Saturday.
> Juan regresó el doce de mayo. John returned (on) May 12.
> Voy a llegar tarde para el almuerzo. I'll be (arrive) late for lunch.
> Ya son las doce y media. It is already twelve-thirty.
> Los vi la semana pasada. I saw them last week.

> BUT: Hoy es lunes. Today is Monday.
> Es otoño. It is autumn.

el lunes – on Monday
los lunes – on Mondays

4. With parts of the body, articles of clothing, and other things closely associated with a person, in place of the possessive adjective when the reference is clear:

> Marta se lavó las manos. Martha washed her hands.
> Nos quitamos los zapatos. We took off our shoes.
> Yo he perdido el reloj. I have lost my watch.
> Ella tiene el pelo rubio. She has blond hair (Her hair is blond).

5. With the name of a language, except after **de** and **en** or immediately after **hablar** (and sometimes after such verbs as **aprender, comprender, escribir, estudiar, leer, saber**):

El español no es fácil.   Spanish is not easy.
Ana habla bien[1] el francés.   Ann speaks French well.

BUT: ¿Habla Ud. portugués?   Do you speak Portuguese?
Éste es un libro de español.   This is a Spanish book.
La carta está escrita en inglés.   The letter is written in English.

(costs is at)

El café está á
89¢ la libra.

6. With nouns of rate, weight, and measure (English regularly uses the indefinite article):

Cuestan treinta dólares el par.   They cost thirty dollars a pair.
Pagué ochenta centavos la docena.   I paid eighty cents a dozen.

7. With names of rivers and mountains, with proper names and names of places when modified, and with the names of certain countries and cities:

El Amazonas está en el Brasil.   The Amazon (River) is in Brazil.
Conocemos la España moderna.   We know modern Spain.

When you use
def. art. before
country, don't
use a unless
preceding verb
requires a.

Some commonly used names of countries and cities which are preceded by the definite article in conservative literary usage (but which are often used without the article in journalistic and colloquial use) are:

(el) Canadá	(el) Brasil	(el) Perú	(el) Callao
(los) Estados Unidos	(el) Ecuador	(el) Paraguay	(el) Cuzco
(la) Argentina	(la) Florida	(el) Uruguay	(la) Habana

The article is seldom omitted in the case of El Salvador, which means *The Savior.*

Omit def. art. —
1) Apposition, no article
Washington, capi-
tal de los EEUU
es muy bonito.
2) Titles of rulers
Felipe Segundo,
rey de España
vivió en el Escorial.

NOTE: Special use of the definite article el. Feminine nouns which begin with stressed a- or ha- require el in the singular, instead of la, when the article immediately precedes: el agua, *the water,* el hambre, *hunger;* but las aguas, *the waters,* la altura, *the height.*
   Recall the two contractions in Spanish of the masculine singular definite article: a + el = al; de + el = del. Examples: Vamos al cine, *We are going (Let's go) to the movie;* Entro en el cuarto del muchacho, *I enter the boy's room.*

---

[1] When any word other than the subject pronoun comes between forms of hablar and the name of a language, the article is used.

II. Usos del artículo indefinido

The indefinite article **un** (*m.*), **una** (*f.*), *a, an*, is regularly repeated before each noun:

Ella tiene un reloj y una pulsera. She has a watch and bracelet.

The plural form **unos, unas** means *some, any, a few, several, about* (in the sense of approximately). Normally *some* and *any* are expressed in Spanish only when emphasized:

estar a – is at

Ayer vi unas blusas bonitas. Yesterday I saw some (a few) pretty blouses.

El señor Díaz tiene unos sesenta años. Mr. Díaz is about sixty years old.

BUT: **¿Tiene Ud. dinero?** Do you have any money?

No tenemos que tomar notas. We don't have to take (any) notes.

In Spanish the indefinite article is omitted in certain cases in which it is regularly used in English:

1. After **ser,** with an unmodified noun of profession, occupation, religion, nationality, rank, or political affiliation, or in answer to the English *What is* (*he*)?

El padre de Juanita es médico. Jane's father is a doctor.

¿Qué es él? —Es profesor. What is he? —He is a teacher.

The indefinite article is used, however, when a person's identity is stressed, and when these nouns are modified:

¿Quién es ella? —Es una profesora. Who is she? —She is a teacher.

Ella es una buena profesora. She is a good teacher.

2. Often before nouns, particularly in interrogative and negative sentences, after prepositions, and after certain verbs (such as **tener** and **buscar**), when the numerical concept of *a, an* (*one*) is not emphasized:

¿Busca Ud. casa ahora? Are you looking for a house now?

José salió sin sombrero. Joseph went out without a hat.

Marta no tiene coche. Martha doesn't have a (has no) car.

3. With adjectives such as **otro, -a,** *another,* **tal,** *such a,* **cien(to),** *a (one) hundred,* **mil,** *a (one) thousand,* **cierto, -a,** *a certain,* **medio, -a,** *a half,* and with **¡qué!** *what a!* in exclamations:

Tráigame Ud. otra bandeja.   Bring me another tray.
Cierta muchacha me dijo eso.   A certain girl told me that.
¡Qué hombre!   What a man!

Ejercicio   Lean en español, supliendo el artículo—definido o indefinido—cuando sea necesario:

1. Buenos días, _____ señor López. *El*_____ señor Díaz no ha llegado todavía.
2. Hoy es _____ miércoles. Siempre tengo tres clases *los*_____ miércoles.
3. Ellos hablan _____ español. Dicen que *el*_____ español es difícil.
4. Piensan ir a *la*_____ España. Quieren conocer bien *la*_____ España contemporánea.
5. El tío de Ana es _____ autor. Es *un*_____ autor distinguido.
6. ¿Qué es _____ don Carlos? —Creo que es _____ músico.
7. ¿Quién es _____ doña Inés? —Se dice que es *una*_____ secretaria.
8. Felipe no tiene _____ reloj. Vamos a regalarle *un*_____ reloj de oro.
9. ¿Busca Ud. _____ disco hoy? —Sí, busco *un*_____ disco hecho en España.
10. A ella le gustan *las*_____ rosas. Su novio le manda _____ flores cada semana.
11. María habla bien *el*_____ portugués. No habla _____ francés.
12. Carlos siempre toma _____ café aquí. No le gusta *el*_____ café frío.

III. El género (*gender*) y el número de los substantivos

A. Nouns referring to male beings, most nouns ending in **-o,** days of the week, the names of languages, certain nouns ending in **-ma, -pa, -ta,** and infinitives used as nouns, are masculine:

el jueves Thursday   **el español** Spanish   **el mapa** map

BUT: **la mano** hand
      la radio radio (*as a means of communication*)
      la foto (*abbreviation of* **fotografía**) photo

Nouns referring to female beings and most nouns ending in -a (except those ending in -ma, -pa, -ta) or in -(c)ión, -dad, -tad, -tud, -umbre, -ie are feminine:

    la invitación invitation   **la reunión** meeting   **la verdad** truth

    BUT: **el día** day   **el avión** (air)plane

Some nouns ending in -a, particularly in -ista, are either masculine or feminine: **el (la) artista**, *artist* (man or woman). The gender of other nouns must be learned by observation:

    el plan plan   **el jamón** ham   **la suerte** luck   **la leche** milk

Many nouns ending in -o, particularly those of relationship, change o to a for the feminine: **el hijo**, *son*, **la hija**, *daughter.*

B. In general, to form the plural of nouns, add -s to those ending in an unaccented vowel and -es to those ending in a consonant, including y. Most nouns ending in an unstressed syllable ending in -s and most family names do not change in the plural: **el (los) parabrisas**, *windshield(s)*, **el (los) tocadiscos**, *record player(s)*, **el (los) lunes**, *Monday(s)*; **Gómez** (family name), **los Gómez**, *the Gómez family.* **Los señores Gómez** means *Mr. and Mrs. Gómez.*

Singular	Plural
el emparedado sandwich	**los emparedados** sandwiches
el refrán proverb	**los refranes** proverbs
el joven young man	**los jóvenes** young men
el examen examination	**los exámenes** examinations

Note that the accent is not written on the plural **refranes** and that it is added on the plurals **jóvenes** and **exámenes** to keep the stress on the same syllable as in the singular. Nouns ending in -z change the z to c before -es, and those ending in -ión drop the accent in the plural: **el lápiz, los lápices; la lección, las lecciones.**

    Certain nouns denoting rank or relationship may be used in the masculine plural to refer to individuals of both sexes: **los reyes**, *the kings, the king(s) and queen(s)*; **los hermanos**, *the brothers, the brother(s) and sister(s).*

Ejercicios   **A.** Repitan cada oración; luego, repítanla otra vez, cambiando los substantivos al plural y haciendo los otros cambios necesarios.

MODELO: El amigo de ella trae su   El amigo de ella trae su libro.
          libro.   Los amigos de ellas traen sus
                                            libros.

1. La niña tiene el lápiz en la mano.   2. El profesor le explica la lección al estudiante.   3. El poeta va a leer ese poema suyo a la clase.   4. La mujer siempre pasa por la calle los lunes.   5. La profesora de francés no sabe el refrán.   6. El artista nos enseña el cuadro español.   7. La muchacha habla del plan para la próxima reunión.   8. El joven no puede aceptar nuestra invitación.   9. El conferenciante hablará sobre un problema social.   10. El estudiante mira la foto del parque nacional.

B. Para contestar negativamente:

1. ¿Trabajas todo el día en casa?   5. ¿Tiene jardín la casa del señor
2. ¿Es profesora la señorita   Díaz?
   Navarro?   6. ¿Tienes clase los sábados?
3. ¿Es artista la señora Valdés?   7. ¿Son interesantes los refranes?
4. ¿Conoces bien las costumbres   8. ¿Aceptas la invitación para el
   peruanas?   almuerzo?

C. Después de oír el substantivo, repítanlo empleando el artículo definido; luego, repitan la frase en el plural.

MODELO: mapa   el mapa, los mapas

1. hijo.   2. profesora.   3. parque.   4. mano.   5. reunión.   6. universidad.   7. mes.   8. ciudad.   9. viaje.   10. jardín.   11. librería. 12. país.   13. poema.   14. avión.   15. noche.   16. viernes.   17. flor. 18. rey.   19. alma.   20. examen.

IV. Usos de las palabras indefinidas y negativas

Pronouns

algo   something, anything   **nada**   nothing, (not) . . .
                                                  anything

alguien   someone, somebody,   **nadie**   no one, nobody,
   anybody, anyone   (not) . . . anybody (anyone)

Pronoun or Adjective

alguno some(one), any;
  (*pl.*) some
cualquier(a) any
  or anyone (*at all*)

ninguno no, no one, none,
  (not) . . . any (anybody)

Adverbs

siempre always

también also, too

nunca
jamás } never, (not) . . . ever

tampoco neither, (not *or* nor) . . .
  either

Conjunctions

o or
o . . . o either . . . or

ni nor, (not) . . . or
ni . . . ni neither . . . nor,
  (not) . . . either . . . or

Aztec or Mixtecan
mosaic snake

A. Simple negation is expressed by placing **no** immediately before the verb (or the auxiliary in the compound tenses and in the progressive forms of the tenses).

If negatives such as **nada, nadie,** etc., follow the verb, **no** or some other negative word must precede the verb; if they precede the verb or stand alone, **no** is not used. If a negative precedes the verb, all the expressions in the Spanish sentence are negative, rather than indefinite as in English. After **que,** *than,* the negatives are used:

> **Miguel tiene algo.**   Michael has something.
> **No tiene nada** *or* **Nada tiene.**   He has nothing (He doesn't have anything).
> **Él nunca (jamás) trajo nada.**   He never brought anything.
> **Ana salió sin decir nada.**   Ann left without saying anything.
> **No lo hice tampoco** *or* **Tampoco lo hice.**   I didn't do it either (Neither did I do it).
> **¿Qué sabes? —Nada de particular.**   What do you know? —Nothing special.
> **Carlota lee más que nadie (nunca).**   Charlotte reads more than anyone (ever).
> **No veo ni a Juan ni a Marta.**   I don't see either John or Martha (I see neither John nor Martha).
> **Ni Pablo ni Luis pueden[1] hacer eso.**   Neither Paul nor Louis can do that.

If the verb is not expressed, **no** usually follows the word it negates: **Yo no,** *Not I;* **todavía no,** *not yet.*

B. The pronouns **alguien** and **nadie** refer only to persons, unknown or not mentioned before, and the personal **a** is required when they are used as objects of the verb:

> **¿Vio Ud. a alguien?**   Did you see anyone?
> **Nadie me llamó, ni yo llamé a nadie.**   No one called me, nor did I call anybody.

C. **Alguno** and **ninguno,** used as adjectives or pronouns, refer to *someone* or *none* of a group of persons or things already thought of or mentioned. The plural **algunos, -as,** means *some, any, several.* Before a masculine

---

[1] Singular nouns connected by **o** or **ni** which precede the verb normally take a plural verb.

singular noun **alguno** is shortened to **algún**, and **ninguno** to **ningún**. **Ninguno, -a,** is normally used only in the singular:

Alguno de los niños lo dejó aquí.   Someone of the children left it here.
Ninguna de ellas lo[1] sabe todo.   None of them knows everything.
¿Conoces a algunas de las señoritas?   Do you know any of the young ladies?
Ellos pasarán por aquí algún día.   They will come by here some day.
Ningún hombre hará eso.   No man will do that.
No es ningún banquete.   It isn't any banquet.

D. Both **nunca** and **jamás** mean *never*, but in a question **jamás** means *ever* and a negative answer is expected. When neither an affirmative nor negative answer is implied, **alguna vez**, *ever, sometime, (at) any time*, is used:

Tomás nunca (jamás) me llama.   Tom never calls me.
¿Has visto jamás tal cosa? —No, nunca.   Have you ever seen such a thing? —No, never.
¿Ha estado Ud. alguna vez en México?   Have you ever (at any time) been in Mexico?

E. The plural **algunos, -as,** means *some, several, a few*; **unos, -as,** with the same meanings is more indefinite and expresses indifference as to the exact number. In some cases **unos, -as,** corresponds to *a pair of, two*; its place is taken by **algunos, -as,** with a **de**-phrase:

Hay algunos cuadros en la pared.   There are some pictures on the wall.
Él leerá algunos poemas suyos.   He will read some poems of his.
Unos (Algunos) niños están en el jardín.   Some children are in the garden.
Marta tiene unos ojos bonitos.   Martha has two (a pair of) pretty eyes.
Algunos de ellos están cogiendo flores.   Some of them are picking flowers.

---

[1] When **todo**, *everything*, is the direct object of a verb, the direct object pronoun **lo** is also used.

Remember that unemphatic *some* and *any* are not regularly expressed in Spanish:

> **¿Tiene Ud. dinero en el bolsillo?**   Do you have some (any) money in your pocket?

An emphatic way to express *any (at all)* is to place **alguno, -a**, after the noun:

> **Él hizo eso sin razón alguna.**   He did that without any reason at all.

only drop a before feminine noun !

F. **Cualquiera** (*pl.* **cualesquiera**), which may drop the final **a** before a noun, means *any, anyone* in the sense of *any at all, just any:*

> **Me conformo con cualquier cosa.**   I'm satisfied with anything (at all).
>
> **Cualquier persona puede hacer eso.**   Any person (at all) can do that.
>
> **Cualquiera de ellos me conoce bien.**   Anyone of them knows me well.

G. **Algo** and **nada** are sometimes used as adverbs, meaning *somewhat, rather*, and *(not) at all*, respectively:

> **A menudo Juan llega algo tarde.**   Often John arrives rather late.
>
> **Ese libro no es nada interesante.**   That book isn't at all interesting.

Ejercicios   A. Repitan la frase; luego, cámbienla a la forma negativa.

MODELO: Ramón tiene algo.   Ramón tiene algo. Ramón no tiene nada.

1. Veo algo sobre la mesa.   2. Juan le dio algo a su profesor de español.
3. Había algo en la nevera.   4. Alguien ha llamado a Miguel.   5. Hemos visto a alguien en el jardín de María.   6. Hay alguien en la cocina.

7. Alguno de los niños ha gritado mucho.   8. Algún hombre hará el trabajo.   9. Mi mamá ha invitado a alguno de los niños.   10. ¿Viene alguna de las muchachas?

11. ¿Siempre dices algo a alguien? 12. Alguna de ellas irá también.
13. Han visto a Juan o a Pablo. 14. El cuento es algo interesante.

B. Para contestar negativamente:

1. ¿Llamó alguien anoche?
2. ¿Almorzó contigo alguno de ellos?
3. ¿Nos ayudará algún muchacho?
4. ¿Has comprado alguna cosa hoy?
5. ¿Ha estado Ud. jamás en la ciudad de México?
6. ¿Siempre toma Ud. mucho al mediodía?
7. ¿Fueron Uds. al cine con alguien?
8. ¿Queda algo en la nevera?
9. ¿Buscó Ud. a alguna de las niñas?
10. ¿Discutes los planes con alguien?

C. Para completar empleando el equivalente de las palabras inglesas *some* o *any* cuando sea necesario:

1. Algún día pasaré por tu casa. 2. Algunos estudiantes fueron al Club Español. 3. ¿Compró Ud. unos zapatos en esta tienda? 4. El profesor Valdés va a leer algunos poemas suyos. 5. Nos conformaremos con cualquier cosa. 6. No conozco cualquier libro más interesante. 7. Unas mujeres acaban de entrar. 8. ¿Puede quedarse aquí alguna de las muchachas? 9. Algunas de ellas puede poner la mesa. 10. Juan no tiene cuadro alguno en su cuarto. 11. Elena tiene unos zapatos nuevos. 12. Mi mamá quiere preparar algunos emparedados para la reunión del club. 13. ¿Hay algunas tomates en la nevera? 14. No, y no hay ningún jamón tampoco. 15. ¿Quieres café con azúcar? 16. Hoy no voy a tomar ningún postre.

A. Lean en español, supliendo el artículo indefinido cuando sea necesario:

Resumen

1. Luis no tiene _____ servilleta.
2. ¿Busca Ud. _____ nevera ahora?
3. Mi abuelo dice que no necesita un coche en esa ciudad.
4. ¿Toman Uds. _____ café aquí?
5. Marta no quiere una bolsa nueva.
6. No puedo escribir sin _____ lápiz.

7. La mujer es _una_ argentina rica.

8. ¿Qué es ella? —Es _~~una~~_ profesora.

9. ¿Quién es él? —Es _un_ médico.

10. Elena y _una_ otra joven pasaron _una_ media hora en la tienda.

B. Usos del artículo definido. Para expresar en español:

1. We go to church on Sundays.
2. Ann, wash (*fam.*) your hands.
3. Johnny, put on (*fam.*) your shoes.
4. Professor Valdés will leave for Argentina next month.
5. Today is Wednesday, isn't it?
6. The water was not cold (hot).
7. You (*pl.*) like bacon, don't you?
8. The lecturer will talk about contemporary poetry.

C. Usos de las palabras indefinidas y negativas. Para expresar en español:

1. Does he have anything in his hand? 2. I haven't anything (I have nothing). 3. Jane invited someone for lunch. 4. Mary did not see anyone downtown. 5. Some girl lost her wristwatch. 6. None of the boys could find it. 7. We never buy anything in this store. 8. Martha sings better than anyone. 9. Have you (*pl.*) ever (at any time) been in California? 10. Any man (at all) can help us. 11. That novel is not at all bad. 12. That woman never gives any money to anyone.

D. Formen oraciones originales, empleando las frases o palabras siguientes:

1. acordarse de
2. darse prisa
3. poner la mesa
4. cualquier cosa
5. molestarse tanto
6. ni . . . ni

Resumen de palabras y expresiones

acordarse (ue) (de + *obj.*) to remember, recall
al mediodía at noon
el (*also* **la**) **azúcar** sugar
el banquete banquet
calentar (ie) to heat
el (la) conferenciante lecturer, speaker
conformarse (con) to be satisfied (with)
contemporáneo, -a contemporary
cualquier cosa anything (*at all*)
dar la bienvenida a to welcome
darse prisa to hurry
discutir to discuss
la docena (de) dozen
duro, -a hard
faltar to be lacking (missing), be in need of, need
la invitación (*pl.* **invitaciones**) invitation
la lata can
la lechuga lettuce
molestarse tanto to go to so much trouble (bother)
la molestia trouble, bother

muerto, -a de hambre starving (to death)
la nevera refrigerator
el pan bread
para el almuerzo for lunch
pasar por to pass (go, come) by *or* along
el poema poem
la poesía poetry
el poeta poet
poner la mesa to set the table
próximo, -a next
el reloj de pulsera wristwatch
la reunión (*pl.* **reuniones**) meeting
si queda (algo) if (anything) is left *or* remains
la sopa soup
tener ... años to be ... years old
tener (mucha) suerte to be (very) lucky *or* fortunate
tener mucho gusto en to be very glad (pleased) to
todos, -as all, all of them, everybody, everyone
un poco de (leche) a little (milk)

LECTURA IV

Observaciones sobre las comidas hispanoamericanas

Las comidas constituyen una parte esencial de la cultura de los pueblos. En los siguientes párrafos trataremos de dar una idea de algunas comidas típicas de los países al sur del Río Grande.

Las comidas hispanoamericanas reflejan, en general, los cultivos y las condiciones de vida de las diversas regiones. En México y en la América Central, por ejemplo,[1] el maíz[2] ha sido durante siglos la base de la alimentación.[3] No es una sorpresa, por lo tanto,[4] encontrar que con harina de maíz se hacen las tortillas mexicanas, que se necesitan para preparar las enchiladas, tostadas y tacos tan conocidos en el suroeste de nuestro país.

La enchilada es una tortilla de harina de maíz, enrollada,[5] que se rellena de[6] queso o carne y se cuece en el horno. La tostada es una tortilla tostada que se cubre de[7] frijoles refritos, y se aderezatn[8] con lechuga, tomate, cebolla y queso. Se prepara el taco doblando[9] la tortilla tostada y rellenando el interior de carne picada; se cuece en el horno y al servirse se cubre de lechuga, tomate y queso rallado.[10] Como condimento no falta la salsa de chile (un pimiento, o ají, como se llama en América, muy picante).

Otros platos típicos de las mismas regiones son el tamal, los chiles rellenos y el mole de guajolote (el nombre que dan al pavo en México). El tamal cambia con las localidades. En México es una especie de empanada de harina de maíz que se rellena de pescado o carne y se envuelve en hojas de plátano o de la mazorca del maíz; se cuece al vapor[11] o en el horno. La hayaca de Venezuela y la humita del Perú, Chile y la Argentina son variedades del tamal, con ingredientes diferentes. Los chiles rellenos contienen carne picada de vaca o de cerdo, aderezada con almendras, pasas y un poco de chocolate.

---

[1] **por ejemplo,** *for example.*　　[2] To facilitate preparation of this Lectura, see the glossary on page 113 for meanings of words and expressions used here and, with a few exceptions, not elsewhere in the text.　　[3] **alimentación,** *nutrition.*　　[4] **por lo tanto,** *therefore.*　[5] **enrollada,** *rolled.*　　[6] **rellenar,** *to fill, stuff;* **rellenarse de,** *to be filled (stuffed) with.*　[7] **se cubre de,** *is covered with.*　　[8] **se aderaza,** *is garnished.*　　[9] **doblando,** *by folding.*　[10] **rallado,** *grated.*　　[11] **al vapor,** *in steam, steamed.*

El mole es la salsa con que se preparan en México los guisados de carne, como el guajolote, por ejemplo. Es famoso el mole poblano. Se prepara con tomate, cebolla, canela, chile y chocolate, entre otros ingredientes.

Fruit and vegetable department in a modern supermarket, Guadalajara, México

En las regiones marítimas de Hispanoamérica los pescados y los mariscos son una parte importante de las comidas. Un plato muy popular es el escabeche. Se prepara macerando[1] el pescado frito en una salsa de vinagre, aceite, ají, cebolla y pimienta; se sirve frío. Entre los mariscos son corrientes los cangrejos, langostas, langostinos, calamares, almejas y ostiones (el nombre que se da en América a las ostras).

En los países en que abunda el ganado vacuno,[2] como en la Argentina y el Uruguay, encontramos que la carne asada es el plato favorito. Los biftecs de estas regiones, asados al horno o en parrillas,[3] cómo en el caso de la famosa parrillada argentina, son de primera calidad.

Otros platos hispanoamericanos, como el arroz con pollo y la paella, son de origen español. Suelen variar un poco según la localidad.

Los postres, en general, parecen seguir modelos españoles. Como en España los más corrientes son el arroz con leche y el flan. Populares también en Hispanoamérica son las deliciosas conservas de frutas. En México y la América Central una clase de dulce en pasta, hecho de frutas, se llama ate; en forma de jalea, se llama cajeta. Son famosas las cajetas de Celaya (Guanajuato, México).

(*Facing page, top*) Food counter in Libertad market, Guadalajara, México. (*Bottom*) Fish market, Mexico City

---

[1] **macerar,** *to steep, soak.*   [2] **ganado vacuno,** *cattle.*   [3] **parrillas,** *grills.*

Ejercicio   Traduzcan al español las frases siguientes, tratando de imitar las construcciones y fraseología del texto:

1. We would need many paragraphs to describe the typical foods of all the Spanish-American countries.
2. Persons who live in the Southwest are well acquainted with several Mexican dishes, such as the enchilada, the taco, and the tostada.
3. The enchilada is a rolled corn cake which contains meat or cheese; as seasoning chili sauce is used.
4. There are different types of tamales according to the ingredients they contain.
5. In Mexico it is a kind of small pie which is filled with fish or meat and is wrapped in corn husks.
6. Stuffed peppers are prepared with ground pork or beef, garnished with almonds, raisins, and chocolate.
7. In the maritime regions many kinds of fish and shellfish are served; stuffed crab is a very popular dish.
8. To prepare pickled fish one steeps fried fish in a sauce made of vinegar, olive oil, chili, onion, and (black) pepper.
9. In countries in which cattle abound, roast meat is a favorite food, as in the case of the Argentine *parrillada*.
10. We have always liked the desserts which are common in Spain, like rice pudding, custard, and fruit preserves.

Snack bar,
Guanajuato, México

Glosario

el **aceite**   olive oil
el **ají**   chili, pepper (*vegetable*)
la **almeja**   clam
la **almendra**   almond
el **arroz (con leche)**   rice (pudding)
   arroz con pollo   rice with chicken
   asado, -a   roast(ed)
el **ate**   *preserve*
el **biftec**   (beef)steak
la **cajeta**   *kind of jelly*
el **calamar**   squid
la **canela**   cinnamon
el **cangrejo**   crab
la **carne**   meat
   carne asada   roast, roasted meat
   carne de cerdo   pork
   carne de vaca   beef
   carne picada   ground meat
la **cebolla**   onion
   cocer (ue)   to cook
el **condimento**   condiment, seasoning
las **conservas**   preserves
el **chile**   chili, pepper
   salsa de chile   chili sauce
el **dulce**   sweet; candy
la **empanada**   *small meat* (or *fish*) *pie*
la **enchilada**   corn cake with chili
el **escabeche**   pickled fish
los **frijoles (refritos)**   (refried) kidney
   beans
   frito, -a   fried
las **frutas**   fruit
   conservas de frutas   fruit
      preserves
el **guajolote**   turkey (*Mex.*)
el **guisado**   stew
la **harina**   flour
   harina de maíz   cornmeal
la **hayaca**   tamale (*Venezuela*)

el **horno**   oven
   al horno   in an oven
la **humita**   tamale (*South America*)
el **ingrediente**   ingredient
la **jalea**   jelly
la **langosta**   lobster
el **langostino**   prawn, crawfish
el **maíz**   maize, corn
el **marisco**   shellfish; *pl.* seafood, shellfish
la **mazorca**   ear (*of corn*)
   hojas de la mazorca del maíz   corn
      husks
el **mole**   *a sauce*
   mole poblano   *sauce in the style of
      Puebla* (*Mexico*)
el **ostión** (*pl.* **ostiones**)   oyster
la **ostra**   oyster
la **paella**   *a rice dish containing meat,
   vegetables, and shellfish*
la **parrillada**   barbecue
la **pasa**   raisin
la **pasta**   paste (*confection*)
el **pavo**   turkey (*Spain*)
el **pescado**   fish
   picado, -a   minced, chopped, ground
   picante   hot, highly seasoned
la **pimienta**   black pepper
el **pimiento**   pepper (*vegetable*)
el **plátano**   plantain, banana
   hojas de plátano   banana leaves
el **plato**   dish
   relleno, -a   stuffed, filled
la **salsa**   sauce
el **taco**   *a rolled corn cake*
el **tamal**   tamale
la **tostada**   toasted corn cake
   tostar (ue)   to toast
el **vinagre**   vinegar

LECCIÓN CINCO

Las formas, la concordancia y la colocación de los adjetivos.
Expresiones con «hacer, haber» y «tener».   Palabras interrogativas y
exclamaciones

Los nuevos campeones

*(El equipo en que juega Ramón acaba de ganar el campeonato de fútbol. Al volver
a su cuarto Ramón se encuentra con su amigo Enrique.)*

Enrique.	¡Enhorabuena, Ramón! ¡Qué bien jugaron todos!
Ramón.	Gracias, Enrique. Fue un partido muy reñido. Los contrarios tenían unos defensas muy fuertes y muy rápidos.
Enrique.	Casi perdimos las esperanzas cuando el tiro de Roberto pasó por encima de la portería. Parecía un gol seguro.
Ramón.	Pero los delanteros volvieron a atacar con mayor furia y por fin ganamos el partido.
Enrique.	No parece posible. Sólo quedaba un minuto cuando Roberto marcó el gol.
Ramón.	Yo tenía mucho miedo. Como llovía y había mucho lodo, era difícil pasar el fútbol.
Enrique.	Y no debemos olvidar que Arturo, el portero, jugó muy bien.
Ramón.	Tenemos que felicitarle. Hizo unas paradas extraordinarias.
Enrique.	Es el primer campeonato que ha ganado nuestra universidad, ¿verdad?
Ramón.	Sí, pero no será el último.[1] Ninguno de los jugadores se gradúa este año.
Enrique.	¿Echaron en la piscina al entrenador?
Ramón.	¡Pobre hombre! Nos dijo que llevaba un traje nuevo, pero no le permitimos mudarse de ropa.
Enrique.	¡Qué lástima! Los jóvenes deben ser más corteses con los mayores.

[1] **Último, -a,** means *last* (in a series); **pasado, -a,** is used for *last* (just passed): **la semana pasada,** *last week.*

A. Para contestar en español en oraciones completas:

Preguntas sobre el   1. ¿Qué acaba de ganar el equipo en que juega Ramón?   2. ¿Qué le
diálogo   dice Enrique a Ramón?   3. ¿Qué dice Ramón del partido?   4. ¿Cuánto
tiempo quedaba cuando Roberto marcó el gol?   5. ¿Por qué era difícil
pasar el fútbol?   6. ¿Por qué hay que felicitar al portero?   7. ¿Por qué
cree Ramón que volverán a ganar el campeonato al año siguiente?
8. ¿Qué le habían hecho los jugadores al entrenador?

Aplicación del   1. ¿Qué deporte es más popular en este país, el fútbol americano o el
diálogo   fútbol de estilo *soccer*?   2. ¿Cuáles son algunos países en que es muy
popular el fútbol de estilo *soccer*?   3. ¿Tiene esta universidad un
equipo de fútbol de estilo *soccer*?   4. ¿En qué deportes tiene un
equipo la residencia en que Ud. vive?   5. ¿En qué deportes ha ganado
el campeonato la residencia en que Ud. vive?   6. ¿En qué deportes ha
tenido esta universidad equipos excelentes?   7. ¿En qué deportes
toman parte las muchachas en esta universidad?   8. ¿En qué deportes
han ganado el campeonato los equipos de muchachas?

B. Preparen un diálogo original, de unas ocho líneas, para recitar en
clase, empleando las frases y preguntas siguientes como elemento
inicial:

1. **Luis.**   Según el periódico de la universidad, vamos a ganar el
campeonato de fútbol este año.

   Juan.   Me parece difícil. Varios de nuestros mejores jugadores se
graduaron el año pasado, ¿verdad?

2. **Carlos.**   Me dicen que jugaste al fútbol en la escuela superior,
Miguel. ¿No te gustaría formar parte del equipo universitario?

   Miguel.   ¡Hombre! ¡Hay muchos jugadores mejores que yo en esta
universidad!

Pronunciación   The sounds of Spanish **g** (**gu**) and **j** (**x**). At the beginning of a breath-
group or after **n**, Spanish **g** (written **gu** before **e** or **i**) is a voiced velar
stop, like a weak English *g* in *go*. In all other cases, except before **e** or **i**
in the groups **ge**, **gi**, Spanish **g** is a voiced velar continuant; that is, the
breath is allowed to pass between the back of the tongue and the palate.
(The diaeresis is used over **u** in the combinations **güe** and **güi** when the
u is pronounced: **vergüenza**.)

Spanish **g** before **e** and **i**, and **j** in all positions, have no English equivalent. They are pronounced approximately like a strongly exaggerated *h* in *halt* (rather like the rasping German *ch* in *Buch*). Remember that the letter **x** in the words **México, mexicano,** and **Texas,** spelled **Méjico, mejicano,** and **Tejas** in Spain, is pronounced like Spanish **j.** Note also that the consonant **j** is silent in **reloj,** but pronounced in the plural **relojes.**

Pronounce after your teacher:

1. ganamos	graduarse	guitarra	lengua
distinguido	ninguno	con gusto	un gol
2. la guitarra	es grande	Miguel	diálogo
seguir	luego	dos goles	mucho gusto
3. jefe	jamón	junio	extranjero
dirigirse	generalmente	la Argentina	imaginarse

4. Tengo un gato algo glotón.   Gané un reloj de pulsera.
   El viaje de Jorge a Nuevo México.   Ningún jugador se quejó.

Notas gramaticales

I. Las formas, la concordancia (*agreement*) y la colocación de los adjetivos

A. Forms and agreement of adjectives

An adjective, which limits or describes a noun, must agree with the noun in gender and number, whether the adjective modifies the noun directly or is in the predicate. An adjective which modifies two or more singular nouns is put in the plural; if one noun is masculine and the other feminine, the adjective is regularly masculine plural. (The adjective should stand nearest the masculine noun.) Adjectives form their plurals in the same way as nouns (see Lección cuatro, page 99).

The feminine singular of adjectives ending in **-o** is formed by changing final **-o** to **-a.** Adjectives of nationality that end in a consonant and adjectives that end in **-án, -ón, -or** (except the comparatives **mejor, peor, mayor, menor,** and such words as **interior, exterior, superior,** and a few others which are comparatives in Latin) add **-a** for the feminine. Other adjectives have the same form for the masculine and feminine:

Singular		Plural	
Masculine	*Feminine*	*Masculine*	*Feminine*
nuevo	nueva	nuevos	nuevas
mexicano	mexicana	mexicanos	mexicanas
español	española	españoles	españolas
francés	francesa	franceses	francesas
hablador[1]	habladora	habladores	habladoras
mayor	mayor	mayores	mayores
feliz	feliz	felices	felices
joven	joven	jóvenes	jóvenes
cortés	cortés	corteses	corteses

Note the addition of the written accent: **joven-jóvenes**; the dropping of the accent: **cortés-corteses** and **francés-francesa, franceses, francesas**; and the change in spelling: **feliz-felices**.

B. Position of adjectives

Limiting adjectives (articles, unstressed possessives, demonstratives, numerals, indefinites, and other adjectives which show quantity) usually precede the noun.

Adjectives which distinguish or differentiate a noun from others of the same class (adjectives of color, size, shape, nationality, adjectives modified by adverbs, past participles used as adjectives, and the like) regularly follow the noun.

> **veinte estudiantes españoles**   twenty Spanish students
> **algunas muchachas mexicanas**   some Mexican girls
> **otra familia grande**   another large family
> **mis zapatos negros**   my black shoes
> **una pluma y un lápiz rojos**   a red pen and pencil
> **un niño muy feliz**   a very happy little boy
> **muchas cosas interesantes**   many interesting things

When two or more adjectives modify a noun, each occupies its normal position; if they follow the noun, the last two are regularly connected by y. Two or more singular adjectives may modify a plural noun.

> **el distinguido autor mexicano**   the distinguished Mexican author
> **el famoso héroe argentino**   the famous Argentine hero
> **las literaturas española y mexicana**   Spanish and Mexican literatures

---

[1] **hablador, -ora,** *talkative*.

Certain common adjectives (**bueno, mejor, mayor, malo, peor,** and less frequently **pequeño, joven, viejo,** and a few others) often precede the noun, but they may follow the noun to place more emphasis on the adjective than on the noun.

> **una buena muchacha** *or* **una muchacha buena**   a good girl
> **un joven poeta** *or* **un poeta joven**   a young poet

We have already observed that certain adjectives have a different meaning when they precede or follow a noun: for **nuevo, -a,** see page 35, footnote 1. In addition to **grande** (see section C, 2, which follows), two other examples are:

> **el hombre pobre**   the poor man (*not rich*)
> **el pobre hombre**   the poor man (*a man to be pitied*)
>
> **un amigo viejo**   an old friend (*elderly*)
> **un viejo amigo**   an old friend (*of long standing*)

Descriptive adjectives may also precede the noun when they are used figuratively or when they express a quality that is generally known or not essential to the recognition of the noun. In such cases there is no desire to single out or to differentiate. Also, when a certain quality has been established with reference to the noun, the adjective often precedes the noun.

Whenever an adjective is changed from its normal position, the speaker or writer gives a subjective or personal interpretation of the noun. An adjective placed before the noun loses much of its force and expresses its quality as belonging to the noun as a matter of course. When it follows, it indicates a distinguishing quality and it assumes the chief importance. In English this result is attained by a slight pause and the stress of voice:

> **la fuerte personalidad del autor**   the strong personality of the author
> **estas breves notas**   these brief notes
> **un magnífico (famoso) cuadro mexicano**   a magnificent (famous) Mexican picture
> **los altos Andes**   the high Andes
> **la blanca nieve**   white snow

C. Shortened forms of adjectives

1. A few adjectives drop the final **-o** when they precede a masculine

singular noun: **bueno, malo, uno, primero, tercero, postrero** (*last*), **alguno, ninguno. Alguno** and **ninguno** become **algún** and **ningún**, respectively:

el primer mes the first month	**ningún jugador** no player
algún estudiante some student	**un buen coche** a good car

BUT: **los primeros días**   the first days
       una buena idea   a good idea

2. Three common adjectives drop the last syllable under certain conditions:

a. **Grande** becomes **gran** before either a masculine or feminine singular noun, and usually means *great*:

un gran autor   a great author   **una gran sorpresa**   a great surprise

BUT: **dos grandes hombres**   two great men
      estas grandes obras   these great works

When **grande** follows the noun, it regularly means *large, big*:

un país grande   a large country
estos coches grandes   these large cars

b. **Santo** (not **Santa**) becomes **San** before names of all masculine saints except those beginning with **Do-** or **To-**:

San Pablo St. Paul	**San Francisco** St. Francis
BUT: **Santo Tomás** St. Thomas	**Santa María** St. Mary
Santo Domingo St. Dominic	**Santa Inés** St. Agnes

c. **Ciento** becomes **cien** before all nouns, including **millones,** and before the adjective **mil,** but it is not shortened before numerals smaller than one hundred:

cien teléfonos   100 telephones
cien muchachas   100 girls
cien mil personas   100,000 persons
ciento cincuenta hombres   150 men

D. Use of prepositional phrases instead of adjectives

In Spanish a noun is rarely used as an adjective; instead, a prepositional phrase beginning with **de** or **para** is normally used. Such constructions may be considered compound nouns:

> **el campeonato de fútbol**   the football championship
> **el periódico de la universidad**   the university newspaper
> **el reloj de pulsera**   the wristwatch
> **la residencia de estudiantes**   the student dormitory
> **una casa de piedra**   a stone house
> **un programa de televisión**   a TV program
> **estas tazas para café**   these coffee cups
> **un vaso para agua**   a water glass

A. Repitan cada frase; luego, al oír un nuevo substantivo, formen otra   *Ejercicios*
frase haciendo los cambios necesarios.

MODELO: Es una canción mexicana.   Es una canción mexicana.
          canciones   Son canciones (*or* unas
                                canciones) mexicanas.

1. Es un traje bonito.   3. ¿Es hablador el hombre?
     corbata   mujer?
     sombreros   estudiantes?
     blusas   muchachas?

2. Mi amigo es español.   4. Es un día hermoso.
   Mi amiga   noche
   Los jugadores   árboles
   Las señoritas   rosas

B. Repitan cada frase; luego, cámbienla al singular:

1. sus buenos amigos.   2. nuestras buenas amigas.   3. aquellos malos caminos.   4. aquellas niñas muy buenas.   5. otras revistas españolas.
6. nuestros hermanos menores.   7. los primeros días buenos.   8. esas grandes oportunidades.   9. algunos jugadores mexicanos.   10. aquellos grandes profesores.   11. estos pobres muchachos.   12. los nuevos campeones.   13. unos compañeros de clase.   14. estas tazas para té.
15. aquellos programas de televisión.   16. unas paradas extraordinarias.

C. Primero oirán un substantivo; luego, oirán dos adjetivos, separados por una pausa. Combínenlos en una sola frase, según los modelos.

MODELOS: casa—una, nueva   una casa nueva
          edificio—aquel, tercer   aquel tercer edificio

1. hermano—nuestro, mayor   5. jugador—otro, buen
2. día—el, primer   6. ciudades—cuatro, españolas
3. señorita—aquella, simpática   7. autor—otro, gran
4. muchachos—varios, corteses   8. estudiante—algún, extranjero

II. Expresiones con «hacer, haber» y «tener»

A. **Hacer** is used impersonally with certain nouns in Spanish in speaking of the state of the weather and the temperature, while *to be* is used in English:

¿Qué tiempo hace hoy?   What kind of weather is it today?
Hace buen (mal) tiempo.   It is good (bad) weather.
Hizo (mucho) calor ayer.   It was (very) warm yesterday.
Hará (mucho) fresco mañana.   It will be (very) cool tomorrow.
Ha hecho (mucho) frío.   It has been (very) cold.
Hacía (mucho) viento.   It was (very) windy.
Hace mucho sol hoy.   It is very sunny (The sun is shining brightly) today.

Since **calor, fresco, frío, viento, sol** are all nouns in these expressions, they are modified by the adjective **mucho**, not by the adverb **muy**.

B. **Haber,** used impersonally, also applies to certain natural phenomena, especially those that are seen:

Hay mucho sol.   It is very sunny.
Hay luna esta noche.   The moon is shining (It is moonlight) tonight.
Hay mucho lodo (polvo).   It is very muddy (dusty).
Hay pocas nubes en el cielo.   There are few clouds in the sky.
Había niebla (neblina).   It was foggy (misty).

C. In speaking of a person, or anything living, **tener** is used with certain nouns:

Juan tiene (mucho) frío.   John is *or* feels (very) cold.
Tenemos (mucho) calor.   We are *or* feel (very) warm.

Compare the use of **estar** or **ser** with an adjective when referring to a changeable or inherent quality:

Está nublado (despejado).   It is cloudy (clear).
El agua estaba muy fría.   The water was very cold.
El hielo es frío.   Ice is cold.

Other common idiomatic expressions with **tener** are:

tener cuidado   to be careful
tener hambre   to be hungry
tener sed   to be thirsty
tener miedo   to be afraid, frightened
tener prisa   to be in a hurry
tener razón   to be right
no tener razón   to be wrong
tener sueño   to be sleepy
tener suerte   to be lucky, fortunate
tener vergüenza   to be ashamed

With all the above nouns, **mucho, -a,** translates English *very, (very) much.* **Mucha** is used with the feminine nouns **hambre, sed, prisa, razón, suerte, vergüenza.**

Some additional expressions with **tener** are:

¿Cuántos años tienes (tiene Ud.)?   How old are you?
Tengo dieciocho años.   I am eighteen (years old).
¿Qué tiene Carlos?   What is the matter (What's wrong) with Charles?
Tienen ganas de ir a casa.   They feel like going (are anxious to go) home.
Aquí tiene Ud. (el libro).   Here is (the book). (*Handing someone something.*)
Pablo tenía la culpa.   Paul was at fault (to blame).
Tenemos que darnos prisa.   We have to (must) hurry (up).

NOTE: **Tener prisa** means *to be in a hurry,* while **darse prisa** means *to hurry (up.)*

Ejercicios   **A.** Para contestar en español:

1. ¿Qué tiempo hace hoy?   2. ¿Qué tiempo hizo ayer?   3. ¿Qué tiempo ha hecho esta semana?   4. ¿En qué estación del año hace más calor? 5. ¿En cuál de las estaciones hace más frío?   6. ¿Qué tiempo hace en el otoño?   7. ¿Dónde hace frío todo el año?   8. ¿Qué tomamos cuando hace mucho calor?

9. ¿Hay sol hoy?   10. ¿Habrá luna esta noche?   11. ¿Hay mucho polvo ahora?   12. ¿Cuándo hay lodo?   13. ¿Hay niebla aquí a veces?

14. ¿Tiene Ud. frío en este momento?   15. ¿Qué hace Ud. cuando tiene hambre?   16. ¿Qué toma Ud. cuando tiene mucha sed?   17. ¿Tiene Ud. sueño en clase a veces?   18. ¿Tiene Ud. miedo de los animales? 19. ¿Tiene Ud. ganas de ir al cine esta noche?   20. ¿Cuántos años tiene Ud.?

B. Para expresar en español:

1. Are you (*pl.*) very sleepy?   2. The boys are in a hurry.   3. What's the matter with Paul?   4. How old is your (*fam. sing.*) sister?   5. Here is the football; take (*fam. sing.*) it.   6. We are not at fault.   7. I am hungry and thirsty.   8. He doesn't feel like studying.   9. Hurry up (*pl.*); it is late.   10. The children are not afraid.   11. It has been cloudy today.   12. There are no clouds in the sky.

III. Palabras interrogativas y exclamaciones

A. Interrogative words

1. **¿Quién?** (*pl.* **¿Quiénes?**) *Who? Whom?* refers only to persons; it requires the personal (or distinctive) **a** when used as the object of a verb:

   ¿Quién llamó?   Who called?
   ¿A quiénes vio Ud. anoche?   Whom did you see last night?

Whose? can only be expressed by **¿De quién(es)?** and the verb **ser:**

   ¿De quién es esta cinta?   Whose tape is this?

All interrogatives bear the written accent in both direct and indirect questions:

No sé quién trajo las bandejas. I don't know who brought the trays.

2. **¿Qué?** *What? Which?* is both a pronoun and an adjective; as an adjective it may mean *Which?* For a definition, **¿Qué?** is used with **ser:**

¿Qué le enviaste a Marta? What did you send (to) Martha?
¿Qué cuadro le gusta a Ud.? Which picture do you like?
¿Qué es un examen? What is an examination?
¿Qué es Roberto?—Es abogado. What is Robert?—He is a lawyer.

3. **¿Cuál?** (*pl.* **¿Cuáles?**) *Which one (ones)? What?* asks for a selection and is regularly used only as a pronoun. With **ser,** use **¿Cuál(es)?** for *What?* unless a definition or identification is asked for:

¿Cuál de los cuadros le gusta a Ud.? Which (one) of the pictures do you like?
¿Cuál es la capital de Chile? What (*i.e.,* Which city) is the capital of Chile?

4. Other interrogative words are:

¿cuánto, -a? how much?
¿cuántos, -as? how many?
¿dónde? where?
¿adónde? where? (*with verbs of motion*)
¿cómo? how? (in what way?)
¿cuándo? when?
¿por qué? why? (for what reason?)
¿para qué? why? (for what purpose?)
¿qué clase de . . . ? what kind of . . . ?
¿por dónde se va . . . ? how (*i.e.,* by what route) does one go?

¿Cuántas personas hay aquí? How many persons are there here?
¿Adónde iban ellos? Where were they going?
¿Cómo se puede hacer eso? How can one do that?
¿Cómo te gusta el café? ¿Con azúcar? How do you like your coffee? With sugar?

The last sentence refers to one's taste. *How do you like?* in the sense of *What do you think of?* is expressed by **¿Qué le (te) parece(n) . . . ?**

¿Qué te parece esta cafetera? —Me gusta mucho. How do you like this coffeepot? —I like it very much.

B. Exclamations

1. **¡Qué!** + a noun means *What a (an)* . . . ! When an adjective follows the noun, either **más** or **tan** must precede the adjective:

> **¡Qué lástima (sorpresa)!**   What a pity (surprise)!
> **¡Qué obra más (tan) interesante!**   What an interesting work!

When the adjective precedes the noun, **más** or **tan** is omitted; before plural nouns **¡qué!** means *what!*

> **¡Qué buena idea!**   What a good idea!
> **¡Qué hermosas flores!**   What beautiful flowers!

¡Qué! followed by an adjective or adverb means *how!*

> **¡Qué guapo es!**   How handsome he is!
> **¡Qué bien canta María!**   How well Mary sings!
> **¡Qué suerte has tenido!**   How lucky (fortunate) you have been!

NOTE: In the last example, **suerte** is a noun in Spanish but an adjective in English; the expression means literally: *What luck you have had!*

2. All interrogatives may be used in exclamations if the sense permits:

> **¡Quién haría eso!**   Who would do that!
> **¡Cuántas flores tiene ella!**   How many flowers she has!

With verbs, **¡cuánto!** means *how!*

> **¡Cuánto me alegro de saber eso!**   How glad I am to know that!
> **¡Cuánto lo sentimos!**   How we regret it (sorry we are)!

Ejercicios   **A.** Para leer en español supliendo ¿**qué**? o ¿**cuál(es)**?:

1. ¿ _Qué_ pasó en el partido?   2. ¿A _qué_ hora terminó él?
3. ¿_Cuáles_ jugadores jugaron mejor?   4. ¿_Cuál_ de ellos se gradúan este año?   5. ¿_Qué_ otro deporte le gusta a Ud.?   6. ¿_Qué_ clases tiene Ud. hoy?   7. Allí vienen dos jóvenes extranjeros. ¿_Cuál_ es Luis Sierra?   8. ¿_Qué_ es el señor Martínez, abogado o médico?
9. ¿A _cuál_ de los cafés prefieres ir?   10. ¿_Cuáles_ de tus amigos te acompañan?

B. Escuchen cada frase; luego, cámbienla a una exclamación, usando
¡qué! o ¡cuánto!

MODELOS: Las flores son   ¡Qué hermosas son las
          hermosas.   flores!
          La noche es muy   ¡Qué noche más (tan)
          bonita.   bonita!
          Siento mucho no   ¡Cuánto siento no saberlo!
          saberlo.

1. El día es malo.   7. Ramón jugó bien.
2. Juan tiene buena suerte.   8. El jardín es bonito.
3. Hace buen tiempo.   9. La muchacha está triste.
4. Luis es guapo.   10. Me alegro de estar aquí.
5. Es una sorpresa muy   11. Gritamos cuando él marcó
   agradable.   el gol.
6. Doña Marta es simpática.   12. Nos divertimos allí.

A. La colocación de los adjetivos. Para expresar en español: **Resumen**

1. My older brother has several good Mexican friends.   2. They like
to go to football games.   3. Our players are the new champions this
year.   4. It is the first championship that our team has won.   5. It was
a very hard-fought game.   6. Our backs were very strong and fast.
7. Arthur is an excellent goalkeeper.   8. He made some extraordinary
stops.   9. None of the good players graduates this year.   10. The coach
was wearing a new suit.   11. They threw the poor man into the pool.
12. Young people should be more courteous with older people (their
elders).

B. Para leer en español, supliendo la forma correcta de **estar, haber,
hacer, ser** o **tener.** Usen el tiempo presente si no se indica otro
tiempo:

1. ¿Qué tiempo _hace_ hoy?   2. _Hace_ fresco y mucho viento.
3. Nosotros _tenemos_ mucho calor en este edificio.   4. No _ha hecho_ (pres.
perf.) mucho frío aquí este otoño.   5. A veces _hay_ mucho polvo.
6. No _habrá_ (future) luna esta noche.   7. _Ten_ (fam. sing. command) mucho cuidado y no _tengas_ miedo.   8. Ud. _tiene_ razón;
parece que él siempre _tiene_ mucho frío.   9. _Había_ (imp.) niebla
cuando salimos de casa.   10. El hielo _es_ frío, pero a menudo el
agua _está_ caliente.

C. Usos de las palabras interrogativas y las exclamaciones. Para expresar
en español:

1. Whom did she call this
   morning?
2. Which (ones) of the boys are
   going to the game?
3. Who are the good players?
4. Which one is the best goalkeeper?
5. What universities have
   student dormitories?
6. What a fast game!
7. How fortunate our team is!
8. What a great surprise!
9. How glad the students are to
   have a good team!
10. Why didn't the coach change
    his clothes?

D. Repitan cada frase; luego, al oír un nuevo substantivo, formen otra frase haciendo los cambios necesarios:

1. un día hermoso. (noche)
2. un pueblo español. (ciudad)
3. aquel niño cortés. (niños)
4. su hermano mayor. (hermanas)
5. mi amigo feliz. (amigas)
6. el cuento francés. (cuentos)
7. un hombre hablador. (mujer)
8. ese camino largo. (calles)

Resumen de palabras y expresiones

al año siguiente (in) the following year
atacar to attack
el campeón (*pl.* **campeones**) champion
el campeonato championship
el contrario opposing player; *pl.* the other side, opposing players
el defensa back (*soccer*)
el delantero forward (*soccer*)
despejado, -a clear (*weather*)
echar (en) to throw *or* toss (into)
encontrarse (ue) con to run across (into), meet
¡enhorabuena! congratulations (to you)!
el entrenador coach, trainer
el equipo team
la escuela superior high (secondary) school
la esperanza (*also pl.*) hope
extraordinario, -a extraordinary
felicitar to congratulate

fuerte strong
la furia fury
el gol goal (*soccer*)
graduarse (ú) (*like* **continuar**) to graduate
el lodo mud
marcar to make (*a score*)
los mayores older people, (their) elders
muchas veces often, many times
nublado, -a cloudy
oír hablar de to hear of (about)
la parada stop
por encima de *prep.* over, above
la portería goal (*soccer*)
el portero goalkeeper (*soccer*)
¡qué lástima! what a pity (shame)!
reñido, -a hard-fought
tener (mucho) miedo to be (very) frightened *or* afraid
el tiro shot
universitario, -a university (*adj.*)

LECTURA V

El fútbol visto desde Hispanoamérica

Entre todos los deportes que se practican en los países hispano-americanos el que suscita el mayor interés y el mayor apasionamiento[1] es el balompié, o fútbol de estilo *soccer*. En los Estados Unidos, donde el fútbol «americano», el básquetbol y el béisbol son los deportes de máxima atracción popular, nos causa extrañeza[2] saber que el único deporte que se practica en casi todas las naciones del mundo es el balompié. Más de 143 países lo tienen como su deporte nacional. Se calcula que más de doscientos millones de personas observaron por televisión los partidos del último campeonato mundial, celebrados en la Alemania Occidental en 1974.

En Rusia hay dos millones de futbolistas, entre aficionados[3] y profesionales. En Francia hay un millón doscientos mil balompedistas; en el pequeño Chile hay medio millón. En los alrededores de Londres[4] hay todas las semanas unos ochocientos partidos de carácter más o menos oficial. Hasta en el África más primitiva se juega al *soccer*.

Hay que añadir que el balompié parece ser el deporte que va ganando partidarios más rápidamente en las escuelas y universidades de nuestro país. Se calcula que se juega en unas tres mil escuelas secundarias y en la mayoría de las universidades.

En Hispanoamérica, México, Chile, la Argentina y el Uruguay han tenido equipos excelentes. Los equipos uruguayos, que han ganado tres campeonatos mundiales en este deporte, gozan de[5] extraordinario prestigio y tienen muchos admiradores. El Estadio Centenario, en Montevideo, tiene una capacidad para más de ochenta mil personas. En los grandes torneos sus amplias instalaciones se ven colmadas de[6] enormes masas de espectadores, atraídos por la importancia de los conjuntos[7] que intervienen en los partidos.

Las noticias siguientes, que aparecieron en periódicos sudamericanos, darán una idea más gráfica del fútbol hispanoamericano.

---

[1] apasionamiento, *enthusiasm.*   [2] nos causa extrañeza, *it surprises us.*   [3] aficionados, *amateurs.*   [4] alrededores de Londres, *environs of London.*   [5] gozan de, *enjoy.*   [6] colmadas de, *crowded with.*   [7] conjuntos, *teams.*

El fútbol extranjero

BOGOTÁ. El partido de fútbol disputado[1] esta tarde entre River Plate, campeón profesional de Argentina, y Millonarios, vice-campeón de fútbol profesional de Colombia, se resolvió por un empate a un tanto por lado,[2] luego de haber terminado el primer tiempo en empate a cero.[3]

La guerra de los goles

SANTIAGO. En un torneo veraniego[4] y triangular, el equipo brasileño Vasco da Gama venció, primero, a Nacional de Monte-video, por 2 goles a 1, y después a Colo Colo por 3 goles a 2. Cuando primeramente jugaron Vasco y Nacional, la sentencia de los críticos fue casi unánime: el fútbol de Vasco era un fútbol ultramoderno, de esos que no gustan,[5] pero con el cual se gana. Así fue. Vasco da Gama ganó ese triangular de verano, pero no gustó.

En general, se admite que Colo Colo jugó pésimo[6] porque cometió muchas torpezas[7] y fallaron los jugadores considerados llaves;[8] como, por ejemplo, Hormazábal, que no hizo un solo pase bien hecho y hubo que sacarlo de la cancha,[9] y Jorge Robledo, que, si no avisan por los altoparlantes que estaba jugando, nadie se hubiera dado cuenta.[10]

Los jugadores del equipo brasileño no dieron, precisamente, un curso de buen comportamiento,[11] se hicieron los desagra-dables,[12] enviaron la pelota a las tribunas,[13] y, en fin,[14] su com-portamiento no fue ni mucho menos cortés.[15] Al final provocaron un incidente de mayor consideración,[16] que terminó en puñetes[17]—un espectáculo que hacía mucho tiempo no se veía[18] en una cancha santiaguina.[19]

---

[1] **disputado,** *contested, played.*   [2] **un empate . . . lado,** *a one to one tie (for each side).*
[3] **luego de . . . cero,** *after the first period had ended in a zero to zero tie.*   [4] **veraniego,** *summer.*
[5] **de esos que no gustan,** *of those which are not pleasing (entertaining).*   [6] **pésimo,**
very badly, miserably.   [7] **torpezas,** *stupid mistakes.*   [8] **fallaron . . . llaves,** *the key
players failed "to come through."*   [9] **hubo que . . . cancha,** *had to be taken (it was
necessary to take him) from the field.*   [10] **si no avisan . . . cuenta,** *if they had not an-
nounced over the loudspeakers that he was playing, no one would have realized it.*
[11] **no dieron . . . comportamiento,** *didn't exactly give a course in (offer an example of) good
behavior.*   [12] **se hicieron los desagradables,** *they became unpleasant.*   [13] **tribunas,**
grandstands.   [14] **en fin,** *in short.*   [15] **no fue ni mucho menos cortés,** *was far from
courteous.*   [16] **de mayor consideración,** *of greater significance.*   [17] **en puñetes,** *in a
fistfight.*   [18] **que hacía mucho tiempo no se veía,** *which had not been seen for a long
time.*   [19] **santiaguina = de Santiago.**

Soccer match,
University Stadium,
Mexico City

"El Campín" Stadium,
Bogotá, Colombia

Escriban tres oraciones sobre cada uno de los temas siguientes: *Ejercicio*

1. El deporte nacional de unas 143 naciones.
2. El fútbol hispanoamericano y los campeonatos mundiales.
3. Un torneo veraniego y triangular en Santiago.

LECCIÓN SEIS

El tiempo futuro.   El tiempo condicional.   El futuro y el condicional
para expresar probabilidad.   Uso del infinitivo después de una
preposición.   Verbos seguidos del infinitivo sin preposición.
Verbos que necesitan preposición ante un infinitivo

El periódico de la universidad

(*Luis y Carlos están revisando los materiales que han de aparecer en el número
del día siguiente.*)

Luis.   ¿Dónde estará Ricardo? Dijo que estaría aquí a las nueve, ¿verdad?

Carlos.   Cuando estábamos para salir, le mandó llamar el profesor. Como
tardaba mucho en aparecer, decidí no esperarle más.

Luis.   ¿Habrá terminado el artículo que nos prometió?

Carlos.   Creo que sí. Le dije que era importante. Ha de aparecer en la página
editorial.

Luis.   Y, ¿qué me dices de la primera plana? ¿Falta algo?

Carlos.   Me parece que no. Tenemos dos artículos sobre las elecciones, con
fotos de los candidatos, y una extensa sección de noticias.

Luis.   ¿Cuál será el tema del artículo de Ricardo?

Carlos.   Se queja de la apatía de los estudiantes respecto de la reforma
universitaria. Sólo una docena de estudiantes asistieron a la reunión
de ayer.

Luis.   ¿Habrá espacio para las críticas de los estrenos en el cine y en el
teatro?

Carlos.   Y, ¿dónde pondremos el artículo sobre la exposición de dibujos que
se abrió en estos últimos días?

Luis.   ¿No sería bastante reservar un par de columnas en la última página?

Carlos.   Está bien. En la sección de deportes tendremos que poner una
noticia sobre el partido de ayer.

Luis.   No puede faltar. Los jugadores se quejan de que no les damos
bastante publicidad.

Carlos.   ¡Bah! No se puede satisfacer a todos. Pero oigo entrar a Ricardo.

A. Para contestar en español en oraciones completas:

Preguntas sobre el diálogo

1. ¿Qué están haciendo Carlos y Luis?   2. ¿A quién están esperando?
3. ¿Por qué es importante el artículo de Ricardo?   4. ¿Qué materiales
tienen para la primera plana?   5. ¿Cuál será el tema del artículo de
Ricardo?   6. ¿Dónde pondrán el artículo sobre la exposición de dibujos?   7. ¿Qué tendrán que poner en la sección de deportes?   8. ¿De
qué se quejan los jugadores?

Aplicación del diálogo

1. ¿Cuántas páginas tiene el periódico de la universidad?   2. ¿Tiene
el periódico cierta independencia editorial?   3. ¿Diría Ud. que el
periódico representa el pensamiento de la mayoría de los estudiantes?
4. ¿Tiene el periódico una extensa sección de noticias?   5. ¿Le parecen
a Ud. interesantes los artículos que se publican en el periódico de la
universidad?   6. ¿De qué se quejan los estudiantes que escriben cartas
al periódico?   7. ¿Trata Ud. de leer el periódico de la universidad todos
los días?   8. ¿Prefiere Ud. el periódico de la universidad o el periódico
de la ciudad?

B. Preparen un diálogo original, de unas ocho líneas, para recitar en
clase, empleando las frases y preguntas siguientes como elemento
inicial:

1. **Miguel.**   ¿Has visto la foto que aparece en la primera plana del
   periódico?
   Juan.   Será una broma; pero ¿tú crees que merece todo este
   espacio en la primera plana?

2. **María.**   Acabo de leer la crítica del estreno de anoche. Me parece
   claro que el autor no comprendió la comedia.
   Dorotea.   ¿Quién escribiría la crítica? ¿Sería Ricardo?

Pronunciación

A. The sounds of **s**. Spanish **s** is a voiceless, alveolar continuant, somewhat like the English hissed *s* in *sent*. Before voiced **b, d, g, l, ll, m, n,
r, v, y,** however, Spanish **s** becomes voiced and is pronounced like
English *s* in *rose*. Pronounce after your teacher:

1. desayuno   José   residencia   visitar   has estado
2. antes de   buenos días es grande   las listas   las muchachas

B. The sounds of **x.** Historically **x** is equivalent to English *ks* and it is pronounced this way sometimes in affected pronunciation. In normal usage, however, it is pronounced the following ways:

1. Before a consonant it is pronounced *s*: **expresar.**
2. Between vowels it is pronounced *gs*: **examinar (eg-sa-mi-nar).**
3. In a few words, **x** may be pronounced *s*, even between vowels, as in **exacto** and **auxiliar** and in words built on these words. Pronounce after your teacher:

1. explicar	excursión	extranjero	texto	exactamente
2. examen	existencia	éxito	exhibir	taxi

C. Silent consonants. A few consonants are dropped in Spanish pronunciation:

1. As stated earlier, the consonant **j** is silent in **reloj,** but is pronounced in the plural **relojes.**
2. The consonant **p** is silent in **septiembre.**
3. The consonant **t** is silent in **istmo.**
4. Spanish **d** tends to fall in the ending **-ado,** and final **d** is regularly dropped, in familiar speech, in the word **usted.**
5. The letter **h** is silent in modern Spanish: **ahora.**

I. El tiempo futuro

A. Meaning

In general, the future tense in Spanish corresponds to the English future tense, translated by *shall* or *will*:

> **Ana dice que esperará aquí.**   Ann says (that) she will wait here.
> **¿Dónde pondremos el artículo?**   Where shall we put the article?

B. Substitutes for the future

1. The present indicative tense is often substituted for the future (particularly if an expression of time is included) to make the statement more vivid, to imply greater certainty that the action will take place, and in questions, when immediate future time is involved:

Notas gramaticales

El partido empezará a las dos.   The game will begin at two.
El partido empieza a las dos.   The game begins at two.
Vuelvo en seguida.   I'll return at once (be right back).
¿Escuchamos un disco ahora?   Shall we listen to a record now?

2. **Ir a** plus an infinitive is used in the present indicative tense to refer to the near future. (The imperfect **iba a, ibas a,** etc., is similarly used to replace the conditional, especially in Spanish America.)

Van a llegar a la ciudad mañana.   They are going to arrive at the city tomorrow.
Él dijo que iba a venir hoy.   He said that he would (was going to) come today.

3. **Haber de** plus an infinitive, which denotes what *is,* or *is supposed, to* (happen), is sometimes the equivalent of the future tense, often with a sense of obligation. (In the imperfect, this expression may be used to represent the conditional.)

Había   _was_

Ha de aparecer en la página editorial.   It is to appear on the editorial page.
¿Qué he de hacer?   What am I to do (shall I do)? (What am I supposed to do?)
Yo sabía que él no había de pagar (= **pagaría**).   I knew that he wouldn't pay.

4. In **si**-clauses the present indicative tense is normally used in Spanish, as in English, even though the action is to be completed in the future:

Si él vuelve mañana, me llamará.   If he returns tomorrow, he will call me.

NOTE: Do not confuse the use of **querer** plus an infinitive in asking a favor, which corresponds to English *will, be willing to,* with the true future. Similarly, **no querer** plus an infinitive may express *be unwilling to, will not:*

¿Quiere Ud. abrir la ventana?   Will you open the window?
¿Quieres ir al cine conmigo?   Will you (Are you willing to) go to the movie with me?
Ellos no quieren esperar.   They won't (are unwilling to) wait.

The future must be used, however, in cases such as: *(not immediate future)*

> **¿Estarás en casa esta noche?**   Will you be at home tonight?

II. El tiempo condicional

A. Meaning

The conditional tense expresses a future action from the standpoint of the past and is translated in English by *should* or *would*. (Its use in conditional sentences will be discussed in Lección nueve.)

> **Él dijo que estaría aquí pronto.**   He said that he would be here soon.

Remember that English *would* (*used to*) is often used to express repeated action in the past, in which case the imperfect indicative tense is used, as explained in Lección tres:

> **A veces dábamos paseos por el campo.**   At times we would take walks in the country.

In the preterit, **no querer** plus an infinitive may express *would not* (*refused to*), *was unwilling to:*

> **Ricardo no quiso decir nada de las críticas.**   Richard would not (refused to) say anything about the reviews.

B. The conditional may be used to express a polite or softened future statement: *(with querer, past subj. is usually used.)*

> **Me gustaría acompañarlos.**   I should like to accompany them.
> **¿No sería bastante reservar un par de columnas en la última página del periódico?**   Wouldn't it be sufficient to reserve a couple of columns on the last page of the newspaper?

A. Repitan cada frase; luego, empiecen la frase con **Luis dice que**,   *Ejercicios* cambiando el verbo en cursiva al futuro:

podrá   *habrá*

1. *Puede* escribir un artículo.   2. *Hay* espacio para las críticas.

tendrá

3. *Tiene* que poner una noticia.   5. No se *queja* de los estudiantes.

quejará

4. *Sale* después de comer.   6. No *ha* terminado el informe.

saldrá   *habrá*

B. Repitan cada frase; luego, al oír otra forma del verbo, formen una nueva frase, según el modelo.

MODELO: Yo *sé* que Juan lo hará.   Yo sé que Juan lo hará.
        (*sabía*)   Yo sabía que Juan lo haría.

sabría 1. Yo *creo* que él sabrá revisar los materiales. (*creía*)
habría 2. Carlos *sabe* que habrá espacio para la noticia. (*sabía*)
sería   3. Luis *dice* que será bastante reservar un par de columnas. (*dijo*)
quejaría 4. *Creemos* que ella se quejará de la apatía de los estudiantes. (*Creíamos*)
tendríamos 5. *Sabemos* que tendremos que escribir algo sobre el partido de ayer. (*Sabíamos*)
harían 6. Él *está* seguro de que ellos harán el trabajo esta noche. (*estaba*)

C. Repitan la frase; luego, repítanla empleando el futuro, según los modelos.

MODELOS: Van a salir mañana.   Van a salir mañana. Saldrán mañana.

         Ana ha de cantar hoy.   Ana ha de cantar hoy. Ana cantará hoy.

Pondré   *Tendremos*

1. He de poner algo en esta sección. 2. Hemos de tener un artículo sobre el partido. 3. Ha de *aparecerá* aparecer en la sección de deportes. 4. ¿Qué *dirán* van a decir de la primera plana? 5. ¿De qué van a *se quejarán* quejarse ahora los *será* estudiantes? 6. ¿Cuál va a ser el tema del artículo de Roberto?

D. Después de oír la pregunta, contesten empleando formas de mandato afirmativas y negativas con **Ud.** como sujeto, y substituyendo el substantivo con el pronombre correspondiente.

MODELO: ¿Pongo *el artículo* aquí?   Sí, póngalo Ud. allí.
                                       No, no lo ponga Ud. allí.

1. ¿Espero más *a Carlos*?
2. ¿Reviso *los materiales* ahora?
3. ¿Escribo *la crítica* hoy?

4. ¿Empiezo a escribir *la noticia*?
5. ¿Hago *el trabajo* esta tarde?
6. ¿Busco *las fotos* esta noche?

III. El futuro y el condicional para expresar probabilidad

The future is often used to indicate probability, supposition, or conjecture concerning an action or state in the present time:

¿**Dónde estará Ricardo?** I wonder where Richard is. (Where do you suppose Richard is?)
Estará en casa. He is probably (must be) at home.
¿**Cuál será el tema del artículo?** What do you suppose is the subject of the article? (What can the subject of the article be?)

Similarly, the conditional indicates probability or conjecture with reference to the past:

¿**Quién escribiría la crítica?** Who probably (do you suppose) wrote the review?
¿**Sería Ricardo?** Do you suppose it was Richard? (I wonder if it was Richard.)
Serían las dos cuando salieron. It was probably two o'clock when they left.

Probability or conjecture may also be expressed by the future perfect tense and occasionally by the conditional perfect:

¿**Adónde habrá ido Carlos?** Where can Charles have gone? (Where has Charles probably gone? Where do you suppose Charles has gone?)
¿**Habrá terminado el trabajo ya?** Do you suppose he has finished the work already?
¿**Qué habría hecho él?** What could he have done?

A. Repitan; luego, cambien el verbo al futuro para expresar probabilidad:

Ejercicios

1. ¿Quién es aquel hombre?
   será
2. ¿Dónde está Ricardo?
   estará

3. ¿Adónde van los estudiantes
   irán
   tan tarde?

4. ¿Quién tiene el periódico de *tendrá*
la mañana?
5. Los niños están jugando. *estarán*

6. Hay mucha gente en el *habrá*
cine.

Cambien el verbo al condicional:

7. ¿Qué hora era? *sería*
8. Eran las diez y media de la
noche. *serían*

9. ¿Adónde iban los dos niños? *irían*
10. ¿Dónde estaban Ana y María
el domingo pasado? *estarían*

Cambien el verbo al futuro perfecto:

11. Ya han llegado a la reunión. *habrán*
12. Él ha vuelto de la excursión
a la sierra. *has. habrá*

13. ¿Ha estado Juan en el campo? *habrá*
14. ¿Han terminado el artículo
sobre el partido de ayer? *habrán*

B. Para expresar en español:

1. What time can it be? 2. Paul probably has many friends there.
3. Do you suppose Jane is ill? 4. I wonder who has the photos. 5. The students have probably written the news items. 6. Who do you suppose wrote this review? 7. Where did they probably go? 8. John probably returned home early.

IV. Uso del infinitivo después de una preposición

In Spanish the infinitive is used after a preposition; in English the present participle is often used. **Al** plus an infinitive is the Spanish equivalent of English *Upon* (*On*) plus the present participle, or occasionally of a clause beginning with *When*. The infinitive may have a subject (which follows the infinitive), an object, or both:

Ricardo salió sin verme.   Richard left without seeing me.
Al saberlo yo, le escribí.   Upon finding it out (When I found it out), I wrote to him.
Después de leer el artículo, él lo revisó. After reading the article, he checked it.
Además de hacer eso, escribió una crítica.   Besides doing that, he wrote a review.

V. Verbos seguidos del infinitivo sin preposición

A. Verbs that do not require a preposition before an infinitive

A few of the many verbs which do not require a preposition before an infinitive when there is no change in subject are: **decidir, desear, esperar, necesitar, pensar (ie)** (when it means *to intend, plan*), **poder, preferir (ie, i), prometer, querer, saber, sentir (ie, i)** (*to be sorry, regret*), **temer.** *to fear*

> **No se puede satisfacer a todos.**   One cannot satisfy everybody.
> **Siento no poder ir con Uds.**   I'm sorry I cannot go (I am sorry not to be able to go) with you.

The infinitive follows impersonal expressions without a preposition:

> **Es bueno (posible) asistir a la reunión.**   It is well (possible) to attend the meeting.

See Appendix E, pages 331–333, for a more complete list of verbs of the types mentioned in this section and in section VI which follows.

B. Some special uses of the infinitive

1. After **oír** and **ver** the infinitive is regularly used in Spanish, while the present participle is often used in English. Note the word order in the first example:

> **Oigo entrar a Ricardo.**   I hear Richard coming in (enter).
> **Los vimos salir.**   We saw them leave (leaving).

2. **Dejar, hacer, mandar,** and **permitir** are usually followed by the infinitive when the subject of the verb which follows is a pronoun. (Some exceptions to this usage will be discussed later.)

> **Déjeme (Permítame) Ud. llamarle.**   Let me (Permit me to) call him.
> **Le mandé escribir un artículo.**   I ordered him to (had him) write an article.

While usage varies, with **dejar** and **hacer** personal objects are usually direct; with other verbs they are usually indirect.

Often the infinitive is translated by the passive voice, especially when its subject is a thing:

Él hizo facturar la maleta.   He had the suitcase checked.
Las mandé (hice) poner en el coche.   I ordered *or* had them put in the car.
Le mandó llamar el profesor.   The teacher had him called (sent for him).
Hice revisar el artículo.   I had the article checked.

VI. Verbos que necesitan preposición ante un infinitivo

A. Verbs which take **a** before an infinitive

All verbs expressing motion or movement to a place, the verbs meaning *to begin*, and certain others such as **atreverse**, *to dare*, **aprender**, *to learn*, **enseñar**, *to teach, show,* **ayudar**, *to help, aid,* and **obligar**, *to oblige,* require **a** before an infinitive. The last three verbs have the subject of the infinitive expressed:

Fueron (Corrieron) a ver el coche.   They went (ran) to see the car.
Él aprendió (empezó) a cantar la canción.   He learned (began) to sing the song.
Él me enseñó (ayudó) a hacer eso.   He taught (helped) me to do that.

Volver a plus an infinitive means (*to do*) *again*:

Vuelva Ud. a leer la noticia.   Read the news item again.

B. Verbs which take **de** before an infinitive

Three common verbs which require **de** are **acordarse (ue) (de),** *to remember* (*to*), **alegrarse (de),** *to be glad* (*to*), and **olvidarse (de),** *to forget* (*to*). (**Olvidar** plus an infinitive also means *to forget* [*to*].)

Nos alegramos de verte.   We are glad to see you.
Juan se olvidó de llamar a Juanita.   John forgot to call Jane.

Dejar de plus an infinitive means *to stop, fail to.* **Tratar de** means *to try to,* and **tratarse de** means *to be a question of.* **Acabar de** in the present and imperfect means *have just*, *had just*, respectively:

Dejaron de tocar la guitarra. They stopped playing the guitar.
No dejes de volver temprano. Don't fail to return early.
No se trata de aprender eso. It is not a question of learning that.
Ramón acaba (acababa) de entrar. Raymond has (had) just entered.

Some verbs followed by an adjective or noun require **de** before an infinitive as well as before a noun or noun clause:

Estamos seguros de que él nos ayudará. We are sure that he will help us.
Estamos seguros de poder ayudarlos. We are sure of being able to help them.
Los muchachos están cansados de trabajar. The boys are tired of working.
Tengo miedo de esperar más. I'm afraid to wait any longer.

C. Verbs which take **en** before an infinitive

Common verbs are: **consentir (ie, i) en,** *to consent to, agree to,* **insistir en,** *to insist on,* **pensar (ie) en,** *to think of,* **tardar en,** *to delay in, take long to:*

Él tardaba en aparecer. It was taking him long to appear (He delayed in appearing).

A. Repitan la frase; luego, cámbienla a una forma de mandato con **Ud.** *Ejercicios* o **Uds.** como sujeto:

1. Roberto nos enseña a bailar la rumba.
2. Ana comienza a leer la comedia.
3. Elena aprende a tocar la canción.
4. No dejan de revisar el artículo.
5. María le ayuda a lavar el coche.
6. No se olvidan de hacer el trabajo a tiempo.
7. No tratan de jugar en la calle.
8. No tardan mucho en llegar.

B. Lean en español, supliendo la preposición correcta cuando sea necesario:

1. Hemos __de__ poner estos artículos en la primera plana.   2. Ayúdame tú __a__ revisar esta crítica.   3. Trata tú __de__ darles más publicidad a los jugadores.   4. No es necesario _____ dejar más espacio en esta página.   5. Juan nos obligó __a__ esperar una hora.
6. Pensamos _____ ver la exposición de dibujos hoy.   7. No podemos _____ pasar mucho tiempo allí.   8. Mucho gusto __en__ conocerle a Ud.   9. Mi hermana no consentirá __en__ asistir a la reunión.
10. Ella dice que se trata __de__ terminar una composición para mañana.
11. Vuelva Ud. __a__ leer esta sección de deportes.   12. Estoy seguro __de__ poder hacerlo pronto.   13. ¿Sabes si Tomás prefiere _____ quedarse aquí?   14. ¿Están cansados __de__ aprender tantas palabras?
15. Mi mamá tardó __en__ salir de la tienda.   16. Esperamos _____ divertirnos mucho esta noche.   17. Pablo insiste __en__ pagar la cuenta.   18. Juan acaba __de__ llamar a Carolina.

Resumen   **A.** Usos de verbos para expresar el futuro. Para expresar en español:

1. Where shall I put this long article?
2. Does (Will) today's game begin at two o'clock?
3. Will you (*fam. sing.*) be able to check the news item right away?
4. I believe that it is to appear in the sports section.
5. Shall I leave this photo on the first page?
6. Won't you (*fam. sing.*) write a column for the last page?
7. What are we to do now? Is there anything lacking?
8. Shall we wait longer for Richard?
9. We are supposed to see whether there is an article on the elections.
10. There is probably space for the exhibition of drawings.

B. Repitan la frase; luego, repítanla otra vez, cambiando el verbo al tiempo correspondiente para expresar probabilidad.

MODELOS: ¿Quién es?   ¿Quién es? ¿Quién será?
          ¿Dónde han estado?   ¿Dónde han estado? ¿Dónde
                               habrán estado?

          Eran las cinco.   Eran las cinco. Serían las cinco.

1. ¿Qué tiene Felipe?   3. ¿Cuál es el tema del artículo?
2. Los jóvenes van al partido.   4. ¿Hay espacio para esta crítica?

5. ¿Ha ido Carlos al centro?
6. ¿Dónde han puesto las fotos?

7. Felipe ya ha vuelto.
8. Han visto el estreno en el teatro.

9. ¿Qué hora era?
10. ¿Adónde fueron sus amigos?

11. ¿Eran españolas las dos señoritas?
12. Estuvieron en casa anoche.

C. Usos del infinitivo. Para expresar en español:

1. Let me drive (*formal sing.*) the car this afternoon, please. 2. My father had (made) me wash it this morning. 3. Mother, I shall have the dress cleaned tomorrow. 4. I shall have him write a review of the film he saw last night. 5. We heard Mary singing in Spanish. 6. Paul has just bought a new suit. 7. Don't fail (*fam. sing.*) to come to visit me often. 8. Have you (*pl.*) seen them walking through the park? 9. Upon seeing her, I handed her the two drawings. 10. Besides doing that, I chatted with her about the art exhibition.

National Library, Guatemala City

Cristo Street in old
San Juan, Puerto Rico

D. Formen frases en español usando un infinitivo después de las expresiones siguientes:

1. olvidarse de   3. volver a   5. enseñar a   7. consentir en
2. dejar de   4. tardar en   6. tratar de   8. atreverse a

Resumen de palabras y expresiones

además de *prep.* besides, in addition to
aparecer to appear, show up
la apatía apathy
la broma joke
el candidato candidate
la columna column
la comedia play, comedy
la crítica review
el dibujo drawing
editorial *adj.* editorial
la elección (*pl.* **elecciones**) election
en estos últimos días during these last few days
el espacio space, room
está bien all right, that's fine
estar para to be about to
el estreno première, first performance
la exposición (*pl.* **exposiciones**) exhibition
extenso, -a extensive, large
la independencia independence
le mandó llamar (he) had him called, (he) sent for him

los materiales materials, copy (*printing*)
la mayoría de the majority of, most (of)
me parece que no I think (believe) not
merecer to merit, deserve
(no) esperar más (not) to wait (any) longer
no puede faltar it must appear, it cannot be missing
la noticia news, news item, notice
el pensamiento thought
la plana page (*printing*)
la publicidad publicity
la reforma reform
representar to represent, show, express
respecto de in regard to, concerning
revisar to check (*examine*)
satisfacer (*like* **hacer**) to satisfy
la sección de noticias news section
el tema subject, theme, topic
tratar de + *inf.* to try to
un par de a couple (pair) of

LECTURA VI

La función política de la universidad

¿Tiene la universidad una función política? Se trata de una de las cuestiones más debatidas de nuestro tiempo. Una breve comparación de la universidad norteamericana con la hispanoamericana parece indicar que no hay una sola contestación, válida para todos los países y para todas las circunstancias.

En los Estados Unidos la universidad—sea del estado, del municipio o particular[1]—siempre ha defendido su autonomía frente al[2] gobierno. El principio que se invoca para justificar tal autonomía es significativo: el estado debe abstenerse de[3] intervenir en la organización técnica de la universidad, y la universidad, por su parte,[4] debe observar una completa abstención frente a las cuestiones políticas del estado.

Esto no quiere decir[5] que la universidad deba quedar al margen de[6] la vida nacional. Lo que se quiere es que la universidad sea apolítica, es decir, que sea un centro académico y científico donde se puedan estudiar los problemas de la nación objetivamente, sin partidarismo ni proselitismo[7] de ninguna clase.

Para muchos hispanoamericanos, en cambio,[8] la idea de una universidad apolítica es ilusoria. En su opinión, la universidad, que en Hispanoamérica es un organismo del estado, además de los fines reconocidos por todos—la formación profesional, la organización de la investigación científica y la difusión de la cultura—, tiene una función social de la mayor importancia: la de poner la cultura al servicio de[9] la nación. Si los estudiantes han de ser los hombres de mañana y los futuros profesionales, la universidad tiene la obligación de asumir la alta misión

---

[1] sea . . . particular, *whether it be a state, municipal, or private institution.*   [2] frente a, *in the face (presence) of.*   [3] abstenerse de, *refrain (abstain) from.*   [4] por su parte, *on its part.*   [5] no quiere decir, *doesn't mean.*   [6] al margen de, *on the fringe of.*   [7] sin partidarismo ni proselitismo, *without partisanship or proselitism.*   [8] en cambio, *on the other hand.*   [9] al servicio de, *in the service of.*

política de formar ciudadanos aptos,[1] conscientes de sus derechos y responsabilidades y capaces de enfrentarse con éxito con[2] los problemas nacionales. La universidad debe formar en primer lugar al ciudadano y, partiendo de allí,[3] formará al profesional.

Esta orientación política de la universidad hispanoamericana explica la activa participación de los estudiantes y profesores en la vida nacional. Como en todas partes, las preocupaciones inmediatas son la defensa de la autonomía de la institución, la libertad de cátedra[4] y la reforma y democratización de los sistemas académicos; pero en Hispanoamérica las energías están orientadas también hacia la identificación y resolución de los problemas nacionales.

La actividad política de los estudiantes y profesores tiene una larga tradición en los países hispanoamericanos. Continúa todavía en nuestro tiempo, aunque incidentes como el que se describe en la noticia siguiente ocurren en otras partes también.

Biology student and instructor, University of Guadalajara, México

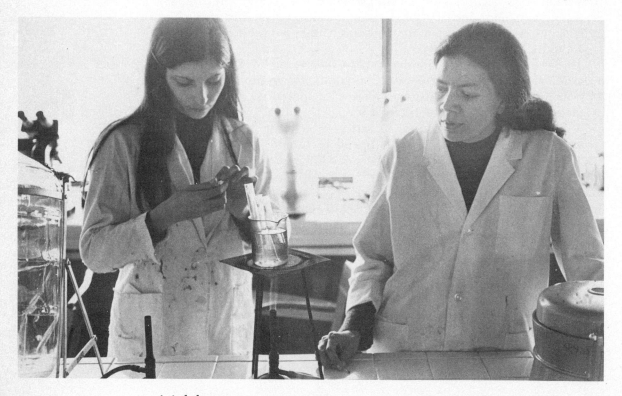

[1] **ciudadanos aptos,** *competent citizens. of successfully facing (coping with).* **tad de cátedra,** *academic freedom.*

[2] **capaces de enfrentarse con éxito con,** *capable* [3] **partiendo de allí,** *beginning there.* [4] **liber-**

Los estudiantes pidieron perdón para 21 profesores y 43 alumnos

PUEBLA (México). Los estudiantes universitarios se apoderaron al mediodía de hoy de[1] 14 autobuses urbanos, y con ellos bloquearon las principales calles de la ciudad y suspendieron por completo[2] la circulación de las 11.00 a las 13.00 horas.[3]

Los vigilantes de tránsito[4] tuvieron que desviar los vehículos por otras calles, en tanto que[5] los estudiantes organizaban un mitin.

Los oradores hablaron para exponer la necesidad que hay de que la Rectoría[6] perdone y haga volver a los 21 profesores de la Preparatoria y de la Escuela de Ciencias Físico-Matemáticas, que por segunda vez[7] han sido expulsados, y a los 43 estudiantes preparatorianos y de diversas Facultades que también quedaron fuera de[8] la Universidad.

Los estudiantes amenazaron con llegar a los extremos[9] en caso de que[10] no se les conceda lo que piden.

Por su parte, el Rector había declarado, antes de la realización del mencionado mitin,[11] que iba a convocar al Consejo Universitario; pero que de antemano[12] considera que el Consejo no modificará los acuerdos tomados, porque menguaría el principio de autoridad.[13]

Escriban un breve resumen, de unas ciento cincuenta palabras, de «La función política de la universidad.»   *Ejercicio*

---

[1] apoderarse de, *to seize, take possession of.*   [2] por completo, *completely.*   [3] de las 11.00 a las 13.00 horas, *from 11 a.m. to 1 p.m.*   [4] vigilantes de tránsito, *traffic policemen.*   [5] en tanto que, *while.*   [6] Rectoría, *Rector's (President's) Office.*   [7] por segunda vez, *for the second time.*   [8] fuera de, *outside of.*   [9] amenazaron ... extremos, *threatened to go to extremes.*   [10] en caso de que, *in case (that).*   [11] antes de ... mitin, *before the above-mentioned meeting was carried out.*   [12] de antemano, *in advance.*   [13] menguaría ... autoridad, *the principle of authority would diminish (be lessened).*

LECCIÓN SIETE

Teoría del modo subjuntivo. **Las formas del presente de subjuntivo.**
El subjuntivo en cláusulas substantivas. **Otras formas de mandato**

Una excursión a la sierra

(Los padres de Ana tienen una casa de campo en un lugar hermoso de la sierra. Ana ha invitado a Elena a pasar las vacaciones con ella.)

Ana. ¿Has llamado a tus padres, Elena? ¿Te permiten ir a la sierra con nosotros?

Elena. Acabo de hablar con ellos. No tienen otros planes. Me piden que te dé las gracias por la invitación.

Ana. De nada, Elena. ¡Cuánto me alegro de que puedas acompañarnos! Dudo que haya[1] un sitio más hermoso en la sierra.

Elena. Habrá mucha nieve en esta estación del año, ¿verdad?

Ana. ¡Ya lo creo! Y como sé que te gustan los deportes de invierno, te aconsejo que lleves tus esquíes.

Elena. ¿Llevo mis patines también?

Ana. Sí, no dejes de llevarlos. Es posible que podamos patinar también.

Elena. Sólo siento no poder quedarme durante las dos semanas. Mis padres quieren que pase unos días en casa de mis abuelos.

Ana. No te había dicho que mi padre vendrá a buscarnos. Yo prefiero que él conduzca cuando hay nieve y hielo en la carretera.

Elena. ¿A qué hora quiere tu padre que salgamos?

Ana. Insiste en que estemos listas a las seis.

Elena. No creo que haya ninguna dificultad en salir a esa hora. Que esté aquí a las seis. Estaré lista, Ana.

Ana. Pues, acostémonos en seguida. ¡Que descanses mucho, Elena! Hasta mañana.

---

[1] Note that the present subjunctive of the impersonal form of **haber,** corresponding to the present indicative **hay,** is **haya,** *there is (are), there may be.*

155

A. Para contestar en español en oraciones completas:

Preguntas sobre el diálogo   1. ¿De qué hablan Ana y Elena en este diálogo?   2. ¿Con quiénes acaba de hablar Elena?   3. ¿Qué le piden a Elena sus padres?   4. ¿De qué se alegra Ana?   5. ¿Qué dice Ana del sitio adonde piensan ir?   6. ¿Qué le aconseja Ana a Elena?   7. ¿Qué siente Elena?   8. ¿A qué hora quiere el padre de Ana que salgan?

Aplicación del diálogo   1. ¿Le gustan a Ud. los deportes de invierno?   2. ¿En qué estación del año hay nieve y hielo en esta parte del país?   3. ¿Qué tiempo hace hoy?   4. ¿Es agradable conducir cuando hay hielo en la carretera?   5. ¿Sabe Ud. patinar?   6. ¿Se puede esquiar por aquí?   7. ¿Piensa Ud. hacer una excursión a la sierra?   8. ¿Le gusta a Ud. ir a la sierra en el[1] verano o en el invierno?

B. Estudien las palabras y expresiones siguientes para emplear algunas de ellas en el diálogo citado o para usarlas en un diálogo nuevo basado sobre el modelo:

a toda velocidad at full speed	**peligroso, -a** dangerous
bajar to descend	**el pico** peak
deslizarse sobre la nieve to glide *or* slide over the snow	**romperse una pierna** to break a (one's) leg
emocionante thrilling	**subir** to ascend, climb up
el esquiador skier	**torcerse (ue) la muñeca (el tobillo)**
la ladera slope	to sprain one's wrist (one's ankle)
nevado, -a snow-covered	

Pronunciación   The pronunciation of **y,** *and.* Recall that within a breath-group the conjunction **y** (phonetically an unstressed **i**) combines with a preceding vowel or consonant or with a following vowel to form one syllable. The principles that govern the pronunciation of **y** are the following:

1. When initial in a breath-group before a consonant or when between consonants, it is pronounced like the Spanish vowel **i**: **Y se marchó (Y-se-mar-chó), tres y tres (tre-s y-tres).**

---

[1] The definite article is often omitted with the seasons in prepositional phrases: **en verano, en invierno; un día de primavera,** *a spring day;* **deportes de invierno,** *winter sports,* used on the preceding page and above.

2. When initial in a breath-group before a vowel or when between vowels, it is pronounced like Spanish y: ¿y usted? (¿y̯ us-ted?), éste y aquél (és-te-y̯ a-quél).

3. Between d, s, or z and a vowel within a breath-group, it is also pronounced like Spanish y: usted y ella (us-ted-y̯ e-lla), éstos y aquéllos (és-tos-y̯ a-qué-llos).

4. Between l, n, or r and a vowel within a breath-group, it is pronounced as the first element of a diphthong, with the preceding consonant, the y, and the following vowel in a single syllable: aquél y éste (a-qué-l y̯ és-te), hablan y escriben (ha-bla-n y̯ es-cri-ben), entrar y esperar (en-tra-r y̯ es-pe-rar).

5. Between a vowel and a consonant, it forms a diphthong with the vowel that precedes it: Marta y Juan (Mar-ta y̯-Juan).

Apply the above principles in the following exercises:

1. Write the following phrases and sentences, dividing them into syllables and underlining the stressed syllables:

Son las tres y cuarto.	Y se fue.
Es rica y elegante.	Y escribe bien.
Son blancos y amarillos.	¿Van Carlos y Arturo?
El español y el francés.	Treinta y seis.

2. Read the following phrases and sentences as single breath-groups:

Lean y traduzcan esta frase.	Iremos Carlos y yo.
Saben leer y escribir.	Sabe el inglés y el francés.
Es fácil y agradable.	Miren y escuchen.
Blanco y negro.	Usted y Arturo van.

Theory

I. Teoría del modo subjuntivo

Notas gramaticales

The word *subjunctive* means *subjoined,* and except for its use in main clauses to express commands, the subjunctive mood is regularly used in subordinate or dependent clauses. The indicative mood expresses *facts,* makes *assertions,* states *certainties,* or asks direct questions. In general, the subjunctive is dependent upon an *attitude,* a *wish,* a *feeling,* or some *uncertainty* in the mind of the speaker, expressed or implied in the main clause. The reference in the dependent clause is to an unaccomplished act or state.

In the case of a dependent clause, the student must observe whether the idea expressed in the principal clause is one which requires the subjunctive in Spanish, then whether the subject of the dependent clause is <u>different</u> from that of the main verb. If this is true in both cases, the subjunctive will generally be used.

The subjunctive is more widely used in English than many persons realize because its forms differ from the indicative mood only in the third person singular and in some irregular verbs. In this and later lessons the subjunctive will be discussed according to its use in noun, adjective, and adverbial clauses. In the examples which follow, note, in the noun clauses, the various English equivalents of the Spanish subjunctive forms: English present tense, the future, use of the modal auxiliary *may,* and the infinitive:

Yo no creo que ella esté aquí.   I do not believe (that) she is (will be) here.
Esperamos que lo hagan.   We hope (that) they may (will) do it.
Yo no quiero que él venga.   I do not wish that he come (I don't want him to come).

II. Las formas del presente de subjuntivo

Recall that in the present subjunctive tense the endings of **-ar** verbs begin with **-e,** while those of **-er** and **-ir** verbs begin with **-a:**

tomar: tome   tomes   tome   tomemos   toméis   tomen
comer: coma   comas   coma   comamos   comáis   coman
abrir: abra   abras   abra   abramos   abráis   abran

In earlier lessons we have used the third person singular and plural and the second person singular forms of the present subjunctive in commands. See Repaso primero, pages 8–11, for uses of these forms, and Appendix D, pages 314–330, for the present subjunctive forms of all types of verbs. Remember that the stem of the present subjunctive of all but six verbs (**dar, estar, haber, ir, saber, ser**) is formed by dropping the ending **-o** of the first person singular of the present indicative.

dar – dé
estar – esté
haber – haya
ir – vaya
saber – sepa
ser – sea

Para contestar afirmativamente, empleando una forma de mandato con   *Ejercicio*
Ud. o **Uds.** como sujeto.

MODELOS: ¿Busco el libro?   Sí, búsquelo Ud.
          ¿Le pedimos algo?   Sí, pídanle Uds. algo.

1. ¿Abro las ventanas?   6. ¿Vamos al centro hoy?
2. ¿Toco el disco ahora?   7. ¿Volvemos antes de las
3. ¿Me siento en la primera   cinco?
   fila?   8. ¿Seguimos leyendo la
4. ¿Pongo la mesa ahora   novela?
   mismo?   9. ¿Servimos refrescos esta
5. ¿Escojo un vestido en esta   noche?
   tienda?   10. ¿Comenzamos a cantar?

III. El subjuntivo en cláusulas substantivas

The subjunctive is regularly used in a noun clause (*i.e.*, a clause used as
the subject or object of a verb) when the verb in the main clause expresses or implies ideas of the speaker such as those of *wish, advice,
request, command, permission, approval, cause, suggestion, preference,
insistence,* and the like, as well as their negatives. Remember that in
English the infinitive is most commonly used after such verbs, but in
Spanish a noun clause, usually introduced by **que,** is regularly used if
the subject of the dependent clause is different from that of the main
clause:

   Ella quiere ir al campo.   She wants to go to the country. (*Subjects
     the same*)
   Ella quiere que yo vaya también.   She wants me to go too. (*Subjects
     different*)
   José prefiere conducir.   Joseph prefers to drive. (*Subjects the same*)
   José prefiere que yo conduzca.   Joseph prefers that I drive. (*Sub-
     jects different*)
   Insiste en que estemos listas a las seis.   He insists that we be ready
     at six.

With certain verbs, *e.g.*, **decir, pedir, aconsejar,** and others which require the indirect object of a person, the subject of the infinitive in
English is expressed as the indirect object of the main verb and understood as the subject of the subjunctive verb in the dependent clause. In

the case of a sentence like *Ask him to come*, think of it as, *Ask of (to) him that he come*:

> **Pídale Ud. a ella que espere un rato.**   Ask her to wait a while.
> **Te aconsejo que lleves tus esquíes.**   I advise you to take your skis.
> **No le digas que me ayude.**   Don't tell him to help me.
> **Le permitiré a Juan que juegue hoy.**   I shall permit John to play today.

In Lección seis we found that **dejar, hacer, mandar,** and **permitir** are usually followed by the infinitive when the subject of a dependent verb is a pronoun. The subjunctive is also used after these verbs, particularly when the dependent verb has a noun subject (last example, above). One also says: **Permitiremos que lleven sus patines,** *We shall permit that they take their skates.*

Ejercicios   **A.** Repitan la oración; luego, al oír la frase con la conjunción (*conjunction*) **que,** formen una nueva oración, según el modelo.

MODELO: Prefiero hacer eso. (que Ud.)   Prefiero hacer eso.
                                            Prefiero que Ud. haga eso.

1. Quiero ir a la sierra.   (que Uds.)
2. Preferimos pasar todo el día allí.   (que ellos)
3. ¿Quieres ir a esquiar?   (que nosotros)
4. ¿Desea Ud. hacer la excursión mañana?   (que yo)
5. No quieren volver antes de las cuatro.   (que tú)
6. ¿A qué hora quiere ella salir?   (que Juan y yo)
7. ¿Deseas pasar unos días en el campo?   (que tus hermanos)
8. Insistirán en comprar una casa de campo.   (en que yo)

B. Después de oír una frase, oirán una oración incompleta; formen una nueva oración introducida por la oración incompleta, según el modelo.

MODELO: ir a casa. (Dígales Ud. que)   Dígales Ud. que vayan a casa.

1. darle las gracias.   (Quiero que ellos)
2. estar listos a las ocho.   (Pídales Ud. que)
3. llevar los patines.   (Le aconsejo a Juan que)

4. venir a buscarnos.   (¿Prefieres que ellos . . . ?)
5. no olvidarse de los esquíes.   (Les diré que)
6. conducir el coche.   (No le permitiré a Carlos que)

IV. El subjuntivo en cláusulas substantivas (continuación)

The subjunctive is used in noun clauses dependent upon verbs or expressions of emotion or feeling, such as *joy, sorrow, fear, hope, pity, surprise,* and the like, as well as their opposites, provided that there is a change in subject from that of the main verb. Some common expressions of emotion are:

alegrarse (de que)   to be glad (that)

esperar   to hope

sentir (ie, i)   to regret, be sorry

ser lástima   to be a pity (too bad)

temer   to fear

tener miedo (de que)   to be afraid (that)

Me alegro de verte.   I am glad to see you. (*Subjects the same*)

¡Cuánto me alegro de que vayas!   How glad I am that you will go! (*Subjects different*)

Siento no poder quedarme.   I'm sorry I cannot (I'm sorry not to be able to) stay.

Sienten que no podamos esperar.   They are sorry (that) we cannot wait.

Tenemos miedo de que Ana no venga.   We are afraid that Ann will not come.

Es lástima que ella no sepa patinar.   It is a pity that she cannot (doesn't know how to) skate.

Repitan la oración; luego, al oír la frase con la conjunción **que,** úsenla para formar una nueva oración, siguiendo el modelo.   *Ejercicio*

MODELO: Espero divertirme mucho.   Espero divertirme mucho.
     (que tú)   Espero que tú te diviertas
                                        mucho.

1. Me alegro de poder ir contigo.   (de que Elena)
2. Temen tener que trabajar mañana.   (que Roberto)
3. Es lástima no saber esquiar.   (que Inés)
4. Esperamos encontrar una casa de campo.   (que los señores Díaz)

5. ¿Sienten Uds. no llegar a tiempo?   (que sus padres)
6. ¿Tienes miedo de patinar allí?   (que nosotros)

V. El subjuntivo en cláusulas substantivas (continuación)

The subjunctive is used in noun clauses after expressions of *doubt,*
uncertainty, belief expressed negatively, and *denial.* Common verbs
of this type are:

dudar to doubt		**no creer** not to believe	
negar (ie) to deny		**no estar seguro de que** not to be sure that	

Creemos que habrá nieve.   We believe (think) there will be snow.
   (*Certainty*)
No creo que haya ninguna dificultad.   I don't believe that there is
   (will be) any difficulty. (*Uncertainty*)
Dudo que haya un sitio más hermoso.   I doubt that there is a more
   beautiful place.
Niegan que yo comprenda eso.   They deny that I understand that.
No estamos seguros de que vayan.   We aren't sure that they are
   going (will go).

Note that **creer** and **estar seguro, -a, de que** express certainty and are
followed by the indicative in a clause, while **no creer que** and **no estar
seguro, -a, de que** express uncertainty or doubt and require the subjunctive in a clause.
   When **creer** is used in questions, the speaker may imply doubt of
the action in the dependent clause, in which case the subjunctive is
used. If no implication of doubt is made, the indicative is used. **No creer
que** in a question implies certainty:

¿Cree Ud. que vuelvan hoy?   Do you believe they will return today?
   (*Doubt in mind of the speaker*)
¿Cree Ud. que habrá nieve?   Do you believe there will be snow?
   (*The speaker has no opinion*)
¿No crees que podemos esquiar?   Don't you believe (think) we can
   ski?

Ejercicio   Para expresar en español:

1. I believe that John's father will buy a country house.   2. Helen
doesn't believe that Mary knows how to skate.   3. We are sure that the

boys will take their skis. 4. Ann is not sure that they will be ready at six. 5. John doesn't believe that there is much snow in the mountains. 6. My friends deny that there is ice on the highway. 7. Do you (*formal sing.*) believe that they will come to pick us up? (*Certainty implied*) 8. I doubt that they will arrive before noon.

VI. El subjuntivo en cláusulas substantivas (fin)

Impersonal expressions that contain ideas of *possibility, necessity, uncertainty, probability, strangeness, doubt,* and the like, require the subjunctive in the dependent clause provided that a subject is mentioned. Impersonal expressions of fact and certainty, such as **Es cierto (verdad, evidente),** *It is certain (true, evident),* require the indicative; when no subject is expressed, the infinitive is used:

Es preciso (mejor) llamarlos. It is necessary (better) to call them.
Es posible (probable) que patinemos. It is possible (probable) that we shall skate.
Puede (ser) que Ana se quede en casa. It may be that Ann will stay at home.
Será fácil que aprendas eso. It will be easy for you to learn that.
No es cierto (verdad) que haya nieve en la sierra. It isn't certain (true) that there is snow in the mountains.

Some common impersonal expressions which often require the subjunctive are:

basta it is sufficient (enough)
conviene it is fitting (advisable)
es bueno it is well
es difícil it is difficult
es dudoso it is doubtful
es extraño it is strange
es fácil it is easy
es importante it is important
es imposible it is impossible
es lástima it is a pity (too bad)
es mejor it is better
es necesario it is necessary
es posible it is possible
es preciso it is necessary
es probable it is probable
importa it is important, it matters
puede (ser) it may be
más vale (vale más) it is better

Es difícil + inf. = it's hard
Es difícil + subj. = it's not likely (same for fácil)

These expressions really fall under sections III, IV, and V, pages 159–162, but they are treated separately for convenience and clarity.

The infinitive may be used after most impersonal expressions if the subject of the dependent verb is a personal pronoun, not a noun. In this case the subject of the dependent verb is the indirect object of the main verb:

Me (les) es mejor ir hoy.   It is better for me (them) to go today.

BUT: **Es extraño que Ana no esté aquí.**   It is strange for Ann not to be here.

Ejercicios   **A.** Repitan cada oración; luego, formen una nueva oración empleando el infinitivo, como en el modelo.

MODELO: Vale más que él vuelva hoy.   Vale más que él vuelva
                                                                                    hoy.
                                                                        Vale más volver hoy.

1. Es preciso que bajemos la ladera.   2. Importa que Ud. no olvide eso. 3. Es posible que lleven los esquíes.   4. No basta que Ud. aprenda el diálogo.   5. Será mejor que busques otro sitio más hermoso.   6. Conviene que hagan planes para el viaje.   7. Puede que él se rompa una pierna.   8. No es fácil que aprendas la canción.   9. No es preciso que se muden de ropa.   10. Es bueno que Uds. tengan cuidado si hay hielo en la carretera.

B. Repitan la frase; luego, al oír una expresión impersonal, formen otra frase cambiando la original, según los modelos.

MODELOS: Juan podrá esquiar hoy.   Juan podrá esquiar hoy.
              (Es posible que)   Es posible que Juan pueda
                                                         esquiar hoy.

              (Es cierto que)   Es cierto que Juan podrá
                                                         esquiar hoy.

1. Ellos tienen otros planes.   (Es lástima que)
2. Ana aprenderá a conducir fácilmente.   (Es probable que)
3. Yo llamaré a Dorotea ahora mismo.   (Será mejor que)
4. Mis abuelos no están aquí.   (Es extraño que)
5. Ellos se quedarán varios días en la sierra.   (Es verdad que)
6. El señor López comprará una casa de campo.   (No es cierto que)
7. Mis padres volverán esta noche.   (No es posible que)
8. Tú te divertirás mucho en la excursión.   (Es evidente que)
9. Juan vendrá a buscarnos pronto.   (Importa que)
10. Estaremos listos a las cinco y media.   (Es cierto que)

VII. Otras formas de mandato

A. The first person plural of the present subjunctive, and sometimes **vamos a** plus the infinitive, express commands equal to *let's* or *let us* plus a verb. **A ver** is regularly used for *Let's see.*

Remember that object pronouns are attached to affirmative commands and to infinitives, but they precede the verb in negative commands:

Llamemos a Elena.   Let's call Helen.
Abrámosla.
Vamos a abrirla. } Let's open it.
No los dejemos allí.   Let's not leave them there.

NOTE: **Vamos** is used for the affirmative *Let's (Let us) go.* The subjunctive **No vayamos** must be used for *Let's not go:* **No vayamos todavía,** *Let's not go yet.* **No vamos a casa** can only mean *We are not going home.*

When the reflexive **nos** is added to this command form, the final **-s** is dropped from the verb:

Vámonos.   Let's be going (Let's go).
Levantémonos (Vamos a levantarnos).   Let's get up.
No nos sentemos.   Let's not sit down.

B. **Que**, equivalent to the English *have, let, may, I wish,* or *I hope,* introduces indirect commands, except in the first person. In such cases object pronouns precede the verb, and a noun or pronoun subject often follows the verb. This construction is really a clause dependent upon a verb of *wishing, hoping, permitting,* etc., with the main verb understood, but not expressed:

Que los traiga Juan.   Have (Let, May) John bring them.
Que esté él aquí a las seis.   Let him be here at six.
¡Que te diviertas mucho!   May you (I want you to, I hope you) have a very good time!

Remember that when *let* means *allow* or *permit,* it is translated by **dejar** or **permitir: Déjele (Permítale) usted a Pablo que vaya a esquiar,** *Let Paul (Allow* or *Permit Paul to) go skiing.*

Ejercicios   **A.** Para contestar dos veces, primero afirmativa, y luego negativamente, según los modelos.

MODELO: ¿Escribimos la frase?   Sí, escribámosla. No, no la escribamos.

1. ¿Llevamos los patines?   3. ¿Buscamos a Elena?
2. ¿Seguimos el coche?   4. ¿Devolvemos los esquíes?

MODELO: ¿Nos acostamos?   Sí, acostémonos. No, no nos acostemos.

5. ¿Nos levantamos?   7. ¿Nos vamos?
6. ¿Nos sentamos?   8. ¿Nos vestimos?

B. Después de oír un mandato, formen otra frase de mandato precedida de la frase **Yo no puedo** o **Nosotros no podemos**, siguiendo los modelos.

MODELOS: Lleve Ud. la comida.   Yo no puedo, que la lleve él.
         Cierren Uds. las ventanas.   Nosotros no podemos, que las cierren ellos.

1. Traiga Ud. los paquetes.   5. Escojan Uds. el sitio.
2. Sirva Ud. el café.   6. Toquen Uds. los discos.
3. Pague Ud. la cuenta.   7. Váyanse Uds.
4. Siéntese Ud.   8. Acérquense Uds.

Resumen   **A.** Repitan la oración; luego, al oír el comienzo (*beginning*) de otra oración, complétenla, según los modelos.

MODELOS: Habrá nieve allí.   Habrá nieve allí.
         (Creo que)   Creo que habrá nieve allí.
         (No creo que)   No creo que haya nieve allí.

1. Mi padre vendrá a buscarnos.   (Yo estoy seguro de que)
2. Ana podrá acompañarnos.   (No estamos seguros de que)
3. Podremos patinar mañana.   (Nuestros amigos creen que)
4. Tú comprarás un par de esquíes.   (Ellos no creen que)
5. Hay hielo en la carretera.   (Dudamos que)

6. Mi hermano irá a la sierra esta tarde.   (Mi mamá niega que)
7. Estaremos listos a las siete.   (¿No crees que . . . ?)
8. Elena se quedará en casa de sus abuelos toda la semana.   (Marta cree que)

(B) Usos del subjuntivo en cláusulas substantivas. Para expresar en español:

1. I want you (*fam. sing.*) to invite Ann to spend her (the) vacation with us.   2. And I advise you to call her now, because she is probably at home.   3. John insists that I go to the meeting with him today.   4. Ask (*fam. sing.*) them to be here before eight o'clock.   5. We are sorry that Robert will not return until tomorrow.   6. How glad I am that he can stay here all week!   7. They are afraid that you (*fam. sing.*) cannot accompany them.   8. We hope that Paul will thank them for the gift right away.   9. We are not sure that Richard will drive his car today.
10. It is important to do that; it will be easy for Henry to do it.   11. It is true that there is snow in the park; it is not certain that there is much ice.
12. It is impossible for me to leave at six (*two ways*).

Mountain climbing in Asturias, Spain.

Winter resort,
Portillo, Chile.

C. Para contestar afirmativamente, usando la forma de mandato con **usted:**

1. ¿Empiezo a leer la carta?
2. ¿Sigo aprendiendo la canción?
3. ¿Le llevo algo al niño?
4. ¿Les doy las gracias ahora?

5. ¿Me siento en esta silla?
6. ¿Me quedo aquí hasta la una?
7. ¿Le digo que vuelva hoy?
8. ¿Me acerco al señor Díaz?

D. Otras formas de mandato. Para expresar en español:

1. Have John wash it.
2. May you (*fam. sing.*) be happy!
3. Have Jane wait a few moments.
4. May you (*pl.*) have a good time!

5. Let's take the skis to them (*two ways*).
6. Let's sit down now (*two ways*).
7. Let's not go to the mountains yet.
8. Let's not put on our hats.

Resumen de palabras y expresiones

la casa de campo country house	**el esquí** (*pl.* **esquíes**) ski
dar las gracias a uno (**por**) to thank one (for)	**esquiar**[1] (**í**) to ski
	insistir en que to insist that
de nada don't mention it, you're welcome	**el patín** (*pl.* **patines**) skate
	patinar to skate
la dificultad difficulty	**por aquí** around (by) here

[1] Conjugated like **enviar** (**í**), Appendix D, page 326.

LECTURA VII

La mujer y los deportes

La participación de la mujer en los deportes tiene una historia relativamente breve en los Estados Unidos. Comenzó en el siglo pasado, cuando la educación física llegó a considerarse como un elemento valioso en los programas de las escuelas y universidades.

Durante la primera mitad del siglo actual la mujer ya tomaba parte en muchos deportes, como en el golf, el tenis, la natación,[1] el hockey, la gimnasia y el básquetbol. Las escuelas de segunda enseñanza[2] y las universidades tenían equipos de muchachas que competían entre sí en torneos regionales y nacionales.

Después de la segunda guerra mundial la participación de la mujer en los deportes ha aumentado enormemente. Hoy día[3] se celebran concursos[4] internacionales en varios deportes y hay jugadoras profesionales que se ganan la vida como deportistas.[5]

Aunque se considera que la educación física es una parte esencial de la formación de la juventud, hasta hace poco se ofrecían becas[6] «atléticas» solamente a estudiantes del sexo masculino. Pero se va rectificando esta injusticia. Media docena de las universidades más prestigiosas de los Estados Unidos han anunciado que a partir de[7] 1974 habrá becas «atléticas» para mujeres que quieran especializarse en los deportes.

Como otro ejemplo de interés histórico puede citarse la decisión de un tribunal de Madrid, que en 1973 concedió a una señorita, María de los Ángeles Hernández, el derecho de torear en las plazas de toros de España.

En general, sin embargo,[8] la mujer hispanoamericana no es tan aficionada a[9] los deportes como su hermana norteamericana. Pero va aumentando el número de mujeres que participan en los deportes en Hispanoamérica, como demuestran las noticias que se citan a continuación.[10]

---

[1] natación, *swimming.*　[2] escuelas de segunda enseñanza, *secondary schools.*　[3] Hoy día, *Nowadays.*　[4] concursos, *contests, meets.*　[5] se ganan la vida como deportistas, *earn a living as sportswomen.*　[6] becas, *scholarships.*　[7] a partir de, *beginning with.*　[8] sin embargo, *nevertheless*　[9] ser aficionado -a, a, *to be fond of.*　[10] a continuación, *below.*

La golfista chilena Sara García venció en el torneo internacional del Uruguay

PUNTA DEL ESTE. En el torneo para parejas de damas,[1] a 36 hoyos, vencieron la chilena Sara García y la uruguaya Madelón Páez Vilaro, con 148 golpes. Ocuparon el segundo lugar las argentinas Oagrane y Helguera, con 149. El tercer lugar lo ocuparon las brasileñas, con 150.

Han comenzado los Juegos Atléticos Iberoamericanos[2]

MADRID. Han comenzado los II[3] Juegos Atléticos Iberoamericanos. La ceremonia de apertura[4] fue presidida por el vicepresidente del Gobierno español, capitán general Muñoz Grande.

Hasta el momento de cerrar esta edición,[5] los ganadores de pruebas[6] han sido: Rolando Cruz, de Puerto Rico, en salto con pértiga,[7] con 4,50[8] metros. Enrique Helf de Argentina, en lanzamiento de peso,[9] con 16,06 metros. Mabel Farina, de Argentina, en salto de longitud,[10] categoría femenina, con 5,58 metros, y Marlene Ahrens, de Chile, en lanzamiento de jabalina[11] femenino, con 45,63 metros.

Deberá defender en Río de Janeiro el título de vicecampeón del mundo

SANTIAGO. El básquet[12] femenino chileno es vicecampeón del mundo y campeón sudamericano invicto.[13] Tiene acumulados gran número de laureles y goza de los mejores prestigios.[14] Por ello el básquet femenino merece una especial atención. Mucho

---

[1] **parejas de damas,** *women's doubles.*   [2] **Juegos Atléticos Iberoamericanos,** *Ibero-American Track and Field Games.*   [3] **II = Segundos.**   [4] **de apertura,** *opening.*   [5] **Hasta ... edición,** *Up to the moment this edition went to press* (lit., *. . . of closing this edition*).   [6] **ganadores de pruebas,** *winners of trials.*   [7] **en salto con pértiga,** *in the pole vault.*   [8] **4,50 = cuatro (metros), cincuenta (centímetros.)** (While the comma has largely been replaced in Spanish numbers by a period, it is still used.)   [9] **lanzamiento de peso,** *shot putting.*   [10] **salto de longitud,** *long jump.*   [11] **lanzamiento de jabalina,** *javelin throw.*   [12] **básquet,** *basketball team.*   [13] **invicto,** *undefeated.*   [14] **mejores prestigios,** *highest prestige.*

más, si cabe,[1] cuando en octubre se disputará en Río de Janeiro el II Campeonato del Mundo.

El equipo para el torneo mundial estará formado, posiblemente, por casi las mismas jugadoras que lo formaron en el Sudamericano[2] de Quito, con la inclusión, quizá, de dos o tres valores[3] nuevos; pero con las figuras estelares[4] ya conocidas. Es, pues, indispensable coordinar un plan de trabajo[5] sin prisas[6]— un trabajo que mantenga en el seleccionado[7] la unidad[8] indispensable.

Traduzcan al español las frases siguientes, tratando de imitar las construcciones y fraseología del texto: *Ejercicio*

1. When did women begin to take part in sports in the Spanish-American countries?
2. In the United States, their participation started in the nineteenth century, when physical education came to be considered an essential part of the programs of schools and universities.
3. Haven't you (*pl.*) seen photographs, taken in the first years of this century, of women's hockey and basketball teams?
4. Nowadays most secondary schools and universities have women's teams that compete in regional and national tournaments.
5. Although courses in (**de**) physical education for women are generally electives (of the elective type), the number of students who take them has increased enormously.
6. The publicity which has been given to certain professional sportswomen probably explains this increase.
7. One must remember also that beginning with 1974 "athletic" scholarships will be granted to girls as well as to boys.
8. Who won the trials in the women's javelin throw in the Ibero-American Track and Field Games?
9. According to the newspaper, the right to fight bulls in Spanish bullrings has been granted to a young lady.
10. The sports section has an interesting article about the Chilean women's basketball team that will participate in an international tournament in October.

---

[1] **si cabe**, *if it is possible.*   [2] **el Sudamericano = el Torneo sudamericano.**   [3] **valores,** *talented players.*   [4] **figuras estelares,** *stars, super players.*   [5] **plan de trabajo,** *training plan.*   [6] **sin prisas,** *unhurriedly, without haste.*   [7] **el seleccionado,** *the team which is selected.*   [8] **unidad,** *unity* (i.e., teamwork).

LECCIÓN OCHO

El (presente) perfecto de subjuntivo.   Las cláusulas adjetivas y los
pronombres relativos.   El subjuntivo en cláusulas adjetivas.   Usos
especiales del objeto indirecto

Carlos se encuentra un poco enfermo

*(Durante el desayuno en la residencia de estudiantes uno de los diez o
doce amigos que se reúnen todos los días a desayunarse en la misma
mesa advierte la ausencia de uno de ellos. Juan le pregunta a un
compañero por el que falta.)*

Juan. ¿Has visto a Carlos? No ha bajado a desayunarse, lo cual me parece
muy extraño.

Luis. No se siente bien esta mañana. Dudo mucho que se haya levantado.

Juan. ¿Qué le pasa?

Luis. Dice que le duele la garganta y que tiene dolor de cabeza.

Juan. ¿Tiene fiebre?

Luis. Le tomé la temperatura y parece que tiene un grado y medio. Me
preguntó si conocemos a algún médico que hable español.

Juan. El médico con quien hablamos en casa del profesor Valdés es
mexicano. Nos dijo que tiene su oficina en un edificio grande a unas
tres cuadras de aquí.

Luis. Es el edificio en cuyo piso bajo se encuentra una farmacia, ¿verdad?

Juan. Creo que sí. ¿Hay alguien que pueda llevarle a la oficina del médico?

Luis. Yo le llevaré. Hoy no tengo clases por la mañana.

Juan. Si no me equivoco, el médico se llama Solís. Trata de llamarle antes
de ir a su oficina.

Luis. Lo haré en seguida. Así sabremos si puede recibirle pronto.

Juan. Espero que no sea más que un resfriado. Si es algo grave, tendremos
que llamar a la madre de Carlos, la cual vive en San Agustín.

Luis. Ya veremos. De todos modos habrá que hacer lo que diga el médico.

175

A. Para contestar en español en oraciones completas:

Preguntas sobre el diálogo

1. ¿Qué le parece extraño a Juan?   2. ¿Qué contesta Luis?   3. ¿Qué le pasa a Carlos?   4. ¿Tiene fiebre Carlos?   5. ¿Dónde tiene su oficina el médico mexicano?   6. ¿Quién va a llevar a Carlos a la oficina del médico?   7. ¿Qué hará Luis antes de ir a la oficina del médico?   8. Si es algo grave, ¿qué tendrán que hacer los estudiantes?

Aplicación del diálogo

1. ¿Dónde se desayuna Ud.?   2. ¿Se desayuna Ud. con los mismos amigos todos los días?   3. ¿Qué le preguntamos a un compañero cuando nos parece que no se siente bien?   4. Si parece que está enfermo, ¿qué le aconsejamos?   5. ¿Qué debe hacer uno cuando tiene un resfriado?   6. ¿Tiene la universidad una oficina a que puedan ir los estudiantes cuando están enfermos?   7. ¿Hay en la oficina un médico que hable español?   8. ¿Cuántas veces ha necesitado Ud. un médico este año?

B. Preparen un diálogo original, de unas diez líneas, para recitar en clase, empleando las frases y preguntas siguientes como elemento inicial:

1. **María.**   Me dice Luisa que no podrá asistir al concierto esta noche.
   Dorotea.   ¡Qué lástima! ¿Tiene un resfriado?

2. **Carlos.**   ¿Qué te pasa, Juan? Estás muy pálido.
   Juan.   Creo que me he torcido el tobillo jugando al básquetbol. No puedo andar.

Pronunciación

Intonation. Review the section on intonation in Appendix A, pages 300–302. In a series or enumeration, which may consist of three or more members (nouns, adjectives, phrases or clauses), each member of the series constitutes a separate breath-group. The intonation pattern varies depending on the position of the series in the sentence.

a. If the series begins the sentence, all the breath-groups end with a slight fall of the voice except the last group, in which the voice rises to a pitch above the normal tone (level 3).

b. If the series occurs at the end of a sentence, the last two groups follow the pattern of the contrasting rise and fall of a declarative sentence of two members, but the preceding groups all end with a fall of the voice slightly below the normal tone. If the series is left incomplete (that is, if the last two members are not connected by the conjunction y), all the groups will end with a slight fall in the voice. Practice the following examples:

Series at the beginning:

Los lunes, los martes y los jueves ceno en casa.

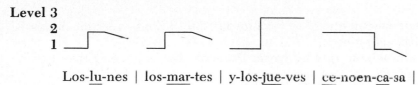

Los-lu-nes | los-mar-tes | y-los-jue-ves | ce-noen-ca-sa |

Series at end:

Ceno en casa los lunes, los martes y los jueves.

Ce-noen-ca-sa-los-lu-nes | los-mar-tes | y-los-jue-ves |

Incomplete series, at end:

Su novia es guapa, rica, elegante . . .

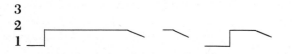

Su-no-viaes-gua-pa | ri-ca | e-le-gan-te |

I. El (presente) perfecto de subjuntivo

Notas gramaticales

The present perfect subjunctive tense is formed by the present subjunctive of **haber** with the past participle. After verbs in the main clause which require the subjunctive in the dependent clause, Spanish uses the present perfect subjunctive tense to translate English *have (has)* plus the past participle:

Singular	Plural

haya ⎤
hayas ⎬ tomado, comido, vivido
haya ⎦

hayamos ⎤
hayáis ⎬ tomado, comido, vivido
hayan ⎦

Dudo mucho que él se haya levantado.   I doubt very much that he has gotten up.
Siento mucho que no hayan llegado.   I'm very sorry they haven't arrived.
Es posible que Ana haya estado enferma.   It's possible that Ann has been ill.

Ejercicio   Repitan la oración; luego, repítanla otra vez, cambiando el verbo de la cláusula subordinada al perfecto de subjuntivo.

MODELO: Yo dudo que él esté aquí.   Yo dudo que él esté aquí.
                                                            Yo dudo que él haya estado
                                                            aquí.

1. Espero que Juan baje a comer.   2. Es lástima que él no se sienta bien.   3. No creo que él tenga un resfriado.   4. Me alegro de que tú abras todas las ventanas.   5. Él duda que Uds. lean el cuento.   6. Sentimos mucho que ella no se ponga los guantes.   7. Tengo miedo de que ellos no lleven sus patines.   8. Me parece extraño que Uds. no vayan a la sierra.

II. Las cláusulas adjetivas y los pronombres relativos

An adjective clause modifies a noun or pronoun and is introduced by a relative pronoun. In the sentence *I know a boy who can help us*, the adjective clause *who can help us* modifies *boy*. *Who* is a relative pronoun and *boy* is the antecedent of the clause.

A. Simple relative pronouns

1. **Que,** *that, which, who,* and when used as direct object of a verb, *whom,* is invariable and refers to persons or things. Used as the object of a preposition, **que** refers normally to things and only occasionally to persons. The relative pronoun is sometimes omitted in English when used as the object of a verb, but not in Spanish:

> **la casa que compró**   the house (that) he bought
> **los amigos que se reúnen**   the friends who meet (gather)
> **el partido de que trata el artículo**   the game with which the article deals
> **los jóvenes que vimos**   the young men (whom) we saw

2. **Quien** (*pl.* **quienes**), *who, whom,* refers only to persons. It is used mainly as the object of a preposition, always meaning *whom,* and sometimes instead of **que** when the relative pronoun *who* is separated from the antecedent by a comma. The personal **a** is required when **quien(es)** is the direct object of a verb:

> **el médico con quien hablamos**   the doctor with whom we talked
> **el señor Díaz, quien me llamó, quiere . . .**   Mr. Díaz, who called me, wishes . . .
> **los hombres a quienes vimos ayer**   the men (whom) we saw yesterday

In the last sentence **que** may replace **a quienes,** and in conversation it is more widely used.

3. **El cual (la cual, los cuales, las cuales),** *that, which, who, whom,* is used to clarify which one of two possible antecedents the clause modifies, and after prepositions such as **sin, por,** and those of more than one syllable. Be sure that the long relative agrees with its antecedent. (These long relatives are much more widely used in literary style than in everyday conversation.)

> **la madre de Carlos, la cual vive en . . .**   Charles' mother, who lives in . . .
> **el coche cerca del cual están jugando**   the car near which they are playing

El que (la que, los que, las que) may be substituted for forms of **el cual**, particularly after prepositions, as in the second example.

4. **Lo cual** (sometimes **lo que**), *which* (*fact*), a neuter form, is used to refer back to an idea, statement, or situation, but not to a specific noun:

> **No ha bajado a desayunarse, lo cual me parece extraño.**   He hasn't come down for breakfast, which (fact) seems strange to me.

B. Compound relative pronouns

1. **El (la) que,** *he (she) who, the one who* (*that, which*), and **los (las) que,** *those* or *the ones who* (*that, which*), may refer to persons or things. These forms are often called compound relatives because the definite article (which originated from the Latin demonstrative) serves as the antecedent of the **que**-clause. (Do <u>not</u> use forms of **el cual** in this construction.)

> **Juan pregunta por el que falta.**   John asks about the one who is missing.
> **Estas muchachas y las que están ausentes . . .**   These girls and the ones (those) who are absent . . .
> **Los que se reúnen aquí . . .**   Those who meet here . . .

Quien (*pl.* **quienes**), which refers only to persons, sometimes means *he (those) who, the one(s) who,* particularly in proverbs:

> **Quien mucho duerme, poco aprende.**   He who sleeps much, learns little.

2. **Lo que,** *what, that which,* a neuter form, refers only to an idea or statement:

> **Lo que dice Juan es verdad.**   What (That which) John says is true.
> **Yo sé lo que Uds. quieren hacer.**   I know what you want to do.

3. **Cuyo, -a, -os, -as,** *whose, of whom, of which,* is a relative possessive adjective. It agrees with the noun it modifies in gender and number:

> **el edificio en cuyo piso bajo**   the building on the first floor of which (on whose first floor)
> **la mujer cuyos hijos**   the woman whose children (the children of whom)

Remember that **¿De quién(es)?** expresses *Whose?* in a question: **¿De quién es esta casa?** *Whose house is this?* (*lit.*, Of whom is this house?)

A. Después de oír las dos frases, combínenlas, usando el pronombre relativo **que**, según el modelo.   *Ejercicios*

MODELO: Ella tenía un libro. Era nuevo.   El libro que ella tenía era
                                                 nuevo.

1. Ana compró un vestido. Es muy bonito.
2. Juanita sirvió unos refrescos. Eran excelentes.
3. Vimos a los niños. Estaban en el parque.
4. Conocimos al hombre ayer. Es médico.
5. Invité a varios jóvenes. Son estudiantes.

Combinen las dos frases, usando el pronombre relativo **quien**, según el modelo.

MODELO: Vimos al joven. Es   Vimos al joven, quien es mexicano.
            mexicano.   El joven a quien vimos es mexicano.

6. Saludé a la joven. Es española.
7. Hablamos con la muchacha. Es estudiante de esta universidad.
8. Charlamos con aquel señor. Trabaja en esta tienda.
9. Llamé a aquella niña. Está jugando en el patio.
10. Anoche conocimos a aquella señorita. Es profesora de inglés.

Combinen las dos frases, usando **el cual** o una de sus formas, según el modelo.

MODELO: La madre de Carlos vive   La madre de Carlos, la cual
            en San Agustín. Vendrá   vive en San Agustín,
            a visitarle pronto.   vendrá a visitarle pronto.

11. Los amigos de Marta estudian en la biblioteca. Tienen un examen
     mañana.
12. La tía de Miguel viaja por México. Le envió una carta.
13. El abuelo de Inés ha escrito libros sobre México. Vive en San
     Antonio.
14. Las hijas de la señora Díaz corren hacia el parque. Son muy simpá-
     ticas.

B. Lean en español, supliendo el pronombre relativo:

1. La casa de campo _que_ compraron es hermosa.   2. Los patines _que_ tengo son de Roberto.   3. El niño _que / el que_ (*two ways*) vieron Uds. es mi hermanito.   4. El señor Navarro, _quien / el cual_ (*two ways*) es español, dio la conferencia.   5. El edificio del _cual / del que_ hablan es muy grande.   6. Las señoras con _quienes_ charla mi mamá son mexicanas. 7. Me gusta la casa cerca de _la cual_ juegan los muchachos.   8. Los amigos de Juan, _quienes / los que, los cuales_ se reúnen aquí, son estudiantes de esta universidad.   9. ¿Hiciste _lo que_ dijo el médico?   10. Los jóvenes no han vuelto, _lo cual_ nos parece extraño.   11. Estos esquíes y _los que_ tiene Ana son nuevos.   12. Esta tarjeta y _la que_ recibí la semana pasada son de mis padres.   13. Mi tío construyó este edificio y _el que_ está en la esquina.   14. _Quien_ busca, halla.

III. El subjuntivo en cláusulas adjetivas

When the antecedent of an adjective clause is indefinite or negative, that is, when the adjective clause refers back to someone or something that is uncertain, unknown, indefinite, or nonexistent, the subjunctive is used in it. In general, if *any, whatever,* or *whoever* can be applied to the antecedent, the subjunctive is required. The idea of futurity is often involved.

The indicative is used, however, when the antecedent refers back to someone or something that is certain or definite. This includes an action that occurs as a general rule:

> **¿Hay alguien que pueda llevarle a la oficina del médico?**   Is there anyone who can take him to the doctor's office?
> **¿Tiene ella un amigo que haya estado en México?**   Does she have a friend who has been in Mexico?
> **Queremos una casa que sea más grande.**   We want a (any) house that is larger.
> **Haremos lo que diga el médico.**   We shall do what(ever) the doctor says (may say).
> **No hay nadie que haya jugado mejor.**   There is no one who has played better.
> **Ana no ve nada que le guste.**   Ann doesn't see anything (sees nothing) that she likes.

> BUT: **Ana encuentra algo que le gusta mucho.**   Ann finds something that she likes a great deal.

(

>**Yo siempre hago lo que me piden.**   I always do what (that which) they ask of me.
>
>**Ricardo tiene un tío rico que vive en San Agustín.**   Richard has a rich uncle who lives in St. Augustine.

In adjective clauses the personal **a** is omitted when a noun does not refer to a specific person (first example below). It is used, however, before the pronouns **alguien** and **nadie,** and before forms of **alguno** and **ninguno** when referring to a person and when used as direct objects:

>**Necesito un hombre que me ayude mañana.**   I need a man who will (may) help me tomorrow.
>
>**No conozco a nadie que diga eso.**   I don't know anyone who says (will say) that.
>
>**¿Conoce Ud. a algún médico que hable español?**   Do you know a (any) doctor who speaks Spanish?

A. Repitan cada frase; luego, al oír el comienzo de otra frase, completen la nueva frase, según el modelo.   *Ejercicios*

MODELO: Tiene un traje que le gusta.   Tiene un traje que le gusta.
         (Quiere un traje)   Quiere un traje que le guste.

1. Buscamos al joven que habla bien el español. (Buscamos un joven)
2. Tienen una casa que tiene ocho cuartos. (Necesitan una casa)
3. Cerca de aquí hay un sitio que es más hermoso. (Cerca de aquí no hay ningún sitio)
4. Deseamos reunirnos en el café donde sirven comidas mexicanas. (Deseamos reunirnos en algún café)
5. Quiero encontrar a la señorita que ha vivido en México. (Quiero encontrar una señorita)
6. Espero ver al niño que ha estado en el museo. (Espero ver un niño)

B. Para expresar en español:

1. I see some of the boys who meet here every day.   2. We believe that there is someone who can take him to the doctor's office.   3. We are looking for a secretary who writes Spanish.   4. Do you (*formal sing.*) know anyone who speaks the language well?   5. We prefer a girl who has lived in Mexico or Chile.   6. Mr. Martínez needs a man who can

work in his store.   7. Is there any boy who wants to go to the drugstore now?   8. We do not see anyone who has time (in order) to do it.   9. The girls want to find some dresses that they like.   10. The children will do what(ever) their mother may say.

IV. Usos especiales del objeto indirecto

A. If an action is performed on one person by another, the corresponding indirect object pronoun is used with the verb. This construction most often involves parts of the body, articles of clothing, or things closely related to the person. Note that the definite article replaces the possessive adjective:

> **Le tomé la temperatura.**   I took his temperature (*lit.*, I took to him the temperature).
> **La madre les lavó las manos.**   The mother washed their hands.

Remember that the reflexive pronoun is used when the subject acts upon itself:

> **Mi madre se tomó la temperatura.**   My mother took her (own) temperature.
> **Juanito se lavó las manos.**   Johnny washed his hands.

B. The verb **doler,** *to ache, hurt,* has as its subject a noun expressing a part of the body, and the person is the indirect object:

> **Le (Me) duele la garganta.**   His (My) throat aches (hurts).
> **A ella le duele (Le duele a ella) la cabeza.**   Her head aches.

Ejercicio   Repitan la frase; luego, al oír un nuevo sujeto, formen otra frase, según el modelo.

MODELO: Ana se tomó la temperatura.   Ana se tomó la temperatura.
       (Mi hermana)   Mi hermana le tomó la
                                            temperatura a Ana.

1. Juanito se lavó las manos.   2. Pablo se quitó los zapatos.
   (Yo)   (Ella)

3. Ana se compró un reloj. (Su   5. Juan se sirvió café. (Carolina)
   papá)   6. Luisa se cortó la mano.
4. Marta se puso la ropa. (Su   (Yo no)
   mamá)

A. Repitan cada pregunta; luego, contéstenla negativamente, haciendo   **Resumen**
los cambios necesarios en la cláusula adjetiva.

MODELO: ¿Ve Ud. algo que sea   ¿Ve Ud. algo que sea mejor?
            mejor?   No, no veo nada que sea mejor.

1. ¿Ve Ud. a alguien que pueda llevar la maleta?
2. ¿Hay alguien que tenga un resfriado hoy?
3. ¿Conoce Ud. a algún médico que hable español?
4. ¿Ves algo que Marta pueda comprar?
5. ¿Hay alguna cosa aquí que le guste a él?
6. ¿Hay alguien que conozca a aquel señor?
7. ¿Conoces a alguien que haya ido a la sierra?
8. ¿Ha leído Ud. algo que haya sido más interesante?

B. Usos de los pronombres relativos. Para expresar en español:

1. The young lady whom (*two ways*) we met yesterday is from Colombia.
2. John's sister, who has just arrived, is studying at another university.
3. We can see the building on whose first floor the lawyer has his office.
4. Ask (*fam. sing.*) George what he did with the book of which we were
talking.   5. Our cousins have not returned yet, which (fact) surprises
me.   6. These women and the one who is near the car are friends of
my mother.   7. It can be said that those who (*two ways*) practice much,
learn rapidly.   8. These two articles and the one which Helen read are
well written.

C. Usos del objeto indirecto. Para expresar en español:

1. The children washed their   3. Ann didn't take off her
   hands.   shoes.
2. Their mother washed their   4. Her sister took her shoes off
   hands.   her.

5. The doctor took her
   temperature.
6. Did he take his temperature?
7. Did Jane put on her new hat?

8. I put her hat on her.
9. My head aches (*two ways*).
10. Does your (*fam. sing.*)
    throat hurt?

D. Repaso. Repitan cada oración; luego, repítanla otra vez, cambiando
el verbo al pretérito de indicativo:

1. Carolina va a la sierra con algunos amigos.   2. José y yo no podemos
acompañarlos.   3. El señor Díaz hace un viaje a México.   4. Los jóvenes nos traen varios regalos.   5. María se sienta en la primera fila.
6. Mi mamá no duerme la siesta.   7. Los muchachos nunca me piden
nada.   8. Oyen cantar a María.   9. Roberto sigue leyendo la novela.
10. ¿Qué te dicen tus amigos?   11. ¿Cuáles de los estudiantes vienen
a la reunión?   12. ¿Es fácil aprender el diálogo?   13. Les doy las
gracias por la invitación.   14. Mi mamá se pone el vestido nuevo.
15. Arturo no se acuerda de eso.   16. Todos se divierten mucho en la
excursión.   17. Mi papá conduce el coche al aeropuerto.   18. Nuestro
tío construye una casa de campo.   19. Los estudiantes advierten la
ausencia de Carlos.   20. María no quiere dar un paseo con Pablo.
21. Yo llego a la universidad a las nueve.   22. Me equivoco; él no sabe
nada de particular.   23. Bárbara tiene que escribir una carta a un amigo
mexicano.   24. Roberto y Carolina andan despacio por la calle.
25. Ella y yo volvemos a casa a las cinco de la tarde.

Resumen de palabras y expresiones

advertir (ie, i) to notice
Agustín Augustine
la ausencia absence
ausente absent
la cuadra block (*city*)
de todos modos at any rate, by all
   means
el dolor ache, pain
equivocarse to be mistaken
la farmacia pharmacy, drugstore
la fiebre fever
la garganta throat
el grado (y medio) degree (and a half)
grave grave, serious
no ... más que only

pálido, -a pale
el piso bajo first floor
¿qué (le) pasa? what's the matter
   with (him, her, you)? what's
   happening to (him, her, you)?
el resfriado cold (*disease*)
la temperatura temperature
reunirse[1] **(ú)** to meet, gather, get
   together
sentirse (ie, i) (bien) to feel (well)
suceder to happen
tener dolor de cabeza to have a
   headache
tratar de + *obj.* to deal with
ya veremos we'll see soon (presently)

[1] See page 326, footnote 1, for forms.

LECTURA VIII

Una encuesta[1] sobre las carreras profesionales

¿Qué carrera profesional recomendaría usted a un joven que va a empezar sus estudios universitarios? Una encuesta realizada recientemente por una empresa norteamericana le ayudará a llegar a una decisión respecto de este problema. La encuesta, que se repite cada cinco años desde[2] 1950, tiene por objeto[3] pedir a individuos de unas trescientas localidades, seleccionadas científicamente, que indiquen cuál de una lista de nueve profesiones principales consideran la mejor para un joven de hoy día. Las nueve profesiones son las de médico, abogado, ingeniero, profesor, industrial o ejecutivo de negocios, dentista, funcionario del gobierno, banquero y clérigo.

En el presente análisis de la encuesta vamos a comparar las respuestas recibidas en 1962 y 1973 de adultos de menos de 30 años de edad. Todos admiten que se han realizado cambios radicales en la sociedad norteamericana—sobre todo[4] en la manera de pensar de los jóvenes—durante los últimos diez años. ¿Se reflejan estos cambios en las ideas de la juventud respecto de las carreras preferidas?

Como en 1962, una cuarta parte de los interrogados opinaron en 1973 que la medicina era la mejor profesión para un joven: el 26 por 100[5] en 1962 y el 25 por 100 en 1973. (Para el público en general, los resultados favorecen aun más la medicina: el 23 por 100 le dio el primer lugar en 1962, y el 28 por 100 en 1973.)

Es muy general la impresión de que las universidades producen un número excesivo de abogados. A pesar de[6] esta impresión, ha habido un aumento considerable en el interés por los estudios de derecho: el 8 por 100 los escogió en 1962 y el 20 por 100 en 1973. (En el público en general el aumento no ha sido tan notable: el 8 por 100 en 1962, y el 14 por 100 en 1973.) No parece difícil explicar este aumento. Los estudios de derecho no sólo preparan al estudiante para una carrera lucrativa como abogado, sino que también constituyen una base ex-

---

[1] encuesta, *poll.*   [2] se repite . . . desde, *which has been repeated . . . since.*   [3] por objeto, *as a purpose.*   [4] sobre todo, *especially.*   [5] el 26 por 100, *26 percent.* (Read: el veintiséis por ciento.)   [6] A pesar de, *In spite of, Despite.*

Student, School of
Mechanical Engineering,
University of Mexico,
Mexico City.

celente para una carrera en el gobierno o en los negocios. Para algunos
estudiantes la abogacía ofrece también un instrumento útil para combatir
los abusos e injusticias de la sociedad.

Otras carreras que han atraído a muchos jóvenes son las de ingeniero
y de profesor. El interés por ellas ha disminuido un poco durante los
últimos diez años. El 17 por 100 escogió la profesión de ingeniero en
1962, y el 14 por 100 en 1973. La profesión de maestro fue la preferida
del 18 por 100 en 1962, y del 14 por 100 en 1973.

Se observa un aumento considerable en el porcentaje de jóvenes que
desean prepararse para una carrera en los negocios. Sólo el 3 por 100 la
escogió en 1962, mientras que el 9 por 100 la eligió en 1973.

La atracción de la carrera de dentista ha aumentado también: el 5
por 100 la escogió en 1962, y el 6 por 100 en 1973. Los puestos en el
gobierno parecen un poco menos atractivos: el 7 por 100 los eligió en
1962 y el 6 por 100 en 1973. No ha habido cambio en cuanto al[1] porcentaje de los que desean ser banqueros: el 2 por 100 escogió esta profesión en las dos encuestas.

Los resultados respecto de la última profesión de la lista parece
indicar un descenso del idealismo en nuestra sociedad actual. Mientras
que el 4 por 100 escogió la carrera de clérigo en 1962, sólo el 1 por 100
la eligió en 1973.

---

[1] **en cuanto a,** *as for, with regard to.*

Spinning yard needed for
the loom—handicraft still
common in smaller towns
in Mexico.

Las cifras siguientes también parecen significativas: en 1962 el 10 por 100 no tenía opinión respecto de su preferencia; en 1973 sólo el 3 por 100 se declaró indeciso.

En cuanto a las profesiones favorecidas por los estudiantes hispanoamericanos, los resultados de una encuesta semejante mostrarían la influencia de diversos factores sociales y económicos. En los países subdesarrollados, por el elevado coste de las instalaciones que se necesitan para la preparación de estudiantes en las carreras técnicas y científicas, como las de médico o ingeniero, el número de estudiantes que pueden prepararse para dichas profesiones es muy limitado. Las universidades, por lo tanto, tienden a favorecer las disciplinas, como el derecho, la pedagogía, las humanidades y las ciencias sociales, en que las instalaciones son menos costosas.

La generalización citada parece válida para Hispanoamérica. Una minoría selecta escoge las profesiones de médico y de ingeniero—las de mayor consideración social—, aunque tenga que efectuar sus estudios en el extranjero.[1] Grandes masas de estudiantes, en cambio, se acumulan en las facultades de derecho y de ciencias sociales, y, según algunos críticos, se da un énfasis excesivo a las humanidades. (¡Se ha dicho que hasta la edad de veinte y dos años todo universitario hispanoamericano aspira a ser poeta o novelista!)

[1] **en el extranjero,** *abroad.*

Potter, San Pedro
de Tlaquepaque,
Jalisco, Mexico.

Las preferencias de los estudiantes graduados que vienen a universidades norteamericanas para continuar sus estudios parecen confirmar las observaciones hechas anteriormente. La mayor parte de ellos vienen a ampliar sus estudios de ingeniería, medicina y agricultura.

No debe olvidarse, además, otra diferencia muy importante: en Hispanoamérica sólo una pequeña minoría de los estudiantes—el uno por 100, aproximadamente—continúa sus estudios en la universidad.

Escriban tres oraciones sobre cada uno de los temas siguientes: *Ejercicio*

1. Observaciones sobre las profesiones incluidas en la encuesta sobre las carreras profesionales.
2. Las dos profesiones más populares entre los estudiantes norteamericanos.
3. Factores que afectan las preferencias de los estudiantes hispanoamericanos respecto de las profesiones.

LECCIÓN NUEVE

Formas del imperfecto de subjuntivo.   El pluscuamperfecto de subjuntivo.   Usos de los tiempos del subjuntivo.   El subjuntivo en cláusulas adverbiales.   El subjuntivo en frases condicionales

Una cámara para el viaje a México

(Son las diez de la noche. Roberto acaba de regresar a su cuarto. Ha ido de compras con su padre y han cenado en el centro. Entra su amigo Jorge.)

Jorge.   ¡Hola, Roberto! Aunque sea tarde, he venido a ver si encontraste la cámara que deseabas.

Roberto.   Pasa, Jorge. Me ha regalado mi papá una cámara de treinta y cinco milímetros. Quiero que la veas.

Jorge.   ¡Hombre! ¿Por qué no me llamaste para que te ayudara a escoger entre tantas marcas buenas? (*Le enseña Roberto la cámara.*) Pero, ¡ésta es magnífica!

Roberto.   Pasé por tu cuarto a eso de las tres, pero habías salido antes de que yo llegara.

Jorge.   ¡Gastas el dinero como si fueras millonario! Con la pantalla y el proyector que te regalaron para tu cumpleaños, ya no te falta nada.

Roberto.   Me gustaría aumentar mi colección de transparencias.[1] Pienso sacar muchas fotografías cuando vaya a México este verano.

Jorge.   También llevarás tu cámara de cine, ¿verdad?

Roberto.   Habrá ocasiones en que podré usar las dos. Cuando haya bailes o fiestas populares, será mejor usar la cámara de cine.

Jorge.   ¿Por qué no metes un rollo de película en la cámara para probarla?

Roberto.   Es una buena idea, aunque no sé si podré hacerla revelar antes que me marche.

Jorge.   Si tuviera dinero, haría el viaje contigo. Si fuésemos juntos, nos divertiríamos mucho.

Roberto.   Si no hubieras ido a Nueva York durante las Navidades, tus ahorros no habrían bajado tanto . . .

Jorge.   Pero si sigo trabajando en la biblioteca, podré reunir el dinero fácilmente. ¿Qué te parece la idea?

Roberto.   ¡Me parece magnífica!

Jorge.   Pues, prometo acompañarte con tal que consiga el dinero.

---

[1] For *slide, transparency,* **la diapositiva** is also used.

A. Para contestar en español en oraciones completas:

Preguntas sobre el   1. ¿De dónde regresa Roberto?   2. ¿Qué le ha regalado su padre?
diálogo   3. Según Jorge, ¿cómo gasta Roberto el dinero?   4. ¿Qué le habían
regalado a Roberto para su cumpleaños?   5. ¿Qué piensa hacer Roberto
en México?   6. ¿En qué ocasiones piensa usar su cámara de cine?
7. ¿Qué haría Jorge si tuviera dinero?   8. ¿Cómo podrá Jorge reunir el
dinero para ir a México?

Aplicación del   1. ¿Le interesan a Ud. las cámaras?   2. ¿Cuántas cámaras tiene Ud.?
diálogo   3. ¿Le gustaría a Ud. que le regalasen una cámara de cine o ya tiene una?
4. ¿Qué marcas de cámaras prefiere Ud.?   5. ¿En qué ocasiones ha
sacado Ud. muchas fotos?   6. ¿Sabe Ud. revelar sus películas o las
manda revelar?   7. ¿Tiene Ud. una colección de transparencias?
8. ¿Cuánto valdrá un proyector bueno?

B. Estudien las palabras y expresiones siguientes para emplear algunas
de ellas en el diálogo citado o para usarlas en un diálogo nuevo basado
sobre el modelo:

el álbum album	**la exposición** (*pl.* **exposiciones**)
la ampliación (*pl.* **ampliaciones**)	exposure
enlargement	**fotogénico, -a** photogenic
ampliar to enlarge	**fotográfico, -a** photographic
el carrete reel	**el fotógrafo** photographer
desenfocado, -a out of	**la instantánea** snapshot
focus	**el lente** lens
enfocado, -a in focus	**la prueba negativa** negative
enfocar to focus	**el trípode** tripod
el enfoque focus(ing)	**el visor** viewfinder

Pronunciación   Review the observations on Spanish intonation (Repaso tres, pages
26–27, Lección dos, pages 57–58, and Lección ocho, pages 176–177;
then read the first four exchanges of the dialogue of this lesson, paying
close attention to the intonation patterns.

Notas   **I. Formas del imperfecto de subjuntivo**
gramaticales

The imperfect subjunctive tense in Spanish has two forms, often referred
to as the -ra and -se forms, and the same two sets of endings are used for
the three conjugations. To form the imperfect subjunctive of all verbs,

regular and irregular, drop **-ron** of the third person plural preterit indicative and add **-ra, -ras, -ra, -´ramos, -rais, -ran** or **-se, -ses, -se, -´semos, -seis, -sen.** Only the first person plural form has a written accent. Remember that the **-er** and **-ir** verbs have the same endings in all tenses except in the present indicative. The two imperfect subjunctive tenses are interchangeable in Spanish, except in conditional sentences (section V of this lesson) and in softened statements (Lección diez, page 221):

tomar:	tomara	tomaras	tomara	tomáramos	tomarais	tomaran
	tomase	tomases	tomase	tomásemos	tomaseis	tomasen
comer:	comiera	comieras	comiera	comiéramos	comierais	comieran
vivir:	viviese	vivieses	viviese	viviésemos	vivieseis	viviesen

See Appendix D, pages 319–330, for the imperfect subjunctive forms of irregular and stem-changing verbs. For easy reference, the infinitive, third person plural preterit, and the first person singular imperfect subjunctive forms of some common irregular verbs are listed here:

Inf.	3rd Pl. Pret.	Imp. Subj.
andar	anduvieron	anduviera, -se
caer	cayeron	cayera, -se
conducir	condujeron	condujera, -se
construir	construyeron	construyera, -se
creer	creyeron	creyera, -se
dar	dieron	diera, -se
decir	dijeron	dijera, -se
estar	estuvieron	estuviera, -se
haber	hubieron[1]	hubiera, -se
hacer	hicieron	hiciera, -se
ir	fueron	fuera, -se
oír	oyeron	oyera, -se
poder	pudieron	pudiera, -se
poner	pusieron	pusiera, -se
querer	quisieron	quisiera, -se
saber	supieron	supiera, -se
ser	fueron	fuera, -se
tener	tuvieron	tuviera, -se
traer	trajeron	trajera, -se
ver	vieron	viera, -se

[1] See page 260 for the preterit forms of **haber.**

Stem-changing verbs, Class I (which end in **-ar** and **-er**), have no stem change in the imperfect subjunctive. In Class II verbs (**sentir, dormir**), the stem vowel **e** becomes **i** and **o** becomes **u** in the third person singular and plural of the preterit and in the entire imperfect subjunctive. In Class III verbs (**pedir, reír**) the stem vowel **e** becomes **i** in the same forms:

sentir (ie, i)	sintieron	sintiera, -se
dormir (ue, u)	durmieron	durmiera, -se
pedir (i, i)	pidieron	pidiera, -se
reír (i, i)	rieron	riera, -se

II. El pluscuamperfecto de subjuntivo

The pluperfect subjunctive is formed by using either the **-ra** or **-se** imperfect subjunctive form of **haber** plus the past participle:

hubiera	hubiese	
hubieras	hubieses	
hubiera	hubiese	
		tomado, comido, vivido
hubiéramos	hubiésemos	
hubierais	hubieseis	
hubieran	hubiesen	

Yo sentía mucho que él ya hubiera (hubiese) comido.   I was very sorry that he had already eaten.

III. Usos de los tiempos del subjuntivo

When the main verb in a sentence which requires the subjunctive in a dependent clause is in the present, future, or present perfect tense, or is a command, the verb in the dependent clause is regularly in the present or present perfect subjunctive tense:

Quiero que veas la cámara.   I want you to see the camera.
Le diré (he dicho) que vuelva pronto.   I shall tell (have told) him to return soon.
Pídales Ud. que nos enseñen la pantalla.   Ask them to show us the screen.
Es posible que se hayan marchado.   It is possible that they have left.

When the main verb is in the preterit, imperfect, conditional, or pluperfect tense, the verb in the dependent clause is usually in the imperfect subjunctive, unless the English past perfect tense is used in the dependent clause, in which case the pluperfect subjunctive is used in Spanish:

Le pedí (pedía) que me lo diera. I asked (was asking) him to give it to me.

No había nadie que pudiese ayudarnos. There was no one who could help us.

Yo dudaría que Ana hubiese ido de compras. I would doubt that Ann had gone shopping.

Contrary to the above statements, the imperfect subjunctive may follow the present, future, or present perfect tense when, as in English, the action of the dependent clause took place in the past:

No creo que Juan regresara anoche. I don't believe John returned last night.

Ejercicios

A. Lean en español, supliendo la forma correcta del verbo entre paréntesis; cuando sea necesario el imperfecto de subjuntivo, usen las dos formas:

1. Carolina insiste en que yo (ir) de compras con ella.   2. Ella insistió en que yo (estar) en su casa a las dos.   3. Mi hermano quiere que yo le (comprar) un rollo de película.   4. Yo quería que él lo (meter) en su cámara nueva para probarla.   5. Carolina busca un regalo que le (gustar) a su mamá.   6. Ella deseaba encontrar algo que no (costar) demasiado.   7. No creo que Ricardo (haber) ido a clase hoy.   8. Yo no creía que él se (haber) marchado.

B. Repitan cada oración; luego, al oír una nueva frase inicial, completen la oración, haciendo los cambios necesarios:

1. Yo no quiero que se marchen todavía. (Yo no quería)
2. Les pediré que vuelvan a reunirse pronto. (Les pediría)
3. Desean buscar una casa que sea más cómoda. (Deseaban)
4. No hay nadie que se dé cuenta de eso. (No había nadie)
5. Es posible que Juan pueda reunir el dinero. (Era posible)

6. José duda que Jorge siga trabajando en la biblioteca. (José dudaba)
7. Será mejor que Roberto escoja la cámara para su cumpleaños. (Sería mejor)
8. No estamos seguros de que hayan hecho el viaje. (No estábamos seguros de)

IV. El subjuntivo en cláusulas adverbiales

An adverbial clause, which modifies a verb and indicates *time, purpose, concession, condition, result, negative result,* and the like, is introduced by a conjunction, often a compound with **que** as the last element. If the action has taken place or is an accepted fact, the indicative mood is used; if the action may take place but has not actually been accomplished, the subjunctive is normally used in the clause.

A. Time clauses

The subjunctive is used after conjunctions of time if the action in the dependent clause has not been completed at the time indicated by the main clause, that is, when the time referred to in the clause is indefinite and future, and therefore uncertain, from the standpoint of the time expressed in the main clause. **Antes (de) que,** *before,* always requires the subjunctive since the action indicated in the clause cannot have taken place.

When the time clause expresses an accomplished fact in the present or past, or a customary occurrence, the indicative is used.

Common conjunctions which introduce time clauses are:

antes (de) que before	**en cuanto** as soon as
así que as soon as	**hasta que** until
cuando when	**luego que** as soon as
después (de) que after	**mientras (que)** while, as long as

Yo estudié hasta que regresó Felipe.   I studied until Philip returned.
Cuando yo veo a Juan, le saludo.   When I see John, I greet him.
En cuanto yo le vea, le saludaré.   As soon as I see him, I shall greet him.
Cuando haya bailes, será mejor usar la cámara de cine.   When there are dances, it will be better to use the movie camera.

Tú habías salido antes de que yo llegara. You had left before I
  arrived.
Ana quería leer hasta que Pablo la llamara. Ann wanted to read
  until Paul called (should call) her.

B. Concessive and result clauses

Aunque, *although, even though, even if,* is followed by the subjunctive
mood unless the speaker wishes to express a statement as a certainty or
is indicating an accomplished fact, in both of which cases the indicative
mood is used:

Aunque sea tarde, he venido a verte. Even though it may be late,
  I have come to see you.
Aunque es tarde, he venido a verte. Although it is late, I have come
  to see you. (*Certainty implied*)
Aunque yo estaba cansado, fui con él. Although I was tired, I went
  with him. (*A fact*)

Two other conjunctions, **de manera que** and **de modo que,** both meaning
so that, may express result, in which case they are followed by the indicative mood. They may also express purpose, in which case the subjunctive is used. Compare the following sentences (also see section C,
which follows):

Juan habló de manera (modo) que le entendimos. John spoke so
  that (in such a way that) we understood (did understand) him.
Hable Ud. de manera (modo) que le entendamos. Speak so that we
  may understand you. (*No certainty that we will*)

NOTE: In certain adverbial constructions, if there is no change in subject,
the corresponding preposition plus the infinitive is used instead of a
clause with the subjunctive:

¿Por qué no metes un rollo en la cámara para probarla? Why don't
  you put a roll in the camera to (in order that you may) try it?
Aprendan el diálogo de memoria para poder repetirlo. Learn the
  dialogue by heart in order to be able to (so that you can) repeat it.

C. Purpose, proviso, conditional, negative result clauses

Certain conjunctions denoting *purpose, proviso, condition, negative result,* and the like, always require the subjunctive because they cannot introduce a statement of fact. By their very meaning they indicate that the action in the clause is uncertain or that the action may not, or did not, actually take place. In addition to **de manera que** and **de modo que,** *so that* (see section B), some other conjunctions of these types are:

a fin de que	in order that	**para que**	in order that
a menos que	unless	**siempre que**	provided that
con tal (de) que	provided that	**sin que**	without

> **¿Por qué no me llamaste para que te ayudara?** Why didn't you call me in order that I might help you?
>
> **Prometo acompañarte con tal que consiga el dinero.** I promise to go with you provided that I get (obtain) the money.
>
> **Los niños salieron sin que los oyera su mamá.** The children went out without their mother's hearing them.

Ejercicios   **A.** Para leer en español, supliendo la forma correcta del verbo entre paréntesis:

1. Siempre empieza la clase en cuanto (entrar) el profesor.
2. Eran las diez de la noche cuando Roberto (regresar) a su cuarto.
3. Vamos a enseñarles la cámara en cuanto (llegar) ellos.
4. La compré aunque me (costar) demasiado.
5. Aunque (llover) esta noche, tendremos que ir al teatro.
6. Dijeron que se marcharían mañana aunque (hacer) mal tiempo.
7. Quédense Uds. en casa hasta que (volver) yo del mercado.
8. No llegarán a tiempo a menos que (darse) prisa.
9. Hable Ud. de modo que le (oír) bien todos los estudiantes.
10. Traeré el proyector para que Ud. lo (ver).
11. Mi papá me lo compró para que yo (poder) mirar las películas.
12. Tráigame Ud. café con tal que (estar) caliente.
13. Habíamos comido antes de que ellos (haber) vuelto a casa.
14. Juan no podrá ir con Uds. sin que yo le (dar) el dinero.
15. No ganará mucho mientras que (trabajar) en esta tienda.

B. Repitan cada pregunta; luego, contéstenla afirmativamente, agregando (*adding*) una cláusula introducida por la frase **aunque Pablo,** según el modelo.

MODELO: ¿Hará Ud. el viaje?   ¿Hará Ud. el viaje? Sí, aunque
                                      Pablo lo haga.

1. ¿Escogerá Ud. una cámara?   4. ¿Mirará Ud. las
2. ¿Buscará Ud. una pantalla?   transparencias?
3. ¿Sacará Ud. muchas   5. ¿Irá Ud. de compras hoy?
   fotografías?   6. ¿Seguirá Ud. trabajando allí?

C. Para expresar en español:

1. When I take a trip, I take many photographs.   2. As soon as I have
time, I shall buy two or three rolls of film.   3. Mary's aunt will stay
with Jane while her parents are (may be) in Mexico.   4. It will be
better to use the movie camera when there are (may be) popular dances.
5. Before you (*fam. sing.*) leave, I want you to put a roll of film in the
camera in order to try it.   6. I waited for Helen in order that she might
help me to select a dress.   7. Robert said he would come to my room
provided that I should show him some slides.   8. Richard promised to
accompany us unless he should have to work in his father's store.

V. El subjuntivo en frases condicionales

In earlier lessons we have used simple conditions in which the present
indicative is used in the English *if*-clause and the same tense in the
Spanish **si**-clause (see Lección seis, page 138):

> **Si Juan está en su cuarto,**   **está estudiando.**
>   If John is in his room,   he is studying.
> **Si ellos tienen dinero,**   **harán el viaje.**
>   If they have (the) money,   they will take the trip.

Simple conditions are also expressed in past time:

> **Si Ana recibió (ha recibido) el cheque,**   **compró el vestido.**
>   If Ann received (has received) the check,   she bought the dress.

In a **si**-clause which implies that a statement is contrary to fact (*i.e.*, not
true) in the present, Spanish uses either form of the imperfect subjunctive. A contrary-to-fact sentence may also be expressed in the past, in
which case the pluperfect subjunctive is used in the **si**-clause (see the
second example which follows).

The conclusion or main clause of a conditional sentence is usually expressed by the conditional (or conditional perfect), as in English. (In reading you will also find the -ra form of the imperfect or pluperfect subjunctive in the main, or result, clause; in the exercises of this text only the conditional or conditional perfect will be used.)

Si yo tuviera (tuviese) dinero,	**haría el viaje.**
If I had (the) money (*but I don't*),	I would take the trip.
Si Pablo hubiese (hubiera) venido,	**me habría llamado.**
If Paul had come (*but he didn't*),	he would have called me.

Como si, *as if,* also expresses a contrary-to-fact condition, in which case the conclusion, or main clause, is understood:

always takes imperfect or pluperfect subj.

    ¡Gastas el dinero como si fueras millonario!   You spend money as if you were a millionaire!

Similarly, either form of the imperfect subjunctive is used in the **si**-clause to express a condition that may (might) not be fulfilled in the future. Whenever the English sentence has *should* or *were to* in the *if*-clause, the imperfect subjunctive is used in Spanish:

Si fuésemos (fuéramos) juntos,	**nos divertiríamos mucho.**
If we should (were to) go together,	we would have a very good time.
Si vinieran (viniesen) mañana,	**harían el trabajo.**
If they should (were to) come tomorrow,	they would do the work.

NOTE: The future and conditional indicative and the present subjunctive tenses are not used after **si** meaning *if.* When **si** means *whether,* the indicative must be used: **No sé si podrán venir,** *I do not know whether they will be able to come.*

Ejercicios   **A.** Repitan cada frase; luego, al oír otra cláusula con **si,** completen la frase:

1. Si Carlos tiene dinero, comprará un traje.
   Si Carlos tuviera dinero,
   Si Carlos hubiera tenido dinero,

2. Si ella ve a Marta, le dará la cámara.
   Si ella viese a Marta,
   Si ella hubiese visto a Marta,
3. Si vamos juntos, nos divertiremos.
   Si fuéramos juntos,
   Si hubiéramos ido juntos,

B. Repitan la frase; luego, cambien la forma de los verbos, según el modelo.

MODELO: Si tienen tiempo, irán   Si tienen tiempo, irán al cine.
          al cine.   Si tuvieran tiempo, irían al cine.

1. Si José vuelve a casa, nos llamará.
2. Si María está en su cuarto, escribirá la composición.
3. Si vamos a México, sacaremos muchas fotografías.
4. Si no es tarde, charlaré con Ud. un rato.

MODELO: Si la compras, podrás   Si la compras, podrás usarla.
          usarla.   Si la comprases, podrías usarla.

5. Si metes un rollo de película, podrás probar la cámara.
6. Si lo llevas mañana, lo revelarán pronto.
7. Si traen el proyector, veremos las transparencias.
8. Si sigo trabajando, reuniré bastante dinero para el viaje.

MODELO: Si han venido, le   Si han venido, le habrán visto.
          habrán visto.   Si hubieran venido, le habrían visto.

9. Si ella ha ido de compras, habrá comprado muchas cosas.
10. Si han encontrado algo, se lo habrán enviado a su mamá.

A. Repitan cada frase; luego, al oír una nueva conjunción, substitúyanla **Resumen**
en la frase:

1. *En cuanto* yo tenga tiempo, voy a escoger un proyector. (*Cuando*)
2. *Después que* llegue Miguel, nos marcharemos. (*Antes de que*)
3. No podré acompañarte *a menos que* él me preste el dinero. (*sin que*)
4. Todos se reunirán aquí *con tal que* vengan los otros. (*después que*)
5. Yo traje la cámara *para que* Ud. la viera. (*de modo que*)

6. Decidieron ir al campo *aunque* lloviese. (*a menos que*)
7. Ellos querían quedarse aquí *hasta que* llegase el médico. (*aunque*)
8. Se lo di a Luisa *de manera que* pudiera comprar un regalo. (*para que*)

B. Lean en español; luego, repitan cada frase, comenzando con las palabras entre paréntesis y cambiando el verbo de la cláusula subordinada a la forma del imperfecto de subjuntivo que termina en **-ra**:

1. Queremos que ellos *vayan* de compras con nosotros. (Queríamos)
2. Yo no creo que Felipe *haya* podido hacer el viaje. (Yo no creía)
3. Pídale Ud. al señor Díaz que *traiga* su proyector. (Jorge le pidió)
4. No será posible que *vuelvan* antes del mes de mayo. (No sería)
5. No vemos a nadie que *tenga* cámara de cine. (No vimos)
6. ¿Hay alguien que *conozca* a aquel señor? (¿Había alguien . . . ?)
7. Ella dice que saldrá en cuanto *vuelvan* los niños. (Ella dijo que saldría)
8. Yo le llamaré para que te *ayude* a escoger una maleta. (Yo le llamé)
9. Creen que él irá a verlos aunque *sea* tarde. (Creían que él iría)
10. Ana quiere esperar hasta que *lleguen* sus amigas. (Ana quería esperar)

C. Usos del subjuntivo en frases condicionales. Para expresar en español:

1. If Robert has the money, he will buy a camera.   2. If Robert were to go to Mexico, he would take many photographs.   3. If he had had time, he would have tried out the camera.   4. If Charles arrives before six o'clock, we shall eat supper downtown.   5. If he should come earlier, we would look at some slides.   6. If I had seen a good projector, I would have bought it.   7. Raymond talks as if he had a cold.   8. I know that if he stayed at home, he was ill.

D. Repaso de algunas expresiones usadas en las Lecciones siete, ocho y nueve. Para expresar en español:

1. You are welcome.
2. I should say so!
3. He thanked me for the gift.
4. What's the matter with him?
5. Pick us up (*fam. sing.*) at five, please.
6. Jane doesn't feel well.
7. She is absent today.

8. Martha only has a cold.
9. It is nothing serious.
10. I believe so.
11. At any rate.

12. He left at about four
    o'clock.
13. How do you like the idea?
14. I think it is wonderful!

Resumen de palabras y expresiones

a eso de   at about (*time*)
el ahorro   economy; *pl.* savings
aumentar   to increase, augment
bajar   to decline
la cámara (de cine)   (movie) camera
**la cámara de treinta y cinco milí-
    metros**   35-millimeter camera
gastar   to spend (*money*), waste,
    use (up)
juntos, -as   together
la marca   brand, make, kind
meter   to put (in)

el milímetro   millimeter
el millonario   millionaire
las Navidades   Christmastime
la pantalla   screen
pasa (tú)   come in
probar (ue)   to try out, test
el proyector   projector
reunir (ú)   to collect, get (together)
revelar   to reveal, develop (*film*)
el rollo   roll (*of film*)
la transparencia   slide, transparency
ya no   no longer

LECTURA IX

Una conversación sobre el turismo en México

(Luisa y Ramón se casaron durante su tercer año en la universidad. Luisa consiguió participar en un concurso de televisión y gracias a sus conocimientos de historia y de geografía ha ganado un premio fantástico: un viaje de quince días[1] a México para ella y su esposo. Los dos están conversando con un profesor mexicano sobre el turismo en México.)

Profesor. México está admirablemente organizado para ofrecer a los visitantes las máximas comodidades. ¿Qué partes del país figuran en su itinerario?

Ramón. Volaremos directamente a la ciudad de México, donde nos quedaremos cinco días. Desde allí iremos a Yucatán. Y de regreso a[2] los Estados Unidos pararemos un par de días en Acapulco y en Puerto Vallarta.

Luisa. En la ciudad de México pondrán un coche a nuestra disposición.

Profesor. Lo van a necesitar. Desde la capital se extiende una red de carreteras en excelentes condiciones en todas las direcciones. Pero además existen miles de kilómetros de líneas férreas y el servicio de autobuses es excelente.

Luisa. Tenemos muchos deseos de[3] visitar el Parque de Chapultepec y el Museo Nacional de Antropología.

Profesor. En el Museo podrán repasar toda la historia de México. Se considera como uno de los museos más ricos y mejor organizados del mundo.
Y como tendrán coche, hay muchas excursiones que podrán hacer: a Cuernavaca, a las pirámides, a Taxco y a otros lugares bellos de los alrededores, como el balneario de San José de Purúa.

Ramón. Debiéramos pasar los quince días en la ciudad de México, ¿verdad? ¿No podría ser el centro de todas nuestras actividades turísticas?

Profesor. Es cierto que la capital es una amalgama de todo lo mexicano: desde el México de los huaraches y el sarape hasta el más lujoso y refinado. Pero el país tiene también otras facetas que interesan al turista. Trataré de abrirles el apetito[4] para que piensen en volver varias veces. Comencemos por la zona más cercana a nosotros. ¿Han visitado Uds. la Baja California?

Ramón. Hemos estado en Tijuana y en Ensenada.

---

[1] **quince días,** *fifteen days, two weeks.*   [2] **de regreso a,** *returning to.*   [3] **Tenemos muchos deseos de,** *We are very eager to.*   [4] **abrirles el apetito,** *to whet your appetite.*

Profesor. Hasta hace poco la Baja California era una de las zonas más pobres y aisladas del país. Pues, se ha inaugurado recientemente una nueva carretera, de más de mil millas, que une Tijuana con La Paz y Cabo San Lucas. La creciente afluencia de turistas—sobre todo de deportistas

House of the
Governors,
Uxmal, Mexico

aficionados a la pesca—ha favorecido la construcción de hoteles cómodos a lo largo de[1] la carretera. La gran atracción es la pesca de peces marinos como la aguja de mar[2] y una especie de pez espada volante.[3]

Ramón. Desgraciadamente[4] tendremos que reservar eso para otra ocasión. Pero dos playas de la costa occidental de México figuran en nuestro itinerario.

Luisa. Sí, Acapulco y Puerto Vallarta.

Profesor. Acapulco es el balneario más moderno y elegante de México. Es famoso por sus hermosas playas, hoteles lujosos y clubes sociales y deportivos, que sirven de marco[5] para las más brillantes y alegres reuniones. Las atracciones de las playas y clubes, los deportes náuticos y los paseos por los alrededores hacen de Acapulco un lugar de descanso y entretenimiento de excepcional categoría.

Luisa. Pasaremos dos días también en Puerto Vallarta.

Profesor. A pesar de sus hoteles elegantes y la belleza de los barrios residenciales, Puerto Vallarta es todavía un pueblo de pescadores, rodeado de selvas.[6] Yo, personalmente, prefiero Mazatlán, donde las playas, los excelentes hoteles y restaurantes y los deportes de todas clases mantienen despierto el interés del visitante. Y no hay que olvidar el pequeño puerto de Manzanillo, entre Acapulco y Puerto Vallarta, donde se ha construido recientemente un hotel de lujo, Las Hadas, que se considera como una de las maravillas del hemisferio.

Ramón. El viaje a Yucatán también será muy interesante.

Profesor. La península de Yucatán es un mundo completamente diferente. Durante siglos la región yacía casi olvidada del mundo. Pero todo va cambiando ahora. Hay hoteles cómodos en Mérida y van convirtiéndose en centros turísticos lugares tan poco conocidos como las islas de Cozumel e Isla Mujeres. Las ruinas mayas de Uxmal, Chichén Itzá y Tulún se cuentan entre los monumentos más notables del mapa turístico de México.

Luisa. Es claro que nos espera un viaje inolvidable.

Profesor. Volverán encantados con México. ¡Buen viaje[7] y que se diviertan muchísimo!

Ejercicio

Escriban un breve resumen, de unas ciento cincuenta palabras, de «Una conversación sobre el turismo en México.»

---

[1] **a lo largo de,** *along.*   [2] **aguja de mar,** *sailfish.*   [3] **pez espada volante,** *marlin.*
[4] **Desgraciadamente,** *Unfortunately.*   [5] **sirven de marco,** *serve as a setting.*   [6] **rodeado de selvas,** *surrounded by forests.*   [7] **¡Buen viaje . . . !** *(Have) a good trip . . . !*

LECCIÓN DIEZ

Repaso de los adjetivos y pronombres demostrativos.   Los adjetivos
posesivos.   Los pronombres posesivos.   Otros usos del subjuntivo.
Usos de los adjetivos como substantivos.   Los diminutivos

Comprando un radio[1]

(*Ricardo y Tomás entran en una tienda donde venden aparatos de radio. Se acerca un dependiente.*)

Dependiente.	Buenos días, señores. ¿En qué puedo servirles?
Ricardo.	Busco un radio de onda corta. ¿Quiere enseñarme algunos modelos de este año, por favor?
Dependiente.	¿Le interesa a usted un aparato con tocadiscos o uno de radio solo?
Ricardo.	No me interesa el tocadiscos; nuestro televisor tiene uno.
Dependiente.	Pues aquí hay dos de la misma marca. Éste tiene doce tubos, y ése, ocho. ¿Quiere usted que yo ponga éste o ése?
Ricardo.	Ponga usted el pequeñito, por favor.
Dependiente.	A ver si puedo sintonizar una emisora mexicana. A esta hora es difícil a causa de la estática...
Tomás.	No se oye bien...
Dependiente.	Un momentito... Trataré de sintonizar una emisora de Nueva York. ¡Ah, sí! ¿Qué les parece?
Tomás.	(*Dirigiéndose a Ricardo.*) El tono es maravilloso. Me recuerda el mío.
Ricardo.	(*Al dependiente.*) Pues, antes de decidirme, quisiera escuchar el otro. (*El dependiente lo pone y lo escuchan unos momentos.*)
Tomás.	No me gusta tanto como el de ocho tubos.
Dependiente.	Ni a mí tampoco.[2] Como ustedes pueden ver, tenemos modelos de otras marcas. Ése tiene frecuencia modulada. Voy a ponerlo...
Tomás.	(*A Ricardo.*) Los de esa marca son excelentes. Un amigo mío tiene uno y está encantado con él.
Ricardo.	(*Al dependiente.*) Este último me parece el mejor. ¿Cuánto cuesta?
Dependiente.	Ochenta dólares. Y a ese precio es una ganga.
Ricardo.	¡Dios mío! Tal vez usted tenga razón; pero antes de comprarlo quisiera consultarlo con mi padre.
Dependiente.	Como usted quiera,[3] pero no debiera esperar mucho. Es un modelo muy popular.

[1] For *radio* (*set*), **el radio** is used; for *radio* as a means of communication, **la radio** is used.
[2] **Ni a mí tampoco,** *Neither do I.* Remember that the prepositional form must be used when the verb (**gustar** here) is understood.   [3] Note the use of the subjunctive here after the conjunction **como,** *as,* expressing indefiniteness.

A. Para contestar en español en oraciones completas:

Preguntas sobre el diálogo

1. ¿Qué les pregunta el dependiente a Ricardo y a Tomás?   2. ¿Qué contesta Ricardo?   3. ¿Le interesa a Ricardo un aparato con tocadiscos? 4. ¿Cuál de los dos radios escuchan primero?   5. ¿Por qué no se oye bien la emisora mexicana?   6. ¿Qué dice Tomás del tono del aparato? 7. ¿Qué aparato pone por fin el dependiente?   8. ¿Por qué no lo compra Ricardo?

Aplicación del diálogo

1. ¿Cuántos aparatos de radio tiene Ud.?   2. ¿Tiene Ud. un radio de onda corta?   3. ¿Tiene frecuencia modulada?   4. ¿Qué programas extranjeros ha escuchado Ud.?   5. ¿Tiene Ud. televisor en su cuarto? 6. ¿Qué programas de televisión le gustan a Ud.?   7. ¿Tiene Ud. tocadiscos?   8. ¿Se oyen emisoras mexicanas desde esta parte del país?

B. Preparen un diálogo original, de unas diez líneas, para recitar en clase, empleando las frases y preguntas siguientes como elemento inicial:

1. **María.**   Mi radio no funciona. ¿Crees que podrán arreglármelo?
   Carlos.   No creo que valga la pena, María. Hay tantos modelos superiores a ése en las tiendas.

2. **Ricardo.**   ¿Te molestará si pongo el radio? Quiero escuchar la emisora de la universidad.
   Enrique.   ¡Al contrario! El decano va a anunciar sus recomendaciones respecto del nuevo plan de estudios, ¿verdad?

Notas gramaticales

I. Repaso de los adjetivos y pronombres demostrativos

A. A demonstrative adjective agrees in gender and number with the noun it modifies and, in Spanish, is repeated before nouns in a series. **Este** points out persons or things near the speaker; **ese,** persons or things near to, or associated with, the person addressed; **aquel,** persons or things distant from the speaker or person addressed, or unrelated to either. (Do not confuse the demonstrative, which points out the noun to which it refers, with the relative pronoun **que,** *that.*)

Singular

Masculine	Feminine	
este	esta	this
ese	esa	that (*nearby*)
aquel	aquella	that (*distant*)

Plural

Masculine	Feminine	
estos	estas	these
esos	esas	those (*nearby*)
aquellos	aquellas	those (*distant*)

este hombre y esta mujer   this man and woman
esos aparatos cerca de Ud.   those sets near you
aquella joven allí   that young lady there (*distant*)

B. The demonstrative pronouns are formed by placing an accent on the stressed syllable of the adjectives: **éste, ése, aquél,** etc. The use of the pronouns corresponds to that of the adjectives, except that singular forms often mean *this (one), that (one).* They may be used as subject or object of the verb, or they may stand alone.

There are three neuter pronouns (**esto,** *this,* **eso,** *that,* **aquello,** *that*) which are used when the antecedent is a statement, a general idea, or something which has not been identified. Since there are no neuter adjectives, an accent is not required on these three forms:

Me gustan ese radio y éste.   I like that radio (set) and this one.
¿Quiere Ud. que yo ponga éste o ése?   Do you want me to turn on this one or that one?
Este modelo y aquéllos son nuevos.   This model and those (*yonder*) are new.
¿Cuál de las marcas prefieres? ¿Ésta?   Which one of the brands do you prefer? This one?
¿Qué es esto?   What is this?
Eso no es muy interesante.   That isn't very interesting.

C. The demonstrative pronoun **éste** is used to indicate *the latter* (that is, the nearer), and **aquél**, *the former.* Contrary to English usage, in Spanish, when both are used, *the latter* always comes first:

Ana y Marta no vienen porque ésta no se siente bien.   Ann and Martha aren't coming because the latter doesn't feel well.
Ricardo y su hermana van de compras; ésta busca un radio y aquél, un tocadiscos.   Richard and his sister go shopping; the former is looking for a record player and the latter, a radio.

D. We found in Lección ocho that the Spanish definite article replaces the demonstrative before **que.** Similarly, it replaces the demonstrative before **de. El (la, los, las) de** means *that (those) of, the one(s) of (with, in)*; sometimes in English this construction is expressed by a possessive (first two examples):

mi abrigo y el de Felipe   my topcoat and Philip's (that of Philip)
estas blusas y las de Ana   these blouses and Ann's (those of Ann)
las del pelo rubio   the ones (girls) with (the) blond hair
la del sombrero rojo   the one with (in) the red hat

The neuter article **lo** followed by **de** means *that (matter, affair) of:*

Lo de su amigo me interesa.   That (affair) of your friend interests me.

Ejercicios   **A.** Para contestar afirmativamente, empleando el pronombre demostrativo correspondiente.

MODELOS: ¿Quiere Ud. este traje?   Sí, quiero ése.
          ¿Es buena esta marca?   Sí, ésa es buena.

1. ¿Le gusta a Ud. este radio?
2. ¿Le interesan a Ud. estos aparatos?
3. ¿Tiene buen tono esa marca?
4. ¿Escuchas aquellas canciones?

5. ¿Son caras esas cámaras?
6. ¿Son mexicanos esos discos?
7. ¿Prefieres aquel radio de onda corta?
8. ¿Sintoniza Ud. aquella emisora?

B. Para expresar en español:

1. This building and that one (*distant*) are new.   2. Those radios and these have a marvelous tone.   3. I prefer this very small one (*m.*) to that one (*nearby*).   4. Shall I turn on this television set or that one (*distant*)?   5. Here are two brands; this one has ten tubes, and that one, eight.   6. The clerk says it is a bargain, but I do not believe that. 7. John and Mary entered the store; the latter was looking for a record player.   8. Jane's dress and Helen's are very pretty.   9. Who is that boy, the one with red hair?   10. That girl (*distant*) and the one in the green hat are cousins of Paul.

II. Los adjetivos posesivos

Possessive adjectives agree in gender and number with the thing possessed (that is, with the noun modified), not with the possessor, as in English. The short, or unstressed, forms precede the nouns, and they are repeated before nouns in a series in Spanish:

Singular	Plural	
mi	mis	my
tu	tus	your (*fam.*)
su	sus	his, her, its, your (*formal*)
nuestro, -a	nuestros, -as	our
vuestro, -a	vuestros, -as	your (*fam.*)
su	sus	their, your

The long, or stressed, forms follow the noun. They are used for clearness and emphasis, in direct address, to translate *of mine, of his,* etc., after the verb ser, and in a few set phrases. These forms are:

mío, mía	míos, mías	my, of mine
tuyo, tuya	tuyos, tuyas	your (*fam.*), of yours
suyo, suya	suyos, suyas	his, her, your (*formal*), its, of his, of hers, of yours, of its
nuestro, nuestra	nuestros, nuestras	our, of ours
vuestro, vuestra	vuestros, vuestras	your (*fam. pl.*), of yours
suyo, suya	suyos, suyas	their, your (*pl.*), of theirs, of yours

¿Traes tus libros?   Are you bringing your books?
Carlos, ¿son suyas estas cosas?   Charles, are these things yours?
Ana tiene dos libros míos.   Ann has two books of mine.
Bárbara y una amiga suya vienen.   Barbara and a friend of hers are
  coming.
Ellos son buenos amigos míos (nuestros).   They are good friends of
  mine (ours).
Querida (amiga) mía: My dear (friend):
¡Dios mío!   Heavens!

Since **su(s)** and **suyo** (**-a, -os, -as**) have several meanings, the forms **de
él, de ella,** etc., may be substituted to make the meaning clear. (The
prepositional form is not used for any long possessive other than **suyo,
-a, -os, -as.**)

Me gusta su casa.   I like his (her, your, their) house.
Me gusta la casa de él (de ella, de usted).   I like his (her, your) house.
¿Es de ellos este coche? —No, es de él.   Is this car theirs? —No, it
  is his.

Ejercicios   A. Repitan cada frase; luego, repítanla otra vez empleando una frase con
una forma de **suyo,** según el modelo.

MODELO: Carlos y una amiga *de él*   Carlos y una amiga de él
                                             Carlos y una amiga suya

1. este traje *de él*   5. aquel tocadiscos *de ellos*
2. ese radio *de ella*   6. esta cámara *de él*
3. aquellas transparencias *de ellos*   7. esas películas *de ustedes*
4. esos discos *de usted*   8. varias fotografías *de ella*

B. Para contestar afirmativamente, según los modelos.

MODELOS: ¿Es nuestra esta cámara?   Sí, es nuestra (*or* es suya).
         ¿Son míos esos libros?   Sí, son suyos.
         ¿Son suyas esas compras?   Sí, son mías.

1. ¿Es nuestro aquel disco?   3. ¿Son suyas estas trans-
2. ¿Son míos estos   parencias?
   lápices?   4. ¿Es suyo este radio?

5. ¿Es nuestra aquella guitarra? 7. ¿Es tuyo ese televisor?
6. ¿Son nuestros aquellos dibujos? 8. ¿Son mías esas revistas?

III. Los pronombres posesivos

The possessive pronouns are formed by using the definite article with the long forms of the possessive adjectives. Remember that after **ser** the article is usually omitted:

el mío; la mía; los míos; las mías	mine
el tuyo; la tuya; los tuyos; las tuyas	yours (*fam.*)
el suyo; la suya; los suyos; las suyas	his, hers, its, yours (*formal*)
el nuestro; la nuestra; los nuestros; las nuestras	ours
el vuestro; la vuestra; los vuestros; las vuestras	yours (*fam.*)
el suyo; la suya; los suyos; las suyas	theirs, yours

 mi radio; el mío, el nuestro my radio; mine, ours
 nuestra casa; la mía, la nuestra our house; mine, ours
 Ana, yo tengo los libros míos y los tuyos. Ann, I have <u>my</u> books and
  yours.
 Señor López, ¿tiene usted los suyos? Mr. López, do you have
  yours?
 Juan tiene la pluma suya y las mías. John has <u>his</u> pen and mine.

Since **el suyo (la suya, los suyos, las suyas)** may mean *his, hers, its, yours* (formal), *theirs*, these pronouns may be clarified by using **el de él, el de ella,** etc. The article agrees with the thing possessed:

 Carlos mira el suyo. Charles looks at his (hers, yours, theirs).
 El coche de ellos y el de ustedes están aquí. Their car and yours
  are here.
 Nuestros padres y los de ella vienen. Our parents and hers are
  coming.

Ejercicios

A. Repitan cada frase; luego, repítanla otra vez, substituyendo el substantivo con el pronombre posesivo, o con la frase **el (la) de él (de ella,** etcétera).

MODELOS: Lleva *su equipaje.*   Lleva su equipaje. Lleva el suyo.
         Tengo la *maleta de*   Tengo la maleta de Juan. Tengo la
         Juan.   de él.

1. La hermana de Ana   5. El *jardín de mi mamá* es bonito.
   tiene *su blusa.*   6. Las *flores de Inés* son hermosas.
2. Pablo y yo vamos a   7. ¿Quieres ver *nuestras*
   nuestra casa.   *películas*?
3. ¿Tiene ella *su bolsa*?   8. Juan, no conduzcas *tu coche*
4. Pablo lleva *mis cámaras.*   hoy.

B. Para contestar afirmativamente, según los modelos.

MODELOS: ¿Tienes tu cámara?   Sí, tengo la mía.
         ¿Quieren ellos sus fotos?   Sí, quieren las suyas.

1. ¿Ve Ud. su coche?   5. ¿Mira Ana su televisor?
2. ¿Escuchan Uds. su tocadiscos? 6. ¿Tiene Carlos sus compras?
3. ¿Traen Uds. sus composiciones? 7. ¿Desean ellas sus regalos?
4. ¿Buscas tus guantes?   8. ¿Lleva él su maleta?

C. Para expresar en español:

1. I want you (*formal*) to bring your camera and mine.   2. Tell (*formal*)
them to take their skates and yours.   3. John doubts that his sister and
mine will go to the movie.   4. Wait (*formal*) a moment in order that I
may give you her composition and his.   5. Let (*formal*) me bring my
skis and hers tomorrow morning.   6. Whose records are these? —Do
you (*fam. sing.*) have mine?

IV. Otros usos del subjuntivo

Uses of the subjunctive as the main verb in a sentence, other than in
formal commands and in negative familiar commands (see Repaso
primero, pages 8–9, 11), are:

A. After **tal vez** and **quizá**(s), and less commonly **acaso**, all meaning
perhaps, when doubt or uncertainty is implied:

Quizás él ha llegado.   Perhaps he has arrived. (*Certainty implied*)

Tal vez tenga Ud. razón.   Perhaps you may be right. (*Uncertainty implied*)

B. To make a statement or question milder or more polite (sometimes called a softened statement or question), the **-ra** imperfect subjunctive forms of **deber, querer,** and sometimes **poder,** are used:

Debo ayudar a mi mamá.   I must (ought to) help my mother. (*Strong obligation*)

Yo debiera llamarla.   I should call her. (*Milder obligation*)

Quiero ir al cine.   I want to go to the movie. (*Strong wish*)

Yo quisiera ir contigo.   I should like to go with you. (*More polite*)

¿Pudieras esperar un momento?   Could you wait a moment? (*Polite question*)

NOTE: Remember that the conditional of **gustar** also means *should (would) like* and may be used instead of **quisiera,** etc.: **Nos (Me) gustaría verlos,** *We (I) should like to see them.*

C. After **¡Ojalá!,** with or without **que,** *Would that! I wish that!* the present subjunctive is used in an exclamatory wish which refers to something which may happen in the future. The imperfect subjunctive is used to express a wish concerning something that is contrary to fact in the present, and the pluperfect subjunctive to express a wish concerning something that was contrary to fact in the past:

¡Ojalá (que) ella me llame!   Would that she call me!

¡Ojalá que supiesen eso!   Would that they knew that!

¡Ojalá hubieran vuelto antes!   (How) I wish they had returned before!

When used alone, **¡Ojalá!** means *God grant it! I hope so!*

¿Viene Juan mañana? —¡Ojalá!   Is John coming tomorrow? —I hope so!

Ejercicios

A. Para contestar negativamente, agregando una frase introducida por **pero quisiera,** y substituyendo el objeto del verbo con el pronombre correspondiente.

MODELO: ¿Has visto el radio   No, pero quisiera verlo.
         de él?

1. ¿Has llamado a tu hermana?   3. ¿Has oído mis discos?
2. ¿Has comprado el televisor?   4. ¿Has sintonizado aquella emisora?

B. Para cambiar al imperfecto de subjuntivo, según los modelos.

MODELOS: Quiero probar la cámara.   Quisiera probar la cámara.
         Quiero que tú saques   Quisiera que tú sacaras
           la foto.   la foto.
         Debo llamar a mi mamá.   Debiera llamar a mi mamá.

1. Quiero enseñarle este modelo   5. Queremos que Uds. oigan
   ahora.   aquél.
2. Queremos escuchar el otro.   6. Debo consultar eso con mi
3. Quieren comprar el más   padre.
   grande.   7. Debemos ayudar a Carlos.
4. ¿Quieres que yo ponga ése?   8. No deben esperar mucho.

C. Para contestar con una oración introducida por **tal vez** (**quizás**).

MODELO: ¿Volverán ellos esta   Tal vez (Quizás) vuelvan esta
         noche?   noche.

1. ¿Vendrá ella mañana?   3. ¿Les interesará el tocadiscos?
2. ¿Encontrarán una ganga allí?   4. ¿Escogerán otra marca?

D. Para cambiar al presente de subjuntivo después de **¡Ojalá que!**

MODELO: ¿Leerán la novela?   ¡Ojalá que lean la novela!

1. ¿Llegarán esta noche?   3. ¿Se divertirán en la fiesta?
2. ¿Podrá ella visitarnos?   4. ¿Buscará él otra casa?

Para cambiar al imperfecto y al pluscuamperfecto de subjuntivo después
de **¡Ojalá que!**, siguiendo los modelos.

MODELOS: No creen lo que él   ¡Ojalá que creyeran lo que él
         dijo.   dijo!
         No han llegado a   ¡Ojalá que hubieran llegado a
         tiempo.   tiempo!

5. No están en casa.   8. No van a Nueva York.
6. Ella no sabe la canción.   9. No han vuelto del viaje.
7. No pueden pasar por aquí.   10. Él no ha visto la exposición.

V. Usos de los adjetivos como substantivos

Many adjectives may be used with the definite article, demonstratives, numerals, and other limiting adjectives to form nouns. In this case the adjective agrees in gender and number with the noun understood. Remember that adjectives of nationality are also used as nouns: **Luis es mexicano,** *Louis is (a) Mexican.*

Este último me parece el mejor.   This last one seems to me (to be) the best (one).
No me gusta tanto como el otro.   I don't like it so much as the other one.
Ponga Ud. el más pequeño.   Turn on the smaller one.
Una joven compró las blancas.   A young lady bought the white ones (*f.*).

Repitan cada frase; luego, repítanla otra vez, empleando el adjetivo como substantivo.   *Ejercicio*

MODELO: ¿Te gusta la blusa roja?   ¿Te gusta la blusa roja?
                                       ¿Te gusta la roja?

1. La casa amarilla es del señor Díaz.   2. Me gusta este televisor grande.   3. Quieren buscar una casa más grande.   4. Prefiero ver unos zapatos negros.   5. Esta última blusa es muy bonita.   6. ¿Puede Ud. sintonizar una emisora mexicana?   7. ¿Cuánto cuesta la otra marca? 8. Miramos varios aparatos nuevos.   9. Yo quisiera escuchar algunos discos españoles.   10. ¿Qué les parece a Uds. este radio pequeñito?

VI. Los diminutivos

In Spanish, diminutive endings are often used to express not only small size but also affection, pity, scorn, ridicule, and the like. The most common endings are: -ito, -a; -illo, -a; -(e)cito, -a; -(e)cillo, -a. Frequently, the use of these suffixes with nouns precludes the need for adjectives. For the choice of ending rely upon observation. A final vowel is often dropped before adding the ending:

hermana	sister	**hermanita**	little sister
hermano	brother	**hermanito**	little brother
Juan	John	**Juanito**	Johnny
pueblo	town	**pueblecito**	small town, village
señora	lady, woman	**señorita**	young lady (woman)
ventana	window	**ventanilla**	ticket window

Applied to baptismal names these endings indicate affection, with no implication of size: **Juanita,** *Jane*; **Anita,**[1] *Annie*; **Tomasito,** *Tommy*. Sometimes a change in spelling is necessary to preserve the sound of a consonant when a final vowel is dropped: **Diego,** *James*, and **Dieguito,** *Jimmie*. Similarly, note the change in spelling in the adverb **poco,** *little* (quantity), and **poquito,** *very little*; also, in the noun **taza,** *cup*, and **tacita,** *small (tiny) cup*.

Ejercicio   Give the base word to which each diminutive suffix has been added:

casita	small house, cottage	**mesita**	small table, stand
cosilla	small thing, trifle	**momentito**	(short) moment
florecita	small (tiny) flower	**mujercita**	pleasant little woman
golpecito	slight blow, tap	**pequeñito, -a**	very small, tiny
hijito	(dear) son	**piedrecita**	small stone, pebble
hombrecito	nice little man	**pobrecito**	poor boy (man, thing)
jovencito	nice young fellow	**regalito**	small gift

Resumen   A. Repitan la frase; luego, repítanla otra vez, siguiendo el modelo.

MODELO: mi casa y la casa de Ana   mi casa y la casa de Ana
                                       mi casa y la de Ana

---

[1] The diminutives given in the rest of this section are not listed in the end vocabulary unless they are used elsewhere in this text. Watch for similar and other uses of diminutives in reading.

1. estos jardines y el jardín de mi madre.   2. estas mujeres y la mujer del vestido amarillo.   3. este edificio y el edificio de piedra.   4. esta señorita y la señorita del pelo negro.   5. este radio y el radio de mi hermano.   6. aquellos discos y los discos de música mexicana.   7. este lugar y el lugar que visitó él.   8. estas dos marcas y la marca que nos ha enseñado Ud.   9. estos modelos y los modelos que él me mostró. 10. aquella emisora de Nueva York y las emisoras que oímos ayer.

B. Para completar, empleando el pronombre posesivo correspondiente, según los modelos.

MODELOS: Éstos son *mis lápices.*   Estos lápices son míos.
            Marta tiene *su libro.*   Luis tiene el suyo.

1. Éste es *nuestro disco.* Este disco es *el nuestro*
2. Éstos son *mis discos.* Estos discos son *los míos*
3. Ésa es *mi revista.* Esa revista es *la mía.*
4. Ésas son *sus transparencias.* Esas transparencias son *las suyas*
5. Aquélla es *nuestra guitarra.* Aquella guitarra es *la nuestra*
6. Aquél es *tu televisor.* Aquel televisor es *el tuyo*
7. Juan tiene *su dibujo.* Marta tiene *la suyo*
8. Ellos escuchan *su radio.* Ud. escucha *el suyo*
9. Nosotros llevamos *nuestras cámaras.* Ana lleva *la suya*
10. Yo vivo en *mi apartamento.* Nosotros vivimos en *el nuestro*

C. Otros usos del subjuntivo y usos de los adjetivos como substantivos. Para expresar en español:

1. I should like to buy the white blouse, not the green one.
2. You (*formal sing.*) ought to look at this red hat, not the blue one.
3. Would that she liked this one as much as the other one!
4. Perhaps he may prefer small cars to larger ones.
5. Would you (*formal sing.*) like to take her those yellow roses instead of the red ones?
6. Which of the brands do you (*formal sing.*) like, this one or the other one?

D. Usos de los adjetivos y pronombres posesivos. Para expresar en español:

1. Is he a friend of yours (*formal sing.*)? —Yes, he is a friend of mine.
2. Is this camera ours? —Yes, it is ours, not hers.　　3. This composition is not mine. Is it yours (*formal sing.*) (*two ways*)?　　4. They listen to their radio, and we listen to ours.　　5. These rolls of film are mine, and that one is yours (*fam.*).　　6. This hat is Jane's; it is not yours (*fam.*). 7. Heavens! I have put on your (*fam.*) gloves, not mine.　　8. Mary and several (girl)friends of hers are going to the meeting.

Modern steel works, San Nicolás, Argentina

Resumen de palabras y expresiones

a causa de *prep.* because of
al contrario on the contrary
al mismo tiempo at the same time
el aparato (de radio) (radio) set
arreglar to adjust, fix, regulate
consultar to consult, discuss
el decano dean
decidirse to make up one's mind
¡Dios mío! heavens! for heaven's sake!
la emisora broadcasting station
¿en qué puedo servirle(s)? what can I do for you?
es que the fact is that
esperar mucho to wait long (a long time)
en vez de *prep.* instead of, in place of
la estática static
la frecuencia frequency
frecuencia modulada FM

funcionar to function, work, run (*said of something mechanical*)
la ganga bargain
el juego de béisbol baseball game
maravilloso, -a marvelous
pequeñito, -a very small, tiny
el pequeñito very small one (*m.*)
el plan de estudios curriculum
poner (el radio) to turn on (the radio)
el radio de onda corta short-wave radio (*set*)
la recomendación (*pl.* **recomendaciones**) recommendation
recordar (ue) to remind (one of)
sintonizar to tune in
superior a superior to
el televisor television (TV) set
el tono tone
el tubo tube
valer la pena to be worth while

LECTURA X

Hispanoamérica en el último tercio del siglo XX

Los problemas económicos y sociales que los países hispanoamericanos tendrán que resolver durante las próximas décadas son
sumamente graves. A pesar de los esfuerzos de los últimos años, la
América latina no ha logrado progresar con la rapidez deseada.

El problema más evidente es el de la debilidad económica y política
de los países hispanoamericanos frente a la gran república norteamericana. En parte se debe al fraccionamiento[1] geográfico del territorio;
pero también se debe a fuertes sentimientos nacionalistas que se han
opuesto a[2] los intentos de unificación propuestos desde la época de
Simón Bolívar, el libertador del norte de la América del Sur. Como
veremos más adelante,[3] alguna forma de integración económica será
necesaria para garantizar un futuro de paz y de bienestar para nuestros
vecinos al sur del Río Grande.

Otro problema urgente es el de la injusta distribución de la riqueza
y del poder. La disparidad entre las clases ricas y las masas es excesiva.
Las clases ricas defienden sus privilegios desesperadamente y no se
preocupan suficientemente con los sufrimientos de las clases bajas. En
muy pocos países se practica la democracia y para mantener el orden se
ha acudido a[4] los gobiernos militares.

Para que puedan desarrollarse en Hispanoamérica las ideas demo-
cráticas habrá que dedicar atención especial a la educación de las masas.
En los últimos años se han construido miles de escuelas; pero es penoso[5]
observar que el índice de analfabetismo[6] todavía pasa del[7] 50 por 100
en muchos países, sobre todo en aquellos en que la población indígena
es numerosa.

Otro problema gravísimo es el del rápido aumento de la población,
el cual, entre otras dificultades, ha creado la necesidad de aumentar

[1] **se debe al fraccionamiento,** *it is due to the fractioning (division).*   [2] **que se han
opuesto a,** *which have opposed.*   [3] **más adelante,** *later (farther) on.*   [4] **se ha acudido
a,** *they have resorted to.*   [5] **penoso,** *distressing.*   [6] **analfabetismo,** *illiteracy.*
[7] **pasar de,** *to exceed.*

Sisal drying near the factory, Yucatán, Mexico

proporcionalmente la producción alimenticia.[1] Si la población continúa creciendo al ritmo actual[2] (aproximadamente el 3 por 100 al año[3]), llegará a los seiscientos millones de habitantes en el siglo entrante. Hispanoamérica no tiene hoy día los recursos económicos para construir las viviendas y las escuelas que se necesitan. ¿Qué medios podrán encontrarse para elevar el nivel de vida[4] en el siglo XXI?

En general, se ha considerado la industrialización como el medio más eficaz para elevar el nivel de vida en las regiones subdesarrolladas.

[1] **alimenticia,** (*of*) *food.*   [2] **al ritmo actual,** *at the present rate.*   [3] **al año,** *yearly.*
[4] **nivel de vida,** *standard of living.*

En la América hispana, sin embargo, los obstáculos que encuentra la
industrialización son muy graves. Uno de los más importantes es la falta
de recursos económicos. En la economía de los países hispanoamericanos el comercio exterior[1] ha sido una de las principales fuentes de
ingresos,[2] por el estímulo que constituye para las actividades indus-
triales y comerciales. Pues, a pesar de los esfuerzos de los últimos
años, el comercio exterior no sigue aumentando con suficiente rapidez.
Desgraciadamente la exportación de productos básicos—como el café
o los minerales—no varía mucho de un año a otro. Además, en la nueva
edad industrial y tecnológica en que vivimos, la exportación de productos básicos no tiene la importancia que tiene la de artículos manufacturados. Los países industrializados, por consiguiente,[3] comercian
con países del mismo tipo, en perjuicio de[4] los países subdesarrollados.
Es evidente que Hispanoamérica no puede continuar en el papel[5] de
productora de materias básicas. Además de diversificar y de aumentar   Social Security
la producción agrícola, tendrá que desarrollar la capacidad de competir   Building,
en la producción de artículos manufacturados.   Guatemala City,
                                                                         Guatemala

[1] **comercio exterior,** *foreign trade.*   [2] **fuentes de ingresos,** *sources of income (revenue).*
[3] **por consiguiente,** *consequently.*   [4] **en perjuicio de,** *to the detriment (damage) of.*
[5] **papel,** *role.*

Para contrarrestar[1] la disminución de las exportaciones ha habido un esfuerzo por aumentar la demanda interior,[2] por la creación de mercados nuevos. Es claro que para efectuar una intensa activación del comercio interior habrá que comenzar con una honda[3] transformación de la sociedad, para hacer posible una distribución más equitativa de la riqueza. Las reformas sociales son urgentes no sólo por razones políticas y humanitarias, sino también por razones económicas.

Las inversiones[4] domésticas y el crédito exterior han constituido las principales fuentes de financiación del déficit comercial. El ritmo de las inversiones no ha bastado para asegurar el progreso rápido de la industrialización; será necesario, por consiguiente, aumentar el crédito exterior extendido a Hispanoamérica. Sin el capital[5] necesario no pueden importarse los bienes de equipo[6] y los otros productos indispensables para estimular la producción industrial. (Continuará.)[7]

A busy street in downtown Guatemala City, Guatemala

[1] **contrarrestar,** *to counteract, offset.*   [2] **demanda interior,** *domestic demand.*   [3] **honda,** *profound, far-reaching.*   [4] **inversiones,** *investments.*   [5] **el capital,** *capital* (money). [6] **bienes de equipo,** *capital goods.*   [7] **Continuará,** *To be continued.* (See Lectura XII, page 271.)

Traduzcan al español las frases siguientes, tratando de imitar las cons-   *Ejercicio*
trucciones y fraseología del texto:

1. In the last third of the twentieth century the Spanish-American
   countries will have to solve many economic and social problems.
2. The economic and political weakness of most of those countries is
   due in part to the geographic division of the territory.
3. It can also be explained by the strong nationalistic feelings which
   have opposed all plans of unification.
4. Other urgent problems are that of the unjust distribution of wealth
   and power and that of the rapid increase of population.
5. The rapid increase of population has created the need of increasing
   proportionately the production of food.
6. Besides stimulating industrialization and the export of manufactured products, it will be necessary to diversify and to increase
   agricultural production.
7. Although certain attention has been given to the education of the
   masses, unfortunately the rate of illiteracy still exceeds fifty
   percent in many Spanish-American countries.
8. In the economy of Spanish America, foreign trade has been one of
   the principal sources of income.
9. Despite the efforts of the last few years, foreign trade has not increased sufficiently from one year to another.
10. It is evident that domestic investments and foreign credit are
    necessary in order that the governments of those countries can
    carry out reforms in the future.

LECCIÓN ONCE

Comparación de los adjetivos y de los adverbios. Comparaciones de igualdad. «Hacer» en expresiones de tiempo. La traducción de *must*. Formas de mandato correspondientes a «vosotros, -as»

¿Qué parte del concierto te ha gustado más?

(María se encuentra con dos amigos, Luis y Antonio, durante el intermedio de un concierto en el Teatro Universitario. María y Luis han estudiado en la Universidad de Madrid y emplean formas peninsulares.)

María.	¡Luis! ¡Antonio! ¡Vosotros por aquí! Hacía tiempo que no os veía en un concierto de música sinfónica.
Luis.	No exageres, María.
Antonio.	¿No nos vimos hace dos semanas en el concierto de la Orquesta Universitaria?
María.	Con este gentío no se oye nada. ¡Hablad más alto, por favor!
Luis.	¡Acercaos un poco más! Pero, mirad. En aquel rincón hay poca gente. ¡Venid por aquí! *(María y Antonio acompañan a Luis.)*
María.	Pues, me parece que la mayor parte de los estudiantes de nuestra clase han venido al concierto.
Antonio.	Nos dijo el profesor que no debiéramos perder el segundo número, de Carlos Chávez.
María.	Es que Chávez es el representante más ilustre de la música mexicana de nuestros días.
Antonio.	*(A María.)* ¿Qué parte del concierto te ha gustado más?
María.	La composición de Chávez me ha parecido muy impresionante. Es la primera vez que oigo una obra suya.
Luis.	Es diferente de lo que yo esperaba. Los ritmos son más definidos y es más fácil percibir las melodías.
María.	¡Claro! Las fuentes de su música son más populares. Deben de relacionarse con tonadas tradicionales de México.
Luis.	Y no olvidéis que es un compositor más moderno que los otros.
Antonio.	Tal vez por eso no hayan resultado los otros números tan interesantes como el suyo.
María.	Es posible . . .
Antonio.	Pero se apagan las luces, María. A ver si la segunda parte del programa nos gusta tanto como la primera.

A. Para contestar en español en oraciones completas:

Preguntas sobre el diálogo

1. ¿Quiénes se encuentran en el intermedio de un concierto?   2. ¿Qué les dice María a sus amigos al verlos en el concierto?   3. ¿Qué les había dicho el profesor respecto del concierto?   4. ¿Qué dice María de Carlos Chávez?   5. ¿Qué dice María acerca de la composición de Chávez?   6. Según María, ¿con qué deben de relacionarse las fuentes de la música de Chávez?   7. Según Luis, ¿qué no deben olvidar sus compañeros?   8. ¿Cómo se anuncia el comienzo de la segunda parte del concierto?

Aplicación del diálogo

1. ¿Cuántos cursos de música ha tomado Ud.?   2. ¿Hay, en general, muchos o pocos estudiantes en las clases de música?   3. ¿Pone o quita Ud. el radio cuando comienza a estudiar?   4. ¿Forma Ud. parte de una comparsa musical?   5. ¿Tiene la universidad una orquesta sinfónica?   6. ¿Cuánto tiempo hace que no va Ud. a un concierto de música sinfónica?   7. ¿Prefiere la mayor parte de los estudiantes la música sinfónica o la música popular?   8. ¿Se presentan conciertos de música popular en el teatro universitario?

B. Estudien las palabras siguientes para emplear algunas de ellas en el diálogo citado o para usarlas en un diálogo nuevo basado sobre el modelo:

el argumento plot (*of music or drama*)	**la fuerza** force, strength
el carácter (*pl.* **caracteres**)[1] character	**impresionar** to impress, move
clásico, -a classic	**indígena** *m. and f. adj.* native
el desenlace ending, denouement	**la inspiración** (*pl.* **inspiraciones**) inspiration
el elemento element, part	**la leyenda** legend
la emoción (*pl.* **emociones**) emotion	**producir** to produce
encantar to charm, delight	**sencillo, -a** simple
el espíritu spirit	**típico, -a** typical

[1] Normally the addition of -s or -es in forming the plural of nouns does not change the spoken stress of the words. One of the few exceptions is the plural form **caracteres,** with a shift of the stress one syllable toward the end of the word.

I. Comparación de los adjetivos y de los adverbios

A. When one makes unequal comparisons in English, one says, for example, *tall, taller, tallest; expensive, more (less) expensive, most (least) expensive.* In Spanish, place **más,** *more, most,* or **menos,** *less, least,* before the adjective. The definite article is used when *the* is a part of the meaning, and the adjective must agree with the noun in gender and number: **el más alto, la más alta, los más altos, las más altas.** Sometimes the possessive adjective (**mi, tu,** etc.) replaces the definite article.

One can tell from the context when an adjective in Spanish has comparative or superlative force, that is, whether **más** means *more* or *most* and whether **menos** means *less* or *least.* Even though an adjective modified by **más** or **menos** usually follows the noun, in reading you will note exceptions to this practice (also see Lección cinco, page 118). After a superlative, *in* is translated by **de.** *Than* is translated by **que** before a noun or pronoun. After **que,** *than,* the negatives **nadie, nunca, nada, ninguno, -a,** replace **alguien, siempre, algo, alguno, -a,** respectively:

> **Los ritmos son más definidos.** The rhythms are more definite.
> **Es un compositor más moderno que los otros.** He is a more modern composer than the others.
> **Es el representante más ilustre de la música mexicana de nuestros días.** He is the most famous representative of Mexican music in our time.
> **Ella habla más que nunca (nadie).** She talks more than ever (anyone).

Than is translated by **de** before a numeral or numerical expression in an affirmative sentence; if the sentence is negative, either **que** or **de** may be used, the preference being for **que.** Theoretically, **no . . . más que** means *only* and **no . . . más de** means *not . . . more than*:

> **¿Has escrito más de diez composiciones?** Have you written more than ten compositions?
> **No necesito más que cinco dólares.** I need only five dollars.
> **No necesito más de cinco dólares.** I do not need more than five dollars. (*Five at the most*)

When *than* is followed by an inflected verb form, it is expressed by **de** + the definite article + **que,** that is, by **del que, de la que, de los que, de las que,** really meaning *than the one(s) who (which, that),* if the point of comparison is a noun which is the object of the first verb and is elliptically omitted in the second member:

> **Él tiene más flores de las que vende.**   He has more flowers than he sells.
> **Hace más frío hoy del que hizo ayer.**   It is colder today than it was yesterday.
> **Yo escribo más cartas de las que recibo.**   I write more letters than I receive.

When *than* is followed by an inflected verb form, but the second member is elliptical in such a way that the verb of the first member must be repeated in order to complete the idea, **que** is replaced by **de lo que.** (In such sentences the verb which follows **de lo que** often expresses a mental state.)

> **Ella es más bonita de lo que crees.**   She is prettier than (what) you believe (she is).
> **El concierto es mejor de lo que me imaginaba.**   The concert is better than I imagined (it would be).
> **Es diferente de lo que yo esperaba.**   It is different than (from what) I expected (it to be).

B. The comparative of adverbs is also regularly formed by placing **más** or **menos** before the adverb. The article is not used in the superlative, except that the neuter form **lo** is used when an expression of possibility follows:

> **Es más fácil percibir las melodías.**   It is easier to perceive the melodies.
> **Vuelvan Uds. del concierto lo más pronto posible.**   Return from the concert the soonest possible (as soon as possible).

C. Six adjectives and four adverbs, most of which have already been used in this text, are compared irregularly:

Adjectives

bueno good	**(el) mejor**	(the) better, best
malo bad	**(el) peor**	(the) worse, worst

grande   large

- (el) **más grande**   (the) larger, largest
- (el) **mayor**   (the) greater, older, greatest, oldest

pequeño   small

- (el) **más pequeño**   (the) smaller, smallest
- (el) **menor**   (the) smaller, younger, smallest, youngest

mucho(s)   much (many)   **más**   more, most
poco(s)   little (few)   **menos**   less, fewer

Mejor and **peor** precede the noun, just as **bueno, -a,** and **malo, -a,** regularly precede it, except when emphasized. Used with the definite article, the forms are:

    el mejor (peor)   los mejores (peores)
    la mejor (peor)   las mejores (peores)

Grande and **pequeño, -a,** have regular forms which refer to size, while the irregular forms **mayor** (*m.* and *f.*) and **menor** (*m.* and *f.*) usually refer to persons and mean *older* and *younger*, respectively.

Most (of), *The greater part of*, is translated by **La mayor parte de;** the verb normally agrees with the noun following this expression: **La mayor parte de los estudiantes van a los conciertos,** *Most (of the) students go to the concerts.*

Adverbs

    bien   well   mejor   better, best
    mal   bad, badly   peor   worse, worst
    mucho   much   más   more, most
    poco   little   menos   less, least

D. A high degree of quality, without any element of comparison (sometimes called the absolute superlative), is expressed by the use of **muy** before the adjective or adverb or by adding the ending **-ísimo** (**-a, -os, as**) to the adjective. When **-ísimo** is added, a final vowel is dropped. **Muchísimo,** rather than **muy mucho,** is used for the adjective or adverb *very much (many):*

Ella es muy hermosa (hermosísima).   She is very beautiful.
Se divirtieron muchísimo.   They had a very good time.

Ejercicios   **A.** Completen las frases con la forma comparativa del adjetivo o del adverbio.

MODELO: Este concierto es bueno,   Este concierto es bueno,
            pero el otro fue _____.   pero el otro fue mejor.

1. Este edificio es grande, pero aquél es _____.   2. Esta música es buena, pero la otra es _____.   3. Esta obra es larga, pero la última fue _____.   4. Aquella casa blanca es pequeña, pero la amarilla es _____.   5. Aquellas calles son cortas, pero ésta es _____.   6. Yo estoy cansado, pero mi mamá está _____.   7. José tiene dos años más que Pablo; éste es el _____.   8. Marta tiene un año menos que Ana; aquélla es la _____.   9. Carolina toca bien, pero su hermana toca _____.   10. Juan baila mal, pero Miguel baila _____.   11. A mí me interesa mucho la música, pero a él le interesa _____.   12. Ellos tienen poco tiempo, pero yo tengo _____.

B. Para contestar afirmativamente, siguiendo los modelos.

MODELOS: ¿Es grande el parque?   Sí, es más grande que éste.
            ¿Son difíciles las frases?   Sí, son más difíciles que éstas.

1. ¿Son hermosas las flores?   4. ¿Es mala la novela?
2. ¿Es larga la carretera?   5. ¿Está contenta la muchacha?
3. ¿Es bueno el hotel?   6. ¿Es popular la música?

MODELO: ¿Es bonita la casa?   Sí, es la casa más bonita de
                                 todas.

7. ¿Es sencillo el argumento?   9. ¿Es ilustre el compositor?
8. ¿Es típica la leyenda?   10. ¿Es interesante la obra?

MODELO: ¿Es hermosa Carolina?   Sí, es muy hermosa; es
                                 hermosísima.

11. ¿Son altos los árboles?   13. ¿Son malas las obras?
12. ¿Es guapo su novio?   14. ¿Es grande la emoción?

C. Lean en español, supliendo la palabra o frase equivalente a *than*:

1. Creo que hay más _____ mil estudiantes en el teatro.   2. Este concierto es mejor _____ el último.   3. Hay más fuentes en México _____ tenemos en este país.   4. Pablo tiene más amigos en la ciudad _____ tú crees.   5. Marta ha escrito más composiciones _____ me imaginaba.   6. Hoy ella tocará más números _____ tocó la semana pasada.   7. Esta música es diferente _____ yo esperaba.   8. No olvides que este compositor es más moderno _____ el otro.

II. Comparaciones de igualdad (*equality*)

Tan + an adjective or adverb + **como** means *as (so) . . . as.* **Tan** used without **como** means *so,* sometimes *as:*

> **Pablo es tan fuerte como Enrique.**   Paul is as strong as Henry.
> **¿Por qué está ella tan contenta?**   Why is she so happy?

Before an adjective **tan** is used instead of **tal** to mean *such (a):*

> **¡Es un día tan hermoso!**   It is such a beautiful day!
> **Nunca he leído cuentos tan interesantes.**   I have never read such interesting stories.
>
> BUT: **¿Has visto jamás tal cosa?**   Have you ever seen such a thing?

Tanto, -a (-os, -as) + a noun + **como** means *as (so) much (many) . . . as.* **Tanto** is also used as a pronoun or adverb, with or without **como,** meaning *as (so) much (many) (. . . as):*

> **No hay tantos conciertos como antes.**   There aren't so many concerts as before.
> **Ella tiene muchos discos; yo no tengo tantos.**   She has many records; I do not have so many.
> **Dígales Ud. a los niños que no corran tanto.**   Tell the children not to run so much.
> **Nos gusta la segunda parte tanto como la primera.**   We like the second part as much as the first.

A. Repitan cada oración; luego, al oír un substantivo o un adjetivo,   *Ejercicios*
substitúyanlo en la oración original, haciendo los cambios necesarios:

1. Esta casa no es tan *vieja* como aquélla.
   (*nuevo, pequeño, grande, cómodo, bonito*)
2. Elena tiene tantas *blusas* como Luisa.
   (*sombreros, tiempo, amigos, ropa, vestidos*)
3. Ella recibe muchas *revistas*, pero yo no recibo tantas.
   (*periódicos, dinero, cartas, invitaciones, regalos*)

B. Oirán una frase, luego una o más palabras. Formen una frase nueva empleando **tan . . . como,** según el modelo.

MODELO: Luis está ocupado. (Carlos)   Luis está tan ocupado como
                                          Carlos.

1. La composición es impresionante. (la otra)
2. Los ritmos son definidos. (los de Chávez)
3. Este concierto es emocionante. (el de la música mexicana)
4. Las muchachas están contentas. (la profesora)
5. El primer número fue maravilloso. (el segundo)
6. Juan y yo estábamos cansados. (Roberto)

Formen frases nuevas empleando **no . . . tanto, -a (-os, -as) . . . como,** según el modelo.

MODELO: Yo toco muchos números.   Yo no toco tantos números como
                                      Ana.

7. Bárbara escucha muchas orquestas.
8. Aquel compositor usa muchos ritmos.
9. Ricardo pasa mucho tiempo tocando.
10. Antonio ha escrito muchas composiciones.
11. Marta conocía muchas tonadas tradicionales.
12. Nosotros percibimos muchas melodías.

III. «Hacer» en expresiones de tiempo

A. In Spanish, **hace** followed by a period of time (**minuto, hora, día, mes,** etc.) plus **que** and a verb in the present tense, or a present tense plus **desde hace** followed by a period of time, indicates that an action began in the past and that it is still going on in the present. When **desde hace** is used, the word order in Spanish is the same as in English. Note that in English the present perfect tense is used:

Hace una hora que estoy aquí *or* **Estoy aquí desde hace una hora.** I have been here for an hour (*lit.*, It makes an hour that I am here).

¿Cuánto tiempo hace que viven aquí? How long have they been living (*lit.*, How long does it make that they live) here?

Hace varios días que Ricardo busca un puesto. Richard has been looking for a position for several days (For several days Richard has been looking for a position).

Hace tiempo que no te veo en un concierto. I haven't seen you at a concert for a long time.

Hacía followed by a period of time plus **que** and a verb in the <u>imperfect tense,</u> or the <u>imperfect tense</u> plus **desde hacía** followed by a period of time, indicates that an action <u>had been going on</u> for a certain length of time and <u>was still continuing</u> when something else happened. The pluperfect tense is used in English:

Hacía un mes que yo vivía allí cuando la conocí *or* **Yo vivía allí desde hacía un mes cuando la conocí.** I had been living there (for) a month when I met her (*lit.*, It made a month that I was living there . . .).

Hacía tiempo que (yo) no os veía. I had not seen you for a long time.

B. When **hace** is followed by a period of time after a verb in a past tense, it regularly means *ago, since*. If the **hace**-clause comes first in the sentence, **que** usually (although not always) introduces the main clause:

Llegué hace una hora *or* **Hace una hora que llegué.** I arrived an hour ago *or* It is an hour since I arrived.

Nos vimos hace dos semanas. We saw each other two weeks ago.

Ejercicios

A. Después de oír una oración, oirán una expresión de tiempo; combinen los dos elementos en una nueva oración, siguiendo el modelo.

MODELO: Leo el libro. (Hace una hora)   Hace una hora que leo el libro.

1. Viven en México. (Hace cinco meses)
2. Estudio el español. (Hace más de un año)
3. Estamos en el teatro. (Hace una hora y media)
4. No te veo en la biblioteca. (Hace tiempo)

5. No vamos al cine. (Hace una semana)
6. Estoy esperando a Marta. (Hace quince minutos)

B. Después de oír una pregunta, oirán una expresión de tiempo; úsenla para contestar la pregunta, según los modelos.

MODELO: ¿Cuánto tiempo hace que lees?   Leo desde hace una hora.
(una hora)

1. ¿Cuánto tiempo hace que vives aquí? (seis meses)
2. ¿Cuánto tiempo hace que conoce Ud. a María? (un mes y medio)
3. ¿Cuánto tiempo hace que tocas la guitarra? (cuatro años)
4. ¿Cuánto tiempo hace que ella habla por teléfono? (veinte minutos)

MODELO: ¿Cuándo salió ella?   Ella salió hace media hora.
(hace media hora)   Hace media hora que ella salió.

5. ¿Cuándo volviste a casa? (hace tiempo)
6. ¿Cuándo fueron Uds. al centro? (hace varios días)
7. ¿Cuándo llovió aquí? (hace una semana)
8. ¿Cuándo viste a Carlota? (hace un rato)
9. ¿Cuándo vino Miguel a este país? (hace varios meses)
10. ¿Cuándo llegaste a la clase? (hace diez minutos)

C. Para expresar en español:

1. The concert began fifteen minutes ago.   2. We have been here for an hour.   3. My sister has studied Spanish music for several years.   4. How long have you (*formal sing.*) been playing the guitar?   5. I began to play it three months ago.   6. Charles and I attended a symphony concert three days ago.   7. We had been waiting for a long time when they turned off the lights.   8. The orchestra has been playing in the University Theater for many years.

IV. La traducción de *must*

When *must = to have to*, expressing a strong obligation or necessity, **tener que** + an infinitive is used. The impersonal form is **hay (había, habrá,** etc.) **que** + an infinitive:

Ellos tienen que esperar.   They must (have to) wait.
Hay que hacer eso.   One must (It is necessary to) do that.

When *must = is (was) to, is (was) supposed to*, expressing a mild obligation or commitment, **haber de** + an infinitive is used:

Hemos de reunirnos esta noche.   We must (are to) meet tonight.
Habían de salir a las dos.   They were (supposed) to leave at two.

For a moral obligation, duty, customary action, etc., **deber** is used:

Ella debe llamar a su mamá.   She must (ought to) call her mother.

When *must* expresses probability in the present, it is indicated by the future (or future perfect) of the verb (see Lección seis, page 141) or by **deber (de)** + an infinitive:

Estarán en el café.   They must be (probably are) at the café.
Deben de estar allí.   They must be there.
Juan habrá leído la novela.   John must have read the novel.
Debe de haberla leído.   He must have read it.
Deben de relacionarse con tonadas tradicionales.   They must be related to traditional airs.

Después de oír una pregunta, oirán un verbo o una frase; contesten afirmativamente, usando la forma correcta del verbo correspondiente.   *Ejercicio*

MODELOS: ¿*Son* las dos? (*deber de*)   Sí, deben de ser las dos.
    ¿*Has de* ir tú ahora? (*tener que*)   Sí, tengo que ir ahora.

1. ¿*Están* ellos en la biblioteca? (*deber de*)
2. ¿*Es* la una? (*deber de*)
3. ¿*Va* Juan *a* tocar la guitarra? (*haber de*)
4. ¿*Iban a* reunirse temprano? (*haber de*)
5. ¿*Es necesario* llegar a tiempo? (*haber que*)
6. ¿*Será preciso* decidir eso pronto? (*haber que*)
7. ¿*Debemos* ir al concierto esta noche? (*tener que*)
8. ¿*Has de* apagar las luces? (*tener que*)
9. ¿Creían que *podían* esperar un rato? (*deber*)
10. ¿*Han de* pagar la cuenta ahora? (*tener que*)

V. Formas de mandato correspondientes a «vosotros, -as»

Recall that in this text we have followed the practice, which is common in Spanish America, of using the formal **ustedes** with the third person plural present subjunctive in familiar plural commands. Since the familiar plural forms are used in much of Spain, they are needed for recognition in reading. (For commands used with **usted, ustedes,** and **tú,** see Repaso primero, pages 8–9, 11.)

To form the affirmative familiar plural command (the plural imperative) of all verbs, drop **-r** of the infinitive and add **-d.** For the negative familiar plural command, use the second person plural of the present subjunctive. The subject **vosotros, -as,** is usually omitted. (See Appendix D, pages 314–330, for forms of all types of verbs.)

	Affirmative	Negative
tomar:	tomad	no toméis
comer:	comed	no comáis
abrir:	abrid	no abráis
hacer:	haced	no **hagáis**
salir:	salid	no **salgáis**
tener:	tened	no **tengáis**
buscar:	buscad	no **busquéis**
cerrar:	cerrad	no cerréis
contar:	contad	no contéis
volver:	volved	no volváis
jugar:	jugad	no **juguéis**
sentir:	sentid	no **sintáis**
dormir:	dormid	no **durmáis**
pedir:	pedid	no **pidáis**

In forming the familiar plural commands of reflexive verbs, final **-d** is dropped before the reflexive pronoun **os,** except for **idos (irse).** All **-ir** reflexive verbs except **irse** require an accent on the **i** of the stem of the verb: **vestíos.**

	Affirmative	Negative
levantarse:	levantaos	no os levantéis
sentarse:	sentaos	no os sentéis
ponerse:	poneos	no os **pongáis**
vestirse:	vestíos	no os **vistáis**
irse:	**idos**	no os **vayáis**

Cambien el infinitivo a la forma de mandato correspondiente a **vosotros,**   *Ejercicio*
-as; luego, expresen el mandato negativamente:

1. Hablar en inglés.   2. Comer antes de las seis.   3. Escribir las cartas
hoy.   4. Venir a verme mañana.   5. Quitarse los zapatos.   6. Ponerse
los guantes.   7. Vestirse pronto.   8. Acercarse al coche.

A. Repitan cada oración; luego, formen otra oración, empleando **no . . .**   **Resumen**
tan . . . como, siguiendo el modelo.

MODELO: Elena es más alta que Ana.   Elena es más alta que Ana.
　　　　　　　　　　　　　　　　　　Ana no es tan alta como Elena.

1. Margarita lee más despacio   3. Esta música es más clásica
　　que yo.   que ésa.
2. Yo me levanté más tarde que   4. Él pronuncia más correcta-
　　ellos.   mente que Ud.

Usen **no . . . tanto, -a (-os, -as) . . . como,** siguiendo el modelo.

MODELO: Yo tengo más flores que   Yo tengo más flores que ella.
　　　　　ella.   Ella no tiene tantas flores
　　　　　　　　　　　　　　　　　　　como yo.

5. María lee más novelas que   7. Allí hay más fuentes que
　　su hermana.   aquí.
6. Ana escucha más música que   8. Esa obra tiene más
　　Pablo.   melodías que ésta.

B. Usos de las formas comparativas de los adjetivos y de los adverbios.
　　Para expresar en español:

1. This building is large; it is larger than that one (*distant*); it is the
　　largest one in the state.
2. Our house is small; it is smaller than the yellow one; it is the smallest
　　one in the block.
3. We ran across John's older brother and Mary's younger sister down-
　　town yesterday.
4. There are more than one hundred foreign students here; there are
　　more than I imagined.

5. John says that he has already written more compositions this semester than he wrote last year.
6. Most of the students in (of) our Spanish class speak better than you (*pl.*) believe.

C. Comparaciones de igualdad. Para expresar en español:

1. This concert is as exciting as the last one.
2. I have never heard such definite rhythms.
3. There aren't so many people here tonight as the last time.
4. Most people do not have so much interest in concerts as I.
5. Robert plays the guitar better than I, but I do not practice so much.
6. Let's see if the second part of the program is as interesting as the first.

D. Para traducir *must, to have to, to be to,* etc. Para expresar en español:

1. They must be (*two ways*) at the movie now.   2. Jane and Paul must have arrived (*two ways*) late.   3. My parents are (supposed) to look for a

Several aspects of Mexican history blend in modern Mexico City: from left to right, Veracruz Church, the Palacio de Bellas Artes, and the Latin American Tower.

television set today.   4. Henry says that I am to turn off the lights at
eleven.   5. We must always greet our teacher in Spanish.   6. My roommate had to write a long composition last night.   7. One must remember
that Chávez is a great composer.   8. The sources of his music must be
related to traditional airs.

E. Para expresar en español, empleando la forma de mandato correspondiente a **vosotros, -as:**

1. Speak up.   2. Look at the map.   3. Say that in Spanish.   4. Sit down
in the corner.   5. Don't put on your gloves yet.   6. Don't leave the
room.   7. Have a good time tonight!   8. Do that tomorrow morning.

Resumen de palabras y expresiones

apagar   to turn off, lower (*lights*)
¡claro!   clearly! certainly! of course!
el comienzo   beginning
el compositor   composer
el concierto de música sinfónica
   symphony concert
¿cuánto tiempo hace?   how long
   (much time) has it been?
de nuestros días   in (of) our time,
   of today
deber de + *inf.*   must, probably + *verb*
definido, -a   definite
en general   in general, generally
exagerar   to exaggerate
la forma   form
la fuente   fountain; source
el gentío   crowd, mob
hablar más alto   to speak up (louder)
hace tiempo   it is a long time, for a
   long time; a long time ago
ilustre   illustrious, famous
impresionante   impressive, moving

el intermedio   intermission
la luz (*pl.* **luces**)   light
la mayor parte de   most (of), the greater
   part of
(me) parece que   (I) believe that, it
   seems (to me) that
la melodía   melody
peninsular   peninsular (*of Spain*)
percibir   to perceive, comprehend
quitar (el radio)   to turn off (the radio)
relacionarse con   to be related to
el representante   representative
resultar   to result, turn out (to be)
el rincón (*pl.* **rincones**)   corner (*of room*)
el ritmo   rhythm
según   according to
sinfónico, -a   symphonic, symphony
   (*adj.*)
la tonada   air, song
tradicional   traditional
(venir) por aquí   (to come) this way
¡(vosotros) por aquí!   (you) here!

LECTURA XI

Observaciones sobre la música en la América española

El amor por la música es una de las características de la América latina. Desde la época colonial ha habido dos corrientes distintas: la popular, que representa la expresión espontánea del pueblo, y la culta, que muestra influencias europeas.

Las variedades de la música popular son infinitas; cada país tiene una rica tradición musical, con formas propias. En algunos casos se han mezclado elementos indígenas y extranjeros. La música popular de México, por ejemplo, es en gran parte[1] de procedencia andaluza, y su estilo es arcaico, como en las danzas llamadas jarabe[2] y zapateado.[3] La rumba, la conga y otras formas de la música popular de Cuba y de las demás islas del Mar Caribe, en cambio, muestran una fuerte influencia de la música negra. En los países donde la población india es grande, la influencia indígena es muy notable.

En México hay grupos de músicos, los mariachis, que ejecutan la música típica popular. Originalmente del Estado de Jalisco, se han extendido por todo el país. Entre las canciones más bellas de su repertorio pueden citarse *Guadalajara* y *¡Ay, Jalisco, no te rajes!*,[4] alegres y bulliciosas, y *La feria de las flores*, más sentimental. Se cree que la palabra mariachi procede de la palabra francesa *mariage* (matrimonio), mal pronunciada, que los franceses, durante su intervención armada en México (en el siglo XIX), dieron a esta música por tocarse en ceremonias matrimoniales de aquella época.

En cuanto a la música culta, en el siglo XX muchos compositores, como los argentinos Juan Carlos Paz y Juan José Castro, el cubano Ernesto Lecuona, el uruguayo Eduardo Fabini y los mexicanos Manuel

---

[1] **en gran parte,** *largely, in large measure.*   [2] **jarabe,** a popular dance, such as the *Mexican Hat Dance.*   [3] **zapateado,** *clog (tap) dance.*   [4] **¡ . . . no te rajes!,** . . . *don't be boastful!*

Religious procession
with marimba musicians,
Guatemala

Musicians of the
Ballet Folklórico,
Mexico City

Ponce, Silvestre Revueltas y Carlos Chávez, han llegado a desarrollar[1] una música de auténticos temas americanos.

Lecuona (1896–1963) se distinguió como pianista, compositor y director de orquesta. Algunas de sus composiciones, como *Malagueña, Danza negra* y *Siboney,* de inspiración popular, llegaron a ser[2] célebres tanto en Norteamérica como en Hispanoamérica. Juan José Castro (1895–1968) compuso la música de escena[3] para *Bodas de sangre,*[4] de García Lorca, poeta y dramaturgo español.

Carlos Chávez (1899–   ) es el fundador de la Orquesta Sinfónica de México. Convencido de que existe una música mexicana con un carácter y un vigor propios, Chávez se ha dedicado a integrar las diversas fuentes de la tradición nacional. Aunque la esencia de su música es mexicana, sus temas son originales y se ha asimilado completamente el elemento indígena. Su técnica y su genio inventivo le han asegurado un puesto muy alto en el mundo musical.

El chileno Claudio Arrau (1903–   ) es uno de los grandes pianistas de nuestros días. Es considerado como uno de los mejores intérpretes de la obra pianística de Beethoven.

Entre los compositores más jóvenes hay algunos muy notables, como el chileno Juan Antonio Orrego Salas (1919–   ), profesor del Conservatorio Nacional de Chile, y el argentino Alberto Ginastera (1916–   ), director del Conservatorio de Música de su país. Entre las composiciones de Ginastera merecen citarse su poema sinfónico, *Ollantay*[5] (1948), y su ópera *Bomarzo,* estrenada en Washington en 1967.

Escriban tres oraciones sobre cada uno de los temas siguientes: *Ejercicio*

1. Elementos indígenas y extranjeros en la música de Hispanoamérica.
2. Los mariachis de México.
3. Compositores argentinos del siglo XX.

---

[1] **han llegado a desarrollar,** *have succeeded in developing.*   [2] **llegaron a ser,** *became.*
[3] **música de escena,** *background music.*   [4] **Bodas de sangre,** *Blood Wedding.*
[5] **Ollantay,** originally a controversial drama of uncertain authorship and date, possibly written first in Quechua verse in pre-Hispanic days, was presented in Spanish in the eighteenth century. The action, set in Cuzco, the ancient Inca capital, deals with the love of Ollantay, an Inca chieftain of humble birth, and the Inca princess Cusi Coyllur.

LECCIÓN DOCE

Resumen de los usos de «para» y «por». Usos del participio pasado.
El pretérito anterior de indicativo. Usos del participio presente.
Las conjunciones «e» y «u». Usos de «pero, sino» y «sino que». El
artículo neutro «lo». El pronombre neutro «lo». La formación de los
adverbios. Verbos auxiliares para expresar el modo

Planes para el futuro

(*Dos estudiantes llegan temprano a la clase de español y charlan animadamente
mientras esperan al profesor.*)

Juan. Estamos para terminar el semestre. ¿Qué planes tienes para las
vacaciones, Luis?

Luis. ¡Hombre! ¡No puedes imaginarte lo contento que estoy! Concluidos
los exámenes, salgo para Washington.

Juan. ¿Has conseguido un puesto allí?

Luis. Hace unos meses solicité un puesto en el Cuerpo de Paz y parece que
me lo van a conceder.

Juan. ¿A qué país te mandarán?

Luis. Depende de los proyectos que se propongan. Cuando se decida,
tomaremos un curso de orientación.

Juan. ¿Cuánto tiempo estarás en Washington?

Luis. No lo sé todavía, pero es posible que esté allí siete u ocho semanas.

Juan. Puede que te manden a algún país hispanoamericano.

Luis. Como sabes, no sólo he estudiado el español, sino que he tomado
también muchos cursos de inglés. Podré enseñar el inglés en algún
país.

Juan. Como recordarás, el profesor Díaz dirigió un programa del Cuerpo
de Paz en Bolivia. ¿Has estado en contacto con él?

Luis. Él pasó el semestre pasado en Chile, pero apenas hubo regresado, le
llamé por teléfono. Tengo una cita con él mañana.

Juan. Sin duda él podrá darte muchos informes útiles. Que tengas mucha
suerte, Luis. Y no trates de hacer lo imposible.

Luis. Gracias, Juan. No será fácil; pero me entusiasma la posibilidad de
contribuir algo al entendimiento mutuo entre las naciones del mundo.

255

A. Para contestar en español en oraciones completas:

Preguntas sobre el diálogo

1. ¿Qué le pregunta Juan a Luis?   2. ¿Cuándo irá Luis a Washington? 3. ¿Qué había solicitado Luis?   4. ¿A qué país le mandarán?   5. ¿Qué ha estudiado Luis en la universidad?   6. ¿Qué dice Juan del profesor Díaz?   7. ¿Por qué quiere Luis consultar con el profesor Díaz?   8. ¿Qué le entusiasma a Luis?

Aplicación del diálogo

1. ¿Cuándo termina el semestre en esta universidad?   2. ¿Qué planes tiene Ud. para las vacaciones?   3. Dénos Ud. algunos informes sobre sus estudios universitarios.   4. ¿Ha pensado Ud. en solicitar un puesto en el Cuerpo de Paz?   5. ¿Cuántos amigos suyos han solicitado un puesto en el Cuerpo de Paz?   6. ¿A qué países extranjeros los han mandado?   7. ¿En qué países extranjeros le interesaría a Ud. trabajar? 8. ¿Qué profesores podrían dar buenos informes acerca de Ud.?

B. Preparen un diálogo original, de unas diez líneas, para recitar en clase, empleando las frases y preguntas siguientes como elemento inicial:

1. **Carlos.**   Siento mucho no haber podido pasar por tu casa hasta ahora. ¿Has decidido marcharte?

    María.   Sí, Carlos. Salgo mañana en el avión de las dos. ¿Qué quieres que les diga a tus amigos en Buenos Aires?

2. **Enrique.**   Como Ud. sabe, me gustaría conseguir un puesto en algún país de la América española.

    Sr. Díaz.   No me parece difícil. Pero primero quiero que me dé Ud. algunos informes sobre sus estudios universitarios.

Notas gramaticales

I. Resumen de los usos de «para» y «por»

A. Para is used:

1. To express the purpose, use, person, or place for which persons or things are intended or destined:

> **¿Qué planes tienes para las vacaciones?**   What plans do you have for vacation?
> **Esta carta es para Miguel.**   This letter is for Michael.
> **Ya han partido para México.**   They have already left for Mexico.

2. To express a point or farthest limit of time in the future, often meaning *by*:

> **Este diálogo es para mañana.**   This dialogue is for tomorrow.
> **Que estés aquí para las cinco.**   May you be here by five o'clock.

3. With an infinitive to express purpose, meaning *to, in order to*:

> **Me ofreció el dinero para hacer el viaje.**   He offered me the money (in order) to make the trip.
> **Estamos para terminar el semestre.**   We are about to finish (on the point of finishing) the semester.

4. To express *for* in a comparison that may be understood or stated:

> **Juanito habla bien para un niño.**   Johnny talks well for a child.
> **Para Uds., esto será fácil.**   For you, this will be easy.

B. Por is used:

1. To express *for* in the sense of *because of, on account of, for the sake of, on behalf of, in exchange for, about, as*:

> **Por falta de dinero él no pudo ir.**   For lack of money he couldn't go.
> **¿Lo harás por mí?**   Will you do it for (because of) me?
> **Pagué diez dólares por la camisa.**   I paid ten dollars for the shirt.
> **No te preocupes por mí.**   Don't worry about me.
> **Le tomaron por español.**   They took him for (as) a Spaniard.

2. To express the space of time during which an action continues (*for, during*):

> **Estaré en México por un mes.**   I'll be in Mexico for a month.
> **Ella saldrá mañana por la tarde.**   She will leave tomorrow afternoon.

3. To show *by what* or *by whom* something is done; also *through, along*:

> **Juan habló con ella por teléfono.**   John talked with her by telephone.
> **El viaje fue arreglado por Luis.**   The trip was arranged by Louis.
> **Han viajado por Hispanoamérica.**   They have traveled through Spanish America.

4. To indicate the object of an errand or search, *for*, after such verbs as **ir, enviar, mandar, preguntar, venir:**

Han enviado (venido, ido) por Ana. They have sent (come, gone) for Ann.
Preguntaron por ella. They asked for (about) her.

5. With an infinitive to express uncertain outcome (often to denote striving for something) or something yet to be done:

Luchaban por ganar la paz. They were struggling to win peace.
La carta todavía está por escribir. The letter is still to be written.
Estoy por pedirle eso. I feel like asking (am inclined to ask, am in favor of asking) him for that.

6. To form certain idiomatic expressions (some of which could be placed under the above headings):

por aquí (around, by) here	**por falta de** for lack of
por cierto certainly, for sure	**por favor** please
por completo completely	**por fin** finally, at last
por consiguiente consequently	**por lo general** in general, generally
por desgracia unfortunately	**por lo menos** at least
¡por Dios! for heaven's sake!	**por lo tanto** therefore
por ejemplo for example	**por medio de** by means of
por encima de over, above	**por primera vez** for the first time
por eso because of that, therefore, that's why	**por supuesto** of course, certainly
	por último finally, ultimately

¿Por qué? means *Why? For what reason?*, while **¿para qué?** means *why? for what purpose?*

Ejercicio   Para leer en español, supliendo la preposición **para** o **por:**

1. ¿Cuándo partirán _____ la Argentina? 2. ¿Tiene Ud. muchos planes _____ el verano? 3. Yo le di las gracias a María _____ todo. 4. Arturo me dijo que vendría _____ mí a las ocho. 5. ¿Por qué se preocupa Ud. tanto _____ Ricardo? 6. Su mamá hizo el vestido _____ ella (*i.e., for her use*). 7. ¿_____ quién es este billete? —Es _____ mí. 8. Es _____ el concierto que van a presentar el sábado _____ la noche. 9. Estoy seguro de que está _____ llover pronto.

10. Tráeme tú una taza _____ té, _____ favor.   11. Los muchachos jugaron _____ dos horas.   12. Anduvieron despacio _____ la calle. 13. Escoja Ud. una tarjeta _____ Dorotea.   14. ¿Cuánto pagaste _____ ese reloj?   15. Parece que todo el mundo lucha _____ ganar más dinero.   16. ¿Es verdad que comemos _____ vivir?   17. ¿Crees que le tomaron _____ argentino?   18. _____ fin podemos hacer planes _____ la reunión.   19. Tendremos que darnos prisa _____ llegar a tiempo.   20. ¿_____ qué sirven los amigos?   21. Voy a enviar _____ Antonio _____ entregarle estas cartas.   22. Que vuelvan Uds. _____ el mediodía.   23. Este artículo, que fue escrito _____ Ana, es _____ el periódico de hoy.   24. _____ una persona que se siente muy bien, ella se queja mucho.

II. Usos del participio pasado

A. The past participle is most commonly used with the appropriate tense of **haber** to form the perfect tenses, in which case the participle always ends in **-o.** It is also frequently used as an adjective, including its use with **estar** and similar verbs to express a state or condition which results from a previous action, and with **ser** to form the passive voice. In the latter two constructions, the past participle agrees in gender and number with the noun or pronoun it modifies:

> **Hemos visto la película.**   We have seen the film.
> **La puerta estaba (se encontraba) abierta.**   The door was open.
> **Los vasos fueron rotos por Juanito.**   The glasses were broken by Johnny.

B. The past participle also may be used independently with a noun or pronoun to express *time, manner, means,* and the like. (This is sometimes called the absolute use of the past participle.) Used thus, the participle precedes the noun or pronoun it modifies and agrees with it in gender and number. The translation depends on the context:

> **Concluidos los exámenes, salgo para Washington.**   Once the exams are ended (After the exams are ended), I shall leave for Washington.
> **Salido el avión, volví a casa.**   After the plane had left (The plane having left), I returned home.

NOTE: **De** often replaces **por** with verbs other than **estar** or **ser** to introduce an agent dependent upon a past participle: **Parto para Buenos**

Aires, acompañado de mi hermano Juan, *I'll leave for Buenos Aires, accompanied by my brother John.* Compare the normal use of **por** in the passive voice (see Lección primera, pages 39–40).

Ejercicio　Escuchen la oración; luego, cámbienla, usando el participio pasado, según el modelo.

MODELO:　*Al escribir la carta,* Ana se la　　Escrita la carta, Ana se la
　　　　　　　envió a Marta.　　　　　　　　envió a Marta.

1. *Al cerrar la puerta,* la profesora empezó a hablar en español.
2. *Al concluir el dibujo,* Miguel lo vendió.
3. *Después de leer los artículos,* Luisa los revisó.
4. *Al comprar la maleta,* Roberto la metió en el coche.
5. *Después de hacer los planes,* los estudiantes los anunciaron.
6. *Al entregar el informe,* Carolina fue a la biblioteca.

III. El pretérito anterior (*preterit perfect*) de indicativo

The preterit perfect tense is formed with the preterit of **haber** and the past participle. It is translated like the English past perfect tense, but is used only after conjunctions such as **cuando, en cuanto, después que, apenas** (*scarcely, hardly*). In the case of **apenas,** the word *when* is carried over to the following clause in English; it is not expressed in Spanish:

	Singular			Plural	
hube	⎫		**hubimos**	⎫	
hubiste	⎬	hablado, comido, vivido	**hubisteis**	⎬	hablado, comido, vivido
hubo	⎭		**hubieron**	⎭	

　　En cuanto (Cuando) él hubo metido el rollo, cerró la cámara.　As soon as (When) he had put in the roll, he closed the camera.
　　Apenas él hubo llegado, le llamé por teléfono.　Scarcely had he returned, when I telephoned him.

In spoken Spanish the simple preterit often replaces the preterit perfect. The Spanish pluperfect is used to translate the English past perfect in other cases: **Habían vuelto,** *They had returned.*

IV. Usos del participio presente

The present participle, also called the gerund, has a number of important functions.

1. **Estar** is used with the present participle to express the progressive forms of the tenses, that is, to express the action of the verb as continuing at a given moment (see Lección primera, page 38):

> **Los niños están (estaban) gritando.** The children are (were) shouting.
> **¿Qué estás leyendo ahora?** What are you reading now?

2. Verbs of motion, particularly **ir, andar, venir,** are used with the present participle to give a more graphic representation of an action in progress. These verbs normally retain something of their literal meaning. **Seguir** and **continuar,** *to continue, keep on,* are followed by the present participle. (The progressive forms of **ir, salir, venir** are seldom used.)

> **Él iba (venía) cantando.** He was (went along, came) singing.
> **Sigan (Continúen) Uds. charlando.** Continue *or* Keep on chatting.

Ir + a present participle is also equivalent to the English *to go on* or *keep on* + present participle, *do something gradually (slowly, more and more)*:

> **Ellos van aprendiendo a hablar bien.** They keep on learning (are gradually learning) to speak well.
> **La temperatura iba subiendo.** The temperature was rising (slowly, more and more).

3. Referring to the subject, expressed or understood, the present participle may be used to convey a variety of adverbial relationships:

> **Pasan mucho tiempo jugando en el parque.** They spend much time playing in the park.
> **Andando rápidamente, llegué a tiempo.** By walking rapidly, I arrived on time.

Repitan cada oración; luego, al oír un verbo, substituyan la forma correcta del verbo seguida del participio presente, según los modelos.   *Ejercicio*

MODELOS: Luis mira un mapa. (estar)   Luis mira un mapa. Luis está
mirando un mapa.

            Andaban despacio. (ir)   Andaban despacio. Iban
andando despacio.

1. Roberto visita a sus abuelos. (estar)
2. Luis hacía un viaje por Hispanoamérica. (estar)
3. Los niños corren hacia nosotros. (venir)
4. Ellos se acercaban al patio. (ir)
5. Nosotros aprendemos la lengua poco a poco. (ir)
6. Los precios suben mucho, ¿verdad? (ir)
7. Ella anda rápidamente por la calle. (venir)
8. En este momento Juan solicita un puesto en México. (estar)
9. Luis se preocupa mucho por el proyecto. (ir)
10. Lea Ud. hasta las cuatro. (seguir)

V. Las conjunciones «e» y «u»

Before words beginning with **i-**, **hi-** (but not **hie-**), Spanish uses **e**, *and*,
for **y**. Before words beginning with **o-** or **ho-**, Spanish uses **u**, *or*, for **o**:

> **Luis habla español e inglés.**   Louis speaks Spanish and English.
> **Juanita hizo eso siete u ocho veces.**   Jane did that seven or eight
> times.

> BUT: **nieve y hielo**   snow and ice

VI. Usos de «pero, sino» y «sino que»

The English conjunction *but* is usually expressed by **pero** in Spanish.
When *but* means *on the contrary, but instead,* **sino** is used in place of
pero in an affirmative statement which contradicts a preceding negative
statement. Usually no verb—other than an infinitive—may be used after
sino:

> **Me probé el traje pero no lo compré.**   I tried on the suit but did not
> buy it.
> **No fueron en autobús, sino en avión.**   They didn't go by bus, but by
> plane.
> **No vimos a Roberto, sino a Jorge.**   We didn't see Robert, but George.
> **Yo no quiero jugar, sino descansar.**   I don't want to play, but to rest.

If the sentence contains different clauses, **sino que** is used:

> **No sólo he estudiado el español, sino que he tomado también muchos cursos de inglés.**   I have not only studied Spanish, but I have also taken many courses in English.

Para leer en español, supliendo la conjunción **pero, sino** o **sino que:**   *Ejercicio*

1. Traté de llamar a Felipe, _____ nadie contestó.   2. A Carlos le gusta la música clásica, _____ a mí no.   3. Estas melodías no son mexicanas, _____ argentinas.   4. Ellos no fueron en autobús, _____ en coche.   5. Los niños no andaban despacio, _____ corrían rápidamente.   6. Mis amigos van a México, _____ no pueden visitar a Monterrey.   7. Inés dice que no quiere estudiar, _____ dormir la siesta.   8. He de quedarme aquí, _____ no se preocupen ustedes por mí.

VII. El artículo neutro «lo»

1. The neuter article **lo** is used with masculine singular adjectives, with adverbs, and with past participles used as adjectives, to form an expression almost equivalent to an abstract noun. The translation of this abstract idea or concept varies according to context:

> **Lo malo es que no están aquí.**   What is bad (The bad thing *or* part) is that they aren't here.
> **Lea Ud. lo escrito.**   Read what is (has been) written.

2. The neuter article **lo** used with an adjective or adverb followed by **que** translates *how:*

> **¿Sabes lo contentas que están ellas?**   Do you know how happy they are?

3. Remember the uses of the neuter article **lo** explained earlier: **lo que** meaning *what, that which*; **lo de** meaning *that (matter, affair) of* (see Lección diez, page 216), **de lo que,** *than,* in certain comparisons, and **lo (más pronto) posible,** *the soonest possible* (see Lección once, page 238).

Ejercicio   Después de oír una oración, oirán una frase; substituyan la frase en la oración, según el modelo.

MODELO: *Lo malo* es que ya han   Lo peor es que ya han salido.
               salido. (*Lo peor*)

1. *Lo bueno* es que Luis aceptó el puesto. (*Lo mejor*)
2. *Lo importante* es hablar correctamente. (*Lo necesario*)
3. Hay que recordar *lo dicho*. (*lo hecho*)
4. No traten Uds. de hacer *lo difícil*. (*lo imposible*)
5. Repitan Uds. *lo escrito*. (*lo leído*)
6. Arregle Ud. *lo nuestro*. (*lo suyo*)
7. Siempre andan *lo más despacio* posible. (*lo más rápidamente*)
8. Parece que vuelven *lo más tarde* posible. (*lo más pronto*)
9. Sabemos *lo contentos que* están ellos. (*lo tristes que*)
10. No puedes imaginarte *lo largas que* son las lecciones. (*lo difíciles que*)

VIII. El pronombre neutro «lo»

In addition to its use as a pronoun object meaning *it* (**No lo creo,** *I don't believe it*), the neuter pronoun **lo** is used:

1. To complete the sentence when no direct object is expressed, with verbs such as **advertir, decir, pedir, preguntar, saber,** and the like (see Lección tres, page 82):

> **Como ellos no lo saben, yo se lo diré.**   Since they don't know it, I'll tell them.
> **¿Podrías ir? —No lo sé. Pregúntaselo a ella.**   Could you go? —I don't know. Ask her.

2. With certain verbs such as **ser** and **parecer,** in answer to a question or to refer back to a noun, adjective, or whole idea, sometimes with the meaning of *so*:

> **¿Es Ud. estudiante? —Sí, lo soy.**   Are you a student? —Yes, I am.
> **Él estará cansado, pero no lo parece.**   He must be tired, but he doesn't seem so.

Para contestar afirmativamente, usando el pronombre neutro **lo**.   *Ejercicio*

MODELO: ¿Es profesora la señorita Gómez?   Sí, lo es.

1. ¿Es abogado el señor Díaz?   4. ¿Soy yo profesor (profesora)?
2. ¿Son norteamericanos sus   5. ¿Parecen ellos estar
   padres?   contentos?
3. ¿Son Uds. estudiantes?   6. ¿Parece ser sencilla la obra?

IX. La formación de los adverbios

In Spanish, adverbs of manner are formed by adding **-mente** (compare
the English suffix *-ly*) to the feminine singular of adjectives. Adverbs
may also be formed by using **con** plus a noun:

    claro clear   **claramente** clearly   **con cuidado** carefully
    fácil easy   **fácilmente** easily   **con frecuencia** frequently

When two or more adverbs are used in a series, **-mente** is added only to
the last one:

    Ella habla rápida y correctamente.   She speaks rapidly and correctly.

Occasionally, adjectives are used in Spanish as adverbs, particularly in
the spoken language and regularly in poetry, with no change in form
other than the usual agreement:

    Ellos vivían felices.   They were living happily.
    Todas iban muy contentas.   All (*f.*) were going very contentedly.

Den los adverbios que correspondan a los adjetivos: *Ejercicio*

1. fuerte.   2. animado.   3. general.   4. sencillo.   5. triste.   6. típico.
7. cortés.   8. exacto.   9. social y económico.   10. claro y rápido.

X. Verbos auxiliares para expresar el modo (*modal auxiliaries*)

A. Translation of *can* and *may*

If *can* expresses physical ability, the present tense of **poder** is used; **saber** indicates mental ability:

> **Yo dudo que él pueda dirigir el programa.** I doubt that he can direct the program.
>
> **¿Sabe Ud. jugar al golf?** Can you (Do you know how to) play golf?

Some of the ways in which *may* is expressed are:

> **Puedes salir ahora si quieres.** You may go out now if you wish.
>
> **Es posible que él lo concluya.** He may (It is possible that he may) finish it.
>
> **Puede (ser) que se vayan hoy.** They may (It may be that they will) leave today.
>
> **Aunque le vea yo, no se lo diré.** Even though I may see him, I'll not tell him.
>
> **Que sean Uds. felices.** May you be happy.
>
> **¿Se puede entrar?** May I (we, one) come in?

B. Translation of *could* and *might*

Could, meaning *would be able to, might,* is translated by the imperfect, preterit, or conditional indicative, or by the imperfect subjunctive of **poder:**

> **Ella podía cantar bien.** She could (was able to) sing well.
>
> **Pablo no pudo terminar el trabajo.** Paul couldn't finish the work.
>
> **¿Podrías ayudarnos?** Could you (Would you be able to) help us?
>
> **Dijeron que podrían esperar.** They said they could (might be able to) wait.
>
> **Era posible que vinieran (pudiesen venir).** It was possible that they might come.

C. Translation of *should (ought to), should like*

Deber may be used in all tenses to express various degrees of obligation. When *should* indicates a mild obligation (not so strong as that expressed by the present tense of **deber**), the **-ra** imperfect subjunctive, the imperfect, or the conditional indicative tense of **deber** is used:

Ud. debiera ir a verlos.   You should (ought to) go (to) see them.
Yo sabía que debía buscarle.   I knew that I should look for him.
Creíamos que Ana debía (debiera, debería) venir.   We thought
  Ann should come.

The preterit of **deber** expresses an obligation at a time previous to
another past action:

Ud. debió proponer el plan.   You should (ought to) have proposed
  the plan.

In a sentence that expresses a contrary-to-fact condition or an improbable
condition in the future (see Lección nueve, page 204), *should* is translated by the conditional indicative tense in the main clause, and by the
imperfect subjunctive tense in the si-clause:

Si yo tuviera tiempo, iría allá.   If I had (should have) time, I should
  (would) go there.

Should like may be translated by the **-ra** imperfect subjunctive forms of
querer, or by the conditional indicative of **gustar:**

Me gustaría (Yo quisiera) ir con él.   I should like to go with him.

Para expresar en español: *Ejercicio*

1. Can you (*fam. sing.*) go to the office with me?   2. Jane can play the
guitar well, but she cannot play it today because she is ill.   3. What
can I do for you (*pl.*)?   4. You (*pl.*) may sit down if you wish.   5. May
they have a good time tonight.   6. You (*fam. sing.*) should look at
several brands of radios if you should go to that store.   7. The clerk
said last week that he could show you some new models.   8. Betty
knows that she must call us today.   9. I should like (*two ways*) to drive
your (*fam. sing.*) new car.   10. If I were John, I would apply for a position in the Peace Corps.

A. Escuchen el modelo; luego, formen dos frases nuevas, una em-   **Resumen**
  pleando la voz pasiva, y la otra empleando **estar** con el participio
  pasado, según el modelo.

MODELO: Juan escribió la carta.   La carta fue escrita por Juan.
                                   La carta está escrita.

1. Mi padre solicitó el puesto.   4. Mi hermana puso la mesa.
2. Mi tía concluyó los proyectos.   5. El estudiante abrió las ventanas.
3. José arregló todo eso.   6. Yo pagué la cuenta.

B. Usos del participio pasado, del participio presente y del pretérito
anterior de indicativo. Para expresar en español:

1. Continue (*pl.*) playing in the patio until I call you.   2. The students
are (gradually) learning some Spanish songs.   3. Robert was walking
(*progressive*) rapidly towards Jane's house.   4. As soon as they had
returned home, they sent for us.   5. By working six or eight hours, I
can finish this composition.   6. The composition written, I shall turn
it in to the teacher.   7. The exercises finished, I listened to some
Mexican records.   8. The trip of Louise and Inez was arranged by their
uncle.   9. Someone forgot to open the door; therefore, it was still
closed.   10. Richard, accompanied by some friends of his, was making
(*progressive*) plans for (the) vacation (*pl.*) in South America.

C. Usos del artículo y del pronombre neutro **lo.** Para expresar en
español:

1. The best thing is to leave for Argentina next week.
2. That matter of Robert seems very strange to me.
3. Come (*formal pl.*) to see us the soonest possible.
4. That is what Thomas and I intend to do.
5. Is Mr. López a musician? —Yes, he is.
6. Is Mary an art student? —No, she isn't.
7. Can you (*fam. sing.*) tell Barbara that? —Yes, I shall tell her (it).
8. Did he turn in the report? —I did not ask him (it).

D. Para contestar afirmativamente en español:

1. ¿Sabes jugar al golf?   2. ¿Puedes jugar conmigo hoy?   3. ¿Podrías
llevarle a Ana la bandeja?   4. ¿Deben Uds. escribirles a sus padres?
5. ¿Debieran Uds. visitar a sus tíos?   6. ¿Quisieran Uds. ir a México
este verano?   7. ¿Es posible que tu padre te ofrezca el dinero para ir

allá?   8. ¿Sería posible que él te lo ofreciera?   9. ¿Puede ser que tú consigas el puesto que deseas?   10. ¿Podría ser que tú lo consiguieras? 11. ¿Irá Ud. a la sierra si alguien le (la) invita?   12. ¿Iría Ud. a México si alguien le (la) invitara?

Resumen de palabras y expresiones

allá   there (*often after verbs of motion*)
animadamente   animatedly
conceder   to grant, give
concluir   to conclude, end, finish
contribuir   to contribute
el **Cuerpo de Paz**   Peace Corps
el **curso de orientación**   orientation course
depender (de)   to depend (on)
dirigir   to direct
en contacto con   in contact with
el **entendimiento**   understanding
entregar   to turn in, deliver
entusiasmar   to make enthusiastic, thrill, excite very much

el **futuro**   future
Hispanoamérica   Spanish America
mutuo, -a   mutual
la **nación** (*pl.* **naciones**)   nation
no sólo . . . sino que   not only . . . but
¿para qué sirven los amigos?   what are friends for?
poco a poco   little by little
la **posibilidad**   possibility
proponer (*like* **poner**)   to propose
el **proyecto**   project
sin duda   doubtless, without a doubt
solicitar   to solicit, apply for
útil   useful

LECTURA XII

Hispanoamérica en el último tercio del siglo XX (conclusión)

Con las reformas de los últimos años ha habido un aumento notable en las responsabilidades y obligaciones de los gobiernos hispanoamericanos. Algunos países han acelerado sus programas para satisfacer las aspiraciones del pueblo respecto de la educación, la sanidad,[1] la urbanización, etcétera. En pocos años se han construido miles de escuelas y de viviendas y se han distribuido miles de libros; muchos lugares ya tienen servicios de alcantarillado,[2] hospitales y centros de salud. Para realizar estas mejoras ha sido necesario introducir cambios en el sistema burocrático y, sobre todo, en el sistema tributario.[3] Los esfuerzos de las clases poderosas por retardar reformas como las citadas revelan uno de los puntos más débiles en la nueva estructuración de Hispanoamérica; se está emprendiendo un vasto programa social sin haber efectuado un cambio radical en la estructura de la sociedad.

No debemos olvidar que se presentan diversas etapas[4] de evolución económica y social en Hispanoamérica. En algunos países—México, Bolivia y Cuba—los procesos[5] revolucionarios han producido cambios radicales en la estructura social. En otros países van surgiendo diversos tipos de sociedades, caracterizados, en general, por una fuerte clase media, con ingresos relativamente elevados. Hay que reconocer, sin embargo, que la mayoría de los hispanoamericanos todavía viven bajo regímenes en que el poder y la riqueza se encuentran concentrados en pocas manos. Para asegurar el bienestar de los países hispanoamericanos y fortalecer el desarrollo de los sistemas democráticos, habrá que emprender una serie de reformas económicas y sociales que eliminen los privilegios y la discriminación, den énfasis a la movilidad social y proporcionen a las generaciones jóvenes la motivación suficiente para adquirir la preparación científica y técnica que necesiten para competir en la sociedad moderna.

[1] **sanidad,** *health, sanitation.* [2] **alcantarillado,** *sewage system.* [3] **tributario,** *of (pertaining to) taxation.* [4] **etapas,** *stages.* [5] **procesos,** *processes, progressive movements.*

Como ya hemos indicado, será difícil que los países hispanoamericanos puedan llevar a cabo[1] programas como los descritos si continúan dentro de sus estrechas fronteras actuales. La integración económica de Hispanoamérica es necesaria no sólo para estimular las relaciones comerciales, sino también para hacer posibles las vastas operaciones científicas y técnicas que habrá que emprender en el futuro—operaciones que sólo pueden ser realizadas por naciones de grandes recursos económicos. Sin la integración indicada, los países hispanoamericanos no podrán asumir el puesto que les corresponde en la comunidad de naciones.

Es grato observar que se han dado ya los primeros pasos[2] hacia la integración económica. La creación del Banco Centroamericano de Integración Económica, por ejemplo, ha estimulado las relaciones comerciales en Centroamérica. Un paso aún más importante ha sido el establecimiento, en 1960, por el Tratado de Montevideo, de la Asocia-

---

[1] **llevar a cabo,** *carry out.*   [2] **se han dado ya los primeros pasos,** *the first steps have already been taken.*

ción Latinoamericana de Libre Comercio, cuyo objeto es el libre comercio en la América latina. Se espera que el libre comercio acelere la industrialización y contribuya al desarrollo económico general, ampliando los mercados y estimulando las inversiones. Nueve naciones han aprobado el Tratado: la Argentina, el Brasil, Chile, Colombia, el Ecuador, México, el Perú, el Paraguay y el Uruguay. En conjunto,[1] forman uno de los mercados más importantes del mundo, con una población de más de 222 millones.

Entre las entidades internacionales que han contribuido a elevar el nivel de vida de Hispanoamérica y a fomentar el desarrollo económico general, la más importante es la Organización de los Estados Americanos (OEA). El resultado de un proceso evolutivo que se inició hace más de un siglo, la OEA fue creada, en su forma actual, en 1948 como un organismo regional dentro de las Naciones Unidas. Desde entonces la OEA ha cumplido sus objetivos de manera ejemplar,[2] manteniendo la paz entre sus miembros, esforzándose por resolver los problemas políticos, jurídicos, sociales y económicos de los respectivos países e impulsando su desarrollo económico, social y cultural.

Al concluir esta larga, pero incompleta, discusión, hay que insistir en el hecho de que los problemas que hemos descrito son nuestros también; las soluciones y remedios que encuentren los países hispanoamericanos afectarán sus relaciones con todas las naciones del mundo libre. Los Estados Unidos ha demostrado que quiere cooperar en la busca de dichas[3] soluciones—pero sin imponer condiciones y sin el papel dominante que ha dañado nuestras relaciones en el pasado. Es preciso que las dos Américas alcancen el máximo grado posible de cooperación y ayuda mutua.

Escriban un breve resumen, de unas ciento cincuenta palabras, de «Hispanoamérica en el último tercio del siglo XX (conclusión).»   *Ejercicio*

---

[1] **En conjunto,** *As a whole.*   [2] **de manera ejemplar,** *in an exemplary way.*   [3] **dichas,** *the aforementioned.*

CARTAS ESPAÑOLAS

In the following pages some of the essential principles for business and personal letters in Spanish will be given. Even though many formulas used in Spanish letters are less formal and flowery than formerly, in general they are still less brief and direct than in English letters, and at times they may seem rather stilted. No attempt is made to give a complete treatment of Spanish correspondence, but study of the material included should suffice for ordinary purposes.

The new words and expressions whose English equivalents are given in this section (including the **Vocabulario útil**, pages 283–284) are not listed in the Spanish–English vocabulary unless used elsewhere in the text. However, meanings are listed for words used in Exercises A, B, and C (page 284).

A. Address on the envelope

The title of the addressee begins with **señor (Sr.)**, **señora (Sra.)**, or **señorita (Srta.)**. **Sr. don (Sr. D.)** may be used for a man, **Sra. doña (Sra. Dª·)** for a married woman, and **Srta.** for an unmarried woman:

Señor don Carlos Morelos	**Sr. D. Pedro Ortega y Moreno**
Srta. Isabel Alcalá	**Sra. Dª. María López de Martín**

In the third example note that Spanish surnames often include the name of the father (**Ortega**), followed by that of the mother (**Moreno**). Often the mother's name is dropped (first two examples). A woman's married name is her maiden name followed by **de** and the surname of her husband (fourth example).

The definite article is not used with the titles **don** and **doña**, which have no English equivalents.

275

Two complete addresses follow:

Sr. D. Luis Montoya   Srta. Elena Pérez
Calle de San Martín, 25   Avenida Bolívar, 245
Santiago, Chile   Caracas, Venezuela

Business letters are addressed to a firm:

Suárez Hermanos (Hnos.)
Apartado (Postal) 867
Buenos Aires, Argentina

Señores (Sres.) López Díaz y Cía., S.A.
Paseo de la Reforma, 12
México, D.F., México

In an address in Spanish one writes first **Calle** (**Avenida**, *Avenue*; **Paseo**, *Boulevard*; **Camino**, *Road*; **Plaza**, *Square*) (**de**), then the house number. **Apartado** (**Postal**), *Post Office Box*, may be abbreviated to **Apdo.** (**Postal**); in Spanish America **Casilla postal** is commonly used for *Post Office Box*. The abbreviation **Cía.** = **Compañía**; **S.A.** = **Sociedad Anónima**, equivalent to English *Inc.* (*Incorporated*); and **D.F.** = **Distrito Federal**, *Federal District*.

Airmail letters are marked **Vía aérea, Correo aéreo**, or **Por avión**. Special delivery letters are marked **Urgente**, and registered letters, **Certificada**. Other directions on the envelope may be: **Particular**, *Private, Personal*; **Lista de correos**, *General Delivery*; **Para reexpedir**, (*Please*) *Forward*; **Impresos**, *Printed Matter*; **No doblar**, *Don't Fold*.

B. Heading of the letter

The usual form of the date line is:

México, D.F., 27 de enero de 1975

The month is usually not capitalized unless it is given first in the date. For the first day of the month, 1° (**primero**) is commonly used; the other days are written 2, 3, 4, etc. Other less common forms for the date line are:

Lima, Junio 15 de 1975
Bogotá, 1° agosto 1976

The address which precedes the salutation of the business and formal social letter is the same as that on the envelope. In familiar letters only the salutation need be used.

C. Salutations

Appropriate salutations for business letters or those addressed to strangers, equivalent to *My dear Sir, Dear Sir, Dear Madam, Gentlemen, etc.*, are:

Muy señor (Sr.) mío: (*from one person to one gentleman*)
Muy señores (Sres.) míos: (*from one person to a firm*)
Muy señor nuestro: (*from a firm to one gentleman*)
Muy señores nuestros: (*from one firm to another firm*)
Muy señora (Sra.) mía: (*from one person to a woman*)
Muy señorita (Srta.) nuestra: (*from a firm to a young woman*)

Formulas which may be used in less formal letters are:

Estimado(s) señor(es): Dear Sir (Gentlemen):
Distinguido(s) señor(es): Dear Sir (Gentlemen):
Muy estimado Sr. Salas: Dear Mr. Salas:
Mi distinguido amigo (colega): Dear Friend (Colleague):

Forms used in addressing relatives or close friends, equivalent to (*My*) *dear brother, friend, etc.*, are:

Querido hermano (Luis):   **(Mi) querida hija:**
Querida amiga mía: **Queridísima[1] mamá:**
Apreciado amigo: **Estimada amiga:**

Great care must be taken to be consistent in the agreement of salutations and conclusions in Spanish letters, keeping in mind whether the letter is addressed to a man, woman, or firm, and whether it is signed by one person or by an individual for a firm.

D. The body of business letters

The Spanish business letter usually begins with a brief sentence which

[1] **Queridísima,** *Dearest.*

indicates the purpose of the letter. Some examples, with English translations, follow. Note that the sentences cannot always be translated word for word:

Acabo (Acabamos) de recibir su carta del 10 de septiembre.
I (We) have just received your letter of September 10.
Le acusamos recibo de su atenta[1] del 2 del corriente . . .
We acknowledge receipt of your letter of the 2nd (of this month) . . .
He (Hemos) recibido con mucho agrado su amable carta . . .
I was (We were) very glad to receive your (good) letter . . .
Nos referimos a su favor de . . .
We are referring to your letter of . . .
Tenemos a la vista su carta de fecha 8 del actual . . .
We have (at hand) your letter of the 8th (of this month) . . .
Tengo (Tenemos) el honor de acusar recibo de la mercancía . . .
I am (We are) happy to acknowledge receipt of the merchandise . . .
Tenemos el placer de informar a usted[2] que . . .
We are pleased to inform you that . . .
Me (Nos) es grato comunicarle(s) que . . .
I am (We are) pleased to inform you that . . .
Rogamos a Uds. se sirvan[3] enviarnos a vuelta de correo . . .
We ask that you kindly send us by return mail . . .
Les agradeceremos se sirvan comunicarnos . . .
We shall be grateful if you will please let us know . . .
Mucho agradeceré a Ud. el mandarme . . .
I shall be very glad if you will send me . . .
Obra en mi (nuestro) poder su grata de 30 de marzo p. pdo.[4] . . .
I (We) have at hand your letter of March 30 . . .
Le doy a Ud. las gracias por el pedido que se sirvió hacerme . . .
Thank you for the order which you kindly placed with me . . .
Le envío giro postal por $30.00 . . .
I am sending you a postal money order for $30.00 . . .
Con fecha 8 del actual me permití escribir a usted, informándole . . .
On the 8th of this month I took the liberty of writing to you, informing you . . .

---

[1] **Carta** is often replaced with **favor, grata, atenta.**   [2] Since **usted** is technically a noun (coming from **vuestra merced,** *your grace*), the object pronoun **le** may be omitted. This practice is noted particularly in letter writing.   [3] After such verbs as **rogar, pedir, suplicar, esperar, agradecer** the relative **que** is often omitted.   [4] **p. pdo. = próximo pasado,** *last.*

Tengo el agrado de dirigirme a usted para agradecerle el envío de . . .

    I have the pleasure of writing to thank you for sending me . . .

En respuesta a su atenta carta del 15 del corriente, nos es grato remitirles adjunto lista de precios y condiciones de venta.

    In reply to your letter of the 15th, we are pleased to send you (enclosed) our price list and conditions of sale.

Le(s) ruego tenga(n) la bondad de indicarme, a la mayor brevedad posible, el precio de una habitación con una (dos) cama(s) con baño.

    Kindly let me know as soon as possible the price of a room with one (two) bed(s) and with bath.

Sírva(n)se reservarme para el 10 del corriente (del próximo) una habitación con dos camas y con baño. La estancia será de ocho días.

    Please reserve for me for the 10th of this month (of next month) a room with two beds and with bath. The length of stay will be for one week.

E. Conclusions

The Spanish conclusion usually requires more than a mere *Very truly yours*, or *Sincerely yours*. However, there is a tendency nowadays to shorten conclusions of business letters, particularly as correspondence continues with an individual or firm. Appropriate conclusions for business letters or those addressed to strangers are:

Queda[1] (Quedo) de Ud(s). atento y seguro servidor,
    I remain,
                  Sincerely (Respectfully) yours,
Aprovecho esta oportunidad para saludarle(s) atentamente,
    I am taking advantage of this opportunity to remain,
                          Sincerely yours,
Aprovechamos esta ocasión para ofrecernos sus attos.[2] y ss. ss.,
    We take advantage of this occasion to remain,
                          Sincerely yours,

---

[1] **Queda** is in the third person if the signee is the subject of the verb. Note similar use of other verbs in other examples.   [2] Abbreviations used in the conclusions given are: **atto.** = **atento; attos.** = **atentos; s. s.** or **S. S.** = **seguro servidor** (*sing.*), lit., *your servant*; **ss. ss.** or **SS. SS.** = **seguros servidores** (*pl.*); **afmo. (afma.)** = **afectísimo (afectísima),** *sincere(ly), affectionate(ly)*; **afmos. (afmas.)** = **afectísimos (afectísimas); atte.** = **atentamente.**

Me repito[1] su afmo. s. s. *or* **Nos repetimos sus afmos. ss. ss.,**
   I (We) remain,
                    Sincerely,
Quedamos de ustedes attos. y SS. SS.,
   We remain,
                    Very truly yours,
En espera de sus gratas noticias, les saluda atentamente,
   Awaiting the expected good news from you, I remain,
                              Sincerely,
Anticipándoles las gracias, nos reiteramos de Ud(s). atte.,
   Thanking you in advance, we remain,
                      Sincerely yours,
Les agradecemos su atención, y nos repetimos de Uds. attos. ss. ss.,
   We thank you for your attention (to the matter), and we remain,
                      Sincerely yours,
Le saludan (muy) atentamente,
   We are (remain),
                    Sincerely yours,

Some conclusions, with many possible variations, for informal social letters equivalent to *Cordially yours, Affectionately yours, etc.,* for members of the family are:

Suyo (Tuyo) afectísimo (afmo.) *or* **Suya (Tuya) afectísima (afma.),**
Suyos afectísimos (afmos.) *or* **Suyas afectísimas (afmas.),**
Queda (Quedo) suyo afmo. (suya afma.),
Le saluda cariñosamente[2] (muy atentamente),
Le saluda muy cordialmente (su servidor y amigo),
Se despide afectuosamente[3] (cordialmente),
(Con el cariño[4] de) tu buen amigo (buena amiga),
Cariñosos saludos[5] de tu amigo (amiga),
Sinceramente, Afectuosamente,
(Un abrazo[6] de) tu hijo, *(one boy signs)*
Tu hijo (hija), que te quiere, *(one boy or girl signs)*
Con todo el cariño de tu hermano (hermana),

---

[1] After the first letter (in which the verb **aprovechar** may have been used) **Me repito** is a good expression.   [2] **cariñosamente,** *affectionately.*   [3] **afectuosamente,** *affectionately.* [4] **cariño,** *affection.*   [5] **saludos,** *greetings.*   [6] **abrazo,** *embrace.*

Other phrases which may accompany these formulas are:

Dé (Da) mis mejores recuerdos a toda su (tu) familia,
   Give my best regards to all your family,
Salude afectuosamente de mi parte a sus padres,
   Give my affectionate (cordial) greetings to your parents,
Con mis mejores deseos para Ud. y los suyos, me despido,
   With my best wishes for you and your family, I am (remain),

F. Sample letters

The following letters translated freely from Spanish to English will
show how natural, idiomatic phrases in one language convey the same
idea in another. Read the following letters aloud for practice, and be
able to write either of them from dictation. The teacher may want to
test comprehension by asking questions in Spanish on the content of
the letters. At the end of this section are listed some words and phrases,
not all of which are used in the sample letters, which should be useful
in composing original letters.

1

12 de marzo de 1975

Librería de Porrúa Hnos. y Cía.
Apartado 7990
México, D.F., México

Muy señores míos:

   Tengo el gusto de avisarles a ustedes que acabo de recibir su atenta
del 8 del actual y el ejemplar de su catálogo con la lista de precios que
se sirvieron remitirme por separado.

   Sírvanse ustedes enviarme a la mayor brevedad posible la lista de
libros que envío anexa. También hallarán adjunto un cheque por pesos
96,40[1] en pago de la factura del 20 del pasado.

   Quedo de ustedes su atto. y S. S.,

---

[1] Read **noventa y seis pesos, cuarenta centavos**. While the comma between the **pesos** and
centavos has largely been replaced in Spanish by a period, it is still used. The English
comma is often written as a period in Spanish: **pesos 1.250,35.**

March 12, 1975

Porrúa Brothers and Co., Bookstore
Post Office Box 7990
Mexico City, Mexico

Gentlemen:

I am glad to inform you that I have just received your letter of
March 8 and the copy of your catalogue with the list of prices which you
kindly sent me under separate cover.

Please send me as soon as possible the list of books which I am including (in this letter). Also you will find enclosed a check for $96.40
(96.40 pesos) in payment of your bill of February 20 (of the 20th of last
month).

Sincerely yours,

2

16 de marzo de 1975

Muy señor nuestro:

Acusamos recibo de su favor del 12 del presente, en que hallamos
adjunto su cheque por pesos 96,40, que abonamos en su cuenta, y por
el cual le damos a usted las gracias.

Hoy le enviamos a vuelta de correo el pedido de libros que se sirvió
hacernos, cuyo importe cargamos en su cuenta.

En espera de sus nuevos gratos pedidos, nos repetimos sus afmos.
attos. y ss. ss.,

March 16, 1975

Dear Sir:

We acknowledge receipt of your letter of March 12, in which we
found enclosed your check for 96.40 pesos, which we are crediting to
your account, and for which we thank you.

Today we are sending by return mail the order for books which you
kindly sent us (made of us), the amount of which we are charging to
your account.

Awaiting other kind orders from you, we remain,

Sincerely yours,

Vocabulario útil

abonar   to credit
adjunto, -a   enclosed, attached
agradecer   to be grateful for, thank for
anexo, -a   enclosed, attached
aprovechar   to take advantage of
el buzón   mailbox
la cantidad   quantity, amount
cargar   to charge
la casa de correos   post office
el catálogo   catalogue
certificar   to register
comunicar   to inform, tell
dirigir   to address, direct
el ejemplar   copy
el envío   shipment, remittance
la estampilla   (postage) stamp (*Am.*)
la factura   bill, invoice
la firma   signature
el folleto   folder, pamphlet
el franqueo   postage
el gerente   manager
el giro   draft

grato, -a   kind, pleased
el importe   cost, amount
la muestra   sample
las noticias   news, information
ofrecer(se)   to offer, be, offer
  one's services
el pago   payment
el pasado   last month
el pedido   order
permitirse   to take the liberty (to)
el recibo   receipt
referir (ie, i)   to refer
referirse (ie, i) a   to refer to
remitir   to remit, send
rogar (ue)   to ask, beg
el saldo   balance
el sello   (postage) stamp (*Spain*)
servirse (i, i)   to be so kind as to
el sobre   envelope
la solicitud   request
suplicar   to beg, ask
el timbre   (postage) stamp (*Am.*)

a la mayor brevedad posible   as soon as possible
a las órdenes de Ud(s).   at your service
a vuelta de correo   by return mail
acusar recibo de   to acknowledge receipt of
al cuidado de (a/c)   in care of (c/o)
anticipar las gracias   to thank in advance
de acuerdo con   in compliance with
del corriente (actual)   of the present month
echar al correo   to mail
en contestación a   in reply to
en espera de   awaiting
en pago de   in payment of
en su cuenta   to one's account
estar encargado, -a de   to be in charge of

giro postal   money order
hacer un pedido   to place (give) an order
haga(n) Ud(s). el favor de + *inf.*   please + *verb*
lista de precios   price list
me repito (nos repetimos)   I (we) remain
(nos) es grato   (we) are pleased
nos place   we are pleased
paquete postal   parcel post
por separado   under separate cover
sírva(n)se + *inf.*   please + *verb*, be pleased to + *inf.*
tener el agrado (gusto, placer) de + *inf.*   to be pleased + *inf.*
tener la bondad de + *inf.*   to have the kindness to + *inf.*, please + *verb*

Ejercicios   **A.** Address envelopes to the following:

1. Mr. Richard Castillo
   10 Santa Ana Square
   Madrid 10, Spain

3. Professor George Medina
   Box 546
   Buenos Aires, Argentina

2. Mrs. Louis Ortiz
   25 Bolívar Avenue
   Lima, Peru

4. López Brothers
   45 Madero Street
   Mexico City, Mexico

B. Give the following date lines and salutations:

1. Buenos Aires, December 10, 1976; Dear Mr. Aguilar: 2. Bogotá,
January 1, 1974; Dear Mrs. Rivas: 3. La Paz, October 12, 1978; Dear
Miss Ortega: 4. Mexico City, July 14, 1970; Dear Mother: 5. Sevilla,
April 20, 1972; Dear Robert: 6. Barcelona, August 15, 1975; Dear
daughter:

C. Give in Spanish:

1. Dear Sir: (*from one person*)   2. Dear Sir: (*from a firm*)   3. Dear
Madam: (*from one person*)   4. Gentlemen: (*from one person*)
5. Gentlemen: (*from a firm*)   6. My dear Madam: (*to a young woman
from one person*)

D. Read in Spanish, then give in correct business English:

1. He recibido su atenta carta del 9 de octubre.
2. Acabo de recibir el libro que se sirvió usted enviarme.
3. Le doy a Ud. las gracias por el pedido que se sirvió hacerme.
4. Tengo el gusto de comunicarle que me fue muy grato recibir su atenta del 16 del corriente.
5. De acuerdo con su solicitud, le remitimos hoy . . .
6. Adjunta le remitimos una muestra.
7. Ruego a ustedes tengan la bondad de darme informes . . .
8. Su carta del 11 del corriente fue referida a nuestro gerente.
9. Tengo el gusto de referirme a su atenta carta del 31 del pasado.
10. Acusamos a usted recibo de su giro postal por la cantidad de . . .

E. Give approximate translations for the following conclusions and indicate whether the signature would be that of an individual or a firm:

1. Aprovecho esta oportunidad para quedar de usted como su afectísimo y s. s.,
2. Me pongo a las órdenes de ustedes para todo lo que pueda servirles,
3. En espera de sus noticias, quedo a sus órdenes y le saludo muy cordialmente,
4. Esperando poder servirles en otra ocasión, nos repetimos, atentamente,
5. Agradeciéndoles su atención, saluda a Uds. muy atentamente,

F. Suggestions for original letters in Spanish:

1. Write to a foreign student, describing some of your daily activities. Try to use words which you have had in this text or some previous text.
2. Write to a member of your family, describing some shopping you have done.
3. Assume that you are the Spanish secretary for an American exporting firm. Write a reply to a Spanish-American firm which has asked for a recent catalogue and prices.
4. Write to an individual, thanking him for his check, which has been received in payment of an invoice of a certain date. Give the balance which remains in his account.

LA PINTURA EN LA
AMÉRICA ESPAÑOLA

La nota característica del arte en la América hispana es la incorporación de elementos americanos a los estilos importados de Europa. Aun antes de la llegada de los españoles, las civilizaciones indígenas de América habían producido maravillosas obras de arte, como el *Mosaico de plumas*, hecho en el Perú, y la *Pintura azteca*, que se hallan reproducidos en las primeras páginas de esta sección.

Desde los primeros años del período colonial se cultivó la pintura tan intensamente en la América española como en Europa. Los focos más importantes de actividad artística fueron los virreinatos de la Nueva España (México) y del Perú y la región ecuatoriana.

El pintor Baltasar de Echave, de origen vasco, que emigró a México hacia 1590, es considerado como el fundador de la escuela mexicana. Su mejor obra existente es quizás la *Oración en el huerto*.[1] En el siglo XVIII se destacó el pintor mexicano Miguel Cabrera (1695–1768), que nació en Oaxaca. Entre otros cuadros excelentes, fue autor de *La Virgen y el Niño coronados* (1762). Es uno de los pintores mexicanos más populares.

Durante la primera mitad del siglo actual surgió la gran escuela muralista de México, que, con Diego Rivera, José Clemente Orozco y David Alfaro Siqueiros, ha florecido hasta nuestros días. En México la Revolución de 1910 ha servido de base para la obra artística de los pintores citados, que han producido una larga serie de pinturas murales que decoran las paredes de muchos edificios públicos. Las artes, las fiestas populares, la vida de los indios y las nuevas ideas sociales les han proporcionado una gran variedad de temas.

Las ideas sociales y políticas de Diego Rivera (1886–1957) le llevaron a hacer de la pintura un medio de propaganda para educar al pueblo. El hombre y el mundo contemporáneo son también el tema general de José Clemente Orozco (1883–1949), que se interesó especialmente por los aspectos más sórdidos y tristes de la vida mexicana. Se ha dicho que ningún otro pintor le ha superado en la expresión del aspecto eterno, humano y trágico de las luchas civiles de su país.

[1] **Oración en el huerto,** *Christ in the Garden* (lit., *Prayer in the Garden*).

Los temas revolucionarios adquieren un vigor extraordinario en las obras de Siqueiros (1898–1974), quien se ha esforzado por abrir nuevos caminos al muralismo. Ha experimentado con el uso de materiales nuevos, así como con la fusión de la pintura y la escultura.

El pintor mexicano Rufino Tamayo (1899–   ) representa una forma moderada del muralismo de su país, expresado en términos de valores universales.

Hacia 1920 empezó también en el Perú un movimiento indígena en el arte. Aunque se desarrolló bajo la influencia del muralismo mexicano, difiere de éste por su tono más moderado. José Sabogal (1888–1956), jefe de la nueva expresión artística de su país, ha buscado su inspiración en el paisaje, en los tipos indígenas y en las costumbres rurales del Perú, empleando como fondo los majestuosos Andes. Aunque también ha interpretado la vida por los ojos del indio, no se observa en sus obras la nota de propaganda, como en las de los artistas mexicanos.

Notables representantes de las corrientes artísticas de influencia europea en Hispanoamérica hoy día son el pintor guatemalteco Carlos Mérida (1893–   ), el cubano Wifredo Lam (1902–   ) y el uruguayo Joaquín Torres García (1874–1948). Mérida ha sido uno de los exponentes más importantes de la pintura abstracta en América. Lam desarrolla su obra en relación con los principios del surrealismo.

La contribución de Torres García ha sido la más importante en relación con las tendencias actuales. En 1928 llegó a crear un estilo nuevo, de formas rectangulares, basado en el principio de la acumulación de imágenes, por medio de las cuales aspiraba a expresar un simbolismo místico, de valor universal.

Hoy día el arte vanguardista es cultivado intensamente en muchos países de Hispanoamérica. En Chile, por ejemplo, el *Grupo Rectángulo*, fundado en 1954, por Ramón Vergara Grez (1923–   ), ha rechazado[1] el *informalismo* y las demás derivaciones de la pintura surrealista (las cuales aspiraban a acabar con todas las normas en el arte) y se esfuerza por dar un enfoque racionalista y un valor ético al arte. Desde 1963 el grupo se llama *Forma y Espacio* y hace concesiones al arte cinético.[2] Tendencias semejantes se encuentran en las producciones del venezolano Jesús Soto (1923–   ) y del argentino Eduardo Mac Entyre (1929–   ). Los dos buscan nuevas formas de expresar aspectos positivos e imaginativos de nuestra época tecnológica.

[1] **ha rechazado,** *has rejected.*   [2] **cinético,** *kinetic* (consisting in or depending upon motion).

Dos notables pintores mexicanos pueden representar las tendencias vanguardistas en su país: Pedro Friedeberg (1937–   ) y José Luis Cuevas (1934–   ). La precisión en la invención matemática, la nota de crítica social y la preocupación por lo sobrenatural son elementos importantes de su arte.

En nuestros días la vitalidad de las artes visuales en Hispanoamérica es extraordinaria. El hecho más importante es que el arte hispanoamericano ha dejado de ser nacional y se ha incorporado a la escena internacional.

Ejercicio oral   Para contestar en oraciones completas:

1. ¿Cuál es la nota característica del arte en la América hispana? 2. ¿Quién es considerado como el fundador de la escuela de pintura en México?   3. ¿Qué pintor mexicano se destacó en el siglo XVIII?

4. ¿Cuándo surgió la gran escuela muralista de México?   5. ¿Qué ha servido de base para la obra artística de los muralistas mexicanos? 6. ¿Qué hizo de la pintura Diego Rivera?   7. ¿Qué se ha dicho del pintor José Clemente Orozco?   8. ¿Cuáles son algunos caminos nuevos que Siqueiros ha tratado de abrir al muralismo?   9. ¿Qué representa el pintor mexicano Rufino Tamayo?

10. ¿En qué ha buscado su inspiración el pintor José Sabogal? 11. ¿Qué corrientes artísticas representan los pintores Mérida, Lam y Torres García?   12. ¿Cuál de ellos ha ejercido mayor influencia en relación con las tendencias actuales?   13. ¿Qué aspira a expresar Torres García por medio de las imágenes que acumula en sus cuadros?

14. ¿Dónde se fundó el *Grupo Rectángulo* y cómo se llama el grupo ahora?   15. ¿Qué aspectos de nuestro tiempo tratan de expresar los pintores Jesús Soto y Eduardo Mac Entyre?   16. ¿Cuáles son algunos elementos importantes de las obras de Pedro Friedeberg y de José Luis Cuevas?

Ejercicio escrito   Escriban un breve informe, de 120–150 palabras, sobre uno de los temas siguientes:

1. La pintura en la América española durante la época colonial.
2. La escuela muralista de México.
3. El arte vanguardista en Hispanoamérica.

LA PINTURA EN LA AMÉRICA ESPAÑOLA

CABEZA DE JAGUAR (detalle)
Mosaico de plumas, hecho en el Perú, hace novecientos años
Cortesía, The Brooklyn Museum
The A. Augustus Healy Fund
Fotografía de Andreas Feininger

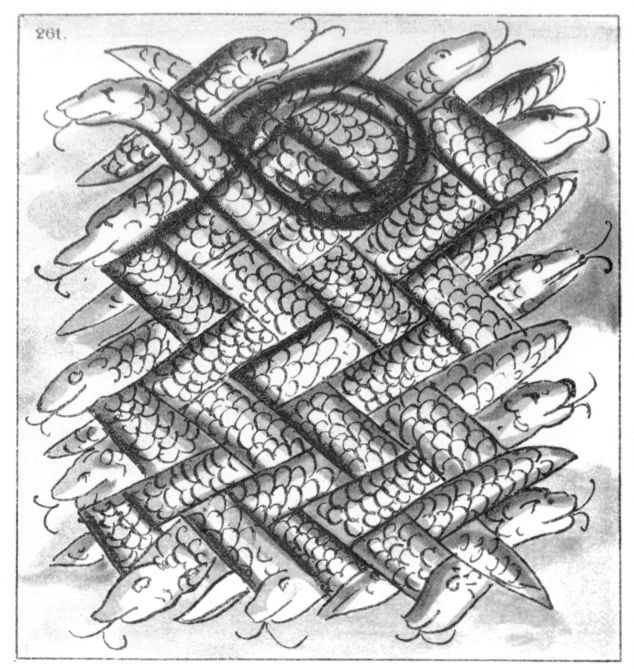

PINTURA AZTECA
Obra de un artista de la época prehispana
Cortesía, Biblioteca, Museo Nacional de Antropología e Historia, México, D. F.
Fotografía de Bradley Smith, New York

LA ORACIÓN EN EL HUERTO
Cortesía, Museo de San Carlos
Colección, Instituto Nacional de
Bellas Artes, México, D. F.

CABRERA

LA VIRGEN Y EL NIÑO CORONADOS, 1762
Cortesía, Philadelphia Museum of Art
Dr. Robert H. Lamborn Collection
Fotografía de Alfred J. Wyatt

Anónimo EL NACIMIENTO DE CRISTO
Cortesía, Instituto Nacional de Bellas Artes, México, D. F.

RIVERA

COMPOSICIÓN CON RELOJ, 1926-27
Cortesía, Museo Nacional de Bellas Artes,
Buenos Aires, Argentina

REVOLUCIÓN, GERMINACIÓN (mural), 1926-27
Cortesía, Escuela Nacional de Agricultura, Chapingo, México
Fotografía de Bradley Smith, New York

OROZCO

LAS SOLDADERAS, ca. 1930
Cortesía, Museo Nacional de Arte Moderno, Chapultepec, I.N.B.A., México, D. F.
Fotografía de Bradley Smith, New York

ECO DE UN GRITO, 1937

Collection, The Museum of Modern Art, New York. Gift of Edward M. M. Warburg

TAMAYO

VENDEDORAS DE FRUTAS, 1952
Cortesía, Albright-Knox Art Gallery,
Buffalo, New York
Gift of Seymour H. Knox

LA LLAMADA DE LA REVOLUCIÓN, 1935
Colección de Pascual Gutiérrez Roldán
Fotografía de Bradley Smith, New York

José Sabogal AGUADORAS (Water Bearers), 1951
Cortesía, San Francisco Museum of Art
Gift of Mr. and Mrs. Garfield Warner

ESTAMPA DEL «POPOL-VUH»
Fragmento del Capítulo XVI del Libro Sagrado
Cortesía, Carlos Mérida

EL JOVEN REY, 1936
Cortesía, Carlos Mérida
From the collection of Mr. and Mrs. Stanley Markus

EL PRESENTE ETERNO, 1944
Cortesía, Museum of Art, Rhode Island School of Design, Providence, R. I.

TORRES GARCÍA

ARTE CONSTRUCTIVO, 1942
Cortesía, Museo Nacional de Bellas Artes,
Buenos Aires, Argentina

1943 AMÉRICA, 1943
Cortesía, Museum of Art, Rhode Island
School of Design, Providence, R. I.

VERGARA GREZ

EL SOL EN LA LUNA, 1964
Cortesía, R. Vergara Grez y Antonio R. Romera,
Santiago, Chile

SIMETRÍA DINÁMICA
Cortesía, R. Vergara Grez y Antonio R. Romera,
Santiago, Chile

CURVAS INMATERIALES VERDES Y NEGRAS, 1966
(madera y metal)
Cortesía, Museum of Art, Rhode Island School of Design, Providence, R. I.

MAC ENTYRE

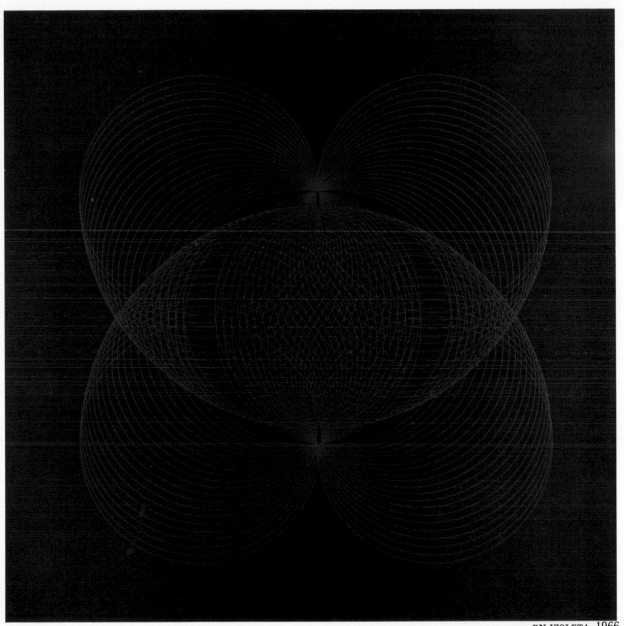

EN VIOLETA, 1966
Cortesía, Museum of Art, Rhode Island School of Design, Providence, R. I.

FRIEDEBERG

CONFESIONES DE UN ERIZO ICONOCLASTA
*Cortesía, Consejo Nacional de Turismo de México y
Galería Antonio Souza, México, D. F.*

CUEVAS

AUTORRETRATO
Cortesía, José Luis Cuevas y Galería de Arte Mexicano

APPENDICES

APPENDIX A

Pronunciation   ## The Spanish Alphabet

LETTER	NAME	LETTER	NAME	LETTER	NAME
a	a	j	jota	r	ere
b	be	k	ka	rr	erre
c	ce	l	ele	s	ese
ch	che	ll	elle	t	te
d	de	m	eme	u	u
e	e	n	ene	v	ve, uve
f	efe	ñ	eñe	w	doble ve
g	ge	o	o	x	equis
h	hache	p	pe	y	ye, i griega
i	i	q	cu	z	zeta

In addition to the letters used in the English alphabet, **ch, ll, ñ,** and **rr** represent single sounds in Spanish and are considered single letters. In dictionaries and vocabularies, words or syllables which begin with **ch, ll,** and **ñ** follow words or syllables that begin with **c, l,** and **n,** while **rr,** which never begins a word, is alphabetized as in English. **K** and **w** are used only in words of foreign origin. The names of the letters are feminine: **la be,** (*the*) *b*; **la jota,** (*the*) *j.*

The Spanish alphabet is divided into vowels (**a, e, i, o, u**) and consonants. The letter **y** is a vowel when final in a word, and when used as the conjunction **y,** *and.*

The Spanish vowels are divided into two groups: strong vowels (**a, e, o**) and weak vowels (**i, u**).

General Remarks. Definition of Phonetic Terms

Even though Spanish uses practically the same alphabet as English, few sounds are identical in the two languages. In describing the Spanish sounds, it will sometimes be necessary to make comparisons between the familiar English sounds and the unfamiliar Spanish ones in order to show how Spanish is pronounced. The student should avoid, of course, the use of English sounds in Spanish words; he should strive to follow the explanations of the text and imitate the pronunciation of the teacher and of the tapes.

In general, Spanish pronunciation is much clearer and more uniform than the English. The vowel sounds are clipped short and are not followed by the diphthongal glide which is commonly heard in English, as in *no* (*no*^{u}), *came* (*ca*^{i}*me*), *why* (*why*^{e}). Even unstressed vowels are pronounced clearly and distinctly; the slurred sound of English *a* in *fireman,* for example, never occurs in Spanish.

Spanish consonants, likewise, are usually pronounced more precisely and distinctly than English consonants, although a few (especially **b, d,** and **g** between vowels) are pronounced very weakly. Several of them (**t, d, l,** and **n**) are pronounced farther forward in the mouth, with the tongue close to the upper teeth and gums. The consonants **p, t,** and **c** (before letters other than **e** and **i**) are never followed by the *h* sound that is often heard in English: *pen* (*p*^{h}*en*), *task* (*t*^{h}*ask*), *can* (*c*^{h}*an*).

To allow for greater accuracy in the description of Spanish speech sounds, it will be helpful to be familiar with the phonetic terms explained in the following paragraphs:

Voiced and voiceless sounds. A sound is said to be voiceless when, during its articulation, the breath passes through the larynx without the vibration of the vocal cords. When the sound is accompanied by the vibration of the vocal cords, it is called voiced. All vowels are normally voiced sounds; consonants, however, may be voiced or voiceless.[1]

Stop and continuant consonants. A stop consonant is one in the making of which the passage of the air through the mouth is for a brief moment entirely stopped, after which the stoppage is released and the air is allowed to pass; such are the consonants in English *pat, cub, dog.* Continuants are consonants in the production of which there is a continuous passage of air and, consequently, a continuous sound, capable of being prolonged, such as the consonants in English *thief, save.*

Place of articulation. Sounds are also classified according to the position or place where the chief obstruction to the passage of the breath is made. If this obstruction is formed between the two lips, the sound is called bilabial: *p* in English *pen.* If the obstruction is made between the teeth, the sound is called interdental: English *th* in *thin.* If the tip

---

[1] The following Spanish consonants are normally voiced: **b, d, g, l, ll, m, n, ñ, r, rr, v, y.** One can easily learn to perceive the distinction between voiced and voiceless consonants by covering the ears with one's hands during the articulation of the sounds. After covering the ears, pronounce first, for example, the *z* of English *daze* and then the *ss* of English *hiss;* the distinction between voiced *z* and voiceless *ss* can be readily felt.

of the tongue forms the obstruction back of the teeth, the sound is called dental: **t** in Spanish **tú**. If the obstruction is formed at the alveolar ridge (that is, the ridge that covers the base of the upper teeth), the sound is called alveolar: *t* in English *ten*. If the obstruction is between the tongue and the hard palate, the sound is called palatal: *ch* in English *church*. If it is between the tongue and the soft palate or velum, the sound is called velar: *c* in English *cut*.

Division of Words into Syllables

Spanish words are hyphenated at the end of a line and are divided into syllables according to the following principles:

a. A single consonant (including **ch, ll, rr**) is placed with the vowel which follows: **pa-pel, mu-cho, ca-lle, pi-za-rra**.

b. Two consonants are usually divided: **tar-de, es-pa-ñol, tam-bién**. Consonants followed by **l** or **r**, however, are generally pronounced together and go with the following vowel: **li-bro, pa-dre, a-pren-do**. Exceptions are the groups **nl, rl, sl, tl, nr, sr: Car-los, En-ri-que**.

c. In combinations of three or more consonants, only the last consonant or the two consonants of the inseparable groups just mentioned (consonant plus **l** or **r**, with the exceptions listed) begin a syllable: **ins-pi-ra-ción, in-glés, en-tra**.

d. Two adjacent strong vowels (**a, e, o**) are in separate syllables: **le-o, tra-e, cre-e**.

e. Combinations of a strong and weak vowel (**i, u**) or of two weak vowels normally form single syllables. Such combinations of two vowels are called *diphthongs*. (See page 298 for further discussion of diphthongs.) Examples: **bue-nos, bien, es-tu-dio, gra-cias, ciu-dad, Luis**.

f. In combinations of a strong and weak vowel, a written accent mark on the weak vowel divides the two vowels into separate syllables: **dí-a, pa-ís, tí-o**. An accent on the strong vowel of such combinations does not result in two syllables: **lec-ción, tam-bién**.

Word Stress[1]

a. Most words which end in a vowel, or in **n** or **s** (plural endings of verbs and nouns, respectively), are stressed on the next to the last syllable: *cla*-se, *to*-mo, *ca*-sas, *en*-tran, *or*-den.

b. Most words which end in a consonant, except **n** or **s**, are stressed on the last syllable: **pro-fe-***sor,* **ha-***blar,* **pa-***pel,* **ciu-***dad,* **es-pa-***ñol.*

c. Words not pronounced according to these two rules have a written accent on the stressed syllable: **ca-***fé,* **in-***glés,* **lec-***ción,* **tam-***bién,* **lá-**piz.

The written accent is also used to distinguish between two words spelled alike but different in meaning (**si,** *if,* **sí,** *yes*; **el,** *the,* **él,** *he,* etc.) and on the stressed syllable of all interrogative words (**¿qué?** *what?*).

Vowels

a is pronounced between the *a* of English *ask* and the *a* of *father*: *ca*-sa, *ha*-bla, *A*-na.

e is pronounced like *e* in *café,* but without the glide sound that follows the *e* in English: *me*-sa, *cla*-se, us-*ted.*

i (y) is pronounced like *i* in *machine*: **Fe-***li*-pe, **sí,** *dí*-as, **y.**

o is pronounced like *o* in *obey,* but without the glide sound that follows the *o* in English: **no,** *so*-lo, cho-co-*la*-te.

u is pronounced like *oo* in *cool*: us-*ted,* *u*-no, a-*lum*-no.

The vowels **e** and **o** also have sounds like *e* in *let* and *o* in *for.* These sounds, as in English, generally occur when the **e** and **o** are followed by a consonant in the same syllable: *él, ser, son,* es-pa-*ñol.* In pronouncing the **e** in **él** and **ser** and the **o** in **son** and **español,** the mouth is opened wider and the distance between the tongue and the palate is greater than when pronouncing the **e** in **mesa** and **clase** and the **o** in **no** and **solo.** These more open sounds of **e** and **o** occur also in contact with the strongly trilled **r (rr),** before the **j** sound (written **g** before **e** or **i,** and **j**), and in the diphthongs **ei (ey)** and **oi (oy).** Pay close attention to the teacher's pronunciation of these sounds.

Consonants

b and **v** are pronounced exactly alike. Each has two different sounds,

[1] In this and the following four subsections the stressed syllable of Spanish examples is italicized.

a voiced stop sound and a voiced continuant sound. At the beginning of a breath-group (see page 299) or after **m** or **n** (also pronounced **m** in this case), whether within a word or between words, Spanish **b** (or **v**) is a voiced bilabial stop, similar to English *b* in *boy* but somewhat weaker: ***bien, bue**-nas, **va**-mos, **un va**-so.* In all other positions, it is a voiced bilabial continuant; the lips do not close completely, as in stop **b**, but allow the breath to pass between them through a very narrow passage: *li-bro,* **Cu**-ba, *no va*-mos. When between vowels, the articulation is especially weak. Avoid the English *v* sound. Note the two different sounds in **vi**-*vir,* be-*ber.*

c before **e** and **i**, and **z** in all positions, are pronounced like the English hissed *s* in *sent* in Spanish America and in southern Spain. In northern and central Spain this sound is like *th* in *thin.* Examples: **cen**-*ta*-vo, *ci*-ne, *gra*-cias.

c before all other letters, **k**, and **qu** are like English *c* in *cat,* but without the *h* sound that often follows the *c* in English: *ca*-sa, *cla*-se, ki-*ló*-me-tro, *que*-so, *par*-que. Note both sounds of **c** in *cin*-co, lec-*ción.*

ch is pronounced like English *ch* in *church*: *mu*-cho, *le*-che, cho-co-*la*-te.

d has two sounds, a voiced stop sound and a voiced continuant sound. At the beginning of a breath-group or when after **l** or **n**, Spanish **d** is a voiced dental stop, like a weak English *d*, but with the tip of the tongue touching the inner surface of the upper front teeth rather than the ridge above the teeth as in English: *dos, mun*-do, sal-*dré.* In all other cases the tongue drops even lower, and the **d** is pronounced as a voiced interdental continuant, like a weak English *th* in *this*: *ca*-da, *pa*-dre, *to*-do. The sound is especially weak in the ending **-ado** and when final in a word before a pause: es-*ta*-do, us-*ted,* Ma-*drid.*

f is pronounced like English *f*: ca-*fé,* Fe-*li*-pe.

g before **e** and **i**, and **j** in all positions, have no English equivalent. They are pronounced approximately like a strongly exaggerated *h* in *halt* (rather like the rasping German *ch* in *Buch*): *gen*-te, *hi*-jo, *Jor*-ge, re-*gión.* (The letter **x** in the words **México** and **mexicano,** spelled **Méjico** and **mejicano** in Spain, is pronounced like Spanish **j.**)

g in other positions, and **gu** before **e** or **i**, are pronounced alike. Each has two sounds, a voiced stop sound and a voiced continuant sound. At the beginning of a breath-group or when after **n**, Spanish **g** (written **gu** before **e** or **i**) is a voiced velar stop, like a weak English *g* in *go*: *gra*-cias, gui-*ta*-rra, *ten*-go. In all other cases, except before **e** or **i** in the groups **ge, gi,** Spanish **g** is a voiced velar continuant, that is, the sound is much weaker, and the breath continues to pass between the back of the tongue and the palate: a-*pa*-ga, *ha*-go, la gui-*ta*-rra. (In the combinations **gua**

and **guo** the **u** is pronounced like English *w* in *wet*: *a*-gua, *len*-gua, an-*ti*-guo; when the diaeresis is used over **u** in the combinations **güe, güi,** the **u** has the same sound: ver-*güen*-za, ni-ca-ra-*güen*-se.)

h is always silent: ha-*blar, ham*-bre, *hoy.*

l is pronounced like *l* in *leap*, with the tip and front part of the tongue well forward in the mouth: *Li*-ma, pa-*pel.*

ll is pronounced like *y* in *yes* in most of Spanish America and in some sections of Spain; in other parts of Spain it is somewhat like *lli* in *million*: *e*-lla, *ca*-lle, lla-*mar.*

m is pronounced like English *m*: *to*-ma, *me*-sa.

n is pronounced like English *n*: *no*, a-*pren*-den. Before **b, v, m,** and **p**, however, it is pronounced like *m*: *un-po*-co, con-*Bár*-ba-ra. Before **c, qu, g,** and **j** it is pronounced like English *n* in *sing*: *blan*-co, *ten*-go, con-Jua-*ni*-ta.

ñ is somewhat like the English *ny* in *canyon*: se-*ñor*, ma-*ña*-na, es-pa-*ñol*, ca-*ñón.*

p is pronounced like English *p*, but without the *h* sound that often follows the *p* in English: *pe*-lo, pa-*pel.*

q (always written with **u**): see page 296, under **c, k,** and **qu.**

r and **rr** represent two different sounds. Single **r**, except when initial in a word and when after **l, n,** or **s,** is a voiced, alveolar, single trill, that is, it is pronounced with a single tap produced by the tip of the tongue against the gums of the upper teeth. The sound is much like *dd* in *eddy* pronounced rapidly: *ca*-ra, *o*-ro, ha-*blar*. When initial in a word, when after **l, n,** or **s,** and when doubled, the sound is a multiple trill, the tip of the tongue striking the gums in a series of very rapid vibrations: *ri*-co, *ro*-jo, pi-*za*-rra, En-*ri*-que.

s is a voiceless, alveolar continuant, somewhat like the English hissed *s* in *sent*: *ca*-sa, *es*-tos. Before the voiced **b, d, g, l, ll, m, n, ñ, r, v,** and **y**, however, Spanish **s** becomes voiced and is pronounced like English *s* in *rose*: es-bo-*zar*, des-*gra*-cia, *mis*-mo, los *li*-bros, *es* ver-*dad.*

t is pronounced with the tip of the tongue touching the back of the upper front teeth (rather than the ridge above the teeth as in English); it is never followed by the *h* sound that is often heard in English: *to*-do, *tar*-des, *tiem*-po.

v: see pages 295–296, under **b.**

x is pronounced as follows: (1) before a consonant it is pronounced like Spanish **s**, that is, it is a voiceless alveolar continuant sound, similar to English hissed *s* in *sent*: ex-plo-*rar*, ex-tran-*je*-ro; (2) between vowels it is usually a double sound, consisting of a Spanish velar continuant **g** (as in *a*-gua) followed by a voiceless, hissed *s*: e-*xa*-men (eg-*sa*-men), *é*-xi-to (*ég*-si-to); (3) in a few words **x** may be pronounced **s** (a voiceless alveolar continuant sound) even between vowels, as in **e-***xac***-to, au-xi-***liar*** (and in words built on these words).

y is pronounced like a strong English *y* in *you*: ***ya, yo, ma***-yo. The conjunction **y**, *and*, when combined with the initial vowel of a following word, is similarly pronounced: *Car*-los-*y* **A**-na.

Diphthongs

As stated on page 294, the weak vowels **i** (**y**) and **u** may combine with the strong vowels **a, e, o,** or with each other to form single syllables. Such combinations of two vowels are called diphthongs. In diphthongs the strong vowels retain their full syllabic value, while the weak vowels, or the first vowel in the case of two weak vowels, lose part of their syllabic value.

As the first element of a diphthong, unstressed **i** is pronounced like a weak English *y* in *yes*, and unstressed **u** is pronounced like *w* in *wet*. The Spanish diphthongs which begin with unstressed **i** and **u** are: **ia, ie, io, iu; ua, ue, ui, uo,** as in *gra*-cias, *bien*, a-*diós*, ciu-*dad*; *cua*-tro, *bue*-no, *Luis*, an-*ti*-guo.

The diphthongs in which unstressed **i** and **u** occur as the second element of the diphthong are nine orthographically, but phonetically only six, since **i** and **y** have the same sound here. They are: **ai, ay; au; ei, ey; eu; oi, oy; ou.** They are pronounced as follows:

> **ai, ay** like a prolonged English *i* in *mine*: *bai*-le, *hay*
>
> **au** like a prolonged English *ou* in *out*: *au*-tor, *cau*-sa
>
> **ei, ey** like a prolonged English *a* in *fate*: *seis*, *ley*
>
> **eu** has no close equivalent in English. It consists of a clipped *e*, as in English *eh*, followed closely by a glide sound which ends in *oo*, to sound like *ehoo*: **Eu**-*ro*-pa
>
> **oi, oy** like a prolonged English *oy* in *boy*: *sois*, *soy*
>
> **ou** like a prolonged English *o* in *note*: lo **u**-*sa*-mos

Remember that two adjacent strong vowels within a word do not combine in a single syllable, but form two separate syllables: *le*-e, **Do**-ro-*te*-a. Likewise, when a weak vowel adjacent to a strong vowel has a written accent, it retains its syllabic value and forms a separate syllable: *dí*-a, pa-*ís*. An accent mark on a strong vowel merely indicates stress: lec-*ción*, tam-*bién*.

Triphthongs

A triphthong is a combination in a single syllable of a stressed strong vowel between two weak vowels. Four combinations are of frequent use: **iai, iei, uai (uay), uei (uey)**, as in **es-tu-*diáis*, Pa-ra-*guay*.** To indicate the mew of a cat and the bark of a dog the triphthongs **iau** and **uau** occur: *miau, guau.* In linking vowels between words, four and five vowels may be pronounced in one syllable.

Linking of Words

In reading or speaking Spanish, words are linked together, as in English, so that two or more may sound as one long word. These groups of words are called breath-groups. The pronunciation of certain Spanish consonants depends upon their position at the beginning of, or within, a breath-group. Similarly, the pronunciation of many individual sounds will be modified depending on the sounds with which they are linked within the breath-group. Since the words that make up the breath-group are pronounced as if they formed one long word, the principles which govern the structure of the syllable must be observed throughout the entire breath-group.

In speech, words normally are uttered in breath-groups. Thus it is necessary to practice pronouncing phrases and even entire sentences without a pause between words. Frequently a short sentence will be pronounced as one breath-group, while a longer one may be divided into two or more groups. The meaning of what is being pronounced will help you to determine where the pauses ending the breath-groups should be made.

The following examples illustrate some of the general principles of linking. The syllabic division in parentheses shows the correct linking; the syllable or syllables italicized bear the main stress.

a. Within a breath-group the final consonant of a word is joined with the initial vowel of the following word and forms a syllable with it: **el alumno (e-la-*lum*-no).**

b. Within a breath-group when two identical vowels of different words come together, they are pronounced as one: **el profesor de español (el-pro-fe-*sor*-de es-pa-*ñol*).**

c. When unlike vowels between words come together within a breath-group, they are usually pronounced together in a single syllable. Two cases occur: (1) when a strong vowel is followed or preceded by a weak vowel, both are pronounced together in a single syllable and the result is phonetically a diphthong (see page 298): **su amigo** (su a-*mi*-go), **Juan y Elena** (*Jua*-n y E-*le*-na), **mi padre y mi madre** (mi-*pa*-dre y-mi-*ma*-dre); (2) if both vowels are strong, each loses a little of its syllabic value and both are pronounced together in one syllable: **vamos a la escuela** (*va*-mo-sa-la es-*cue*-la); **¿Cómo está usted?** (*¿Có*-mo es-*tá us-ted*?).

Intonation

The term intonation refers to the variations in pitch which occur in speech. Every language has its characteristic patterns of intonation. The intonation of Spanish is quite different from that of English.

The alternate rise and fall of the pitch depends upon the particular meaning of the sentence, the position of stressed syllables, and whether the sentence expresses command, affirmation, interrogation, exclamation, request, or other factors. In general, three meaningful levels of pitch can be distinguished in Spanish: one below the speaker's normal pitch (level 1); the speaker's normal tone (level 2), and a tone higher than the normal one (level 3). With respect to the use of these levels, the following basic principles should be observed:

a. At the beginning of a breath-group the voice begins and continues in a relatively low pitch (level 1) as long as the first accented syllable is not reached.

b. When the first accented syllable of a breath-group is reached, the voice rises to the speaker's normal tone (level 2) and continues in the same pitch as long as the last accented syllable is not reached.

c. When the last accented syllable of the breath-group is reached, the voice falls or rises, depending on the following circumstances:

(1) At the end of a declarative statement, the voice falls to a pitch even lower than that of the initial unaccented syllable or syllables.
(2) At the end of an interrogative sentence, or of an incomplete sentence interrupted by a pause, the voice rises to a pitch above the normal tone (level 3).

d. In exclamations, and in questions which begin with an interrogative word, the voice begins in a pitch above the normal tone (level 3) and gradually falls in the following syllables as long as the final accented syllable is not reached; when the last accented syllable is reached, the voice falls to a pitch even lower than that of the initial unaccented syllable or syllables, as in the case of the end of a simple declarative sentence, unless special interest or courtesy is intended, in which case the voice rises to the normal tone or even higher.

Examples

Declarative statement

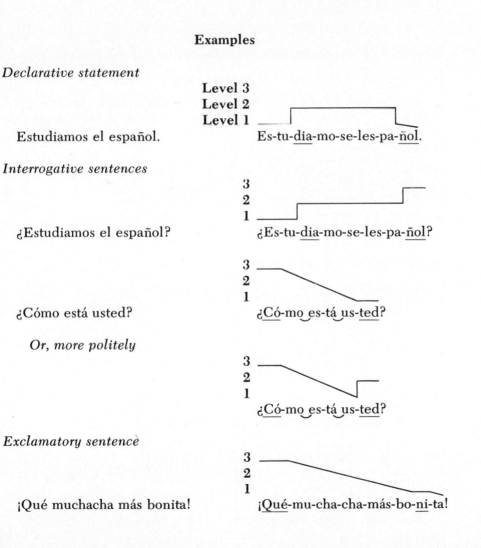

Level 3
Level 2
Level 1

Estudiamos el español.   Es-tu-dia-mo-se-les-pa-ñol.

Interrogative sentences

3
2
1

¿Estudiamos el español?   ¿Es-tu-dia-mo-se-les-pa-ñol?

3
2
1

¿Cómo está usted?   ¿Có-mo es-tá us-ted?

Or, more politely

3
2
1

¿Có-mo es-tá us-ted?

Exclamatory sentence

3
2
1

¡Qué muchacha más bonita!   ¡Qué-mu-cha-cha-más-bo-ni-ta!

Or, with special interest

```
3  _____
2          \
1           \____┐ ┌____
             ¡Qué-mu-cha-cha-más-bo-ni-ta!
```

For additional remarks on Spanish intonation, particularly in a series or enumeration, and for additional intonation patterns, see pages 26–27, 57–58, and 176–177.

Punctuation

Spanish punctuation is much the same as English. The most important differences are:

1. Inverted question marks and exclamation points precede questions and exclamations. They are placed at the actual beginning of the question or exclamation, not necessarily at the beginning of the sentence:

¿Hablan Carlos y Juan?   Are Charles and John talking?
¡Qué muchacha más bonita!   What a pretty girl!
Usted es español, ¿verdad?   You are a Spaniard, aren't you?

2. In Spanish a comma is not used between the last two words of a series, while in English it usually is:

Tenemos plumas, libros y lápices.   We have pens, books, and pencils.

3. A dash is generally used instead of quotation marks to denote a change of speaker in dialogue. It appears at the beginning of each speech, but is omitted at the end:

—¿Es usted peruano?   "Are you a Peruvian?"
—Sí, señor. Soy de Lima.   "Yes, sir. I am from Lima."

If Spanish quotation marks are used, they are placed on the line, as in the example which follows. In current practice English quotation marks are widely used in Spanish:

Juan dijo: «Pasen ustedes.»   John said, "Come in."

Only proper names and the first word of a sentence begin with a capital **Capitalization** letter in Spanish. The subject pronoun **yo** (*I* in English), names of months and days of the week, adjectives of nationality and nouns formed from them, and titles (unless abbreviated) are not capitalized. In titles of books or works of art, only the first word is ordinarily capitalized:

Juan y yo hablamos.   John and I are talking.
Hoy es lunes.   Today is Monday.
Buenos días, señor (Sr.) Pidal.   Good morning, Mr. Pidal.
Son españoles.   They are Spanish.
El sol en la luna   The Sun in the Moon

APPENDIX B

Frases para la clase (*Classroom Expressions*)

A number of expressions and grammatical terms which may be used in the classroom and laboratory are listed below. They are not included in the end vocabularies unless used in the preceding lessons. Other common expressions are used in the text.

Voy a pasar lista.	I am going to call the roll.
Presente.	Present.
¿Qué lección tenemos hoy?	What lesson do we have today?
Tenemos la Lección primera (dos).	We have Lesson One (Two).
¿En qué página empieza?	On what page does it begin?
¿Qué línea (renglón)?	What line?
(La lectura) empieza en la página . . .	(The reading) begins on page . . .
Al principio de la página . . .	At the beginning of (the) page . . .
En el medio (Al pie) de la página . . .	In the middle (At the bottom) of (the) page . . .
Abra(n) usted(es) el (los) libro(s).	Open your book(s).
Cierre(n) usted(es) el (los) libro(s).	Close your book(s).
Lea usted en español.	Read in Spanish.
Empiece usted a leer.	Begin to read.
Siga usted leyendo.	Continue (Go on) reading.
Traduzca usted al español (inglés) . . .	Translate into Spanish (English) . .
Repita usted la frase modelo.	Repeat the model sentence.
Pronuncie usted . . .	Pronounce . . .
Basta.	That is enough, That will do.
Conteste(n) (la pregunta) en español.	Answer (the question) in Spanish.
Vaya(n) usted(es) *or* Pase(n) usted(es) a la pizarra.	Go to the (black)board.
Escuche(n) las instrucciones.	Listen to the directions.
Escriba(n) usted(es) (al dictado).	Write (at dictation).
Usted ha hecho una falta (un error).	You have made a mistake.

Corrija(n) usted(es) la falta.	Correct the mistake.
Borre(n) usted(es) la frase.	Erase the sentence.
Vuelva(n) usted(es) a su(s) asiento(s).	Return to your seat(s).
Siénte(n)se usted(es).	Sit down, Be seated.
Haga(n) usted(es) el favor de (+ *inf.*) . . .	Please (+ *verb*) . . .
Está bien.	All right, That's fine.
¿Qué significa (quiere decir) la palabra . . .?	What does the word . . . mean?
¿Quién quiere hacer una pregunta?	Who wants to ask a question?
¿Cómo se dice . . .?	How does one (do you) say . . .?
Escuche(n) usted(es) bien.	Listen carefully.
Preste(n) usted(es) atención.	Pay attention.
Prepare(n) usted(es) para mañana . . .	Prepare for tomorrow . . .
Ha sonado el timbre.	The bell has rung.
La clase ha terminado.	The class has ended.
Ustedes pueden marcharse.	You may leave (You are excused).

Palabras y expresiones para el laboratorio (*Words and Expressions for the Laboratory*)

el alto parlante	loudspeaker
la audición	playback
los auriculares (audífonos)	ear(head)phones
la cabina	booth
el carrete	reel
la cinta maestra (matriz)	master tape
la cinta (magnetofónica)	(magnetic) tape
la corriente (eléctrica)	power; (electric) current
el disco (fonográfico)	disc, (phonograph) record
empalmar	to splice
el enchufe	plug
la entrada	input
externo, -a	external
la grabadora (de cinta)	(tape) recorder
grabar	to record
el interruptor	switch
el micrófono	microphone
la perilla	knob
reparar	to repair
la salida	output

| el sonido | sound |
| el volumen | volume |

Acérquese (Ud.) más al micrófono.	Get closer to the microphone.
Aleje más el micrófono.	Move the microphone away from you.
Apriete el botón.	Push the button.
Aumente el volumen.	Turn it louder (Increase the volume).
Cuelgue los auriculares.	Hang up the headphones.
Empuje el interruptor hacia la derecha (la izquierda).	Push the switch to the right (left).
Escuche la grabación.	Listen to the recording.
Hable en voz más alta (más baja, natural).	Speak in a louder (lower, natural) voice.
Hable más rápido (despacio).	Speak faster (slower).
Imite usted lo que oiga.	Imitate what you hear.
Mi máquina no funciona.	My machine does not work.
Pare (Apague) su máquina.	Stop (Turn off) your machine.
Ponga en marcha (Encienda) . . .	Start (Turn on) . . .
Póngase (Quítese) los audífonos.	Put on (Take off) your headphones.
Repita usted la respuesta.	Repeat the answer.
Se oirá (Usted oirá) cada frase una vez (dos veces), seguida de una pausa.	You will hear each sentence once (twice), followed by a pause.
Se oirá (Usted oirá) luego la respuesta (correcta).	You will hear the (correct) answer later.
¿Se oye la señal claramente?	Is the signal clear?
Vuelva a enrollar la cinta.	Rewind the tape.

Términos gramaticales (*Grammatical Terms*)

el adjetivo	adjective
demostrativo	demonstrative
posesivo	possessive
el adverbio	adverb
el artículo	article
definido	definite
indefinido	indefinite
el cambio ortográfico	change in spelling
la capitalización	capitalization
la cláusula	clause

la comparación	comparison
el comparativo	comparative
el complemento	object
directo	direct
indirecto	indirect
la composición	composition
la concordancia	agreement
la conjugación	conjugation
la conjunción	conjunction
la consonante	consonant
el diptongo	diphthong
el género	gender
femenino	feminine
masculino	masculine
el gerundio	gerund, present participle
el infinitivo	infinitive
la interjección	interjection
la interrogación	interrogation, question
la letra	letter (*of the alphabet*)
mayúscula	capital
minúscula	small
el modo indicativo (subjuntivo)	indicative (subjunctive) mood
el nombre propio	proper noun
el nombre (substantivo)	noun (substantive)
el número	numeral, number
cardinal (ordinal)	cardinal (ordinal)
el objeto	object
directo	direct
indirecto	indirect
la palabra (negativa)	(negative) word
las partes de la oración	parts of speech
el participio pasado (presente)	past (present) participle
la persona	person
primera	first
segunda	second
tercera	third
el plural	plural
la posición	position
el predicado	predicate
la preposición	preposition

el pronombre	pronoun
interrogativo	interrogative
personal	personal
relativo	relative
la puntuación	punctuation
el radical (la raíz)	stem
el significado	meaning
la sílaba	syllable
penúltima	next to last
última	last
el singular	singular
el subjuntivo	subjunctive
el sujeto	subject
el superlativo (absoluto)	(absolute) superlative
la terminación	ending
el tiempo	tense
el tiempo simple (compuesto)	simple (compound) tense
presente	present
imperfecto	imperfect
pretérito	preterit
futuro	future
condicional	conditional
perfecto	perfect (present perfect)
pluscuamperfecto	pluperfect, past perfect
pretérito anterior	preterit perfect
futuro perfecto	future perfect
condicional perfecto	conditional perfect
el triptongo	triphthong
el verbo	verb
auxiliar	auxiliary
impersonal	impersonal
(in)transitivo	(in)transitive
irregular	irregular
reflexivo	reflexive
regular	regular
la vocal	vowel
la voz	voice
activa	active
pasiva	passive

, coma
; punto y coma
: dos puntos
. punto final
. . . puntos suspensivos
¿ ? signo(s) de interrogación
¡ ! signo(s) de admiración

( ) (los) paréntesis
« » comillas
´ acento escrito
¨ (la) diéresis
˜ (la) tilde
– (el) guión
— raya

Signos de puntuación (*Punctuation Marks*)

adj.	adjective	*m.*	masculine
adv.	adverb	*Mex.*	Mexico
Am.	America	*obj.*	object
cond.	conditional	*part.*	participle
conj.	conjunction	*perf.*	perfect
dir.	direct	*pl.*	plural
e.g.	for example	*p.p.*	past participle
etc.	and so forth	*prep.*	preposition
f.	feminine	*pres.*	present
fam.	familiar	*pret.*	preterit
i.e.	that is	*pron.*	pronoun
imp.	imperfect	*reflex.*	reflexive
ind.	indicative	*sing.*	singular
indef.	indefinite	*subj.*	subjunctive
indir.	indirect	*trans.*	transitive
inf.	infinitive	*U.S.*	United States
lit.	literally	*aux.*	auxiliary

Abreviaturas y signos (*Abbreviations and Signs*)

( ) Words in parentheses are explanatory or they are to be translated in the exercises.

— In the general vocabularies a dash indicates a word repeated, while in the exercises it usually is to be supplied by some grammatical form.

+ = followed by.

APPENDIX C

Cardinal Numerals

0	cero	30	treinta
1	un(o), una	31	treinta y un(o), -a
2	dos	40	cuarenta
3	tres	50	cincuenta
4	cuatro	60	sesenta
5	cinco	70	setenta
6	seis	80	ochenta
7	siete	90	noventa
8	ocho	100	ciento (cien)
9	nueve	101	ciento un(o), ciento una
10	diez		
11	once	110	ciento diez
12	doce	200	doscientos, -as
13	trece	300	trescientos, -as
14	catorce	400	cuatrocientos, -as
15	quince	500	quinientos, -as
16	diez y seis (dieciséis)	600	seiscientos, -as
17	diez y siete (diecisiete)	700	setecientos, -as
18	diez y ocho (dieciocho)	800	ochocientos, -as
19	diez y nueve (diecinueve)	900	novecientos, -as
20	veinte	1.000	mil
21	veinte y un(o), -a (veintiún, veintiuno, veintiuna)	1.020	mil veinte
		1.500	mil quinientos, -as
22	veinte y dos (veintidós)	2.000	dos mil
23	veinte y tres (veintitrés)	100.000	cien mil
24	veinte y cuatro (veinticuatro)	200.000	doscientos, -as mil
25	veinte y cinco (veinticinco)	1.000.000	un millón (de)
26	veinte y seis (veintiséis)	2.000.000	dos millones (de)
27	veinte y siete (veintisiete)	2.500.000	dos millones quinientos, -as mil
28	veinte y ocho (veintiocho)		
29	veinte y nueve (veintinueve)		

Uno and numerals ending in **uno** drop **-o** before a masculine noun; **una** is used before a feminine noun: **un soldado,** *one soldier;* **treinta y un muchachos,** *thirty-one boys;* **veinte y una repúblicas,** *twenty-one republics.*

   Ciento becomes **cien** before nouns and before **mil** and **millones:** **cien dólares,** *one hundred dollars;* **cien mil habitantes,** *one hundred thousand inhabitants.*

Un is regularly not used with **cien(to)** and **mil: mil estudiantes,** *1,000 students*; however, one must say **ciento un mil habitantes,** *101,000 inhabitants.* Un is used with the noun **millón,** which requires **de** when a noun follows: **un millón de dólares,** *$1,000,000.* For *$2,000,000* one says **dos millones de dólares.**

The hundreds agree with a feminine noun: **doscientas muchachas,** *200 girls*; **quinientas cincuenta palabras,** *550 words.* Beyond nine hundred **mil** must be used in counting: **mil novecientos setenta,** *1970.*

Regardless of the English use of *and* in numbers, **y** is regularly used in Spanish only between multiples of ten and numbers less than ten: **diez y seis,** *16*; **noventa y nueve,** *99*; but **seiscientos seis,** *606.*

From 16 through 19, and 21 through 29, the numerals are often written as one word: **dieciséis,** *16.* Note that an accent mark must also be written on the forms **veintiún, veintidós, veintitrés, veintiséis.** Above 29, the one-word forms are not used.

In writing numerals in Spanish a period is often used where a comma is used in English, and a comma is used for the decimal point: *$1.500,75.* In current commercial practice, however, the English method is being used more and more.

Ordinal Numerals

1st **primero (primer), -a**	4th **cuarto, -a**	8th **octavo, -a**
2nd **segundo, -a**	5th **quinto, -a**	9th **noveno, -a**
3rd **tercero (tercer), -a**	6th **sexto, -a**	10th **décimo, -a**
	7th **séptimo, -a**	

Ordinal numerals agree in gender and number with the nouns they modify. **Primero** and **tercero** drop final **-o** before a masculine singular noun: **el primer (tercer) edificio,** *the first (third) building,* but **los primeros días,** *the first days,* **la tercera parte,** *the third part (one-third).*

The ordinal numerals may precede or follow the noun. Contrast the following:

	Lección primera	Lesson One (I)
	el capítulo tercero	Chapter Three
	la Calle Cuarta	Fourth Street
But:	**la primera lección**	the first lesson
	el tercer capítulo	the third chapter
	la cuarta calle	the fourth street

A cardinal number precedes an ordinal when both are used together: **las tres primeras páginas,** *the first three pages.* (Note that Spanish says *the three first,* not *the first three* as in English.)

With titles, chapters of books, volumes, etc., ordinal numerals are normally used through *tenth*. For higher numerals, they are regularly replaced by the cardinal numerals; in these cases all numerals follow the noun. With names of rulers and popes the definite article is omitted in Spanish:

Felipe Segundo	Philip II (the Second)
la página sesenta	page 60
el tomo segundo	Volume Two
el siglo veinte	the twentieth century

Days of the Week

domingo	Sunday		**jueves**	Thursday
lunes	Monday		**viernes**	Friday
martes	Tuesday		**sábado**	Saturday
miércoles	Wednesday			

Months

enero	January		**julio**	July
febrero	February		**agosto**	August
marzo	March		**septiembre**	September
abril	April		**octubre**	October
mayo	May		**noviembre**	November
junio	June		**diciembre**	December

Seasons

la primavera	spring		**el otoño**	fall, autumn
el verano	summer		**el invierno**	winter

Dates

In expressing dates the ordinal numeral **primero** is used for the *first* (day of the month), and the cardinals are used in all other cases. The definite article translates *the, on the,* with the day of the month. (Remember that the definite article translates *on* with a day of the week: **Yo saldré el lunes,** *I shall leave* [*on*] *Monday.*)

Hoy es el primero de enero.   Today is the first of January (January 1).
Nació el dos de mayo.   He was born (on) the second of May (May 2).

A complete date is expressed:

el diez de abril de mil novecientos setenta y cinco   April 10, 1975

¿Qué hora es (era)?   What time is (was) it?

Time of Day

Es (Era) la una.   It is (was) one o'clock.

Son (Eran) las dos.   It is (was) two o'clock.

Es la una y cuarto (media).   It is a quarter after one (half-past one).

Son las nueve menos diez de la mañana.   It is ten minutes before
   nine A.M. (in the morning).

Son las tres de la tarde en punto.   It is three P.M. (in the afternoon)
   sharp.

Eran las ocho de la noche.   It was eight at night (in the evening).

Ella saldrá a la una (a las cuatro).   She will leave at one (at four)
   o'clock.

Acaba de dar la una.   It has just struck one.

Ya han dado las dos.   It has already struck two.

Faltan diez minutos para las once.   It is ten minutes to eleven.

Estarán aquí hasta las cinco.   They will be here until five.

Yo trabajo desde las ocho hasta las doce.   I work from eight until
   twelve.

APPENDIX D

Regular Verbs

INFINITIVE

tomar, *to take*	**comer,** *to eat*	**vivir,** *to live*

PRESENT PARTICIPLE

tomando, *taking*	**comiendo,** *eating*	**viviendo,** *living*

PAST PARTICIPLE

tomado, *taken*	**comido,** *eaten*	**vivido,** *lived*

The Simple Tenses

Indicative Mood

PRESENT

I take, do take, am taking, etc.	*I eat, do eat, am eating, etc.*	*I live, do live, am living, etc.*
tomo	como	vivo
tomas	comes	vives
toma	come	vive
tomamos	comemos	vivimos
tomáis	coméis	vivís
toman	comen	viven

IMPERFECT

I was taking, used to take, took, etc.	*I was eating, used to eat, ate, etc.*	*I was living, used to live, lived, etc.*
tomaba	comía	vivía
tomabas	comías	vivías
tomaba	comía	vivía
tomábamos	comíamos	vivíamos
tomabais	comíais	vivías
tomaban	comían	vivían

PRETERIT

I took, did take, etc.	*I ate, did eat, etc.*	*I lived, did live, etc.*
tomé	comí	viví
tomaste	comiste	viviste
tomó	comió	vivió
tomamos	comimos	vivimos
tomasteis	comisteis	vivisteis
tomaron	comieron	vivieron

FUTURE

I shall (will) take, etc.	*I shall (will) eat, etc.*	*I shall (will) live, etc.*
tomaré	comeré	viviré
tomarás	comerás	vivirás
tomará	comerá	vivirá
tomaremos	comeremos	viviremos
tomaréis	comeréis	viviréis
tomarán	comerán	vivirán

CONDITIONAL

I should (would) take, etc.	*I should (would) eat, etc.*	*I should (would) live, etc.*
tomaría	comería	viviría
tomarías	comerías	vivirías
tomaría	comería	viviría
tomaríamos	comeríamos	viviríamos
tomaríais	comeríais	viviríais
tomarían	comerían	vivirían

Subjunctive Mood

PRESENT

(that) I may take, etc.	*(that) I may eat, etc.*	*(that) I may live, etc.*
tome	coma	viva
tomes	comas	vivas
tome	coma	viva
tomemos	comamos	vivamos
toméis	comáis	viváis
tomen	coman	vivan

-ra IMPERFECT

(that) I might take, etc.	*(that) I might eat, etc.*	*(that) I might live, etc.*
tomara	comiera	viviera
tomaras	comieras	vivieras
tomara	comiera	viviera
tomáramos	comiéramos	viviéramos
tomarais	comierais	vivierais
tomaran	comieran	vivieran

-se IMPERFECT[1]

(that) I might take, etc.	*(that) I might eat, etc.*	*(that) I might live, etc.*
tomase	comiese	viviese
tomases	comieses	vivieses
tomase	comiese	viviese
tomásemos	comiésemos	viviésemos
tomaseis	comieseis	vivieseis
tomasen	comiesen	viviesen

Imperative

take	*eat*	*live*
toma (tú)	come (tú)	vive (tú)
tomad (vosotros)	comed (vosotros)	vivid (vosotros)

The Compound Tenses

PERFECT INFINITIVE

haber tomado (comido, vivido), *to have taken (eaten, lived)*

---

[1] There is also a future subjunctive, used rarely today except in proverbs, legal documents, etc., but which was common in Old Spanish. Forms are:
> tomar: tomare tomares tomare tomáremos tomareis tomaren
> comer: comiere comieres comiere comiéremos comiereis comieren
> vivir: viviere vivieres viviere viviéremos viviereis vivieren

The future perfect subjunctive is: hubiere tomado (comido, vivido), etc.

PERFECT PARTICIPLE

habiendo tomado (comido, vivido), *having taken (eaten, lived)*

Indicative Mood

PRESENT PERFECT	PLUPERFECT	PRETERIT PERFECT
I have taken, eaten, lived, etc.	*I had taken, eaten, lived, etc.*	*I had taken, eaten, lived, etc.*

PRESENT PERFECT		PLUPERFECT		PRETERIT PERFECT	
he		había		hube	
has		habías		hubiste	
ha	tomado	había	tomado	hubo	tomado
	comido		comido		comido
hemos	vivido	habíamos	vivido	hubimos	vivido
habéis		habíais		hubisteis	
han		habían		hubieron	

FUTURE PERFECT		CONDITIONAL PERFECT	
I shall (will) have taken, etc.		*I should (would) have taken, etc.*	

FUTURE PERFECT		CONDITIONAL PERFECT	
habré		habría	
habrás		habrías	
habrá	tomado	habría	tomado
	comido		comido
habremos	vivido	habríamos	vivido
habréis		habríais	
habrán		habrían	

Subjunctive Mood

PRESENT PERFECT		-ra and -se PLUPERFECT	
(that) I may have taken, etc.		*(that) I might have taken, etc.*	

PRESENT PERFECT		-ra and -se PLUPERFECT	
haya		hubiera *or* hubiese	
hayas		hubieras *or* hubieses	
haya	tomado	hubiera *or* hubiese	tomado
	comido		comido
hayamos	vivido	hubiéramos *or* hubiésemos	vivido
hayáis		hubierais *or* hubieseis	
hayan		hubieran *or* hubiesen	

Irregular Past Participles of Regular Verbs

abrir: **abierto**   describir: **descrito**   escribir: **escrito**
cubrir: **cubierto**   descubrir: **descubierto**   romper: **roto**

Comments Concerning Forms of Verbs

INFINITIVE decir	PRES. PART. **diciendo**	PAST. PART. **dicho**	PRES. IND. **digo**	PRETERIT **dijeron**
IMP. IND. decía FUTURE **diré** CONDITIONAL **diría**	PROGRESSIVE TENSES **estoy**, etc. **diciendo**	COMPOUND TENSES **he**, etc. **dicho**	PRES. SUBJ. **diga** IMPERATIVE **di** decid	IMP. SUBJ. **dijera** **dijese**

a. From five forms (infinitive, present participle, past participle, first person singular present indicative, and third person plural preterit) all other forms may be derived.

b. The first and second persons plural of the present indicative of all verbs are regular, except in the cases of **haber, ir, ser.**

c. The third person plural is formed by adding **-n** to the third person singular in all tenses, except in the preterit and in the present indicative of **ser.**

d. All familiar forms (second person singular and plural) end in **-s,** except the second person singular preterit and the imperative.

e. The imperfect indicative is regular in all verbs, except **ir (iba), ser (era), ver (veía).**

f. If the first person singular preterit ends in unaccented **-e,** the third person singular ends in unaccented **-o;** the other endings are regular, except that after **j** the ending for the third person plural is **-eron.** Eight verbs of this group, in addition to those which end in **-ducir**, have a u-stem preterit (**andar, caber, estar, haber, poder, poner, saber, tener**); four have an i-stem (**decir, hacer, querer, venir**); **traer** retains the vowel **a** in the preterit. (The third person plural preterit forms of **decir** and **traer** are **dijeron** and **trajeron**, respectively. The third person singular preterit form of **hacer** is **hizo**.) **Ir** and **ser** have the same preterit forms, while **dar** has second-conjugation endings in this tense.

g. The conditional always has the same stem as the future. Only twelve verbs have irregular stems in these tenses. Five drop **e** of the infinitive ending (**caber, haber, poder, querer, saber**), five drop **e** or **i** and insert **d** (**poner, salir, tener, valer, venir**), and two (**decir, hacer**) retain the Old Spanish stems **dir-, har- (far-)**.

h. The stem of the present subjunctive of all verbs is the same as that of the first person singular present indicative, except for **dar, estar, haber, ir, saber, ser.**

i. The imperfect subjunctive of all verbs is formed by dropping **-ron** of the third person plural preterit and adding the **-ra** or **-se** endings.

j. The singular imperative is the same in form as the third person singular present indicative, except in the case of ten verbs (**decir, di; haber, he; hacer, haz; ir, ve; poner, pon; salir, sal; ser, sé; tener, ten; valer, val** or **vale; venir, ven**). The plural imperative is always formed by dropping final **-r** of the infinitive and adding **-d**. (Remember that the imperative is used only for familiar affirmative commands.)

k. The compound tenses of all verbs are formed by using the various tenses of the auxiliary verb **haber** with the past participle.

Irregular Verbs [1]

1. **andar,** andando, andado, *to go, walk*

PRETERIT	anduve	anduviste	anduvo	anduvimos	anduvisteis	anduvieron
IMP. SUBJ.	anduviera, etc.		anduviese, etc.			

2. **caber,** cabiendo, cabido, *to fit, be contained in*

PRES. IND.	quepo	cabes	cabe	cabemos	cabéis	caben
PRES. SUBJ.	quepa	quepas	quepa	quepamos	quepáis	quepan
FUTURE	cabré	cabrás, etc.		COND.	cabría	cabrías, etc.
PRETERIT	cupe	cupiste	cupo	cupimos	cupisteis	cupieron
IMP. SUBJ.	cupiera, etc.		cupiese, etc.			

[1] Participles are given with the infinitive; tenses not listed are regular.

3. caer, cayendo, caído, *to fall*

PRES. IND.	caigo	caes	cae	caemos	caéis	caen
PRES. SUBJ.	caiga	caigas	caiga	caigamos	caigáis	caigan
PRETERIT	caí	caíste	cayó	caímos	caísteis	cayeron
IMP. SUBJ.	cayera, etc.		cayese, etc.			

4. dar, dando, dado, *to give*

PRES. IND.	doy	das	da	damos	dais	dan
PRES. SUBJ.	dé	des	dé	demos	deis	den
PRETERIT	di	diste	dio	dimos	disteis	dieron
IMP. SUBJ.	diera, etc.		diese, etc.			

5. decir, diciendo, dicho, *to say, tell*

PRES. IND.	digo	dices	dice	decimos	decís	dicen
PRES. SUBJ.	diga	digas	diga	digamos	digáis	digan
IMPERATIVE	di				decid	
FUTURE	diré	dirás, etc.		COND.	diría	dirías, etc.
PRETERIT	dije	dijiste	dijo	dijimos	dijisteis	dijeron
IMP. SUBJ.	dijera, etc.		dijese, etc.			

6. estar, estando, estado, *to be*

PRES. IND.	estoy	estás	está	estamos	estáis	están
PRES. SUBJ.	esté	estés	esté	estemos	estéis	estén
PRETERIT	estuve	estuviste	estuvo	estuvimos	estuvisteis	estuvieron
IMP. SUBJ.	estuviera, etc.		estuviese, etc.			

7. haber, habiendo, habido, *to have* (auxiliary)

PRES. IND.	he	has	ha	hemos	habéis	han
PRES. SUBJ.	haya	hayas	haya	hayamos	hayáis	hayan
IMPERATIVE	he				habed	
FUTURE	habré	habrás, etc.		COND.	habría	habrías, etc.
PRETERIT	hube	hubiste	hubo	hubimos	hubisteis	hubieron
IMP. SUBJ.	hubiera, etc.		hubiese, etc.			

8. hacer, haciendo, hecho, *to do, make*

PRES. IND.	hago	haces	hace	hacemos	hacéis	hacen
PRES. SUBJ.	haga	hagas	haga	hagamos	hagáis	hagan
IMPERATIVE	haz				haced	
FUTURE	haré	harás, etc.		COND.	haría	harías, etc.
PRETERIT	hice	hiciste	hizo	hicimos	hicisteis	hicieron
IMP. SUBJ.	hiciera, etc.		hiciese, etc.			

Like hacer: satisfacer, *to satisfy*

9. **ir, yendo, ido,** *to go*

PRES. IND.	voy	vas	va	vamos	vais	van
PRES. SUBJ.	vaya	vayas	vaya	vayamos	vayáis	vayan
IMPERATIVE	ve				id	
IMP. IND.	iba	ibas	iba	íbamos	ibais	iban
PRETERIT	fui	fuiste	fue	fuimos	fuisteis	fueron
IMP. SUBJ.	fuera, etc.		fuese, etc.			

10. **oír, oyendo,** oído, *to hear*

PRES. IND.	oigo	oyes	oye	oímos	oís	oyen
PRES. SUBJ.	oiga	oigas	oiga	oigamos	oigáis	oigan
IMPERATIVE	oye				oíd	
PRETERIT	oí	oíste	oyó	oímos	oísteis	oyeron
IMP. SUBJ.	oyera, etc.		oyese, etc.			

11. **poder, pudiendo,** podido, *to be able*

PRES. IND.	puedo	puedes	puede	podemos	podéis	pueden
PRES. SUBJ.	pueda	puedas	pueda	podamos	podáis	puedan
FUTURE	podré	podrás, etc.		COND.	podría	podrías, etc.
PRETERIT	pude	pudiste	pudo	pudimos	pudisteis	pudieron
IMP. SUBJ.	pudiera, etc.		pudiese, etc.			

12. **poner,** poniendo, **puesto,** *to put, place*

PRES. IND.	pongo	pones	pone	ponemos	ponéis	ponen
PRES. SUBJ.	ponga	pongas	ponga	pongamos	pongáis	pongan
IMPERATIVE	pon				poned	
FUTURE	pondré	pondrás, etc.		COND.	pondría	pondrías, etc.
PRETERIT	puse	pusiste	puso	pusimos	pusisteis	pusieron
IMP. SUBJ.	pusiera, etc.		pusiese, etc.			

Like **poner:** componer, *to compose*; exponer, *to set forth*; imponer, *to impose*; oponer, *to oppose*; proponer, *to propose*, suponer, *to suppose*.

13. **querer,** queriendo, querido, *to wish, want*

PRES. IND.	quiero	quieres	quiere	queremos	queréis	quieren
PRES. SUBJ.	quiera	quieras	quiera	queramos	queráis	quieran
FUTURE	querré	querrás, etc.		COND.	querría	querrías, etc.
PRETERIT	quise	quisiste	quiso	quisimos	quisisteis	quisieron
IMP. SUBJ.	quisiera, etc.		quisiese, etc.			

14. **saber**, sabiendo, sabido, *to know*

PRES. IND.	sé	sabes	sabe	sabemos	sabéis	saben
PRES. SUBJ.	sepa	sepas	sepa	sepamos	sepáis	sepan
FUTURE	sabré	sabrás, etc.		COND.	sabría	sabrías, etc.
PRETERIT	supe	supiste	supo	supimos	supisteis	supieron
IMP. SUBJ.	supiera, etc.		supiese, etc.			

15. **salir**, saliendo, salido, *to go out, leave*

PRES. IND.	salgo	sales	sale	salimos	salís	salen
PRES. SUBJ.	salga	salgas	salga	salgamos	salgáis	salgan
IMPERATIVE	sal			salid		
FUTURE	saldré	saldrás, etc.		COND.	saldría	saldrías, etc.

16. **ser**, siendo, sido, *to be*

PRES. IND.	soy	eres	es	somos	sois	son
PRES. SUBJ.	sea	seas	sea	seamos	seáis	sean
IMPERATIVE	sé			sed		
IMP. IND.	era	eras	era	éramos	erais	eran
PRETERIT	fui	fuiste	fue	fuimos	fuisteis	fueron
IMP. SUBJ.	fuera, etc.		fuese, etc.			

17. **tener**, teniendo, tenido, *to have*

PRES. IND.	tengo	tienes	tiene	tenemos	tenéis	tienen
PRES. SUBJ.	tenga	tengas	tenga	tengamos	tengáis	tengan
IMPERATIVE	ten			tened		
FUTURE	tendré	tendrás, etc.		COND.	tendría	tendrías, etc.
PRETERIT	tuve	tuviste	tuvo	tuvimos	tuvisteis	tuvieron
IMP. SUBJ.	tuviera, etc.		tuviese, etc.			

Like **tener:** abstener, *to abstain*; contener, *to contain*; mantener, *to maintain*; obtener, *to obtain*.

18. **traer**, trayendo, traído, *to bring*

PRES. IND.	traigo	traes	trae	traemos	traéis	traen
PRES. SUBJ.	traiga	traigas	traiga	traigamos	traigáis	traigan
PRETERIT	traje	trajiste	trajo	trajimos	trajisteis	trajeron
IMP. SUBJ.	trajera, etc.		trajese, etc.			

Like **traer:** atraer, *to attract*.

19. **valer,** valiendo, valido, *to be worth*

PRES. IND.	**valgo**	**vales**	**vale**	**valemos**	**valéis**	**valen**
PRES. SUBJ.	**valga**	**valgas**	**valga**	**valgamos**	**valgáis**	**valgan**
IMPERATIVE	**val** (vale)				valed	
FUTURE	**valdré**	**valdrás,** etc.		COND.	**valdría**	**valdrías,** etc.

Like **valer:** equivaler, *to be equivalent to.*

20. **venir,** viniendo, venido, *to come*

PRES. IND.	**vengo**	**vienes**	**viene**	**venimos**	**venís**	**vienen**
PRES. SUBJ.	**venga**	**vengas**	**venga**	**vengamos**	**vengáis**	**vengan**
IMPERATIVE	**ven**				venid	
FUTURE	**vendré**	**vendrás,** etc.		COND.	**vendría**	**vendrías,** etc.
PRETERIT	**vine**	**viniste**	**vino**	**vinimos**	**vinisteis**	**vinieron**
IMP. SUBJ.	**viniera,** etc.		**viniese,** etc.			

Like **venir:** convenir, *to be fitting;* intervenir, *to take part, intervene.*

21. **ver,** viendo, **visto,** *to see*

PRES. IND.	**veo**	**ves**	**ve**	**vemos**	**veis**	**ven**
PRES. SUBJ.	**vea**	**veas**	**vea**	**veamos**	**veáis**	**vean**
PRETERIT	**vi**	**viste**	**vio**	**vimos**	**visteis**	**vieron**
IMP. IND.	**veía**	**veías**	**veía**	**veíamos**	**veíais**	**veían**

Changes in spelling are required in certain verbs to preserve the sound of the final consonant of the stem. The changes occur in only seven forms of each verb: in the first four types which follow the change is in the first person singular preterit, and in the remaining types in the first person singular present indicative, while all types change throughout the present subjunctive.

Verbs with Changes in Spelling

	a	**o**	**u**	**e**	**i**
Sound of *k*	ca	co	cu	que	qui
Sound of *g*	ga	go	gu	gue	gui
Sound of *s* (*th*)	za	zo	zu	ce	ci
Sound of Spanish **j**	ja	jo	ju	ge, je	gi, ji
Sound of *gw*	gua	guo		güe	güi

1. Verbs ending in **-car** change **c** to **qu** before **e**: buscar, *to look for*

PRETERIT	busqué	buscaste	buscó, etc.			
PRES. SUBJ.	busque	busques	busque	busquemos	busquéis	busquen

Like **buscar**: acercarse, *to approach*; atacar, *to attack*; colocar, *to place*; convocar, *to convoke, call up*; dedicar, *to dedicate*; destacarse, *to stand out*; diversificar, *to diversify*; educar, *to educate*; explicar, *to explain*; indicar, *to indicate*; invocar, *to invoke*; marcar, *to dial* (telephone); modificar, *to modify*; pescar, *to fish*; practicar, *to practice*; provocar, *to provoke*; publicar, *to publish*; rectificar, *to rectify*; sacar, *to take out*; tocar, *to play* (music).

2. Verbs ending in **-gar** change **g** to **gu** before **e**: llegar, *to arrive*

PRETERIT	llegué	llegaste	llegó, etc.			
PRES. SUBJ.	llegue	llegues	llegue	lleguemos	lleguéis	lleguen

Like **llegar**: agregar, *to add*; apagar, *to turn off* (lights); colgar (ue),[1] *to hang* (*up*); entregar, *to hand* (*over*); jugar (ue), *to play* (a game); negar (ie), *to deny*; obligar, *to oblige, force*; pagar, *to pay* (*for*); propagar, *to spread*; rogar (ue), *to ask, beg*.

3. Verbs ending in **-zar** change **z** to **c** before **e**: cruzar, *to cross*

PRETERIT	crucé	cruzaste	cruzó, etc.			
PRES. SUBJ.	cruce	cruces	cruce	crucemos	crucéis	crucen

Like **cruzar**: aderezar, *to garnish*; alcanzar, *to reach*; almorzar (ue), *to take* (*eat*) *lunch*; amenazar, *to threaten*; caracterizar, *to characterize*; centralizar, *to centralize*; comenzar (ie), *to commence, begin*; empezar (ie), *to begin*; esbozar, *to sketch*; esforzarse (ue) por, *to strive to*; garantizar, *to guarantee*; industrializar, *to industrialize*; modernizar, *to modernize*; organizar, *to organize*; realizar, *to realize, carry out*; sintonizar, *to tune in*.

4. Verbs ending in **-guar** change **gu** to **gü** before **e**: averiguar, *to find out*

PRETERIT	averigüé	averiguaste	averiguó, etc.			
PRES. SUBJ.	averigüe	averigües	averigüe	averigüemos	averigüéis	averigüen

Like **averiguar**: menguar, *to lessen*.

5. Verbs ending in **-ger** or **-gir** change **g** to **j** before **a** and **o**: coger, *to pick* (*up*)

PRES. IND.	cojo	coges	coge, etc.			
PRES. SUBJ.	coja	cojas	coja	cojamos	cojáis	cojan

Like **coger**: dirigir, *to direct*; elegir (i, i), *to elect*; escoger, *to choose, select*; surgir, *to surge, arise*.

[1] See pages 327–330 for verbs with stem changes.

6. Verbs ending in **-guir** change **gu** to **g** before **a** and **o**: **distinguir,** *to distinguish*

| PRES. IND. | distingo | distingues | distingue, etc. | | | |
| PRES. SUBJ. | distinga | distingas | distinga | distingamos | distingáis | distingan |

Like **distinguir:** conseguir (i, i), *to obtain, attain*; seguir (i, i), *to follow.*

7. Verbs ending in **-cer** or **-cir** preceded by a consonant change **c** to **z** before **a** and **o**: **vencer,** *to overcome, conquer*

| PRES. IND. | venzo | vences | vence, etc. | | | |
| PRES. SUBJ. | venza | venzas | venza | venzamos | venzáis | venzan |

Like **vencer:** ejercer, *to exert.*

8. Verbs ending in **-quir** change **qu** to **c** before **a** and **o**: **delinquir,** *to be guilty*

| PRES. IND. | delinco | delinques | delinque, etc. | | | |
| PRES. SUBJ. | delinca | delincas | delinca | delincamos | delincáis | delincan |

Verbs with Special Endings

1. Verbs ending in **-cer** or **-cir** following a vowel insert **z** before **c** in the first person singular present indicative and throughout the present subjunctive: **conocer,** *to know, be acquainted with*

| PRES. IND. | conozco | conoces | conoce, etc. | | | |
| PRES. SUBJ. | conozca | conozcas | conozca | conozcamos | conozcáis | conozcan |

Like **conocer:** aparecer, *to appear*; crecer, *to grow*; establecer, *to establish*; favorecer, *to favor*; florecer, *to flourish*; fortalecer, *to strengthen*; merecer, *to merit*; nacer, *to be born*; ofrecer, *to offer*; parecer, *to seem*; pertenecer, *to belong to*; reconocer, *to recognize*; yacer, *to lie* (position).

2. Verbs ending in **-ducir** have the same changes as **conocer,** with additional changes in the preterit and imperfect subjunctive: **conducir,** *to conduct, drive*

PRES. IND.	conduzco	conduces	conduce, etc.			
PRES. SUBJ.	conduzca	conduzcas	conduzca	conduzcamos	conduzcáis	conduzcan
PRETERIT	conduje	condujiste	condujo	condujimos	condujisteis	condujeron
IMP. SUBJ.	condujera, etc.		condujese, etc.			

Like **conducir:** introducir, *to introduce*; producir, *to produce*; traducir, *to translate.*

3. Verbs ending in **-uir** (except **-guir** and **-quir**) insert y except before **i**, and change unaccented **i** between vowels to **y**: **huir**, *to flee*

PARTICIPLES	**huyendo**		**huido**			
PRES. IND.	**huyo**	**huyes**	**huye**	**huimos**	**huís**	**huyen**
PRES. SUBJ.	**huya**	**huyas**	**huya**	**huyamos**	**huyáis**	**huyan**
IMPERATIVE	**huye**				**huid**	
PRETERIT	**huí**	huiste	**huyó**	huimos	huisteis	**huyeron**
IMP. SUBJ.	**huyera**, etc.		**huyese**, etc.			

Like **huir**: concluir, *to conclude, end*; constituir, *to constitute*; construir, *to construct*; contribuir, *to contribute*; disminuir, *to diminish*; distribuir, *to distribute*; substituir, *to substitute*.

4. Certain verbs ending in **-er** preceded by a vowel replace unaccented **i** of the ending by **y**: **creer**, *to believe*

PARTICIPLES	**creyendo**		**creído**			
PRETERIT	creí	**creíste**	**creyó**	**creímos**	**creísteis**	**creyeron**
IMP. SUBJ.	**creyera**, etc.		**creyese**, etc.			

Like **creer**: leer, *to read*.

5. Some verbs ending in **-iar** require a written accent on the **i** in the singular and third person plural in the present indicative and present subjunctive and in the singular imperative: **enviar**, *to send*

PRES. IND.	**envío**	**envías**	**envía**	enviamos	enviáis	**envían**
PRES. SUBJ.	**envíe**	**envíes**	**envíe**	enviemos	enviéis	**envíen**
IMPERATIVE	**envía**				enviad	

Like **enviar**: ampliar, *to enlarge*; desviar, *to divert*; esquiar, *to ski*; variar, *to vary*. However, such common verbs as the following do not have the accented **i**: anunciar, *to announce*; cambiar, *to change*; comerciar, *to trade*; estudiar, *to study*; iniciar, *to initiate*; pronunciar, *to pronounce*.

6. Verbs ending in **-uar** have a written accent on the **u** in the same forms as verbs in section 5:[1] **continuar**, *to continue*

PRES. IND.	**continúo**	**continúas**	**continúa**	continuamos	continuáis	**continúan**
PRES. SUBJ.	**continúe**	**continúes**	**continúe**	continuemos	continuéis	**continúen**
IMPERATIVE	**continúa**				continuad	

Like **continuar**: efectuar, *to carry out*; graduarse, *to graduate*.

[1] **Reunir(se)**, *to gather, meet*, has a written accent on the **u** in the same forms as **continuar**:

PRES. IND.	**reúno reúnes reúne ... reúnen**
PRES. SUBJ.	**reúna reúnas reúna ... reúnan**
IMPERATIVE	**reúne**

7. Verbs whose stems end in **ll** or **ñ** drop the **i** of the diphthongs **ie** (**ié**) and **ió**. Examples, not used in this text, are:

bullir, *to boil*

PRES. PART.	**bullendo**					
PRETERIT	bullí	bulliste	**bulló**	bullimos	bullisteis	**bulleron**
IMP. SUBJ.	**bullera**, etc.		**bullese**, etc.			

reñir (i, i), *to scold*

PRES. PART.	**riñendo**					
PRETERIT	reñí	reñiste	**riñó**	reñimos	reñisteis	**riñeron**
IMP. SUBJ.	**riñera**, etc.		**riñese**, etc.			

Stem-Changing Verbs

CLASS I (-ar, -er)

Many verbs of the first and second conjugations change the stem vowel **e** to **ie** and **o** to **ue** when the vowels **e** and **o** are stressed, *i.e.,* in the singular and third person plural of the present indicative and present subjunctive and in the singular imperative. Class I verbs are designated: **cerrar (ie)**,[1] **volver (ue)**.[2]

cerrar, *to close*

PRES. IND.	**cierro**	**cierras**	**cierra**	cerramos	cerráis	**cierran**
PRES. SUBJ.	**cierre**	**cierres**	**cierre**	cerremos	cerréis	**cierren**
IMPERATIVE	**cierra**					

Like **cerrar**: comenzar, *to commence, begin*; despertar, *to awaken*; empezar, *to begin*; negar, *to deny*; pensar, *to think*; recomendar, *to recommend*; sentarse, *to sit down*.

---

[1] **Errar,** *to err, miss* (a shot), is designated: **errar (ye)**. At the beginning of a verb the initial **i** of the diphthong **ie** is changed to **y**, since no Spanish word may begin with **ie**:

PRES. IND.	**yerro**	**yerras**	**yerra**	erramos	erráis	**yerran**
PRES. SUBJ.	**yerre**	**yerres**	**yerre**	erremos	erréis	**yerren**
IMPERATIVE	**yerra**					

[2] Forms of **oler (ue)**, *to smell* (an odor) follow. Spanish words do not begin with **u** followed by **a, e,** or **o**; thus **h** is written before **ue**:

PRES. IND.	**huelo**	**hueles**	**huele**	olemos	oléis	**huelen**
PRES. SUBJ.	**huela**	**huelas**	**huela**	olamos	oláis	**huelan**
IMPERATIVE	**huele**					

perder, *to lose, miss*

PRES. IND.	**pierdo**	**pierdes**	**pierde**	perdemos	perdéis	**pierden**
PRES. SUBJ.	**pierda**	**pierdas**	**pierda**	perdamos	perdáis	**pierdan**
IMPERATIVE	**pierde**					

Like **perder:** defender, *to defend*; entender, *to understand*; extender, *to extend*; tender, *to tend*.

contar, *to count*; *to relate*

PRES. IND.	**cuento**	**cuentas**	**cuenta**	contamos	contáis	**cuentan**
PRES. SUBJ.	**cuente**	**cuentes**	**cuente**	contemos	contéis	**cuenten**
IMPERATIVE	**cuenta**					

Like **contar:** acordarse, *to remember*; acostarse, *to go to bed*; almorzar, *to take (eat) lunch*; aprobar, *to approve*; colgar, *to hang (up)*; costar, *to cost*; demostrar, *to demonstrate*; encontrar, *to find*; esforzarse por, *to strive to*; mostrar, *to show*; probar, *to try out, test*; recordar, *to recall*; rogar, *to ask, beg*; sonar, *to sound, ring*.

volver,[1] *to return*

PRES. IND.	**vuelvo**	**vuelves**	**vuelve**	volvemos	volvéis	**vuelven**
PRES. SUBJ.	**vuelva**	**vuelvas**	**vuelva**	volvamos	volváis	**vuelvan**
IMPERATIVE	**vuelve**					

Like **volver:** devolver, *to return, give back*; doler, *to ache, pain*; envolver, *to wrap up*; llover, *to rain*; resolver, *to resolve*.

jugar, *to play* (a game)

PRES. IND.	**juego**	**juegas**	**juega**	jugamos	jugáis	**juegan**
PRES. SUBJ.	**juegue**	**juegues**	**juegue**	juguemos	juguéis	**jueguen**
IMPERATIVE	**juega**					

CLASS II (-ir)

Certain verbs of the third conjugation have the changes in the stem indicated below. Class II verbs are designated: **sentir (ie, i), dormir (ue, u).**

PRES. IND.	1, 2, 3, 6	} e > ie	PRES. PART.		} e > i
PRES. SUBJ.	1, 2, 3, 6	} o > ue	PRETERIT	3, 6	
IMPERATIVE	Sing.		PRES. SUBJ.	4, 5	} o > u
			IMP. SUBJ.	1, 2, 3, 4, 5, 6	

[1] The past participles of **volver, devolver, envolver, resolver** are: **vuelto, devuelto, envuelto, resuelto,** respectively.

sentir, *to feel*

PRES. PART.	sintiendo					
PRES. IND.	siento	sientes	siente	sentimos	sentís	sienten
PRES. SUBJ.	sienta	sientas	sienta	sintamos	sintáis	sientan
IMPERATIVE	siente					
PRETERIT	sentí	sentiste	sintió	sentimos	sentisteis	sintieron
IMP. SUBJ.	sintiera, etc.		sintiese, etc.			

Like **sentir**: adquirir,[1] *to acquire;* advertir, *to notice;* consentir, *to consent;* convertir, *to convert;* diferir, *to differ;* divertirse, *to amuse oneself;* preferir, *to prefer.*

dormir, *to sleep*

PRES. PART.	durmiendo					
PRES. IND.	duermo	duermes	duerme	dormimos	dormís	duermen
PRES. SUBJ.	duerma	duermas	duerma	durmamos	durmáis	duerman
IMPERATIVE	duerme					
PRETERIT	dormí	dormiste	durmió	dormimos	dormisteis	durmieron
IMP. SUBJ.	durmiera, etc.		durmiese, etc.			

Like **dormir**: morir,[2] *to die.*

CLASS III (-ir)

Certain verbs in the third conjugation change **e** to **i** in all forms in which changes occur in Class II verbs. These verbs are designated: **pedir (i, i).**

pedir, *to ask*

PRES. PART.	pidiendo					
PRES. IND.	pido	pides	pide	pedimos	pedís	piden
PRES. SUBJ.	pida	pidas	pida	pidamos	pidáis	pidan
IMPERATIVE	pide					
PRETERIT	pedí	pediste	pidió	pedimos	pedisteis	pidieron
IMP. SUBJ.	pidiera, etc.		pidiese, etc.			

Like **pedir**: competir, *to compete;* conseguir, *to obtain, attain;* despedirse, *to take leave;* elegir, *to elect;* repetir, *to repeat;* seguir, *to follow;* servir, *to serve;* vestir, *to dress.*

[1] Forms of **adquirir (ie)** are:

PRES. IND.	adquiero	adquieres	adquiere	adquirimos	adquirís	adquieren
PRES. SUBJ.	adquiera	adquieras	adquiera	adquiramos	adquiráis	adquieran
IMPERATIVE	adquiere					

[2] Past participle: **muerto.**

reír, *to laugh*

PARTICIPLES	**riendo**		reído		
PRES. IND.	**río**	**ríes**	**ríe**	reímos	reís	**ríen**
PRES. SUBJ.	**ría**	**rías**	**ría**	**riamos**	**riáis**	**rían**
IMPERATIVE	**ríe**				**reíd**	
PRETERIT	reí	reíste	**rió**	reímos	reísteis	**rieron**
IMP. SUBJ.	**riera,** etc.		**riese,** etc.			

APPENDIX E

Verbs Followed
by an Infinitive
and Those
Whose Meanings
Change When
Used Reflexively

I. Verbs Followed by an Infinitive, With or Without a Preposition

Many verbs in Spanish are followed directly by an infinitive, as in English. Also, many verbs, as well as certain adjectives and nouns, require a preposition, especially **a, con, de, en,** or **por,** before an infinitive. An occasional verb may be followed by more than one preposition. (Remember that an infinitive is used after many idiomatic expressions, for example, **hay [había] que,** *it is* [*was*] *necessary to*; **tener que,** *to have to, must*.) Since the list is long, only the verbs (including a few which appear in idiomatic expressions) used in this text are listed below.

A. Verbs which may be followed directly by an infinitive

aconsejar   to advise
bastar   to be enough, sufficient
conseguir (i, i)   to succeed in
convenir   to be fitting, advisable
deber   should, ought to, must
decidir   to decide
dejar   to let, allow, permit
desear   to desire, wish, want
esperar   to hope, expect
faltar   to be lacking
gustar   to like, be pleasing to
hacer   to make, have
importar   to matter, be important
interesar   to interest
lograr   to succeed in
mandar   to command, have, order
merecer   to merit, deserve
necesitar   to need

oír   to hear
olvidar   to forget
parecer   to appear, seem
pensar (ie)   to intend, plan
permitir   to permit, allow to, let
poder   to be able, can
preferir (ie, i)   to prefer
prometer   to promise
querer   to wish, want
resolver (ue)   to resolve
resultar   to result, turn out
  (to be)
saber   to know how (to), can
sentir (ie, i)   to regret, be sorry
soler (ue)   to be accustomed to
temer   to fear
ver   to see

331

B. Verbs followed by certain prepositions before an infinitive or other object

a. Verbs which require **a** before an infinitive are:

acudir a   to resort (come) to
aprender a   to learn to
aspirar a   to aspire to
atreverse a   to dare to
ayudar a   to help (aid) to
bajar a   to come (go) down to
comenzar (ie) a   to commence to
contribuir a   to contribute to
correr a   to run to
decidirse a   to make up one's mind to
dedicarse a   to dedicate (devote) oneself to
dirigirse a   to turn to, direct oneself to
empezar (ie) a   to begin to

enseñar a   to teach (how) to, show to
enviar a   to send to
incorporarse a   to incorporate into
invitar a   to invite to
ir a   to go to
llegar a   to come to, become
obligar a   to oblige (force) to
oponerse a   to oppose
pasar a   to go to
salir a   to go (come) out to
tender (ie) a   to tend to
venir a   to come to
volver (ue) a   to return to; to . . . again

Verbs which require **a** before an object are:

acercarse a   to approach
asistir a   to attend
corresponder a   to correspond to

echar a   to throw (toss) into
llegar a   to reach, arrive (at)

b. Verbs which require **con** before an infinitive (but more commonly before an object) are:

amenazar con   to threaten with
conformarse con   to be satisfied with

preocuparse con   to be concerned with (about), be preoccupied with
relacionarse con   to be related to

In addition to the four verbs mentioned, other verbs which require **con** before an object are:

acabar con   to put an end to
encontrarse (ue) con   to run across

enfrentarse con   to face

c. Verbs which require **de** before an infinitive are:

abstenerse de   to refrain from
acabar de   to have just
acordarse (ue) de   to remember
   to
alegrarse de   to be glad to
cansarse de   to become tired of

deber de   must (*probability*)
dejar de   to stop (cease), fail to
haber de   to be (be supposed) to
olvidarse de   to forget to
tratar de   to try to
tratarse de   to be a question of

Verbs which require **de** before an object are:

apoderarse de   to take possession of
burlarse de   to make fun of
constar de   to consist of
despedirse (i, i) de   to take leave of
gozar de   to enjoy

partir de   to leave
pasar de   to exceed
salir de   to leave
servir (i, i) de   to serve as (a)
tratar de   to treat of, deal with

d. Verbs which require **en** before an infinitive are:

consentir (ie, i) en   to consent to,
   agree to
insistir en   to insist on

pensar (ie) en   to think of
   (about)
tardar en   to delay in, take
   long to

Verbs which require **en** before an object are:

convertirse (ie, i) en   to be
   converted into
echar en   to throw (toss) into

entrar en   to enter
fijarse en   to notice

e. Verbs followed by **por** before an infinitive are:

esforzarse (ue) por   to make an
   effort to, strive for
estar por   to be inclined to, be
   in favor of

interesarse por   to become
   interested in
preocuparse por   to worry
   about, be concerned with

II. Verbs (Not Listed in Lección dos) Whose Meanings Change When Used Reflexively

acostumbrar   to accustom

acostumbrarse a   to be (become)
   accustomed to

decidir to decide

dedicar to dedicate

desarrollar to develop

destacar to make stand out, emphasize

dirigir to direct, address

distinguir to distinguish

encontrar (ue) to find

establecer to establish

interesar to interest

ir to go

llevar to take, carry

marchar to march

ocupar to occupy

preparar to prepare

presentar to present, introduce

quitar to remove, take away

reunir to collect

sentir (ie, i) to feel, regret

tratar de to try to (+ *inf.*); to treat of, deal with

ver to see

volver (ue) to return

decidirse a to make up one's mind to

dedicarse a to dedicate oneself to

desarrollarse to be developed

destacarse to stand out

dirigirse a to direct oneself (turn) to

distinguirse to become distinguished

encontrarse (ue) to find oneself, be

establecerse to establish oneself, settle

interesarse (por) to become interested (in)

irse to go away, leave

llevarse to take away, take (with oneself)

marcharse to leave, go away

ocuparse de to take care of

prepararse to be prepared, prepare oneself

presentarse to present oneself, appear

quitarse to take off (oneself)

reunirse to meet, gather

sentirse (ie, i) (bien) to feel (well)

tratarse de to be a question of

verse to be (seen)

volverse (ue) to become

MAPS

ESPAÑA

FRANCIA

Mar Cantábrico

Golfo de León

Oceáno Atlántico

Mar Mediterráneo

ÁFRICA

PORTUGAL

GALICIA
ASTURIAS
LEÓN
VASCONGADAS
NAVARRA
CASTILLA LA VIEJA
ARAGÓN
CATALUÑA
VALENCIA
CASTILLA LA NUEVA
EXTREMADURA
MURCIA
ANDALUCÍA

ISLAS BALEARES
MENORCA
MALLORCA
IBIZA

PIRINEOS
MONTES CANTÁBRICOS
SIERRA DE GUADARRAMA
SIERRA MORENA
SIERRA NEVADA

R. Ebro
R. Duero
R. Tajo
R. Júcar
R. Guadiana
R. Guadalquivir
R. Tinto

La Coruña
Santiago
Padrón
Pontevedra
Vigo
Gijón
Oviedo
Santander
Bilbao
San Sebastián
Vitoria
Pamplona
Burgos
Lerma
Palencia
Valladolid
León
Zamora
Salamanca
Cáceres
Mérida
Badajoz
Coimbra
Lisboa
Polos
Huelva
Sevilla
Jerez
Cádiz
Algeciras
Gibraltar
Ceuta
Córdoba
Jaén
Granada
Málaga
Almería
Cartagena
Murcia
Jijona
Alcoy
Albacete
Socuéllamos
Valdepeñas
Ciudad Real
Mora
Toledo
Madrid
El Escorial
Segovia
Ávila
Cuenca
Teruel
Zaragoza
Lérida
Gerona
Sitges
Tarragona
Castellón
Sagunto
Meca
Valencia
Vinaroz

Estrecho de Gibraltar

ISLAS CANARIAS
LANZAROTE
FUERTEVENTURA
Las Palmas
GRAN CANARIA
TENERIFE
Sto. Cruz de Tenerife
GOMERA
HIERRO
PALMA

ESPAÑA
África

España
Ifni
Sahará español
Senegal
Gambia
Guinea port.
Guinea
Sierra Leona
Liberia
Costa del Marfil
Alto Volta
Ghana
Togo
Dahomey
Nigeria
Níger
Malí
Mauritania
Argelia
Túnez
Camerones
Gabón
Río Muni
Annobón
Fernando Poo

MÉXICO, LA AMÉRICA CENTRAL Y EL CARIBE

Océano Atlántico

San Juan
PUERTO RICO

★REP. DOMINICANA
HAITÍ
★Santo Domingo

Port au Prince★

Kingston

JAMAICA

Mar Caribe

Santiago

CUBA

★La Habana

Golfo de Panamá

PANAMÁ

★Panamá

COSTA RICA

★San José

NICARAGUA

Managua

HONDURAS

Tegucigalpa★

HONDURAS BR.

Belice

Mérida

YUCATÁN

Sisal

Campeche

GUATEMALA

Guatemala★

EL SALVADOR

★San Salvador

Golfo de México

Tampico

Veracruz

Puebla

Cuernavaca

Cholula

MÉXICO

México

Toluca

Pachuca

Jamiquilpan

Querétaro

Oaxaca

Acapulco

SIERRA MADRE ORIENTAL

Laredo

Nuevo Laredo

Monterrey

Saltillo

Zacatecas

San Luis Potosí

Dolores

Guadalajara

Río Grande

El Paso

Ciudad Juárez

Chihuahua

SIERRA MADRE OCCIDENTAL

Nogales

San Diego

La Paz

Golfo de California

Océano Pacífico

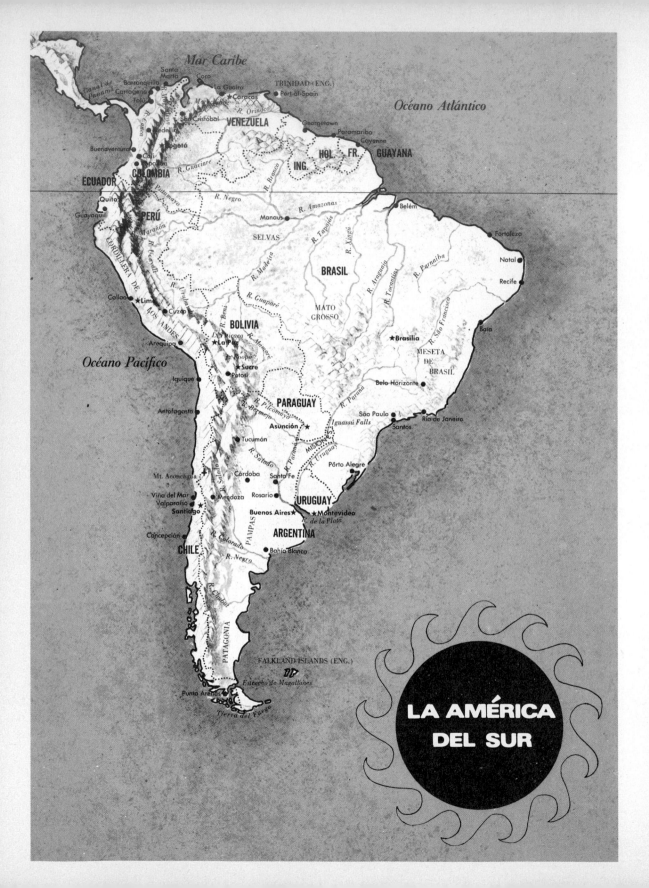

VOCABULARIES

Spanish–English

A

a to, at, in, into, on, from, by, after, *etc.*; *not translated when used before a personal dir. obj.*

abierto, -a *p.p. of* **abrir** *and adj.* open, opened

la abogacía law, legal profession

el abogado lawyer

la abreviatura abbreviation

el abrigo topcoat, overcoat

abrir to open

  abrir el apetito a uno to whet one's appetite

la abstención abstention

abstenerse de to abstain (refrain) from

abstracto, -a abstract

el abuelo grandfather; *pl.* grandparents

la abundancia abundance, large number

abundar to abound, be abundant

el abuso abuse

acabar to end, finish

  acabar con + *obj.* to put an end to, wipe out

  acabar de + *inf.* to have just + *p.p.*

académico, -a academic

acampar to camp

acaso perhaps

el aceite olive oil

acelerar to accelerate, speed up

aceptar to accept

acerca de *prep.* about, concerning

acercar to bring near

  acercarse (a + *obj.***)** to approach, draw near (to), move (toward)

acompañado, -a (de) accompanied (by)

acompañar to accompany, go with

aconsejar to advise

acordarse (ue) (de + *obj.***)** to remember, recall

  acordarse de + *inf.* to remember to

acostar (ue) to put to bed; *reflex.* to go to bed

acostumbrar to accustom

  acostumbrarse a to be (become) accustomed to

la activación activation, promotion

la actividad activity

activo, -a active

actual *adj.* present, present-day

acudir a to resort (come) to

el acuerdo accord, agreement

la acumulación accumulation

acumulado, -a accumulated, piled up

acumular(se) to accumulate, gather

adelante ahead

  más adelante later (farther) on

además *adv.* furthermore, in addition

  además de *prep.* besides, in addition to

aderezar to garnish

adiós goodbye

la adivinanza riddle

adjetivo, -a adjective, adjectival

el adjetivo adjective

la administración administration

admirablemente admirably

el admirador admirer

admirar to admire

admitir to admit

adonde (to) where

¿adónde? where? *(with verbs of motion)*

adquirir (ie) to acquire

el adulto adult

adverbial *adj.* adverbial

el adverbio adverb

advertir (ie, i) to notice

el aeropuerto airport

afectar to affect

aficionado, -a fond; amateur

  (ser) aficionado, -a a (to be) fond of

el aficionado amateur

afirmativamente affirmatively

afirmativo, -a affirmative

la afluencia affluence

el África (*f.*) Africa
agradable agreeable, pleasant
agregar to add
agrícola (*m. and f.*) agricultural
la agricultura agriculture
el agua (*f.*) water
   vaso para agua water glass
la aguadora water bearer
la aguja de mar sailfish
Agustín Augustine
¡ah! ah! oh!
ahora now
   ahora mismo right now, right away
ahorrar to save
el ahorro economy; *pl.* savings
aislado, -a isolated
el ají chili, pepper (*vegetable*)
al = a + el to the
   al + *inf.* on (upon) + *pres. part.*
Alberto Albert
el álbum album
el alcantarillado sewage system
alcanzar to reach, attain
la alcoba bedroom
alegrar to make glad
   alegrarse (de + *obj.*) to be glad (to)
   alegrarse (de que) to be glad (that)
   alegrarse (mucho) de to be (very) glad to
   ¡cuánto me alegro de que . . . ! how glad I am that . . . !
alegre joyful, gay, merry
Alemania Germany
   la Alemania Occidental West Germany
la alfombra rug, carpet
algo *pron.* anything, something; *adv.* somewhat, rather
alguien *pron.* someone, somebody, anyone, anybody
algún *used for* alguno *before m. sing. nouns*
alguno, -a *adj. and pron.* some, any (one), someone; *pl.* some, several, a few
   alguna cosa something, anything
   sin razón alguna without any reason at all
la alimentación nutrition

alimenticio, -a (of) food
el alma (*f.*) soul, heart
la almeja clam
la almendra almond
almorzar (ue) to take (eat) lunch
el almuerzo lunch
   para el almuerzo for lunch
   tomar el almuerzo to take (eat) lunch
¡aló! hello! (*telephone*)
alrededor *adv.* around
los alrededores environs, outskirts, vicinity
   por los alrededores in the vicinity
alto, -a tall, high, lofty
   en voz alta aloud
   hablar más alto to speak up (louder)
el altoparlante loudspeaker
la altura height
el alumno pupil, student
allá there (*often after verbs of motion*)
allí there
la amalgama amalgam
amarillo, -a yellow
   la amarilla the yellow one (*f.*)
el Amazonas Amazon (River)
amenazar con to threaten to
América America
   la América Central Central America
   la América del Sur South America
   la América española Spanish America
   la América hispana Spanish (Hispanic) America
   la América latina Latin America
americano, -a American
la amiga friend (*f.*)
el amigo friend
el amor love
la ampliación (*pl.* ampliaciones) enlargement
ampliar to enlarge, broaden, amplify
amplio, -a large, extensive, broad
Ana Ann, Anne, Anna
el analfabetismo illiteracy
el (la) análisis analysis (*pl.* analyses)
ancho, -a wide, broad
andaluz, -uza Andalusian (*of southern Spain*)

andar   to go, walk

los **Andes**   Andes (*mountains in South America*)

angloamericano, -a (*also noun*) Anglo-American

animadamente   animatedly

animado, -a   animated

el **animal**   animal

anoche   last night

anónimo, -a   anonymous

ante *prep.*   before (*position*)

antemano: de —,   in advance, beforehand

anterior   earlier, preceding

anteriormente   before, previously

antes *adv.*   before

  antes de *prep.*   before

  antes (de) que *conj.*   before

Antonio   Anthony, Tony

la **antropología**   anthropology

anunciar   to announce

añadir   to add

el **año**   year

  al año   yearly, each year

  al año siguiente   (in) the following year

  de los últimos años   of the last (past) few years

  en los últimos años   during (in) the last few years, recently

  tener ... años   to be ... years old

apagar   to turn off, lower (*lights*)

el **aparato**   set

  aparato (de radio)   (radio) set

aparecer   to appear, show up

el **apartamento**   apartment

el **apasionamiento**   enthusiasm, intense emotion

la **apatía**   apathy

apenas   scarcely, hardly

la **apertura**   opening

  de apertura   opening

el **apetito**   appetite

  abrir el apetito a uno   to whet one's appetite

la **aplicación**   application

  aplicación del diálogo   dialogue adaptation

  apoderarse de   to seize, take possession of

apolítico, -a   apolitical

aprender (a + *inf.*)   to learn (to)

  aprender de memoria   to memorize, learn by heart

aprobar (ue)   to approve, pass (*a course or examination*)

aproximadamente   approximately

apto, -a   competent

apurarse   to hurry (up)

aquel, aquella (-os, -as) *adj.*   that, those (*distant*)

aquél, aquélla (-os, -as) *pron.*   that (one), those; the former

aquello *neuter pron.*   that

aquí   here

  por aquí   here, around (by) here

  (venir) por aquí   (to come) this way

  ¡(vosotros) por aquí!   (you) here!

el **árbol**   tree

arcaico, -a   archaic, very old

la **Argentina**   Argentina

argentino, -a (*also noun*)   Argentine

el **argumento**   plot (*of music or drama*)

armado, -a   armed

la **arquitectura**   architecture

arreglar   to adjust, regulate, fix

el **arroz**   rice

  arroz con leche   rice pudding

el **arte**   art; (*f. pl.*) arts, crafts

  artes y oficios   arts and crafts

  las bellas artes   (the) fine arts

el **artículo**   article

el (la) **artista**   artist

artístico, -a   artistic

Arturo   Arthur

asado, -a   roast(ed)

asegurar   to assure

asequible   accessible, available

así   so, thus

  así como   just as, as well as

  así que *conj.*   as soon as

el **asiento**   seat

la **asignatura**   subject (*of study*)

asimilar   to assimilate; *reflex.* to be assimilated

asistir a   to attend

la **asociación**   association

asombrar to astonish, amaze
el aspecto aspect
la aspiración (*pl.* **aspiraciones**) aspiration
aspirar a to aspire to
asumir to assume
atacar to attack
el ate *preserve*
la atención attention
atlético, -a athletic
  Juegos Atléticos Track and Field Games
la atracción (*pl.* **atracciones**) attraction
atractivo, -a attractive
atraer to attract
atraído, -a attracted
atreverse (a) to dare (to)
aumentar to increase, augment
el aumento increase
aun, aún even, still
aunque although, even though, even if
el auricular receiver (*telephone*)
la ausencia absence
ausente absent
auténtico, -a authentic, real
el autobús (*pl.* **autobuses**) bus
  autobús (de las dos) (two-o'clock) bus
  en autobús by bus
  servicio de autobuses bus service
el automóvil automobile
la autonomía autonomy
el autor author
la autoridad authority
el autorretrato self-portrait
auxiliar *adj.* auxiliary
averiguar to find out
el avión (*pl.* **aviones**) (air)plane
  en avión by plane
avisar to announce, inform; to warn
¡ay! oh!
ayer yesterday
  ayer por la tarde yesterday afternoon
  (reunión) de ayer yesterday's (meeting)
la ayuda aid, help
ayudar (**a** + *inf.*) to help (to), aid (to)
azteca (*m. and f.*) Aztec
el (la) azúcar sugar
azul blue

B

el bachiller bachelor (*holder of a degree*)
el bachillerato baccalaureate, bachelor's degree
¡bah! bah!
bailar to dance
el baile dance
la Baja California Lower California
bajar to descend, go (come) down, decline
bajo *prep.* below, under
bajo, -a low, lower
  piso bajo first floor
el balneario spa, bathing resort
el balompedista football player (*soccer*)
el balompié football (*soccer*)
Baltasar Balthasar
el banco bank
la bandeja tray
el banquero banker
el banquete banquet
bañarse to take a bath, go swimming
Bárbara Barbara
el barril barrel
el barrio district
basado, -a based
la base base, basis
básico, -a basic
el básquet basketball, basketball team
el básquetbol basketball
bastante *adj. and adv.* quite, rather, enough, sufficient
bastar to be enough, be sufficient
el batido de leche milk shake
beber to drink
la beca scholarship
Beethoven, Ludwig van (1770–1827) *German composer*
el béisbol baseball
  juego de béisbol baseball game
la belleza beauty
bello, -a beautiful, pretty; fine
  las bellas artes (the) fine arts
la biblioteca library
la bicicleta bicycle
bien *adv.* well

los bienes   wealth, goods
>   bienes de equipo   capital goods
el bienestar   well-being, welfare
la bienvenida   welcome
>   dar la bienvenida a   to welcome
el biftec   (beef)steak
el billete   ticket
>   blanco, -a   white
>   bloquear   to block
la blusa   blouse
>   Bogotá   *capital of Colombia*
>   Bolívar, Simón   (1783–1830) *Venezuelan liberator of northwest South America*
la bolsa   purse
el bolsillo   pocket
>   bonito, -a   pretty, beautiful
la botella   bottle
el Brasil   Brazil
>   brasileño, -a (*also noun*)   Brazilian
>   breve   brief, short
>   brillante   brilliant
la broma   joke
>   buen   *used for* bueno *before m. sing. nouns*
>   bueno *adv.*   well, well now (then), all right, fine, good
>   ¡bueno!   hello! (*telephone*)
>   bueno, -a   good, well
>   ¡buen viaje!   (have) a good trip!
>   lo bueno   what is good, the good thing (part)
>   bullicioso, -a   lively, noisy, boisterous, merry
>   bullir   to boil
>   burlarse (de)   to make fun (of)
>   burocrático, -a   bureaucratic
la busca   search
>   buscar   to look (for), search (for), seek
>   buscar a uno   to come (go) for one, pick one up

C

el caballo   horse
>   caber   to fit, be contained
>   si cabe   if it is possible

la cabeza   head
>   (le) duele la cabeza   (his) head aches
>   tener dolor de cabeza   to have a headache
el cabo   end
>   llevar a cabo   to carry out
>   cada   each
>   caer   to fall
el café   coffee; café
>   taza para café   coffee cup
la cafetera   coffeepot
>   cafetera eléctrica   electric percolator
la cajeta   *kind of jelly*
el calamar   squid
>   calcular   to calculate, estimate
>   calentar (ie)   to heat
la calidad   quality, grade
>   caliente   warm, hot
el calor   heat, warmth
>   hacer (mucho) calor   to be (very) warm (*weather*)
>   tener (mucho) calor   to be (very) warm (*living beings*)
el Callao   Callao (*port near Lima, Peru*)
la calle   street
la cámara   camera
>   cámara de cine (de treinta y cinco milímetros)   (35-millimeter) movie camera
>   cambiar   to change
>   van cambiando   (they) are (gradually) changing
el cambio   change
>   en cambio   on the other hand
la caminata   hike, long walk
el camino   road, way, path, course
la camisa   shirt
el campeón (*pl.* campeones)   champion
el campeonato   championship
el campo   field, country
>   casa de campo   country house (home)
el Canadá   Canada
la canción (*pl.* canciones)   song
la cancha   field (*sport*)
el candidato   candidate
la canela   cinnamon
el cangrejo   crab
>   cansado, -a   tired

cansar to tire (*someone*); *reflex.* to become (get) tired
cantar to sing
el **cañón** (*pl.* **cañones**) canyon
la **capacidad (de)** capacity (to)
capacitado, -a competent, qualified
capacitar to qualify, enable
capaz (*pl.* **capaces**) capable
el **capital** capital (*money*)
la **capital** capital (*city*)
el **capitán general** captain general
el **capítulo** chapter
la **cara** face
el **carácter** (*pl.* **caracteres**) character, nature
la **característica** characteristic
caracterizar to characterize
¡**caramba!** gosh! confound it!
cardinal cardinal
Caribe *adj.* Caribbean
Carlos Charles
Carlota Charlotte
la **carne** meat
  carne asada roast, roasted meat
  carne de cerdo pork
  carne de vaca beef
  carne picada ground meat
caro, -a expensive
Carolina Caroline
la **carpintería** carpentry
la **carrera** career
el **carrete** reel
la **carretera** highway, road
el **carro** car (*railroad*)
la **carta** letter
la **casa** house, home
  a casa de (Ana) to (Ann's)
  casa de campo country house (home)
  en casa at home
  en casa de (Juan) at (John's)
  (ir) a casa (to go) home
  (salir) de casa (to leave) home
casado, -a (con) married (to)
el **casado** married man
casarse (con + *obj.*) to marry, get married (to)
casi almost

el **caso** case
  en caso de que in case that
la **cátedra** professorship
  libertad de cátedra academic freedom
la **categoría** category; class, kind; importance, prominence
catorce fourteen
la **causa** cause
  a causa de *prep.* because of
causar to cause
  causar extrañeza a (uno) to surprise (one)
la **cebolla** onion
celebrar to celebrate, hold
célebre celebrated, famous
la **cena** supper
cenar to eat (take) supper
el **centavo** cent (*U.S.*); *also Spanish-American monetary unit*
centenario, -a centennial
el **centímetro** centimeter
central central
  la América Central Central America
centralizar to centralize
el **centro** center
  Centro de Estudiantes Student Center
  (estar) en el centro (to be) downtown
  (ir) al centro (to go) downtown
Centroamérica Central America
centroamericano, -a Central American
cerca de *prep.* near, close to
cercano, -a *adj.* near, close
cerdo: carne de —, pork
la **ceremonia** ceremony
el **cero** zero
  en empate a cero in a zero to zero tie
cerrado, -a closed
cerrar (ie) to close
  hasta el momento de cerrar esta edición until this edition went to press
el **cielo** sky
la **ciencia** science
  ciencias físico-matemáticas physical-mathematical sciences
  ciencias físico-químicas physical-chemical sciences
  ciencias políticas political science(s)

ciencias sociales   social science(s)
científicamente   scientifically
científico, -a   scientific
ciento (cien)   a (one) hundred
   por ciento   percent
cierto, -a   (a) certain, true
   por cierto   certainly, in truth, in fact, for
   sure
la cifra   figure
el cigarro   cigar
cinco   five
cincuenta   fifty
el cine   movie(s)
   cámara de cine   movie camera
cinético, -a   kinetic (*consisting in or depending upon motion*)
la cinta   tape
   grabadora de cinta   tape recorder
la circulación   circulation
circular   to circulate
la circunstancia   circumstance
la cita   appointment, date
citado, -a   cited, above-mentioned
   las citadas   the ones mentioned (listed)
   (*f.*)
citar   to cite, mention, give
la ciudad   city
   ciudad de México   Mexico City
   periódico de la ciudad   city newspaper
el ciudadano   citizen
civil   civil
la civilización (*pl.* civilizaciones)   civilization
Clara   Clara, Clare
claramente   clearly
claro, -a   clear
   ¡claro!   clearly! certainly! of course!
la clase   class, kind
   clase (de español)   (Spanish) class
   compañero (compañera) de clase   classmate
   de ninguna clase   (not) . . . of any kind
   ¿qué clase de . . . ?   what kind of . . . ?
   sala de clase   classroom
clásico, -a   classic
la cláusula   clause
el clérigo   cleric, clergyman, priest

el club   club
cocer (ue)   to cook
la cocina   kitchen
cocinar   to cook
el coche   car
   en coche   by (in a) car
la coexistencia   coexistence
coger   to pick (up), take, gather
la colaboración   collaboration
la colección (*pl.* colecciones)   collection
el colegio   school (*a secondary school which prepares for the university*)
colgar (ue)   to hang (up)
colmado, -a de   crowded with
la colocación   position, place
colocar   to place, put
colombiano, -a (*also noun*)   Colombian
la colonia   colony
colonial   colonial
la colonización   colonization
el color   color
la columna   column
combatir   to combat, fight
combinar   to combine
la comedia   comedy, play
el comedor   dining room
comenzar (ie) (a + *inf.*)   to commence (to), begin (to), start (to)
comer   to eat
comercial   commercial, business, trade
comerciar   to trade, have commercial relations
el comercio   commerce, trade
   comercio exterior (interior)   foreign (domestic) trade
cometer   to commit
la comida   food, meal
el comienzo   beginning
como   as, like; since
   así como   just as, as well as
   como si   as if
   tan + *adj. or adv.* + como   as (so) . . . as
   tanto . . . como   both . . . and; as (so) much . . . as
   tanto, tanta (-os, -as) . . . como   as (so) much (many) . . . as

¿cómo? how? in what way? what?

¡cómo no! of course! certainly!

la comodidad convenience, comfort

cómodo, -a comfortable

la compañera companion (f.)

    compañera de clase classmate (f.)

el compañero companion

    compañero de clase (cuarto) classmate (roommate)

la compañía company

la comparación (pl. comparaciones) comparison

comparar to compare

comparativo, -a comparative

la comparsa group (of actors, musicians)

competir (i, i) to compete

compitiendo pres. part. of competir

completamente completely

completar to complete

completo, -a complete

    por completo completely

componer to compose

el comportamiento behavior, deportment

la composición (pl. composiciones) composition

el compositor composer

la compra purchase

    ir de compras to go shopping

comprar to buy, purchase

comprender to comprehend, understand

compuesto, -a p.p. of componer and adj. compound

compuso pret. of componer

la comunidad community

con with; to

    con tal (de) que conj. provided that

conceder to grant, give

concentrar to concentrate

la concesión (pl. concesiones) concession

el concierto concert

    concierto de música sinfónica symphony concert

concluir to conclude, finish

la conclusión conclusion

la concordancia agreement

el concurso contest, meet

la condición (pl. condiciones) condition

condicional (also m. noun) conditional (tense)

el condimento condiment, seasoning

conducir to drive, conduct

la conferencia lecture; conference

el (la) conferenciante lecturer, speaker

la confesión (pl. confesiones) confession

confirmar to confirm

conformarse (con) to be satisfied (with)

la conga conga (a dance)

la conjunción (pl. conjunciones) conjunction

el conjunto team; whole, entirety

    en conjunto as a whole

conmigo with me

conocer to know, be acquainted with, meet

    mucho gusto en conocerle (-la) a Ud. (I'm very) pleased to meet (know) you

conocido, -a known, well-known, recognized, familiar

    más conocido, -a best-known

el conocimiento knowledge

consciente conscious

conseguir (i, i) to get, obtain, attain; + inf. to succeed in + pres. part.

el consejo council

    el Consejo Board

consentir (ie, i) en to consent to, agree to

conservador, -ora conservative

conservar to conserve, preserve

las conservas preserves

el conservatorio conservatory

considerable considerable

considerablemente considerably

la consideración consideration, regard, respect, significance

considerar to consider, assume; reflex. to be considered

consigo with himself, herself, etc.

consiguiente: por —, consequently, therefore

constar de to consist of, be composed of

constituir to constitute, make up, establish

la construcción (pl. construcciones) construction

constructivo, -a constructive

construido, -a constructed, built

construir to construct, build

consultar to consult, discuss

el contacto contact

  en contacto (con) in contact (with)

contar (ue) to count; to tell, relate; to rate, consider

contemporáneo, -a contemporary

contener to contain

contento, -a contented, happy, pleased; *adv.* contentedly

  lo contentos que están how happy they are

la contestación (*pl.* **contestaciones**) answer, reply

contestar to answer, reply

contigo with you (*fam. sing.*)

la continuación continuation

  a continuación below, which follow

continuar to continue, go (keep) on

  continuará to be continued

contrario: al —, on the contrary

el contrario opposing player; *pl.* the other side, opposing players

contrarrestar to counteract, offset

la contribución contribution

contribuir to contribute

convencido, -a de que convinced that

convenir to be fitting, be advisable

la conversación (*pl.* **conversaciones**) conversation

conversar to converse

convertir (ie, i) to convert

  van convirtiéndose (they) are being converted

la cooperación cooperation

cooperar to cooperate, take part

coordinar to coordinate

la copla popular song, folksong

la corbata necktie, tie

coronado, -a crowned

Coronado *Spanish explorer of the southwestern U.S.*

correctamente correctly, accurately

correcto, -a correct, accurate

correr to run, race, traverse

corresponder (a) to correspond (to), belong (to), concern

correspondiente (a) corresponding (to)

corriente *adj.* current, common, well-known

la corriente current

cortar to cut (off); *reflex.* to cut (oneself)

cortés (*pl.* **corteses**) courteous, polite

la cortesía courtesy

corto, -a short

la cosa thing

  alguna cosa something, anything

la costa coast

costar (ue) to cost

el coste cost

costoso, -a costly, expensive

la costumbre custom

la creación creation

crear to create

crecer to grow, increase

creciente growing

el crédito credit

  crédito exterior foreign credit

creer to believe, think

  creer que sí to believe (think) so

  ¡ya lo creo! of course! I should say so!

cristiano, -a Christian

Cristo Christ

la crítica review, criticism

crítico, -a critical

el crítico critic

cruzar to cross

el cuaderno notebook

la cuadra block (*city*)

el cuadro picture, painting

  cual: el —, la — (los, las cuales) that, which, who, whom

  lo cual which (fact)

¿cuál(es)? which one (ones)? what?

cualquier(a) (*pl.* **cualesquier[a]**) any *or* anyone (at all), just anyone

  cualquier cosa anything (at all)

cuando when

¿cuándo? when?

cuanto: en —, *conj.* as soon as

  en cuanto a *prep.* as for, with regard to

¿cuánto, -a (-os, -as)? how much (many)?

¿**cuánto tiempo?**   how long?
¿**cuántos años?**   how long (many years)?
¡**cuánto** + *verb*!   how . . . !
cuarto, -a   fourth
   una cuarta parte   one fourth
el **cuarto**   room; quarter
   compañero (compañera) de cuarto   room-
      mate (*m. and f.*)
   cuarto de estar   living room
   (**las ocho**) **y cuarto**   a quarter after (eight)
   (**las siete**) **menos cuarto**   a quarter to
      (seven)
cuatro   four
cubano, -a (*also noun*)   Cuban
cubierto, -a (de)   *p.p. of* **cubrir** *and adj.*
   covered (with)
cubrir   to cover
   cubrirse de   to be covered with
la **cuenta**   account, bill
   darse cuenta de   to realize
el **cuento**   (short) story, tale
el **cuerpo**   body
   Cuerpo de Paz   Peace Corps
la **cuestión** (*pl.* **cuestiones**)   question
el **cuidado**   care
   con cuidado   carefully
   tener (mucho) cuidado   to be (very)
      careful
   cuidar de   to take care of
la **culpa**   fault, blame
   tener la culpa   to be at fault, be to blame
cultivar   to cultivate
el **cultivo**   crop; cultivation
culto, -a   cultured, learned
   la **culta**   the cultured one (*f.*)
la **cultura**   culture
   cultural   cultural
el **cumpleaños**   birthday
cumplir   to fulfil, perform, carry out, dis-
   charge
cursiva: en —,   in italics
el **curso**   course
   curso de orientación   orientation course
   dar un curso   to give a course, offer an
      example
la **curva**   curve

cuyo, -a   whose, of whom, of which
el **Cuzco**   Cuzco (*Andean city in Peru, former
   capital of the Inca empire*)

Ch

charlar   to chat, talk
Chávez, Carlos (1899–   )   *Mexican composer and conductor*
el **cheque**   check
el **chile**   chili
   salsa de chile   chili sauce
chileno, -a (*also noun*)   Chilean, of Chile
el **chocolate**   chocolate

D

la **dama**   lady
   parejas de damas   women's doubles
la **danza**   dance
dañar   to harm, hurt
dar   to give
   dar gusto a   to please, give pleasure to
   dar la bienvenida a   to welcome
   dar las gracias a   to thank
   dar un curso   to give a course, offer an
      example
   dar un paseo (una vuelta)   to take a walk
      or stroll
   dar un paso   to take a step
   darse cuenta de   to realize
   darse prisa   to hurry
de   of, from, about, by, to, concerning, with,
   as; in (*after a superlative*); than (*before
   numerals*)
debatido, -a   debated, discussed
deber   to owe; must, ought to, should
   deber de + *inf.*   must, probably + *verb*
   deberse a   to be due to
el **deber**   duty, debt, obligation
debido, -a   just, proper, due
   como es debido   as is proper, as is only
      right
debiera   (I) should, ought to

debiéramos we should, ought to
débil weak
la **debilidad** weakness
la **década** decade
el **decano** dean
decidir to decide; *reflex.* to make up one's
  mind
decir to say, tell
  a decir verdad in truth, really
  diga, dígame hello (*telephone*)
  es decir that is (to say)
  querer decir to mean
la **decisión** (*pl.* **decisiones**) decision
declarar to declare; *reflex.* to declare itself
  (oneself)
decorar to decorate, adorn
dedicar to dedicate, devote
  dedicarse a to dedicate (devote) oneself
  to
defender (ie) to defend
el **defensa** defense; back (*soccer*)
el (los) **déficit** deficit(s)
definido, -a definite
dejar *trans.* to leave (behind), abandon; to
  let, allow, permit
  dejar de + *inf.* to stop (cease) + *pres.*
  part., fail to + *inf.*
  no dejar de + *inf.* not to stop + *pres. part.*,
  not to fail to + *inf.*
del = de + el of (from) the
el **delantero** forward (*in soccer*)
delicioso, -a delicious
delinquir to be guilty
la **demanda** demand
  demanda interior domestic demand
  demás: los (las) —, the other, the rest (of
  the)
demasiado *adv.* too, too much
la **democracia** democracy
democrático, -a democratic
la **democratización** democratization
demostrar (ue) to demonstrate, show
demostrativo, -a demonstrative
el **dentista** dentist
dentro de *prep.* in, inside, within
el **departamento** department

depender (de) to depend (on)
el **dependiente** clerk
el **deporte** sport
  sección de deportes sports section
el **deportista** sportsman
la **deportista** sportswoman
  deportivo, -a (pertaining to) sport, sports
el **derecho** right; law
  el Derecho Law
la **derivación** (*pl.* **derivaciones**) derivation
desagradable disagreeable, unpleasant
desarrollar to develop; *reflex.* to develop,
  be developed
el **desarrollo** development
el **desastre** disaster, catastrophe
desayunarse to eat (take) breakfast
el **desayuno** breakfast
  para el desayuno for breakfast
descansar to rest
el **descanso** rest
el **descenso** decline
describir to describe
descrito, -a *p.p. of* **describir** *and adj.* described
  los descritos the ones described
descubierto *p.p. of* **descubrir**
descubrir to discover
desde from, since; for (*time*)
  desde ... hasta from ... (up) to
deseado, -a desired
desear to desire, wish, want
desenfocado, -a out of focus
el **desenlace** ending, denouement
el **deseo** desire, wish
  tener muchos deseos de to be very eager
  (wish very much) to
desesperadamente desperately, hopelessly
desfavorable unfavorable
la **desgracia** misfortune
  por desgracia unfortunately
desgraciadamente unfortunately
designar to designate, denote
deslizarse to glide, slide
despacio slowly
  lo más despacio posible the slowest
  possible

despedirse (i, i) (de)   to take leave (of), say goodbye (to)

despejado, -a   clear (*weather*)

despertar (ie)   to awaken, wake up; *reflex.* to wake up (oneself)

despierto, -a   awake; alive

después *adv.*   afterward(s), later, then

  después de *prep.*   after

  después (de) que *conj.*   after

destacarse   to stand out

desviar   to divert, turn

el **detalle**   detail

detrás de *prep.*   behind

devolver (ue)   to return, give back

devuelto   *p.p. of* **devolver**

D.F. = Distrito Federal   Federal District

el **día**   day

  al día siguiente   (on) the following day

  buenos días   good morning (day)

  de (en) nuestros días   in (of) our time, (of) today

  hasta nuestros días   up to today, up to the present time

  hoy día   nowadays, today

  otro día   another day

  quince días   fifteen days, two weeks

  todos los días   every day

el **diálogo**   dialogue

  aplicación del diálogo   dialogue adaptation

la **diapositiva**   slide, transparency

el **dibujo**   drawing

el **diccionario**   dictionary

el **dictado**   dictation

  dicho, -a *p.p. of* **decir** *and adj.*   (the) said, (the) aforementioned

  lo dicho   what is (was) said

dieciocho   eighteen

diecisiete   seventeen

Diego   James

diez   ten

diferente   different

diferir (ie, i)   to differ

difícil   difficult, hard

  lo difícil   what is difficult, the difficult thing (part)

  lo difíciles que (son)   how difficult (they are)

la **dificultad**   difficulty

la **difusión**   diffusion

el **diminutivo**   diminutive

dinámico, -a   dynamic

el **dinero**   money

Dios   God

  ¡Dios mío!   heavens! for heaven's sake!

  ¡por Dios!   for heaven's sake!

la **dirección** (*pl.* **direcciones**)   direction

directamente   directly

directo, -a   direct

el **director**   director

dirigir   to direct

  dirigirse (a + *obj.*)   to turn (to), direct oneself (to), go (to), address (*a person*)

la **disciplina**   discipline

el **disco**   record (*phonograph*)

la **discriminación**   discrimination

la **discusión**   discussion

discutir   to discuss, argue, talk about

la **disminución**   diminution, decrease

disminuir   to diminish, decrease

la **disparidad**   disparity, inequality

la **disposición**   disposition, disposal

disputar   to contend (for), contest, fight (play) for, dispute

distinción: a — de   unlike

distinguido, -a   distinguished, famous

distinguir   to distinguish; *reflex.* to distinguish oneself, become distinguished

distinto, -a   distinct, different

la **distribución**   distribution

distribuir   to distribute

diversificar   to diversify

diverso, -a   diverse, varied, different

divertir (ie, i)   to amuse; *reflex.* to amuse oneself, have a good time

  divertirse mucho   to have a very good time

  que se diviertan (Uds.) muchísimo   may you have a very good time

doblar   to fold

doce   twelve

  la de las doce   the one at twelve o'clock

la **docena** (**de**)   dozen (of)
el **dólar**   dollar (*U.S.*)
  doler (**ue**)   to ache, pain, hurt
    le duele (**la garganta**)   (his throat) hurts
el **dolor**   ache, pain
    tener dolor de cabeza   to have a headache
doméstico, -a   domestic
dominante   dominant, dominating, pre-
  vailing
Domingo   Dominic
  Santo Domingo   St. Dominic
el **domingo**   (on) Sunday
  don   Don (*title used before first names of men*)
  donde   where, in which
  ¿dónde?   where?
    ¿por dónde se va . . . ?   how does one
    go . . . ? (*by what route?*)
  doña   Doña (*title used before first names of women*)
  dormir (**ue, u**)   to sleep; *reflex.* to fall asleep,
    go to sleep
    dormir la siesta   to take a nap
Dorotea   Dorothy
dos   two
    los (**las**) **dos**   the two, both
doscientos, -as   two hundred
el **dramaturgo**   dramatist
la **duda**   doubt
    sin duda   doubtless, without a doubt
  dudar   to doubt
  dudoso, -a   doubtful
el **dulce**   sweet, candy
  durante   during, in, for
  durar   to last
  duro, -a   hard

E

  e   and (*used for* **y** *before* **i-, hi-,** *but not* **hie-**)
el **eco**   echo
la **ecología**   ecology
la **economía**   economy
  económico, -a   economic
el **Ecuador**   Ecuador

ecuatoriano, -a   Ecuadorian, of Ecuador
echar (**en, a**)   to throw *or* toss (into)
la **edad**   age
el **edificio**   building
  editorial *adj.*   editorial
Eduardo   Edward
la **educación**   education
  educar   to educate
  educativo, -a   educational
  efectivo, -a   effective
  efectuar   to effect, carry out, bring about
  eficaz   efficacious, effective
  ejecutar   to perform, do, play (*music*)
el **ejecutivo**   executive
  ejemplar *adj.*   exemplary
el **ejemplo**   example
    por ejemplo   for example
  ejercer   to exert, exercise
el **ejercicio**   exercise
  el (*pl.* **los**)   the (*m.*)
    del (**de los**) **que**   than
    el (**los**) **de**   that (those) of, the one(s) of
      (with, in)
    el (**los**) **que**   that, who, which, he (those)
      who (whom), the one(s) who (that, which)
  él   he; him, it (*m.*) (*after prep.*)
la **elección** (*pl.* **elecciones**)   election
  electivo, -a   elective
la **electricidad**   electricity
  eléctrico, -a   electric
  elegante   elegant
  elegir (**i, i**)   to elect, choose, select
el **elemento**   element
    estar en su elemento   to be in one's
    element
Elena   Helen, Ellen
  elevado, -a   elevated, high
  elevar   to elevate, raise, lift
  eliminar   to eliminate
  ella   she; her, it (*f.*) (*after prep.*)
  ello *neuter pron.*   it
  ellos, -as   they, them (*after prep.*)
  embargo: sin —,   nevertheless
  emigrar   to emigrate
la **emisora**   broadcasting station
la **emoción** (*pl.* **emociones**)   emotion

emocionante thrilling, exciting

la empanada *small meat* (or *fish*) *pie*

el emparedado sandwich

el empate tie (*in game*)

empezar (ie) (a + *inf.*) to begin *or* start (to)

el empleado employee

emplear to employ, use

emprender to undertake

  se está emprendiendo (it) is being undertaken

la empresa company, firm, enterprise

en in, on, at, into, of, by, to

  en (el partido) at (the game)

encantado, -a delighted, charmed

  ¡encantado, -a! (I'll be) delighted to!

encantar to charm, delight

encima: por — de *prep.* over, above

encontrar (ue) to encounter, find, meet; *reflex.* to be, be found, find oneself, meet

  encontrarse con to run across (into), meet

la encuesta poll, inquiry

la enchilada corn cake with chili

la energía energy

el énfasis emphasis

enfermo, -a ill, sick; sickly (*with* ser)

enfocado, -a in focus

enfocar to focus

el enfoque focus(ing)

enfrentarse con to face

enfrente de *prep.* in front of

la enhorabuena congratulations

  ¡enhorabuena! congratulations (to you)!

enorme enormous, large

enormemente enormously

Enrique Henry

enrollado, -a rolled

la ensalada salad

la enseñanza education, instruction, teaching

enseñar (a + *inf.*) to teach *or* show (how to)

entender (ie) to understand

el entendimiento understanding

la entidad entity, body, organization

entonces then, at that time

entrante coming, next

entrar (en + *obj.*) to enter, come (go) in

entre between, among, in

entregar to hand (over), turn in, deliver

el entrenador coach, trainer

el entretenimiento entertainment, amusement

entusiasmar to make enthusiastic, thrill, excite very much

enviar to send

envidiar to envy

envolver (ue) to wrap (up)

envuelto *p.p. of* envolver

la época epoch, period, time

el equipaje baggage, luggage

el equipo team

  los bienes de equipo capital goods

equitativo, -a equitable

equivalente *adj. and m. noun* equivalent

equivaler to be equivalent to

equivocarse to be mistaken

el erizo hedgehog

Ernesto Ernest

errar (ye) to err, miss (*a shot*)

la erre *the letter* "rr"

el escabeche pickled fish

la escena scene

  música de escena background music

escoger to choose, select

escribir to write

  está por escribir (it) is to be written

escrito, -a *p.p. of* escribir *and adj.* written

  lo escrito what is (was, has been) written

la escritora writer (*f.*)

el escritorio desk, writing desk

escuchar to listen (to)

la escuela school

  escuela superior high (secondary) school

la escultura sculpture

ese, esa (-os, -as) *adj.* that, those (*nearby*)

ése, ésa (-os, -as) *pron.* that (one), those

la esencia essence

esencial essential

esforzarse (ue) por to strive to, make an effort to

el esfuerzo (por) effort (to)

eso *neuter pron.* that

  a eso de at about (*time*)

  por eso therefore, because of that, for that reason, that's why

el **espacio** space, room
espada: el pez — volante marlin
España Spain
  la Nueva España New Spain (= Mexico)
español, -ola (*also noun*) Spanish; Spaniard
el **español** Spanish (*language*)
  (**departamento**) **de español** Spanish (department)
especial special
especializarse en to specialize in
especialmente especially
la **especie** kind, species
el **espectáculo** spectacle
el **espectador** spectator
la **esperanza** (*also pl.*) hope
  esperar to wait (for); to hope, expect
  esperar mucho to wait long (a long time)
  (**no**) **esperar más** (not) to wait (any) longer
el **espíritu** spirit
espontáneo, -a spontaneous
la **esposa** wife
el **esposo** husband
el **esquí** (*pl.* **esquíes**) ski
el **esquiador** skier
esquiar to ski
la **esquina** corner (*street*)
establecer to establish, set up
el **establecimiento** establishment
la **estación** (*pl.* **estaciones**) station; season
  estación de gasolina service (gas) station
el **estadio** stadium
el **estado** state
  los Estados Unidos United States
la **estampa** stamp, engraving
la **estancia** stay
  estar to be; to look, taste, feel
  cuarto de estar living room, lounge
  está bien all right, that's fine
  ¿**está** (**Carlos**)? is (Charles) in (at home)?
  está por escribir (it) is to be written
  estar al tanto de to be aware of, be informed of
  estar para to be about to, be on the point of
  estar por to feel like, be inclined to, be in favor of
la **estática** static

este, esta (**-os, -as**) *adj.* this, these
éste, ésta (**-os, -as**) *pron.* this (one), these; the latter
estelar stellar, star (*adj.*)
  figura estelar star, super player
el **estilo** style
estimular to stimulate
el **estímulo** stimulus
esto *neuter pron.* this
estratégico, -a strategic
estrecho, -a narrow, close, rigid
estrenar to perform (present) for the first time
el **estreno** première, first performance
estropear to ruin
la **estructura** structure
la **estructuración** building process
el (**la**) **estudiante** student
  Centro de Estudiantes Student Center
  residencia de estudiantes student residence hall (dormitor)
estudiar to study
el **estudio** study
  plan de estudios curriculum
  programa de estudio program of study, curriculum (*pl.* curricula)
la **etapa** stage
etcétera et cetera, etc., and so forth
eterno, -a eternal
ético, -a ethical
Europa Europe
europeo, -a European
evidente evident, obvious
la **evolución** evolution
evolutivo, -a evolutionary
exactamente exactly, correctly
exacto, -a exact
exagerar to exaggerate
el **examen** (*pl.* **exámenes**) exam(ination)
examinar to examine
excelente excellent, fine
excepcional exceptional
excesivo, -a excessive
la **exclamación** (*pl.* **exclamaciones**) exclamation
la **excursión** (*pl.* **excursiones**) excursion, trip

hacer una excursión to make (take) an excursion
exhibir to exhibit, show
exigir to require, demand
la **existencia** existence
existente existent, extant
existir to exist, be, be in existence
el **éxito** success
  con éxito successfully
la **expedición** (*pl.* **expediciones**) expedition
experimentar to experiment
explicar to explain
la **exploración** (*pl.* **exploraciones**) exploration
explorar to explore
el **exponente** exponent
exponer to set forth, state
la **exportación** (*pl.* **exportaciones**) export, exportation
la **exposición** (*pl.* **exposiciones**) exhibition; exposure
expresar to express
la **expresión** (*pl.* **expresiones**) expression
exprimir to squeeze
expulsar to expel
extender(se) (ie) to extend, spread (out)
extendido, -a extended
la **extensión** (*pl.* **extensiones**) extent, range
extenso, -a extensive, large
exterior exterior; foreign
  comercio (crédito) exterior foreign trade (credit)
extranjero, -a strange, foreign
el **extranjero** foreigner; foreign countries, abroad
  en el extranjero abroad
la **extrañeza** surprise
  causar extrañeza a (uno) to surprise (one)
extraño, -a strange, unusual
extraordinario, -a extraordinary
el **extremo** extreme

F

la **faceta** facet, face, aspect
fácil easy

fácilmente easily
el **factor** factor
facturar to check (*baggage*)
la **facultad** school (*in a university*)
la **falta** lack, want
  por falta de *prep.* for (the) lack of
faltar to be lacking (missing), need, be in need of
  no puede faltar it must appear, it cannot be missing
fallar to fail, be wanting
la **familia** family
famoso, -a famous
fantástico, -a fantastic
la **farmacia** pharmacy, drugstore
el **favor** favor
  haga Ud. el favor de + *inf.* please + *verb*
  por favor please (*at end of request*)
favorecer to favor, help
favorito, -a favorite
la **fe** faith
febrero February
fecundo, -a fruitful
la **fecha** date
la **felicidad** happiness
felicitar to congratulate
Felipe Philip
feliz (*pl.* **felices**) happy; *adv.* happily
femenino, -a feminine, women's
la **feminista** feminist
la **feria** fair
férrea: la línea —, railway
el **ferrocarril** railroad
fértil fertile
la **fiebre** fever
la **fiesta** fiesta, festival, party, holiday
la **figura** figure, person
  figura estelar star, super player
figurar to figure, appear, be
fijado, -a fixed, determined
fijar to fix, establish, determine
la **fila** row
la **filosofía** philosophy
el **fin** end, purpose
  a fin de que *conj.* in order that
  por fin finally, at last

el **final**   end
   al **final**   at the end
la **financiación**   financing
físico, -a   physical
físico-matemático, -a   physical-mathematical
físico-químico, -a   physical-chemical
el **flan**   custard
la **flor**   flower
florecer   to flourish
la **Florida**   Florida
el **foco**   focus, center
fomentar   to foment, encourage, promote,
   foster
el **fondo**   background
la **forma**   form
   en **forma de**   in the form of
la **formación**   formation
formar   to form, make (up), be
   formar parte de   to be a member of, form
   a part of
fortalecer   to strengthen, support
la **foto**   photo
   sacar fotos   to take photos
fotogénico, -a   photogenic
la **fotografía**   photograph
fotográfico, -a   photographic
el **fotógrafo**   photographer
el **fraccionamiento**   fractioning, division
el **fragmento**   fragment
francés, -esa   French
el **francés**   French (*language*); Frenchman
   los **franceses**   the French (people)
   (**profesora**) **de francés**   French (teacher)
Francia   France
Francisco   Francis
la **frase**   phrase, sentence
la **fraseología**   phraseology
Fray   Friar (*title*)
la **frecuencia**   frequency
   con **frecuencia**   frequently
   frecuencia modulada   FM (*radio*)
fregar (ie)   to scrub, wash (*dishes*)
frente a *prep.*   in the face (presence) of
el **fresco**   coolness, fresh air
   hacer (mucho) fresco   to be (very) cool
   (*weather*)
los **frijoles refritos**   refried beans

frío, -a   cold
el **frío**   cold
   hacer (mucho) frío   to be (very) cold
   (*weather*)
   tener (mucho) frío   to be (very) cold
   (*living beings*)
frito, -a   fried
la **frontera**   frontier
las **frutas**   fruit(s)
   conservas de frutas   fruit preserves
la **fuente**   fountain; source
fuera de *prep.*   outside of
fuerte   strong
la **fuerza**   force, strength
fumar   to smoke
la **función** (*pl.* **funciones**)   function
funcionar   to function, work, run (*something
   mechanical*)
el **funcionario**   official, public official
el **fundador**   founder
fundar   to found, establish
la **furia**   fury
la **fusión**   fusion
el **fútbol**   football
   (**partido**) **de fútbol**   football (game)
el **futbolista**   football player
futuro, -a   future
el **futuro**   future; future tense
   futuro perfecto   future perfect (*tense*)

G

Gabriela   Gabriela
la **galería**   gallery
la **gana**   desire
   tener ganas de   to feel like, be anxious to
la **ganadería**   livestock raising
el **ganador**   winner
ganar   to gain, earn, win
   ganarse la vida   to earn a (one's) living
   va ganando   (it) is gaining
la **ganga**   bargain
garantizar   to guarantee
García Lorca, Federico   (1898–1936)
   Spanish poet and dramatist

la **garganta** throat
la **gasolina** gas(oline)
    estación de gasolina gas (service) station
    gastar to waste, use (up), spend (*money*)
el **gato** cat
la **generación** (*pl.* **generaciones**) generation
    general *adj.* general
      en general in general, generally
      por lo general in general, generally
la **generalización** generalization
    generalmente generally
el **género** gender
el **genio** genius
la **gente** people
    mucha gente many people
el **gentío** crowd, mob
la **geografía** geography
    geográfico, -a geographic
la **germinación** germination
la **gimnasia** gymnastics
el **glosario** glossary
    glotón, -ona gluttonous
el **gobierno** government
el **gol** goal (*in sports*)
el **golf** golf
la **golfista** golfer (*f.*)
el **golpe** stroke
    gozar (**de** + *obj.*) to enjoy
la **grabadora** recorder
    grabadora de cinta tape recorder
    grabar to tape, record
    gracias thanks, thank you
      dar las gracias a uno (por) to thank one (for)
      gracias a thanks to
      muchas gracias many thanks, thank you very much
el **grado** degree, level
    graduado, -a graduate
    graduarse to graduate
    gráfico, -a graphic
    gramatical grammatical
    gran great, large (*used for* **grande** *before a sing. noun*)
    grande large, big, great
    grato, -a pleasing, pleasant
    grave grave, serious

gravísimo, -a very grave (serious)
    gritar to shout, cry out
el **grito** cry, shout
el **grupo** group, class
    Guadalupe Hidalgo *town near Mexico City where the treaty of February 2, 1848, ceding California, Arizona, and New Mexico to the U.S., was signed*
el **guajolote** turkey (*Mex.*)
el **guante** glove
    guapo, -a handsome, good-looking, pretty
    guatemalteco, -a Guatemalan
la **guerra** war
    Guillermo William
el **guisado** stew
la **guitarra** guitar
    gustar to be pleasing (to), like
      de esos que no gustan of those which are not pleasing (entertaining)
      gustar más to like more (better, best), prefer
      (me) gustaría (I) should like
      ¿qué le gustaría (a Ud.)? what would you like?
el **gusto** pleasure
    con mucho gusto gladly, with great (much) pleasure
    dar gusto a to please, give pleasure to
    mucho gusto en conocerle (-la) a Ud. (I'm very) pleased to meet (know) you
    tener mucho gusto en to be very glad (pleased) to

H

la **Habana** Havana
    haber to have (*auxiliary*); to be (*impersonal*)
    ha habido there has (have) been
    haber de + *inf.* to be (be supposed) to
    había there was (were)
    habrá there will be
    hay there is (are)
    hay (había, hubo, habrá) que + *inf.* it is (was, will be) necessary to, one must (should)
    no hay que olvidar one must not forget

que haya that there may be

¿qué hay (había) de nuevo? what's (what was) new?

el habitante inhabitant

hablador, -ora talkative

hablar to speak, talk

habla (Carlos) this is (Charles), (Charles) is speaking

hablar más alto to speak up (louder)

oír hablar de to hear of (about)

hacer to do, make; to have; to be (*weather*)

¿cuánto tiempo hace? how long (much time) has it been?

desde hace una hora for an hour

hace (media hora) (a half hour) ago

hace poco a short time ago

hace tiempo it is a long time, for a long time

hace una hora que llegué it is an hour since I arrived

hacer buen (mal) tiempo to be good (bad) weather

hacer un viaje (una excursión) to take (make) a trip (an excursion)

hacerlo poner to have it put

hacerse + *noun* to become

hacía tiempo que no (os) veía (I) had not seen (you) for a long time

haga (Ud.) el favor de + *inf.* please + *verb*

¿qué le vamos a hacer? we can't do anything about it, it cannot be helped

¿qué tiempo hace? what kind of weather is it?

hacia toward(s), about (*with date*)

el hada (*f.*) fairy

hallar to find; *reflex.* to be, be found, find oneself

el hambre (*f.*) hunger

a buen hambre when hunger is great

muerto, -a de hambre starving (to death)

tener (mucha) hambre to be (very) hungry

la hamburguesa hamburger

la harina flour

harina de maíz cornmeal

hasta *prep.* until, to, up to, as far as

desde ... hasta from ... (up) to

hasta luego see you later, until (I see you later)

hasta que *conj.* until

hay there is (are)

hay que + *inf.* one must + *verb*, it is necessary to

¿qué hay de nuevo? what's new?

la hayaca tamale (*Venezuela*)

hecho, -a *p.p. of* **hacer** *and adj.* made, done

lo hecho what is (was) done

el hecho fact

el hecho de que the fact that

el hemisferio hemisphere

la herencia inheritance, heritage

la hermana sister

la hermanita little sister

el hermanito little brother

el hermano brother; *pl.* brothers, brother(s) and sister(s)

hermoso, -a beautiful, pretty

la herrería blacksmithing

el hielo ice

la hija daughter

el hijo son; *pl.* children

hispánico, -a Hispanic

hispano, -a (*also noun*) Hispanic, Spanish

la América hispana Spanish (Hispanic) America

Hispanoamérica Spanish America

hispanoamericano, -a (*also noun*) Spanish (Hispanic) American

la hispanoamericana the Spanish American (one) (*f.*)

la historia history

pasar a la historia to become a thing of the past

histórico, -a historical

el hockey hockey

el hogar home

la hoja leaf

¡hola! hello!

el hombre man

¡hombre! man (alive)!

hondo, -a deep, profound, far-reaching

la honra honor

honrado, -a honorable, honest
la hora hour, time (*of day*)
  ¿a qué hora? at what time? when?
  ya es la hora the hour is over
el horno oven
  al horno in the oven
el hospital hospital
el hotel hotel
  hoy today
  hoy día nowadays, today
el hoyo hole
el huarache sandal, huarache
el huerto garden
  huir to flee
las humanidades humanities
  humanitario, -a humanitarian
  humano, -a human
    lo humano what is human, the human thing
la humita tamale (*South America*)
el humo smoke

I

iberoamericano, -a Ibero-American
iconoclasta (*m. and f.*) iconoclastic
la idea idea
el idealismo idealism
la identificación identification
  ido *p.p. of* **ir**
la iglesia church
  a la iglesia to church
la igualdad equality
  igualmente equally
  ilusorio, -a illusory
  ilustre illustrious, famous
la imagen (*pl.* **imágenes**) image
  imaginarse to imagine
  imaginativo, -a imaginative
  imitar to imitate
el imperfecto imperfect (*tense*)
el imperio empire
  impersonal impersonal
  imponer to impose
  importado, -a imported

la importancia importance
  importante important
    lo importante the important thing (part), what is important
  importar to be important, matter; to import
  imposible impossible
    lo imposible the impossible (thing), what is impossible
la impresión (*pl.* **impresiones**) (**de que**) impression (that)
  impresionante impressive, moving
  impresionar to impress, move
  impulsar to impel, move, give impetus to
  inaugurar to inaugurate, open
el incidente incident
  incluido, -a included
la inclusión inclusion
  incompleto, -a incomplete
la incorporación (**a**) incorporation (in, into)
  incorporarse a to be incorporated in
  indeciso, -a indecisive
  indefinido, -a indefinite
la independencia independence
  indicar to indicate
el indicativo indicative (*mood*)
  (**presente**) **de indicativo** (present) indicative
el índice index, rate
  indígena (*m. and f.*) native, Indian, indigenous
  indio, -a (*also noun*) Indian
  indirecto, -a indirect
  indispensable indispensable, absolutely necessary
el individuo individual
  indudablemente undoubtedly
la industria industry
  industrial industrial
el industrial industrialist
la industrialización industrialization
  industrializar to industrialize
  Inés Inez, Agnes
el infinitivo infinitive
  infinito, -a infinite
la influencia influence
el informalismo informalism (*art movement*)

el **informe**   report; *pl.* information, data
la **ingeniería**   engineering
el **ingeniero**   engineer
el **inglés**   English (*language*)
   curso de inglés   English course
el **ingrediente**   ingredient
  ingresar (en + *obj.*)   to enter (*a university*)
los **ingresos**   income, revenue
  inicial   initial
  iniciar   to initiate, start
la **injusticia**   injustice
  injusto, -a   unjust
  inmaterial   immaterial
  inmediato, -a   immediate
el **inmigrante**   immigrant
  inmigratorio, -a   immigration (*adj.*)
  inolvidable   unforgettable
  insistir (en + *obj.*)   to insist (on)
   insistir en que   to insist that
la **inspiración** (*pl.* **inspiraciones**)   inspiration
la **instalación** (*pl.* **instalaciones**)   installation, facility, plant
la **instantánea**   snapshot
la **institución** (*pl.* **instituciones**)   institution
el **instituto**   institute
el **instrumento**   instrument, tool
el **insulto**   insult
la **integración**   integration
  integrar   to integrate
  intensamente   intensely
  intenso, -a   intense, intensive, active
el **intento**   intent, design, plan
el **interés** (*pl.* **intereses**) **(por)**   interest (in)
  interesante   interesting
  interesar   to interest
   interesarse por   to be (become) interested in
  interior *adj.*   interior; domestic
   la demanda (el comercio) interior   domestic demand (trade)
el **interior**   interior, inside
el **intermedio**   intermission
  internacional   international
  interpretar   to interpret
el **intérprete**   interpreter
el **interrogado**   person (party) questioned
  interrogativo, -a   interrogative

la **intervención**   intervention
  intervenir   to intervene, participate, take part
la **introducción**   introduction
  introducir   to introduce
   introducido, -a por   introduced by
la **invención**   invention
  inventivo, -a   inventive
las **inversiones**   investments
la **investigación**   investigation
  invicto, -a   undefeated
el **invierno**   winter
  deportes de invierno   winter sports
  en (el) invierno   in winter
la **invitación** (*pl.* **invitaciones**)   invitation
  invitar (a + *inf.*)   to invite (to)
  invocar   to invoke
  ir (a + *inf.*)   to go (to); *reflex.* to go (away), leave
   ir + *pres. part.*   to be (*progressive form*), go on, keep on, be gradually (+ *pres. part.*)
   (ir) al centro   (to go) downtown
   ir de caza   to go hunting
   ir de compras   to go shopping
   ¿qué le vamos a hacer?   we can't do anything about it, it cannot be helped
   vámonos   let's be going
   vamos   we are going, let's go
   vamos a + *inf.*   we are going to, let's + *verb*
   voy a llegar tarde   I'll be (arrive) late
la **ironía**   irony
  con ironía   ironically, with irony
  irregular   irregular
  Isabel   Isabel, Betty, Elizabeth
la **isla**   island
  Israel   Israel
el **itinerario**   itinerary

J

jabalina: lanzamiento de —,   javelin throw
jactarse (de)   to boast (of)
el **jaguar**   jaguar
Jaime   James, Jim

la jalea jelly
Jalisco *state in west central Mexico*
jamás ever, never, (not) . . . ever
el jamón ham
 emparedado de jamón ham sandwich
el jarabe *a popular dance in Mexico*
el jardín (*pl.* **jardines**) garden
el jefe chief, leader, head
 Jorge George
 José Joseph, Joe
 joven (*pl.* **jóvenes**) young
  el joven young man
  las jóvenes young women
  los jóvenes young men (people)
 Juan John
 Juanita Juanita, Jane
 Juanito Johnny
el juego game
 juego de béisbol baseball game
 Juegos Atléticos Track and Field Games
el (los) jueves (on) Thursday(s)
el jugador player
la jugadora player (*f.*)
 jugar (ue) (**a** + *obj.*) to play (*a game*)
  jugar al (fútbol) to play (football)
 julio July
 junio June
 juntos, -as together
 jurídico, -a juridical, legal
 justificar to justify
la juventud youth

K

el kilogramo kilogram (*2.2 pounds*)
el kilómetro kilometer (*5/8 mile*)
Kino, Eusebio Francisco *Jesuit priest, explorer, founder of missions and forts in Mexico and southwestern U.S.*

L

la (*pl.* **las**) the (*f.*)
 de la(s) que than

la(s) de that (those) of, the one(s) of (with, in)
la(s) que who, that, which, she who, the one(s) *or* those who (that, whom, which)
la *obj. pron.* her, it (*f.*), you (*formal f.*)
la labor (*also pl.*) labor, work
el laboratorio laboratory
la ladera slope
el lado side
 por lado for each side
el lago lake
la langosta lobster
el langostino prawn, crawfish
el lanzamiento de jabalina javelin throw
 lanzamiento de peso shot putting
el lápiz (*pl.* **lápices**) pencil
 largo, -a long
  a lo largo de along
  lo largas que (son) how long (they are)
 las *obj. pron.* them (*f.*), you (*formal f.*) (*also see* **la**)
  de las (seis) of (six) o'clock
la lástima pity
 ¡qué lástima! what a pity (shame)!
 ser lástima to be a pity (too bad)
la lata can
 latino, -a Latin
  la América latina Latin America
 latinoamericano, -a Latin American
el laurel laurel (wreath), honor
 lavar to wash; *reflex.* to wash (oneself)
 le *obj. pron.* him, you (*formal m.*); to him, her, it, you
la lección (*pl.* **lecciones**) lesson
 Lección primera Lesson One
la lectura reading, reading selection
la leche milk
 arroz con leche rice pudding
 batido de leche milk shake
la lechuga lettuce
 leer to read
 leído *p.p. of* **leer** *and adj.* read
  lo leído what is (was) read
 lejos: a lo —, in the distance
la lengua tongue, language
el lente lens
 les *obj. pron.* (to) them, you (*formal pl.*)

las letras   letters (= literature)
   levantar   to raise, lift (up), take up; *reflex.*
      to get up, rise
la ley   law
la leyenda   legend
la liberación   liberation, freedom
   liberación de la mujer   women's "lib"
   liberal   liberal
la libertad   liberty, freedom
el libertador   liberator
   libre   free
la librería   bookstore
el libro   book
   libro de texto   text, textbook
el licenciado   licentiate (*holder of a licentiate
   or master's degree*)
el liceo = *French* lycée, *a secondary school
   which prepares for the university*
el licuado   frappe (made of tropical fruits)
   limitado, -a   limited
   limpiar   to clean
la línea   line
   línea férrea   railway
la lista   list, roll (*class*)
   listo, -a   ready, clever
la literatura   literature
   lo *neuter article*   the; what is (was), *etc.*
      de lo que   than
      lo (contentos, -as) que están   how (happy)
      they are
      lo de   that (matter, affair) of
      lo (malo)   what is (bad), the (bad) part *or*
      thing
      lo más pronto posible   the soonest pos-
      sible, as soon as possible
      lo que   what, that which
   lo *obj. pron.*   him, it (*m. and neuter*), you
      (*formal m.*)
      lo soy   I am
      no lo parece   he doesn't seem so
la localidad   locality, place
el lodo   mud
   haber (mucho) lodo   to be (very) muddy
   lograr   to get, obtain; + *inf.* to succeed in
   + *pres. part.*
   Londres   London

longitud: salto de —,   long jump
los   the (*m.*)
   de los que   than
   los de   those of, the ones of (with, in)
   los que   who, that, which, the ones *or*
      those who (that, whom, which)
los *obj. pron.*   them (*m.*), you (*formal m.*)
lucrativo, -a   lucrative, profitable
la lucha   struggle
   luchar   to struggle
   luego   then, next, later
      hasta luego   see you later, until (I see you)
      later
      luego de *prep.*   after
      luego que *conj.*   as soon as
el lugar   place, site
   en (primer) lugar   in the (first) place
   lugar de veraneo   summer resort
Luis   Louis
Luisa   Louise
el lujo   luxury
   de lujo   deluxe
   lujoso, -a   luxurious
   el más lujoso   the most luxurious (one)
la luna   moon
   hay luna   the moon is shining, it is moonlight
el (los) lunes   (on) Monday(s)
la luz (*pl.* **luces**)   light

Ll

la llamada   call
   llamar   to call, knock; *reflex.* to call oneself,
   be named
      ¿cómo se llama . . . ?   what is the name
      of . . . ? what is (his) name?
      le mandó llamar   (he) had him called,
      (he) sent for him
      llamar por teléfono   to telephone, call by
      telephone
la llave   key
la llegada   arrival
   llegar (a)   to arrive (at), reach, come *or* go
   (to)

llegar a + *inf.* to come to (go so far as to) + *inf.*, succeed in + *pres. part.*
llegar a ser to become, come to be
llegar tarde to arrive (be) late
llevar to take (along), carry, lead; *reflex.* to take (with oneself), take away
llevar a cabo to carry out
llover (ue) to rain

M

macerar to steep, soak
Madelón Madeline
la madre mother
el maestro teacher
magnífico, -a magnificent, fine, wonderful
el maíz maize, corn
   harina de maíz cornmeal
majestuoso, -a majestic
mal *used for* **malo** *before m. sing. nouns*
mal *adv.* bad, badly
la maleta suitcase, bag
malísimo, -a very bad (poor)
malo, -a bad; ill (*with* **estar**)
   lo malo what is bad, the bad thing (part)
la mamá mama, mother
mandar to send, order, command, have
   le mandó llamar (he) had him called, (he) sent for him
el mandato command
la manera manner, way
   de dos maneras in two ways
   de manera ejemplar in an exemplary way
   de manera que *conj.* so that
la mano hand
mantener to maintain, keep
manufacturar to manufacture
mañana *adv.* tomorrow
   mañana (por la noche) tomorrow (night, evening)
la mañana morning
   (ayer) por la mañana (yesterday) morning
   de la mañana in the morning, a.m.

periódico de la mañana morning newspaper
   por la mañana in the morning
el mapa map
el mar sea
   aguja de mar sailfish
la maravilla marvel, wonder
maravillosamente marvelously
maravilloso, -a marvelous
la marca brand, make, kind
   marcar to dial (*telephone*), make (*a score*)
el marco frame, standard, setting
   marchar to march; *reflex.* to leave, go away
Margarita Margaret, Marguerite
margen: al — de on the fringe of
María Mary
los mariachis *musicians who play rousing Mexican popular music*
le mariage (*French*) marriage
marino, -a marine, sea
marítimo, -a maritime
Marta Martha
el (los) martes (on) Tuesday(s)
más more, most; longer
   más conocido, -a best-known
   no esperar más not to wait (any) longer
   no ... más de not ... more than (*before numeral*)
   no ... más que only
   ¡qué obra más interesante! what an interesting work!
   valer más to be better
la masa mass, crowd; *pl.* masses (*people*)
masculino, -a masculine
las matemáticas math(ematics)
matemático, -a mathematical
la materia matter, material
el material (*also pl.*) matter, material; copy (*printing*)
matrimonial marriage (*adj.*)
el matrimonio marriage
máximo, -a maximum, greatest
maya (*m. and f.*) Maya, Mayan
mayo May
la mayonesa mayonnaise
mayor greater, greatest; older, oldest

la mayor parte de the greater part of, most (of)

los mayores older people, elders

la mayoría majority

la mayoría de the majority of, most (of)

la mazorca ear (*of corn*)

hojas de la mazorca del maíz corn husks

me *obj. pron.* me, to me, (to) myself

mecánicamente mechanically

la medicina medicine (*remedy*)

la Medicina Medicine (*science*)

el médico doctor, physician

medio, -a half, a half; middle

hace media hora a half hour ago

la clase media middle class

(las siete) y media half past (seven)

un grado y medio a degree and a half

el medio means, medium; *pl.* means

por medio de by means of

el mediodía noon

al mediodía at noon

mejor better, best

el mejor the better (best) one (*m.*)

lo mejor what is better (best)

la mejora improvement

la melodía melody

la memoria memory

aprender de memoria to memorize, learn by heart

mencionado, -a above-mentioned

menguar to lessen, diminish

menor smaller, smallest, younger, youngest; lesser, least

menos less, least, fewer; except

a menos que *conj.* unless

(las siete) menos cuarto a quarter to (seven)

no fue ni mucho menos (it) was far from

por lo menos at least

la mentira lie

menudo: a —, often, frequently

el mercado market

merecer to merit, deserve

el mes month

la mesa table, desk (*classroom*)

poner la mesa to set the table

meter to put (in)

el método method

el metro meter (39.3 *inches*)

mexicano, -a Mexican

todo lo mexicano everything Mexican

México Mexico

la ciudad de México Mexico City

México, D.F. Mexico City

mezclar to mix, mingle; *reflex.* to be (become) mixed

mi my

mí *pron.* me, myself (*after prep.*)

el miedo fear

tener miedo (de que) to be afraid (that)

tener (mucho) miedo (de) to be (very) frightened *or* afraid (of, to)

el miembro member

mientras (que) *conj.* while, as long as

el (los) miércoles (on) Wednesday(s)

Miguel Michael, Mike

mil a (one) thousand; *pl.* thousands

el milímetro millimeter

militante militant

militar *adj.* military

la milla mile

el millón (*pl.* **millones**) million

(dos) millones de (personas) (two) million (persons)

el millonario millionaire

Millonarios *name of a soccer team in Colombia*

el mineral mineral

mínimo, -a minimum

el ministerio ministry

la minoría minority

el minuto minute

a los pocos minutos after (in) a few minutes

mío, -a *adj.* my, (of) mine

(el) mío, (la) mía, (los) míos, (las) mías *pron.* mine

¡Dios mío! heavens! for heaven's sake!

mirar to look (at)

la misión (*pl.* **misiones**) mission

misionero, -a missionary

mismo, -a same

ahora mismo   right now, right away
las mismas   the same (ones) (*f.*)
los mismos . . . que   the same (ones) . . . as
místico, -a   mystical
Mistral, Gabriela (Lucila Godoy Alcayaga)
　　(1889–1957) *Chilean poetess*
la mitad   half
　　a mitad del camino   halfway
el mitin   meeting, rally
el modelo   model
moderado, -a   moderate
modernamente   recently, lately
modernizar   to modernize
moderno, -a   modern
modificar   to modify, change
el modo   manner, way, means, mode; mood
　　(*grammar*)
　　de modo que *conj.*   so that
　　de todos modos   at any rate, by all means
modulada: frecuencia —,   FM (*radio*)
el mole   *a sauce*
　　mole poblano   *a sauce in the style of
　　Puebla (Mexico)*
molestar   to molest, bother
　　molestarse tanto   to go to so much trouble
　　(bother)
la molestia   bother, trouble
el momentito   (short) moment
el momento   moment; period, time
　　en este (ese) momento   at this (that)
　　moment
la montaña   mountain
Monterrey   *industrial city in northeast
　　Mexico*
Montevideo   *capital of Uruguay*
el monumento   monument
morir (ue, u)   to die
el moro   Moor
el mosaico   mosaic
mostrar (ue)   to show
la motivación   motivation
la movilidad   mobility
el movimiento   movement
la muchacha   girl
　　equipos de muchachas   girls' (women's)
　　teams

el muchacho   boy; *pl.* boys, boy(s) and girl(s)
muchísimo *adv.*   very much
muchísimo, -a (-os, -as)   very much (many)
mucho *adv.*   much, very much, a great deal,
　　hard
　　(esperar) mucho   (to wait) long (a long
　　time)
mucho, -a (-os, -as) *adj.*   much (many);
　　very
　　mucha gente   many people
　　mucho tiempo   long, a long time
mudar   to change
　　mudarse (de)   to change (*one's clothing,
　　etc.*)
la muerte   death
muerto, -a *p.p. of* morir *and adj.*   died, dead
　　muerto, -a de hambre   starving (to death)
la mujer   woman, girl
mundial *adj.*   world(wide), universal
el mundo   world
　　del mundo   world (*adj.*), of the world
　　todo el mundo   everybody
el municipio   municipality, city
la muñeca   wrist
　　torcerse (ue) la muñeca   to sprain one's
　　wrist
mural *adj. and m. noun*   mural
el muralismo   muralism (*painting of murals*)
muralista (*m. and f.*)   muralist, of murals
el museo   museum
la música   music
　　concierto de música sinfónica   symphony
　　concert
musical   musical
el músico   musician
mutuo, -a   mutual
muy   very

N

nacer   to be born
el nacimiento   birth
la nación (*pl.* naciones)   nation
　　las Naciones Unidas   United Nations
nacional   national

nacionalista (*m. and f.*) nationalist(ic)

nada *pron.* nothing, (not) . . . anything; *adv.* (not) at all

   de nada don't mention it, you're welcome

   nada de particular nothing special

nadar to swim

nadie *pron.* no one, nobody, (not) . . . anybody (anyone)

la naranja orange

la natación swimming

náutico, -a nautical

la Navidad Christmas

   las Navidades Christmastime

   las vacaciones de Navidad Christmas vacation

la neblina mist

   hay neblina it is misty

necesario, -a necessary

   lo necesario what is necessary, the necessary thing (part)

la necesidad necessity, need

necesitar to need

negar (ie) to deny

negativamente negatively

negativo, -a negative

los negocios business

   (ejecutivo) de negocios business (executive)

negro, -a black, Negro

neutro, -a neuter

nevado, -a snow-covered

la nevera refrigerator

ni *conj.* neither, nor

   ni . . . ni neither . . . nor, (not) . . . either . . . or

nicaragüense (*m. and f.*) Nicaraguan

la niebla fog

   hay niebla it is foggy

la nieve snow

ningún *used for* **ninguno** *before m. sing. nouns*

ninguno, -a *adj. and pron.* no, no one, none, (not) . . . any (anybody, anyone)

la niña little girl

el niño little boy, child; *pl.* children

el nivel level

en todos los niveles at all levels

nivel de vida standard of living

no *adv.* no, not

   ¡cómo no! of course! certainly!

   (yo) no not (I)

Nobel, Alfred Bernard (1833–1896) *Swedish chemist and manufacturer of explosives; founder of the Nobel Prizes*

la noche night, evening

   (el sábado) por la noche (Saturday) evening *or* night

   esta noche tonight

   mañana por la noche tomorrow night (evening)

   todas las noches every night (evening)

el nombre name

la norma norm, standard

el norte north

   Norteamérica North America

   norteamericano, -a (*also noun*) (North) American

nos *obj. pron.* us, to us, (to) ourselves, (*reciprocal pron.*) (to) one another, each other

nosotros, -as we, us (*after prep.*); ourselves

la nota note

notable notable, noteworthy

   lo más notable the most notable thing

notar to note, observe, see

la noticia news, news item, notice; *pl.* news, information

   sección de noticias news section

novecientos, -as nine hundred

la novela novel

el novelista novelist

noventa ninety

la novia sweetheart, fiancée, girlfriend

el novio sweetheart, fiancé, boyfriend

la nube cloud

nublado, -a cloudy

nuestro, -a *adj.* our, (of) ours

   (el) nuestro, (la) nuestra, (los) nuestros, (las) nuestras *pron.* ours

   lo nuestro our part, what is ours

nueve nine

   sección de las nueve nine-o'clock section

nuevo, -a new, brand-new; another, different

Nueva España New Spain (= Mexico)

Nuevo México New Mexico

¿qué hay (había) de nuevo? what's (what was) new?

el número number

numeroso, -a numerous, large

nunca never, (not) . . . ever

O

o *conj.* or

o . . . o either . . . or

objetivamente objectively

el objetivo objective

el objeto object, purpose

por objeto as a purpose

la obligación (*pl.* obligaciones) obligation

obligar (a + *inf.*) to oblige *or* force (to)

la obra work (*art, literature, etc.*)

obscuro, -a (*also spelled* oscuro, -a) dark

la observación (*pl.* observaciones) observation

observar to observe, note, see, watch

el obstáculo obstacle

obtener to obtain, get

la ocasión (*pl.* ocasiones) occasion, opportunity

occidental west, western

octubre October

ocupado, -a busy, occupied

ocupar to occupy, hold (*a place*)

ocuparse de to take care of

ocurrir to occur, happen

ochenta eighty

ocho eight

ochocientos, -as eight hundred

OEA = Organización de los Estados Americanos Organization of American States

oficial *adj.* official

la oficina office

el oficio craft, trade

artes y oficios arts and crafts

ofrecer to offer

oír to hear

no se oye nada one can't hear anything

oír hablar de to hear of (about)

¡ojalá! (*used alone*) God grant it! I hope so!

¡ojalá (que) + *verb*! would that . . . ! I wish that . . . !

el ojo eye

oler (ue) to smell (*an odor*)

olvidado, -a de forgotten by

olvidar to forget

no hay que olvidar one must not forget

olvidarse (de + *obj.*) to forget

omitir to omit, overlook

once eleven

la onda wave

de onda corta short-wave

Oñate, Juan de *Spanish explorer and founder of present New Mexico*

la ópera opera

la operación (*pl.* operaciones) operation

opinar to be of the opinion, think

la opinión (*pl.* opiniones) opinion

oponer to oppose, face

oponerse a to oppose

la oportunidad opportunity

la oración (*pl.* oraciones) sentence, prayer

el orador orator, speaker

oral oral

el orden (*pl.* órdenes) order, arrangement

la orden (*pl.* órdenes) order, command

el organismo organism, agency, organization

la organización organization

organizar to organize

la orientación orientation

curso de orientación orientation course

orientado, -a orientated

el origen (*pl.* orígenes) origin

original original

la original the original one (*f.*)

originalmente originally

el oro gold

de oro (of) gold

la orquesta orchestra

director de orquesta orchestra director

os *obj. pron.* you (*fam. pl.*), to you, (to) yourselves, (*reciprocal pron.*) (to) one another, each other oscuro, -a   dark

el **ostión** (*pl.* ostiones)   oyster

la **ostra**   oyster

el **otoño**   autumn, fall

otro, -a   other, another

  (el) uno *or* **(la) una a(l) otro, a (la) otra**   (to) each other

  la **otra**   the other one (*f.*)

  los **otros**   the others (other ones)

  otra **vez**   again, another time

  unos (-as) a otros (-as)   (to) one another

P

Pablo   Paul

el **padre**   father; *pl.* parents

la **paella**   *a rice dish containing meat, vegetables, and shellfish*

pagar   to pay, pay for

la **página**   page

el **país**   country (*nation*)

el **paisaje**   landscape, countryside

la **palabra**   word

pálido, -a   pale

el **pan**   bread

la **pantalla**   screen (*movie*)

el **papá**   father, papa, dad

el **papel**   paper; role

el **paquete**   package

el **par**   pair

  un **par de**   a couple (pair) of, two

para *prep.*   for, to, in order to, by (*time*)

  estar **para**   to be about to, be on the point of

  para **que** *conj.*   in order that

  ¿para qué?   why? for what purpose?

el (los) **parabrisas**   windshield(s)

la **parada**   stop

el **Paraguay**   Paraguay

parar *trans.*   to stop

parecer   to seem, appear (to be)

  (me) parece que   (I) think *or* believe that, it seems to (me) that

  me **parece que no**   I think (believe) not

  ¿qué (te) parece . . . ?   what do (you) think of . . . ? how do (you) like . . . ?

la **pared**   wall

la **pareja**   pair, couple

  parejas de damas   women's doubles

el (los) **paréntesis**   parenthesis (*pl.* parentheses)

  entre paréntesis   in (within) parentheses

el **parque**   park

el **párrafo**   paragraph

la **parrilla**   grill

la **parrillada**   barbecue

la **parte**   part, place

  de mi **parte**   for me, on my part

  en gran **parte**   largely, in large measure

  en todas **partes**   everywhere

  formar **parte de**   to be a member of, form a part of

  la mayor **parte de**   the greater part of, most (of)

  por su **parte**   on its part

  una cuarta **parte**   one fourth

la **participación**   participation

participar   to participate

el **participio**   participle

particular   particular; private

  nada de **particular**   nothing special

el **partidario**   partisan, supporter

el **partidarismo**   partisanship

el **partido**   game, match

  partido (de fútbol)   (football) game

partir (de + *obj.*)   to leave, depart

  a **partir de**   beginning with

  partiendo de allí   beginning there

la **pasa**   raisin

pasado, -a   passed, past, last

el **pasado**   past

pasar   to pass, pass on; to happen; to spend (*time*)

  pasa (tú), pase(n) Ud(s).   come in

  pasar **a**   to go to

  pasar a la historia   to become a thing of the past

  pasar al inglés   to pass into (move to) English

  pasar de   to exceed

pasar por to pass (go, come) by *or* along
¿qué (le) pasa? what's the matter with (him)?
el pase pass (*football*)
el paseo walk, ride, stroll, drive
   dar un paseo to take a walk (stroll)
pasivo, -a passive
el paso step
   dar un paso to take a step
la pasta paste (*confection*)
el patín (*pl.* **patines**) skate
patinar to skate
el patio patio, courtyard
la pausa pause
el pavo turkey (*Spain*)
la paz peace
   Cuerpo de Paz Peace Corps
la pedagogía pedagogy, teaching
pedir (i, i) to ask, ask for, request
   pedir a uno to ask (of) one
la película film
peligroso, -a dangerous
el pelo hair
la pelota ball
la pena: valer —, to be worth while
la península peninsula
peninsular peninsular (*of Spain*)
penoso, -a distressing
el pensamiento thought
pensar (ie) to think; + *inf.* to intend, plan
   pensar en + *obj. or inf.* to think of (about)
peor worse, worst
   lo peor what is worse (worst), the worse (worst) thing
pequeñito, -a very small, tiny
   el pequeñito the very small one (*m.*)
pequeño, -a small, little (*size*)
percibir to perceive, see, comprehend
perder (ie) to lose, miss
el perdón pardon
perdonar to pardon
perfecto, -a perfect
el perfecto present perfect (*tense*)
   (futuro) perfecto (future) perfect (*tense*)
   perfecto presente present perfect
el periódico newspaper

el período period
el perjuicio detriment, damage
   en perjuicio de to the detriment of
permitir to permit, allow, let
pero but
el perro dog
la persona person; *pl.* persons, people
personal *adj.* personal
el personal personnel
la personalidad personality
personalmente personally
pertenecer to belong
pértiga: salto con —, pole vault
el Perú Peru
peruano, -a Peruvian
pesar: a — de *prep.* in spite of, despite
la pesca fishing
el pescado fish (*prepared*)
el pescador fisherman
   pueblo de pescadores fishing village
pescar to fish
pésimo, -a very bad(ly), miserably
peso: lanzamiento de —, shot putting
el pez (*pl.* **peces**) fish
   pez espada volante marlin
el pianista pianist
pianístico, -a piano (*adj.*)
picado, -a minced, chopped, ground
picante hot, highly seasoned
el pico peak
la piedra stone
   de piedra (of) stone
la pierna leg
   romperse una pierna to break a (one's) leg
la pimienta black pepper
el pimiento pepper (*vegetable*)
el pintor painter
la pintura painting
la pirámide pyramid
la piscina swimming pool
el piso floor, story
   piso bajo first floor
la pizarra (black)board
el placer pleasure
el plan plan

plan de estudios curriculum (*pl.* curricula)

la plana page (*printing*)

la plata silver

    de plata (of) silver

el plátano plantain, banana

    hojas de plátano banana leaves

el plato plate, dish

la playa beach

la plaza plaza, square

    plaza de toros bullring

la plenitud fullness, abundance

la pluma pen; feather, plume

el plural plural

el pluscuamperfecto pluperfect, past perfect

la población population

    poblano: mole —, *a sauce in the style of Puebla* (*Mexico*)

pobre poor

poco, -a *adj., pron., and adv.* little (*quantity*); *pl.* (a) few

    a los pocos minutos after (in) a few minutes

    al poco rato after a short while

    al poco tiempo after (in) a short time

    en pocos años in only a few years

    hace poco a short time ago

    poco a poco little by little

    un poco a little, a little while

    un poco de a little (of)

poder to be able, can

    ¿pudieras esperar? could you wait?

    puede (ser) it may be

    ¿se puede entrar? may I (we, one) come in?

el poder power

poderoso, -a powerful; wealthy

el poema poem

la poesía poetry

el poeta poet

la poetisa poetess

    político, -a political

el polvo dust

    hay (mucho) polvo it is (very) dusty

el pollo chicken

    poner to put, put in, place, turn on; *reflex.* to put on (oneself)

poner (el radio) to turn on (the radio)

poner la mesa to set the table

ponerse + *adj.* to become

Popol-Vuh *Popol-Vuh, sacred book of the Mayas*

popular popular

    la popular the popular one (*f.*)

populoso, -a populous

por for, during, in, through, along, by, because of, on account of, for the sake of, on behalf of, about, around, over, per, in exchange for, as (a), (+ *inf.*) to be + *p.p.*

    está por escribir (it) is to be written

    por aquí here, around (by) here

    por ciento (100) percent

    por encima de over, above

    por eso therefore, because of that, for that reason, that's why

    por favor please (*at end of request*)

    por fin finally, at last

    ¿por qué? why? for what reason?

    por semana per (each) week

    (venir) por aquí (to come) this way

    ¡(vosotros) por aquí! (you) here!

el porcentaje percentage

porque because, for

portátil portable

la portería goal (*soccer*)

el portero goalkeeper (*soccer*)

el portugués Portuguese (*language*)

posesivo, -a possessive

la posibilidad possibility

posible possible

posiblemente possibly

la posición position

positivo, -a positive

el postre dessert

postrer(o), -a last

la práctica practice

practicar to practice, go in for

precedido, -a de preceded by

el precio price

precisamente precisely, exactly

la precisión precision

preciso, -a necessary

la preferencia preference

preferido, -a preferred
  la preferida the preferred one (*f.*)
preferir (ie, i) to prefer
la pregunta question
  preguntar to ask (*a question*)
    preguntar por to ask for (about), inquire about
prehispano, -a pre-Hispanic (*before the Spanish discoveries in America*)
el premio prize, award
la preocupación (*pl.* **preocupaciones**) (**por**) preoccupation, worry, concern (with, about)
  preocuparse (con, por) to worry (about), be concerned (with, about)
la preparación (*pl.* **preparaciones**) preparation
  preparar to prepare, fix
    prepararse para to prepare (oneself) for, be prepared for
la Preparatoria Preparatory School
preparatoriano, -a of the preparatory school
preparatorio, -a preparatory
la preposición preposition
preposicional prepositional
presenciar to witness, be present at
presentar to present, introduce, give (*program*)
presente *adj.* present
el presente present (*time*), present tense
el presidio garrison of soldiers; fort
  presidir to preside over
  prestar to lend
el prestigio prestige
  los mejores prestigios the highest prestige
  prestigioso, -a prestigious
el pretérito preterit (*tense*)
  pretérito anterior preterit perfect
la prima cousin (*f.*)
  primario, -a primary
la primavera spring
  día de primavera spring day
  primer *used for* **primero** *before m. sing. nouns* first
    en primer lugar in the first place
primeramente first

primero *adv.* first
primero, -a first
  la primera the first (one) (*f.*)
  Lección primera Lesson One
  por primera vez for the first time
primitivo, -a primitive
el primo cousin
principal principal, main
  las principales the principal ones (*f.*)
el principio principle
la prisa haste
  darse prisa to hurry
  sin prisas unhurriedly, without haste
  tener prisa to be in a hurry
privilegiado, -a privileged, favored
el privilegio privilege
la probabilidad probability
probable probable
probar (ue) to try out, test; *reflex.* to try on
el problema problem
la procedencia origin, source
  proceder to proceed, originate, come
el proceso process, progressive movement
  procurar to procure, obtain, get, attain
la producción (*pl.* **producciones**) production
  producir to produce
el producto product
la productora producer
la profesión (*pl.* **profesiones**) profession
profesional professional
el profesional professional, professional person (*m.*)
el profesor professor, teacher, instructor
la profesora professor, teacher, instructor (*f.*)
el programa program
  programa de estudio program of study, curriculum
  progresar to progress
el progreso progress
  prometer to promise
el pronombre pronoun
  pronto soon, quickly
    lo más pronto posible the soonest possible, as soon as possible
la pronunciación pronunciation
  pronunciar to pronounce
la propaganda propaganda

propagar to propagate, spread
propio, -a proper, suitable, (of) one's own
proponer to propose
proporcionalmente proportionately
proporcionar to furnish, provide
propósito: a —, by the way
propuesto, -a *p.p. of* **proponer** *and adj.* proposed
el **proselitismo** proselytism
próspero, -a prosperous
la **provincia** province
provocar to provoke, incite
próximo, -a next
el **proyecto** project
el **proyector** projector
la **prueba** proof, trial
  prueba negativa negative (*film*)
publicar to publish
la **publicidad** publicity
público, -a (*also m. noun*) public
pudiera (I) could
pudieras (you) could
Puebla *Mexican city east of the capital*
el **pueblecito** small town, village
el **pueblo** town, village; people, nation
la **puerta** door
el **puerto** port
pues *adv.* well, well now (then); why
puesto *p.p. of* **poner**
el **puesto** place, position, post, job
la **pulsera** bracelet
  reloj de pulsera wristwatch
  Punta del Este *coastal city in Uruguay*
el **punto** point
  en punto sharp (*time*)
la **puntuación** punctuation
  puñetes: en —, in a fistfight

Q

que that, which, who, whom; than; since;
  indir. command have, let, may, etc.
  de lo que than (what)

del (de la, de los, de las) que than
el (la, los, las) que that, which, who,
  whom, he (she, those) who (*etc.*), the
  one(s) who (*etc.*)
lo + *adj. or adv.* + que how
lo que what, that which, whatever
los mismos . . . que the same (ones) . . .
  as
no . . . más que only
¿qué? what? which?
  ¿para qué? why? for what purpose?
  ¿por qué? why? for what reason?
¡qué + *adj. or adv.*! how . . . ! what . . . !; +
  noun what a (an) . . . !
quebrado, -a broken
quedar(se) to remain, stay; to be
  si queda (algo) if (anything) is left *or*
  remains
quejarse (de) to complain (of, about)
querer to wish, want
  no quieren (esperar) (they) won't *or* are
  unwilling (to wait)
  no quisieron esperar (they) refused to *or*
  would not wait
  querer (a) to love, like
  querer decir to mean
  ¿quieres (quiere Ud.) + *inf.*? will you
  + *verb*?
  quisiera (I) should *or* would like
  quiso hacer eso (he) tried to do that
querido, -a dear
el **queso** cheese
  emparedado de queso cheese sandwich
quien (*pl.* **quienes**) who, whom, he (those)
  who, the one(s) who
¿quién(es)? who? whom?
  ¿de quién(es) es? whose is it?
¡quién! who!
quince fifteen
  quince días fifteen days, two weeks
quisiera (I) should *or* would like
quitar to take away (off), remove; *reflex.* to
  take off (*oneself*)
  quitar (el radio) to turn off (the radio)
Quito *capital of Ecuador*
quizá(s) perhaps

R

el **rabo** tail
racionalista (*m. and f.*) rationalistic
radical radical; (*m. noun*) stem
el **radio** radio (*set*)
la **radio** radio (*communication*)
rajarse to boast (*Mex.*)
rallado, -a grated
Ramón Raymond
rápidamente rapidly, fast
   lo **más rápidamente posible** the fastest possible, as fast (rapidly) as possible
la **rapidez** rapidity, speed
rápido, -a rapid(ly), fast
el **rato** while, short time (while)
   al **poco rato** after a short while
la **razón** (*pl.* **razones**) reason
   no tener razón to be wrong
   sin razón alguna without any reason at all
   tener razón to be right
la **realización** achievement, carrying out
realizar to realize, carry out, accomplish; *reflex.* to be carried out, become fulfilled
el **recado** message
recibir to receive, welcome
reciente recent
recientemente recently
recitar to recite, give
la **recomendación** (*pl.* **recomendaciones**) recommendation
recomendar (ie) to recommend
reconocer to recognize
recordar (ue) to recall, remember, remind (one of)
rectangular rectangular
rectángulo, -a rectangular
rectificar to rectify
el **rector** rector, president
la **rectoría** rector's (president's) office
el **recurso** resource; *pl.* resources, means
rechazar to reject
la **red** network
redundante redundant
refinado, -a refined
   el **más refinado** the most refined (one)

reflejar to reflect
reflexivo, -a reflexive
la **reforma** reform
el **refrán** (*pl.* **refranes**) proverb
el **refresco** refreshment, cold (soft) drink
refrito, -a refried
regalar to give (*as a gift*)
el **regalo** gift
el **régimen** (*pl.* **regímenes**) regime, rule
la **región** (*pl.* **regiones**) region
regional regional
el **reglamento** regulation(s)
regresar to return, come back
el **regreso** return
   de regreso a returning (to), on one's return to
regular regular
reír (i, i) to laugh
la **relación** (*pl.* **relaciones**) relation
   en relación con in relation to
relacionarse (con) to be related (to)
relativamente relatively
relativo, -a relative
religioso, -a religious
el **reloj** watch
   reloj de pulsera wristwatch
rellenar to fill, stuff
   rellenarse de to be filled (stuffed) with
relleno, -a stuffed, filled
el **remedio** remedy
reñido, -a hard-fought
reñir (i, i) to scold
repasar to review
   para repasar for review
el **repaso** review
   Repaso primero Review One, First Review
el **repertorio** repertory, repertoire
repetir (i, i) to repeat
el **representante** representative
representar to represent, show, express
reproducido, -a reproduced
la **república** republic
reservar to reserve
el **resfriado** cold (*disease*)
la **residencia** residence, residence hall

residencia de estudiantes student residence hall (dormitory)

residencial residential

la resolución solution (*of a problem*)

resolver (ue) to resolve, solve, settle, decide; *reflex.* to be solved (resolved)

respectivo, -a respective

respecto de in (with) regard to, concerning

la responsabilidad responsibility

la respuesta answer, reply

el restaurante restaurant

el resultado result

resultar to result, turn out (to be)

el resumen (*pl.* **resúmenes**) summary

retardar to retard, slow down

la reunión (*pl.* **reuniones**) meeting, gathering

reunir to collect, get (together); *reflex.* to meet, gather, get together

revelar to reveal, make known; to develop (*film*)

revisar to check

la revista magazine, journal

la revolución (*pl.* **revoluciones**) revolution

revolucionario, -a revolutionary

el rey king; *pl.* kings, king(s) and queen(s)

Ricardo Richard

rico, -a rich, wealthy; tasty (*food*)

el rincón (*pl.* **rincones**) corner (*of room*)

el río river

el Río Grande *river between the U.S. and Mexico*

la riqueza wealth, riches

el ritmo rhythm; rate

al ritmo (actual) at the (present) rate

Roberto Robert

rodeado, -a de surrounded by

rojo, -a red

Rolando Roland

el rollo roll (*of film*)

el romance ballad

romper to break

romperse una pierna to break a (one's) leg

la ropa clothes, clothing

mudarse de ropa to change one's clothing

la rosa rose

roto, -a *p.p. of* **romper** *and adj.* broken

rubio, -a blond(e)

la ruina ruin

la rumba rumba (*a dance*)

rural rural

Rusia Russia

S

el sábado (on) Saturday

el sábado por la noche Saturday night (evening)

saber to know (*a fact*), know how, can (*mental ability*); *in pret.* to learn, find out

no lo sé I don't know

sacar to take, take out

sacar de la cancha to take off the field

sacar (fotos) to take (photos)

sagrado, -a sacred

la sala de clase classroom

salir (de + *obj.*) to go out, leave

salir a to go (come) out to

salir de casa to leave home

la salsa sauce

el salto jump, leap

salto con pértiga pole vault

salto de longitud long jump

la salud health

centro de salud health center

saludar to greet, speak to, say hello to

El Salvador El Salvador

san *used for* **santo** *before m. saint's name not beginning with* **Do-** *or* **To-**

San Agustín St. Augustine

San Juan (de los Caballeros) *town north of Santa Fe, New Mexico*

San Roque (1295?–1327) *a French saint venerated for his work in a plague in Italy*

la sanidad health, sanitation

Santiago *capital of Chile*

santiaguino, -a of (pertaining to) Santiago

santo, -a saint, holy, St(e).

Sara Sara(h)

el sarape serape, shawl
la sartén (*pl.* **sartenes**) frying pan
satisfacer to satisfy
satisfactoriamente satisfactorily
satisfecho, -a *p.p. of* **satisfacer** *and adj.*
satisfied
se *pron. used for* **le** *or* **les** (to) him, her, it,
them, you (*formal*); *reflex. pron.* (to)
himself, herself, *etc.*; *reciprocal pron.*
(to) each other, one another; *indef.*
subject one, people, *etc.*
la sección (*pl.* **secciones**) section
sección de noticias news section
la secretaria secretary (*woman*)
el sector sector
secundario, -a secondary
la sed thirst
tener (mucha) sed to be (very) thirsty
seguida: en —, at once, immediately
seguido, -a de followed by
seguir (i, i) to follow, continue, go (keep) on
según according to
segundo, -a second, secondary
en segundo lugar in the second place
seguro, -a sure, certain
estar seguro, -a de + *obj.* to be sure of
estar seguro, -a de que to be sure that
seis six
a las seis at six o'clock
seiscientos, -as six hundred
seleccionar to select, choose
el seleccionado the team which is selected
selecto, -a select
la selva forest, woods
la semana week
por semana per (each) week
semejante similar
el semestre semester
sencillo, -a simple
sentado, -a seated
sentar (ie) to seat; *reflex.* to sit down
la sentencia judgment, opinion
sentimental sentimental
el sentimiento sentiment, feeling
sentir (ie, i) to feel, regret, be sorry

¡cuánto lo sentimos! how sorry we are!
how we regret it!
sentirlo mucho to be very sorry
sentirse bien to feel well
señor Mr., sir
los señores (López) Mr. and Mrs. (López)
el señor gentleman
señora Mrs., madam
la señora lady, woman
señorita Miss
la señorita Miss, young lady (woman)
la separación separation
separado, -a separate(d), apart
septentrional northern
septiembre September
ser to be
es decir that is (to say)
es que the fact is that
no fue ni mucho menos (it) was far from
puede (ser) que it may be that
sea . . . o whether it be . . . or
la serie series
Serra, Fray Junípero *founder of California*
missions
el servicio service
al servicio de in the service of
la servilleta napkin
servir (i, i) to serve
al servirse upon being served
¿en qué puedo servirle(s)? what can I do
for you?
¿para qué sirven los amigos? what are
friends for?
servir de to serve as (a)
sesenta sixty
el sexo sex
si if, whether
sí yes
creer que sí to believe (think) so
sí *reflex. pron.* himself, herself, *etc.* (*after*
prep.)
siempre always
siempre que *conj.* provided that
la sierra mountain range, mountains
la siesta siesta, nap
dormir (ue, u) la siesta to take a nap

siete   seven
el siglo   century
el significado   meaning
significativo, -a   significant, meaningful
el signo   sign, mark
siguiente   following, next
　al día siguiente   (on) the following day
silencioso, -a   silent
la silla   chair
el simbolismo   symbolism
la simetría   symmetry
simpático, -a   likeable, charming, nice
sin prep.   without
　sin embargo   nevertheless
　sin que conj.   without
sinfónico, -a   symphonic, symphony (adj.)
　concierto de música sinfónica   symphony
　　concert
el singular   singular
sino   but
　no sólo (solamente) . . . sino que   not
　　only . . . but
　no sólo . . . sino también   not only . . . but
　　also
　sino que conj.   but
sintonizar   to tune in
el sirviente   servant
el sistema   system
el sitio   site, place
la situación (pl. situaciones)   situation
sobre   on, upon, on top of, over, about, con-
　cerning
　sobre todo   especially, above all
sobrenatural   supernatural
　lo sobrenatural   the supernatural
social   social
　ciencias sociales   social sciences
la sociedad   society
el sol   sun
　hace or hay (mucho) sol   it is (very) sunny,
　　the sun is shining (brightly)
　solamente   only
la soldadera   wife of a soldier, camp follower
　(f.)
el soldado   soldier
soler (ue)   to be accustomed to

solicitar   to solicit, apply for
solo, -a   sole, single, alone
sólo adv.   only
　no sólo (solamente) . . . sino que   not
　　only . . . but
　no sólo . . . sino también   not only . . . but
　　also
el soltero   bachelor
la solución (pl. soluciones)   solution
el sombrero   hat
sonar (ue)   to sound, ring
la sopa   soup
sórdido, -a   sordid
sorprendido, -a   surprised
la sorpresa   surprise
　¡qué sorpresa!   what a surprise!
Sr. = señor
Sra. = señora
Srta. = señorita
su   his, her, your (formal), its, their
subdesarrollado, -a   underdeveloped
subir   to ascend, climb (go) up, rise
　iba subiendo   (it) was rising
subjuntivo, -a   subjunctive
el subjuntivo   subjunctive
　el (presente) de subjuntivo   (present)
　　subjunctive
subordinado, -a   subordinate
subrayado, -a   underlined
substantivo, -a (also m. noun)   substantive,
　noun
substituir   to substitute
　substitúyan(lo)   substitute (it)
　substituyendo   substituting
suceder   to happen
sudamericano, -a   South American
　el Sudamericano   the South-American one
　　(team)
el sueño   sleep
　tener (mucho) sueño   to be (very) sleepy
la suerte   luck
　¡qué mala suerte!   what bad luck!
　¡qué suerte (tengo)!   how lucky or for-
　　tunate (I am)!
　tener (mucha) suerte   to be (very) lucky or
　　fortunate

suficiente sufficient, enough
suficientemente sufficiently
el sufrimiento suffering
el sujeto subject
sumamente extremely, exceedingly
superar to surpass, exceed
superior (a) superior (to)
  escuela superior high (secondary) school
suplir to supply
suponer to suppose
supuesto: por —, of course, certainly
el sur south
  la América del Sur South America
surgir to surge, arise, appear
el suroeste southwest
el surrealismo surrealism (*literary and artistic type of the 20th century*)
surrealista (*m. and f.*) surrealist
suscitar to raise, stir up, arouse
suspender to suspend, stop
suyo, -a *adj.* his, her, its, your (*formal*), their, of his (hers, its, yours, theirs)
  (el) suyo, (la) suya, (los) suyos, (las) suyas *pron.* his, hers, its, yours (*formal*), theirs
  lo suyo what is his (hers, *etc.*); his (her, *etc.*) part

T

el taco *a rolled corn cake*
tal such, such a
  con tal (de) que *conj.* provided that
  ¿qué tal? how are you? how goes it?
  tal vez perhaps
el tamal tamale
también also, too
tampoco neither, (not *or* nor) . . . either
  ni (a mí) tampoco neither do (I), nor (I) either
tan as, so, such
  tan + *adj. or adv.* + como as (so) . . . as
  ¡un día tan hermoso! such a beautiful day!
tanto, -a (-os, -as) *adj. and pron.* as (so) much (many); *adv.* as (so) much

en tanto que while, as long as
estar al tanto de to be aware of, be informed of
por lo tanto therefore
tanto . . . como as (so) much . . . as, as well as, both . . . and
tanto como as (so) much as
tanto, -a (-os, -as) + *noun* + como as (so) much (many) . . . as
el tanto point (*in a score*)
tardar to delay
  tardar (mucho) en to take (very) long to, be (very) long in, delay (long) in
tarde late
  lo más tarde posible the latest possible, as late as possible
la tarde afternoon
  (ayer) por la tarde (yesterday) afternoon
  de la tarde p.m., in the afternoon
  por la tarde in the afternoon
  toda la tarde all afternoon
la tarjeta card (*postal*)
el taxi taxi
  en taxi by (in a) taxi
la taza cup
  taza para café (té) coffee (tea) cup
te *obj. pron.* you (*fam.*), to you, (to) yourself
el té tea
  taza para té teacup
el teatro theater
la técnica technique
técnico, -a technical
tecnológico, -a technological
el teléfono telephone
  llamar por teléfono to telephone, call by telephone
  número de teléfono telephone number
  por (el) teléfono by (on the) telephone
la televisión television, TV
  (programa) de televisión television (program)
el televisor television (TV) set
el tema theme, subject, topic
temer to fear
la temperatura temperature

temprano early

la tendencia tendency

tender (ie) a to tend to

tener to have (*possess*), hold; *in pret.* to get, receive

aquí (las) tiene Ud. here (they) are

¿cuántos años tiene (él)? how old is (he)?

no tener razón to be wrong

¿qué tiene (él)? what's the matter (what's wrong) with (him)?

tener ... años to be ... years old

tener dos años más que to be two years older than

tener ganas de to feel like, be anxious to

tener la culpa to be at fault, be to blame

tener (mucha) suerte to be (very) lucky *or* fortunate

tener mucho gusto en to be very glad (pleased) to

tener (mucho) miedo (de) to be (very) frightened *or* afraid (of, to)

tener que + *inf.* to have to (must) + *inf.*

tener razón to be right

tener tiempo para to have time to

el tenis tennis

la teoría theory

tercer *used for* **tercero** *before m. sing. nouns*

tercero, -a third

el tercio third

terminar to end, finish

el término term

el terreno terrain

preparar el terreno to pave the way

el territorio territory

el texto text

libro de texto text, textbook

ti *pron.* you (*fam. sing.*), yourself (*after prep.*)

la tía aunt

el tiempo time (*in general sense*); tense; weather; period (*sports event*)

a tiempo on time

al mismo tiempo at the same time

al poco tiempo after (in) a short time

¿cuánto tiempo hace? how long (much time) has it been?

hace mucho tiempo for a long time, it is a long time (since)

hacer buen (mal) tiempo to be good (bad) weather

hacía tiempo que no (os) veía (I) had not seen (you) for a long time

mucho tiempo long, a long time

¿qué tiempo hace? what kind of weather is it?

tener tiempo para to have time to

la tienda store, shop

la tierra land

el tío uncle; *pl.* uncle(s) and aunt(s)

típico, -a typical

el tipo type

el tiro shot

el título title, degree

título de bachiller bachelor's degree

el tobillo ankle

torcerse (ue) el tobillo to sprain one's ankle

el (los) tocadiscos record player(s)

tocar to play (*music*)

por tocarse because of being played

el tocino bacon

todavía still, yet

todavía no not yet

todo, -a all, every; *pl.* all, all of them, everybody, everyone; *pron.* all, everything

pensamos ir todos all of us (we all) intend to go

sobre todo especially, above all

toda la (lección) all the *or* the whole (lesson)

toda la (tarde) all (afternoon)

todas las noches (tardes) every night *or* evening (afternoon)

todo lo que all that

todos los (días) every (day)

tomar to take, drink, eat

Tomás Thomas, Tom

el tomate tomato

la tonada air, song

el tono tone

torcerse (ue) to twist, sprain

torcerse la muñeca (el tobillo) to sprain one's wrist (ankle)

torear to fight bulls
el torneo tourney, tournament, match, contest
el toro bull
  plaza de toros bullring
la torpeza stupid mistake
la tortilla omelet (*Spain*); corn pancake
    (*Mexico*)
la tostada toasted corn cake
  tostado, -a toasted
  tostar (ue) to toast
  totalmente totally, entirely
  trabajador, -ora industrious
  trabajar to work
    trabajar mucho to work hard (much)
el trabajo work
  plan de trabajo training plan
la tradición (*pl.* **tradiciones**) tradition
  tradicional traditional
la traducción translation
  traducir to translate
    para traducir al español to translate into
      Spanish
  traer to bring
  trágico, -a tragic
el traje suit
la transformación transformation, change
  transformar to transform, change
el tránsito traffic
  vigilantes de tránsito traffic policemen
la transparencia slide, transparency
el tratado treaty
  tratar (de + *obj.*) to treat (of), deal (with)
    tratar de + *inf.* to try to
  tratarse de to be a question of
  trece thirteen
  treinta thirty
    treinta (y seis) thirty-(six)
  tres three
  trescientos, -as three hundred
  triangular *adj.* triangular, three-way
el triangular triangular (three-way) meet
    (match)
la tribuna grandstand
el tribunal tribunal, court
  tributario, -a of (pertaining to) taxation
el trípode tripod
  triste sad

  lo tristes que (están) how sad (they are)
  tristemente sadly
  tu your (*fam.*)
  tú you (*fam.*)
el tubo tube
el turismo tourism
el turista tourist
  turístico, -a tourist (*adj.*)
  tuyo, -a *adj.* your (*fam.*), of yours
    (el) tuyo, (la) tuya, (los) tuyos, (las) tuyas
      pron. yours

U

  u or (*used for* **o** *before* **o-, ho-**)
  Ud(s). = usted(es) you (*formal*)
  último, -a last (*in a series*), latest
    de los últimos años of the last (past) few
      years
    en estos últimos días during these last
      few days
    en los últimos años during (in) the last
      few years, recently
    este último this last one (*m.*)
    la última the last one (*f.*)
    por último finally, ultimately
  ultramoderno, -a ultramodern
  un, una, uno a, an, one
    (el) uno *or* **(la) una a(l) otro, a (la) otra** (to)
      each other
    es la una it is one o'clock
    (hasta) la una (until) one o'clock
  unánime unanimous
  único, -a only
la unidad unity, teamwork
  unido, -a united
    los Estados Unidos United States
    las Naciones Unidas United Nations
la unificación unification
  unir to unite, join
  universal universal
la universidad university
    (periódico) de la universidad university
      (newspaper)
  universitario, -a university (*adj.*)
    la universitaria the university one (*f.*)

todo universitario every university student

unos, -as some, any, a few, several, a pair of, two; about (*quantity*)

unos (-as) a otros (-as) (to) one another

la **uña** fingernail

la **urbanización** urbanization, city growth (planning)

urbano, -a urban, city (*adj.*)

urgente urgent

el **Uruguay** Uruguay

uruguayo, -a (*also noun*) Uruguayan

usado, -a used

usar to use

el **uso** use

usted you (*formal*)

útil useful

utilizado, -a utilized

V

vaca: carne de —, beef

las **vacaciones** vacation

valer to be worth

más vale (vale más) it is better

valdrá más it will be better

valer la pena to be worth while

valer más to be better

válido, -a valid

valioso, -a valuable

el **valor** value; talented player

vámonos let's be going

vamos we are going, let's go

vamos a + *inf.* we are going to, let's + *verb*

vanguardista (*m. and f.*) vanguardist (*term applied to many "new" movements in the 20th century*)

el **vapor** steam

al vapor steamed, in steam

variar to vary

la **variedad** variety

varios, -as several, various

vasco, -a Basque (*of northern Spain*)

el **vaso** glass

vaso para agua water glass

vasto, -a vast, huge, very large

Vd(s). = usted(es) you (*formal*)

el **vecino** neighbor

el **vehículo** vehicle

veinte twenty

veinte (y seis) twenty-(six)

la **velocidad** speed

a toda velocidad at full speed

vencer to overcome, win out, conquer

la **vendedora** vendor (*f.*)

vender to sell

venir (a + *inf.*) to come

(el verano) que viene next (summer)

venir por aquí to come this way

la **ventana** window

la **ventanilla** ticket window

ver to see; *reflex.* to be (seen)

a ver let's see

nos vemos we'll see (be seeing) each other

veraneo: el lugar de —, summer resort

veraniego, -a summer (*adj.*)

el **verano** summer

en (el) verano in summer

ese triangular de verano that summer three-way match

veras: de —, really, truly

el **verbo** verb

la **verdad** truth

a decir verdad in truth, really

es verdad it is true

¿no es verdad? *or* **¿verdad?** isn't it (true)? aren't (you)? doesn't (he)?

la **vergüenza** shame

tener vergüenza to be ashamed

el **vestíbulo** vestibule, lobby, hall

el **vestido** dress

vestir (i, i) to dress (*someone*); *reflex.* to dress (oneself), get dressed

la **vez** (*pl.* **veces**) time (*in a series*)

a veces at times

alguna vez some time, ever, (at) any time

dos veces twice, two times

en vez de instead of, in place of

muchas veces often, many times

otra vez again, another time

por primera (segunda) vez for the first (second) time

tal vez perhaps

viajar to travel

el viaje trip

¡buen viaje! (have) a good trip!

hacer un viaje to take (make) a trip

el vicecampeón vice-champion, second-place winner

Vicente Vincent

el vicepresidente vice-president

la vida life

el nivel de vida standard of living

ganarse la vida to earn a (one's) living

viejo, -a old

el viento wind

hacer (mucho) viento to be (very) windy

el (los) viernes (on) Friday(s)

el vigilante watchman, policeman

el vigor vigor, strength

el vinagre vinegar

violeta (*m. and f.*) violet (*color; dye*)

la Virgen (*pl.* **Vírgenes**) Virgin

el virreinato viceroyalty

el visitante visitor

visitar to visit

el visor viewfinder

la vista sight, view

en vista de in view of

visto *p.p. of* **ver**

visual visual

la vitalidad vitality

la vivienda dwelling, house

vivir to live

el vocabulario vocabulary

la vocal vowel

volante: el pez espada —, marlin

volar (ue) to fly

volver (ue) to return, come back

volver a (levantar) (to lift) again

vosotros, -as *pron.* you (*fam. pl.*), yourselves

la voz (*pl.* **voces**) voice

en voz alta aloud

la vuelta return

dar una vuelta to take a walk (stroll)

vuelto *p.p. of* **volver**

vuestro, -a *adj.* your (*fam. pl.*), of yours

(el) vuestro, (la) vuestra, (los) vuestros, (las) vuestras *pron.* yours

Y

y and

ya already, now, soon, presently, then; *sometimes used for emphasis and not translated*

ya es la hora the hour is over

¡ya lo creo! of course! I should say so!

ya no no longer

yacer to lie (*position*)

yo I

Z

el zapateado clog (tap) dance

el zapato shoe

la zona zone

English–Spanish

A

a, an un, una; *often not translated*
able: be —, poder
abound abundar
about *prep.* de, acerca de, sobre; *for probability use future or cond. tense*
  at about (*time*) a eso de
absent ausente
accept aceptar
accompanied by acompañado, -a de
accompany acompañar
according to *prep.* según
ache doler (ue)
  (my) head aches (me) duele la cabeza, (tengo) dolor de cabeza
acquainted: be well — with conocer bien
across: run —, encontrarse (ue) con
add añadir
administration la administración
advise aconsejar
afraid: be —, tener miedo
  be afraid that tener miedo de que
after *prep.* después de; (*in giving time*) y
  after a short time al poco rato (tiempo)
  at a quarter after (eight) a las (ocho) y cuarto
afternoon la tarde
  all afternoon toda la tarde
  (yesterday) afternoon (ayer) por la tarde
again otra vez, volver (ue) a + *inf.*
ago: (three months) —, hace (tres meses)
agricultural agrícola (*m. and f.*)
air (*music*) la tonada
airport el aeropuerto
all todo, -a; *pl.* todos, -as
  all (afternoon) toda (la tarde)
alliance la alianza
almond la almendra
almost casi
already ya
also también
although aunque

always siempre
America América
  South America la América del Sur
  Spanish America Hispanoamérica, la América española
American: Spanish (Hispanic) —, hispano-americano, -a
amuse divertir (ie, i)
and y, (*before* i-, hi-, *but not* hie-) e
Ann Ana
another otro, -a
  (visit) one another (visitar)se
any *adj. and pron.* alguno, -a, (*before m. sing. nouns*) algún, (*after negative*) ninguno, -a (ningún); *often not translated*
  any student (at all) cualquier estudiante
  without any reason at all sin razón alguna
anyone alguien, (*after negative or comparative*) nadie
anything algo, alguna cosa, (*after negative*) nada, ninguna cosa
  anything at all cualquier cosa
apartment el apartamento
apathy la apatía
appear aparecer
apply for solicitar
approach acercarse (a)
April abril
architecture la arquitectura
Argentina la Argentina
Argentine *adj.* argentino, -a
arrange arreglar
arrive llegar (a)
  arrive on time llegar a tiempo
art el arte
  art (exhibition) (la exposición) de arte
Arthur Arturo
article el artículo
as como, tan
  as (so) + *adj. or adv.* + as tan . . . como

as if como si

as many + *noun* + **as** tantos, -as . . . como

so much (as) *adv.* tanto (como)

so much (many) + *noun* + **as** tanto, -a (-os, -as) . . . como

(students) as well as (educators) tanto (los estudiantes) como (los educadores)

ask (*question*) preguntar; (*request*) pedir (i, i)

ask for pedir (i, i)

I did not ask him (it) no se lo pregunté

asleep: fall —, dormirse (ue, u)

aspect el aspecto

at a, en

at once en seguida

(be) at the bookstore (estar) en la librería

athletic atlético, -a

attend asistir a

attention la atención

August agosto

aunt la tía

author el autor

available asequible

avenue la avenida

awaken (*someone*) despertar (ie)

away: go —, irse, marcharse

away: right —, ahora mismo

B

bachelor (*holder of degree*) el bachiller

back (*soccer*) el defensa

bacon el tocino

bacon (sandwich) (emparedado) de tocino

bad malo, -a, (*before m. sing. nouns*) mal

not at all bad (no) . . . nada malo, -a

bah! ¡bah!

Barbara Bárbara

bargain la ganga

basketball el básquetbol

Chilean women's basketball team el básquet femenino chileno

women's basketball teams equipos de básquetbol femeninos (de muchachas)

be estar, ser; encontrarse (ue), hallarse; (*visible phenomena*) haber; (*weather*) hacer

be able poder

be afraid that tener miedo de que

be (bad) weather hacer (mal) tiempo

be in a hurry tener prisa

be necessary to haber que (ser necesario *or* preciso) + *inf.*

be right tener razón

be to, be supposed to haber de + *inf.*

be (very) fortunate *or* **lucky** tener (mucha) suerte

be very long in tardar mucho en

be (very) sleepy tener (mucho) sueño

here (it) is aquí (lo) tienes (tiene Ud.)

that there is (may be) que haya

there is (are) hay

there is probably habrá

there will be habrá

there would be habría

what's new? ¿qué hay de nuevo?

beautiful bonito, -a, hermoso, -a, bello, -a

because porque

become + *adj.* ponerse; + *noun* hacerse, llegar a ser

bed la cama

go to bed acostarse (ue)

put to bed acostar (ue)

beef la carne de vaca

ground beef carne picada de vaca

before *prep.* antes de; *conj.* antes (de) que

begin (to) comenzar (ie) (a + *inf.*), empezar (ie) (a + *inf.*)

beginning with a partir de, comenzando (empezando) con

believe creer

believe so creer que sí

I believe not me parece que no, creo que no

besides *prep.* además de

best mejor

like best gustar más

the best one (*m.*) el mejor

the best thing lo mejor

better mejor

Betty Isabel

between entre

bicycle la bicicleta

bill la cuenta

black   negro, -a
  black pepper   la pimienta
block (*city*)   la cuadra
blond(e)   rubio, -a
blouse   la blusa
blue   azul
  the blue one (*m.*)   el azul
book   el libro
bookstore   la librería
  at the bookstore   en la librería
box (*post office*)   el apartado
boy   el muchacho, (*sports*) el hombre
bracelet   la pulsera
brand   la marca
break   romper
  he broke his hand   se rompió la mano
  may he not break a (his) leg   que no se rompa
    la pierna
breakfast   el desayuno
  eat breakfast   desayunarse, tomar el desayuno
bring   traer
broad   amplio, -a
brother   el hermano
building   el edificio
bullring   la plaza de toros
bulls: fight —,   torear
bus   el autobús (*pl.* autobuses)
  the (ten o'clock) bus   el autobús (de las diez)
but   pero, (*after negative*) sino, (*after negative
  before inflected verb*) sino que
buy   comprar
by   por, de, para
  by (plane)   en (avión)
  by working   trabajando

C

cake: corn —,   la tortilla
call   llamar, (*telephone*) llamar por teléfono
  be called   llamarse
camera   la cámara
  movie camera   cámara de cine
can   la lata; poder, (*mental ability*) saber; *for
  conjecture use future tense*
candidate   el candidato

car   el coche
card (*postal*)   la tarjeta
Caroline   Carolina
carry out   efectuar, llevar a cabo
case   el caso
cattle   el ganado vacuno
center   el centro
  Student Center   el Centro de Estudiantes
centralize   centralizar
  be centralized in   centralizarse en
century   el siglo
certain: (a) —,   cierto, -a
champion   el campeón (*pl.* campeones)
championship   el campeonato
change   el cambio; cambiar
  change (one's) clothes   cambiarse de ropa
Charles   Carlos
Charlotte   Carlota
charming   simpático, -a
chat   charlar
check (*examine*)   revisar
cheese   el queso
children   los niños
Chilean   chileno, -a
  chili   el chile, el ají
  chili sauce   salsa de chile
chocolate   el chocolate
choose   escoger
church   la iglesia
  to church   a la iglesia
city   la ciudad
Clara   Clara
class   la clase
  class roll   la lista
  Spanish class   la clase de español
  to class   a clase
classmate   el compañero (la compañera) de
  clase
classroom   la sala de clase
clean   limpiar
clearly   claramente
clerk   el dependiente
close   cerrar (ie)
closed   cerrado, -a
clothes   la ropa
  change (one's) clothes   cambiarse de ropa

cloud   la nube
cloudy   nublado, -a
club   el club
coach   el entrenador
coffee   el café
  coffee cup   taza para café
cold *adj.*   frío, -a
cold   el frío, (*disease*) el resfriado
  be cold (*living beings*)   tener frío
  be (very) cold (*weather*)   hacer (mucho) frío
column   la columna
come   venir
  come by   pasar por
  come in   pase(n) Ud(s).
  come this way   venir (pasar) por aquí
  come to be considered   llegar a considerarse
  come to (work)   venir a (trabajar)
comfortable   cómodo, -a
common   corriente
compete   competir (i, i)
complain (of, about)   quejarse (de + *obj.*)
  complain that   quejarse de que
complete   completar
composer   el compositor
composition   la composición (*pl.* composiciones)
concerning   respecto de, sobre
concert   el concierto
congratulate   felicitar
congratulations!   ¡enhorabuena!
consider   considerar
  come to be considered   llegar a considerarse
consist of   constar de
contain   contener
contemporary   contemporáneo, -a
continue   continuar, seguir (i, i)
contribute   contribuir
corn   el maíz
  corn cake   la tortilla
  corn husks   hojas de la mazorca del maíz
corner (*of room*)   el rincón (*pl.* rincones)
Corps: Peace —,   el Cuerpo de Paz
cost   costar (ue)
  could   *imp., pret., or cond. of* poder
  could you (*fam. sing.*) . . . ?   ¿pudieras (podrías) . . . ?

count   contar (ue)
country   el campo, (*nation*) el país
  country house   casa de campo
course   el curso
course: of —!   ¡ya lo creo! ¡cómo no!
courteous   cortés (*pl.* corteses)
cousin   el primo, la prima
crab   el cangrejo
create   crear
credit   el crédito
  foreign credit   el crédito exterior
cup   la taza
  coffee cup   taza para café
curriculum   el programa (plan) de estudio(s)
  curricula   programas (planes) de estudios
custard   el flan
cut   cortar
Cuzco   el Cuzco

D

dance   el baile
dare (to)   atreverse (a + *inf.*)
date   la cita
daughter   la hija
day   el día
  every day   todos los días
deal: a great —,   mucho, muchísimo
deal with   tratar de + *inf.*
dear   querido, -a; *also see letter writing, page 277*
December   diciembre
definite   definido, -a
degree   el título
deny   negar (ie)
department   el departamento
depend on   depender de
describe   describir
desk   la mesa, el escritorio
despite *prep.*   a pesar de
dessert   el postre
determine   fijar
develop   revelar
  have developed   hacer (mandar) revelar
dial (*telephone*)   marcar

dialogue el diálogo
dictionary el diccionario
different diferente, distinto, -a, diverso, -a
difficult difícil
direct dirigir
directly directamente
discuss discutir
dish el plato
distribution la distribución
diversify diversificar
division el fraccionamiento
do hacer; *not translated as auxiliary*
  didn't he? don't they? ¿(no es) verdad?
  what can I do for you? ¿en qué puedo
    servirle(s)?
doctor el médico, (*title*) el doctor
dollar (*U.S.*) el dólar
domestic doméstico, -a
door la puerta
dormitory: student —, la residencia de estudiantes
Dorothy Dorotea
doubt dudar
doubtless sin duda
down: sit —, sentarse (ie)
downtown el centro
  (be) downtown (estar) en el centro
  (go) downtown (ir) al centro
dozen la docena
  a dozen students una docena de estudiantes
drawing el dibujo
dress el vestido
  dress (oneself) vestirse (i, i)
dressed: get —, vestirse (i, i)
drive conducir
drugstore la farmacia
due: be — to deberse a
during durante
  during these last few days en estos últimos
  días

E

each cada
  (see) each other (ver)se

early temprano
earn ganar
easily fácilmente
easy fácil
eat comer
  eat breakfast desayunarse, tomar el desayuno
  eat supper cenar
  eat (take) lunch almorzar (ue), tomar el
  almuerzo
economic económico, -a
economy la economía
education la educación, la enseñanza
  ministry of education ministerio de educación
educational educativo, -a
educator el educador
effort el esfuerzo
eight ocho
  (before) eight o'clock (antes de) las ocho
  before half past eight antes de las ocho y
  media
either o, (*after negative*) tampoco
elders: their —, los mayores
election la elección (*pl.* elecciones)
elective electivo, -a
eleven once
enchilada la enchilada
encounter encontrar (ue)
English (*language*) el inglés
  English course curso de inglés
enormously enormemente
enough *adj.* bastante
enter entrar (en + *obj.*), (*a university*) ingresar
  en
especially especialmente, sobre todo
essential esencial
etc. etc., etcétera
even though *conj.* aunque
ever jamás, alguna vez, (*after negative*) nunca,
  jamás, (*at any time*) alguna vez
every todo, -a
  every (day) todos los (días)
everybody todo el mundo, todos
everything *pron.* todo
evident evidente
examine examinar

exceed   pasar de
excellent   excelente
exciting   emocionante
excursion   la excursión
   take (make) the excursion   hacer la excursión
exercise   el ejercicio
exhibition   la exposición (*pl.* exposiciones)
exist   existir
expect   esperar
expensive   caro, -a
explain   explicar
export   la exportación
express   expresar
extensive   extenso, -a
extraordinary   extraordinario, -a

F

fail: (not) to — to   (no) dejar de + *inf.*
fall   el otoño
fall asleep   dormirse (ue, u)
famous   famoso, -a
fast   rápido, -a
father   el padre, el papá
fault   la culpa
   be at fault   tener la culpa
favorite   favorito, -a
February   febrero
feel like (studying)   tener ganas de (estudiar)
   feel well (better)   sentirse (ie, i) bien (mejor)
feeling   el sentimiento
fever   la fiebre
few: (a) —,   pocos, -as, unos, -as
   during these last few days   en estos últimos
      días
   of the last few years   de los últimos años
Field: Track and — Games   Juegos Atléticos
fifteen   quince
fifty   cincuenta
fight bulls   torear
fill   rellenar
   be filled with   rellenarse de
film   la película
finally   por fin
find   encontrar (ue), hallar

find out (*in pret.*)   saber
finish   terminar, concluir, acabar
first   primero, -a, (*before m. sing. nouns*) primer
   first floor   piso bajo
   the first (*f.*)   la primera
fish   el pescado
   pickled fish   el escabeche
five   cinco
floor   el piso
   first floor   piso bajo
flower   la flor
food   la comida
   of food *adj.*   alimenticio, -a
football   el fútbol, el balompié (*soccer*)
   football game   partido de fútbol
for   por, para
   for (an hour)   desde hace (una hora) *or* hace
      (una hora) que + *verb*
foreign   extranjero, -a, exterior
   foreign credit (trade)   crédito (comercio)
      exterior
forget   olvidar, olvidarse (de + *obj.*)
form   formar
   form a part of   formar parte de
fortunate: be (very) —,   tener (mucha) suerte
   how fortunate (our team) is!   ¡qué suerte
      tiene (nuestro equipo)!
four   cuatro
fried   frito, -a
friend   el amigo, la amiga
frightened: be very —,   tener mucho miedo
from   de, desde
   from ... (up) to   desde ... hasta
fruit   las frutas
   fruit preserves   conservas de frutas
full: at — speed   a toda velocidad
fun: make — of   burlarse de
future   el futuro

G

game   el juego, (*match*) el partido
   today's game   partido de hoy
   Track and Field Games   Juegos Atléticos
garnished (with)   aderezado, -a (con)

general *adj.* general
generally generalmente, en general
gentleman el señor
    gentlemen (*in letters*) muy señores míos (nuestros)
geographic geográfico, -a
George Jorge
get obtener, conseguir (i, i)
    get up levantarse
gift el regalo
girl la muchacha, la mujer
give dar
glad: be (very) — to alegrarse (mucho) de + *inf.*
    how glad I am (that) . . . ! ¡cuánto me alegro (de que) . . . !
    how glad (the students) are (to . . .)! ¡cuánto se alegran (los estudiantes) (de + *inf.*)!
gladly con mucho gusto
glide (over) deslizarse (sobre)
glove el guante
go ir (a + *inf.*)
    don't go to so much trouble no se moleste Ud. tanto
    go away irse, marcharse
    go to bed acostarse (ue)
    go (to Philip's) ir (a casa de Felipe)
goal el gol
goalkeeper el portero
gold el oro
    gold (watch) (reloj) de oro
golf el golf
good bueno, -a, (*before m. sing. nouns*) buen
    have a (very) good time divertirse (ie, i) (mucho)
government el gobierno
gradually *use* ir + *pres. part.*
    (they) are gradually learning van aprendiendo
graduate graduarse
grandparents los abuelos
grant conceder
great gran (*used before sing. noun*); *pl.* grandes
    a great deal mucho, muchísimo
green verde
    the green one (*f.*) la verde
greet saludar

ground picado, -a
group (*musical*) la comparsa
guitar la guitarra

H

hair el pelo
half medio, -a
    half past (seven) (las siete) y media
hall el vestíbulo
ham el jamón
    ham sandwich emparedado de jamón
hamburger la hamburguesa
hand la mano
hand (over) entregar
happy feliz (*pl.* felices), contento, -a
    how happy (he) is lo contento que está
hard-fought reñido, -a
hat el sombrero
have tener; (*auxiliary*) haber
    have (*causative*) hacer *or* mandar + *inf.*
    have *indir. command* que + *pres. subj.*
    have a headache tener dolor de cabeza
    have a (very) good time divertirse (ie, i) (mucho)
    have just acabar de + *inf.*
    have time to tener tiempo para + *inf.*
    have to tener que + *inf.*
he él
head la cabeza
    (my) head aches (me) duele la cabeza, (tengo) dolor de cabeza
headache: have a —, tener dolor de cabeza
hear oír
heat calentar (ie)
heavens! ¡Dios mío!
Helen Elena
help (to) ayudar (a + *inf.*)
    help each other ayudarse
Henry Enrique
her *adj.* su(s); su(s) *or* el (la, los, las) . . . de ella
her *dir. obj.* la; *indir. obj.* le; *after prep.* ella
here aquí
    come by here pasar por aquí
    here (it) is aquí (lo) tienes (tiene Ud.)
hers *pron.* (el) suyo, (la) suya, (los) suyos, (las) suyas *or* el (la, los, las) de ella

highway   la carretera
him *dir. and indir. obj.* le; *after prep.* él
his *adj.*   su(s); su(s) *or* el (la, los, las) . . . de él;
    pron. (el) suyo, (la) suya, (los) suyos, (las)
    suyas *or* el (la, los, las) de él
  of his   suyo(s), -a(s), de él
hockey   el hockey
  women's hockey teams   equipos de hockey
    femeninos (de muchachas)
home   la casa
  (be) at home   (estar) en casa
  (go) home   (ir) a casa
  leave home   salir de casa
hope   esperar
hot   caliente
hour   la hora
house   la casa
  country house   casa de campo
how?   ¿cómo?
  how do you (*pl.*) **like (the house)?**   ¿qué les
    parece (la casa)?
  how long?   ¿cuánto tiempo?
  how much?   ¿cuánto, -a?
  how old is (he)?   ¿cuántos años tiene (él)?
  how + *adj. or adv.*!   ¡qué . . . !; + *verb*
    ¡cuánto . . . !
  how (pretty) (she) is   lo (bonita *or* hermosa)
    que es (ella)
hundred: **a (one) —,**   ciento, (*before nouns and*
  mil) cien
hungry: **be —,**   tener hambre
hurry: **be in a —,**   tener prisa
hurry (up)   apurarse, darse prisa
hurt   doler (ue)
  does your (throat) hurt?   ¿le duele a Ud. (la
    garganta)?
  his throat hurts   le duele la garganta
  my leg hurts   me duele la pierna
husks: **corn —,**   las hojas de la mazorca del maíz

I

I   yo
Ibero-American   iberoamericano, -a
ice   el hielo

idea   la idea
if   si
ill   enfermo, -a, malo, -a
illiteracy   el analfabetismo
imagine   imaginarse
important   importante
  it is important   es importante, importa
  the important thing   lo importante
impossible   imposible
  the impossible   lo imposible
in   en, de, a, por; (*after a superlative*) de
  in order to *prep.*   para
income   los ingresos
increase   el aumento; aumentar, crecer
industrialization   la industrialización
Inez   Inés
information   los informes
ingredient   el ingrediente
insist that   insistir en que
instead of   en vez de
institution   la institución (*pl.* instituciones)
intend   pensar (ie) + *inf.*
interest   el interés
interesting   interesante
intermission   el intermedio
international   internacional
into   a, en
investments   las inversiones
invitation   la invitación (*pl.* invitaciones)
invite   invitar (a + *inf.*)
it *dir. obj.* lo (*m. and neuter*), la (*f.*); *indir. obj.*
  le; (*usually omitted as subject*) él (*m.*),
  ella (*f.*); *after prep.* él (*m.*), ella (*f.*)
item: **news —,**   la noticia

J

Jane   Juanita
January   enero
javelin throw: **women's —,**   lanzamiento de
  jabalina femenino
Jim   Jaime
job   el puesto
John   Juan
Johnny   Juanito

July julio
June junio
just: have —, acabar de + *inf.*

K

kind la clase
know (*facts*) saber
  I don't know no lo sé
  know how to saber + *inf.*

L

laboratory el laboratorio
lack faltar
  be lacking faltar
  is there anything lacking? ¿falta algo?
lady: young —, la señorita, la joven
language la lengua
large grande
  the larger (largest) one (*m.*) el más grande
  the larger ones (*m.*) los más grandes
last pasado, -a, (*in a series*) último, -a
  during these last few days en estos últimos días
  last night anoche
  of the last few years de los últimos años
  the (this) last one (*m.*) el (este) último
late tarde
latter: the —, éste, ésta (-os, -as)
Law el Derecho
lawyer el abogado
learn aprender (a + *inf.*), (*find out*) saber
leave salir (de + *obj.*), partir (de + *obj.*), irse, marcharse (de + *obj.*)
  leave for salir (partir) para
  leave home salir de casa
lecture la conferencia
lecturer el conferenciante
leg la pierna
  my leg hurts me duele la pierna
lend prestar
less menos
lesson la lección (*pl.* lecciones)
let dejar, permitir

let (have) *indir. command* que + *pres. subj.*
let me + *verb* déjeme (permítame) Ud. *or* déjame (permíteme) + *inf.*
let's (let us) + *verb* vamos a + *inf.*, *or first pl. pres. subj.*
let's not go no vayamos
letter la carta
lettuce la lechuga
level el nivel
  at all levels en todos los niveles
library la biblioteca
  at the library en la biblioteca
licentiate el licenciado
light la luz (*pl.* luces)
like como; gustar, (*person*) querer (a)
  how do you like (the house)? ¿qué te (le) parece (la casa)?
  (I) should like (me) gustaría, (yo) quisiera
  like better (best, more) gustar más, preferir (ie, i)
listen (to) escuchar
little (*quantity*) poco, -a
  a little un poco
live vivir
long largo, -a
  be very long in tardar mucho en
  how long (have you been playing)? ¿cuánto tiempo hace (que Ud. toca)?
  (she) has not seen him for a long time hace mucho tiempo que (ella) no le ve
  wait longer esperar más
  (we had been waiting) for a long time hacía mucho tiempo (que esperábamos)
look at mirar
  look at each other mirarse
look for buscar
lose perder (ie)
louder: talk —, hablar más alto
Louis Luis
Louise Luisa
love querer (a)
  love each other quererse
lower (*lights*) apagar
lucky: be (very) —, tener (mucha) suerte
  how lucky (we have been)! ¡qué suerte (hemos tenido)!

lunch   el almuerzo
  eat lunch   almorzar (ue), tomar el almuerzo
  for lunch   para el almuerzo

M

madam   señora, señorita
  (my) dear madam   muy señora (señorita) mía, estimada señora (señorita)
made *adj.*   hecho, -a
magazine   la revista
make   hacer; (*goal*) marcar
  make fun of   burlarse de
  make the trip   hacer el viaje (la excursión)
  make up one's mind   decidirse
man   el hombre
manufactured   manufacturado, -a
many   muchos, -as
  as (so) many ... as   tantos, -as ... como
  so many people   tanta gente, tantas personas
map   el mapa
March   marzo
Margaret   Margarita
maritime   marítimo, -a
Martha   Marta
marvelous   maravilloso, -a
Mary   María
masses (*people*)   las masas
match (*game*)   el partido
matter: that — (of Robert)   lo (de Roberto)
  what's the matter with (Paul)?   ¿qué tiene (Pablo)? ¿qué le pasa a (Pablo)?
may *indir. command* (*wish*)   que + *pres. subj.*; *sign of pres. subj.*; poder
  it may be that   puede (ser) que
  may I wait here?   ¿puedo esperar aquí?
  you may sit down   Ud(s). puede(n) sentarse
May   mayo
me *dir. and indir. obj.*   me; *after prep.* mí
  with me   conmigo
meat   la carne
Medicine   la Medicina
meet   encontrar (ue), (*gather*) reunirse, (*be introduced to*) conocer
meeting   la reunión (*pl.* reuniones)

Mexican   mexicano, -a
Mexico   México
  Mexico City   México, D.F.; la ciudad de México
midnight   la medianoche
Mike   Miguel
mind: make up one's —,   decidirse
mine *pron.*   (el) mío, (la) mía, (los) míos, (las) mías
  of mine *adj.*   mío(s), -a(s)
ministry   el ministerio
minute   el minuto
miss   perder (ie)
Miss   (la) señorita, Srta.
missing: be —,   faltar
  the one who is missing   el que falta
mistaken: be —,   equivocarse
model   el modelo
modernize   modernizar
moment   el momento
  at that moment   en ese (aquel) momento
  at this moment   en este momento
money   el dinero
month   el mes
more   más
morning   la mañana
  in the morning   por la mañana
  (yesterday) morning   (ayer) por la mañana
most   más
  most (of)   la mayoría de, la mayor parte de
mother   la madre, la mamá
mountains   las montañas, la sierra
movie   el cine
  movie camera   cámara de cine
moving *adj.*   impresionante
Mr.   (el) señor, Sr.
  Mr. and Mrs. (Díaz)   los señores (Díaz)
Mrs.   (la) señora, Sra.
much *adj.*   mucho, -a; *adv.* mucho
  how much?   ¿cuánto, -a?
  so much (as) *adv.*   tanto (como)
  so much + *noun* (+ as)   tanto, -a ... (como)
  too much *adv.*   demasiado
  very much *adv.*   mucho, muchísimo
muddy: it was very —,   había mucho lodo
music   la música

musical musical
musician el músico
must deber, haber de + *inf.*, tener que + *inf.*;
   for probability use future (cond., future
   perfect) or deber de + *inf.*
  one must remember hay que recordar
mutual mutuo, -a
my mi(s), mío, -a

N

name el nombre
named: be —, llamarse
nap la siesta
  take a nap dormir (ue, u) la siesta
national nacional
nationalistic nacionalista (*m. and f.*)
near *prep.* cerca de
nearby *adv.* cerca
necessary necesario, -a, preciso, -a
  be necessary to haber que (ser necesario *or*
    preciso) + *inf.*
need la necesidad; necesitar
never nunca, jamás
new nuevo, -a
  New York Nueva York
  what's new? ¿qué hay de nuevo?
news item la noticia
news section la sección de noticias
newspaper el periódico
next próximo, -a
  next (year) (el año) que viene, (el año)
    próximo
night la noche
  last night anoche
  tomorrow night mañana por la noche
nine nueve
  nine o'clock section la sección de las nueve
nineteen diecinueve
no, not *adv.* no; *adj.* ninguno, -a, (*before m.*
  sing. nouns) ningún; *often not translated*
  no one nadie
nobody nadie
none ninguno, -a
noon el mediodía

  at noon al mediodía
  before noon antes del mediodía
not no
  not at all bad (no) . . . nada malo, -a
notebook el cuaderno
nothing nada, ninguna cosa
  nothing special nada de particular
novel la novela
November noviembre
now ahora
  right now ahora mismo
nowadays hoy día
number el número

O

obtain conseguir (i, i), obtener
o'clock: at (ten) —, a las (diez)
  before (four) o'clock antes de las (cuatro)
  the (ten) o'clock (bus) el (autobús) de las
    (diez)
October octubre
of de, en
off: take —, (*someone*) quitar, (*oneself*) quitarse
offer ofrecer
office la oficina
often a menudo, muchas veces
oil: olive —, el aceite
old viejo, -a
  how old is (he)? ¿cuántos años tiene (él)?
older mayor
  older people los mayores
olive oil el aceite
on en, sobre
  on (Sundays) los (domingos)
  on time a tiempo
  put on (*oneself*) ponerse
once: at —, en seguida
one un, uno, una; *indef. subject* se, uno
  no one nadie
  one must (remember) hay que (recordar)
  some one (of them) alguno, -a (de ellos, -as)
  that one (*near person addressed*) ése, ésa,
    (*distant*) aquél, aquélla
  the last one (*m.*) el último

the one in (of, with) el (la) de
the one(s) who (which, that) el (la) que, *pl.*
   los (las) que, quien(es) (*persons only*)
this one éste, ésta
(visit) one another (visitar)se
which one(s)? ¿cuál(es)?
onion la cebolla
only sólo, solamente, no . . . más que
   not only . . . but no sólo . . . sino que
open abrir
oppose oponerse a
or o, (*before* o-, ho-) u
orchestra la orquesta
order: in — that *conj.* para que, a fin de que
   in order to *prep.* para
other otro, -a
   (see) each other (ver)se
   the other one el otro, la otra
ought: (I) — to (yo) debiera
our nuestro, -a
ours *pron.* (el) nuestro, (la) nuestra, (los)
   nuestros, (las) nuestras
   of ours *adj.* nuestro(s), -a(s)
out: carry —, efectuar, llevar a cabo
   try out probar (ue)
over sobre

P

package el paquete
page la página, (*printing*) la plana
   first page (*printing*) la primera plana
   last page la última página
paragraph el párrafo
parents los padres, los papás
park el parque
part la parte, el elemento
   in part en parte
   take part tomar parte
participate participar
participation la participación
past: half — (seven) (las siete) y media
patio el patio
Paul Pablo
pay (for) pagar

pay (a dollar) for pagar (un dólar) por
peace la paz
   Peace Corps el Cuerpo de Paz
people la gente (*requires sing. verb*), las personas; *indef. subject* se, uno
   older people los mayores
   so many people tanta gente, tantas personas
   young people los jóvenes
pepper el chile, el pimiento
   black pepper la pimienta
   stuffed pepper el chile relleno
percent por ciento, por 100
perhaps tal vez, quizá(s), acaso
permit permitir, dejar
person la persona
   persons who las personas que, los que
Peru el Perú
Philip Felipe
photo la foto
   take photos sacar fotos
photograph la fotografía
   take photographs sacar fotografías
physical físico, -a
pick up (one) buscar a (uno)
pickled fish el escabeche
picture el cuadro
pie: small —, la empanada
place (*job*) el puesto
plan el plan, el intento
plane el avión (*pl.* aviones)
play (*game*) jugar (ue) (a + *obj.*), (*music*) tocar
player el jugador
   record player el (los) tocadiscos
pleasant agradable
please haga(n) Ud(s). el favor de + *inf.*, (*after
   request*) por favor
poetry la poesía
political político, -a
pool (*swimming*) la piscina
poor pobre
   very poor hamburger hamburguesa malísima
popular popular
population la población
pork la carne de cerdo
   ground pork carne picada de cerdo
Portuguese (*language*) el portugués

position   el puesto
possible   posible
  the soonest possible   lo más pronto posible
power   el poder
practice   practicar
prefer   preferir (ie, i), gustar más a uno
prepare   preparar
preserves   las conservas
  fruit preserves   conservas de frutas
pretty   bonito, -a, hermoso, -a
primary   primario, -a
principal   principal
probably   probablemente; *use future, cond., or*
  future perfect tense
problem   el problema
product   el producto
production   la producción
professional   profesional
professor   el profesor, la profesora
program   el programa
progress   el progreso
project   el proyecto
projector   el proyector
promise   prometer
proportionately   proporcionalmente
propose   proponer
provided that *conj.*   con tal (de) que, siempre
  que
publicity   la publicidad
publish   publicar
pudding: rice —,   el arroz con leche
purse   la bolsa
put   poner
  let's not put on   no nos pongamos
  put in   meter, poner
  put on (*oneself*)   ponerse
  put on (*someone*)   poner
  put to bed   acostar (ue)

Q

qualify   capacitar
quarter   el cuarto

at a quarter after (eight)   a las (ocho) y cuarto
at a quarter to (seven)   a las (siete) menos
  cuarto
question   la pregunta
quickly   pronto

R

radio (*set*)   el radio
rain   llover (ue)
raisin   la pasa
rapid   rápido, -a
rapidly   rápidamente
rate   el ritmo, el índice
  at any rate   de todos modos
Raymond   Ramón
read   leer
ready   listo, -a
realize   darse cuenta de
reason   la razón (*pl.* razones)
  without any reason at all   sin razón alguna
recall   recordar (ue)
receive   recibir
recommendation   la recomendación (*pl.* recomendaciones)
record (*phonograph*)   el disco
  record player   el (los) tocadiscos
recorder: tape —,   la grabadora (de cinta)
red   rojo, -a
  the red ones (*f.*)   las rojas
reform   la reforma
refrigerator   la nevera
refuse to   *negative pret. of* querer + *inf.*
region   la región (*pl.* regiones)
regional   regional
regret   sentir (ie, i)
  how I regret that!   ¡cuánto siento eso!
related: be — to   relacionarse con
remain (*be left*)   quedar
remember   recordar (ue)
repeat   repetir (i, i)
reply   contestar, responder
report   el informe
represent   representar
representative   el representante

residence hall   la residencia
  student residence hall   residencia de estudiantes
rest   descansar
return (*come back*)   volver (ue), regresar; (*give back*) devolver (ue)
review (*article*)   la crítica
rhythm   el ritmo
rice   el arroz
  rice pudding   el arroz con leche
Richard   Ricardo
right   el derecho
  be right   tener razón
  right away (now)   ahora mismo
river   el río
roast(ed)   asado, -a
Robert   Roberto
roll (*class*)   la lista, (*of film*) el rollo
rolled   enrollado, -a
room   el cuarto
roommate   el compañero (la compañera) de cuarto
rose   la rosa
row   la fila
run across   encontrarse (ue) con

S

St. (Louis)   San (Luis)
same   mismo, -a
sandwich   el emparedado
satisfied: be — with   conformarse con
satisfy   satisfacer
sauce   la salsa
say   decir
  I should say so!   ¡ya lo creo!
scarcely   apenas
scholarship   la beca
school   la escuela, (*of university*) la facultad, la escuela
screen   la pantalla
seasoning   el condimento
seat (*someone*)   sentar (ie)
second   segundo, -a
secondary   secundario, -a

secretary   la secretaria
section   la sección (*pl.* secciones)
  news section   sección de noticias
  nine o'clock section   la sección de las nueve
  sports section   sección de deportes
sector   el sector
see   ver
  let's see   (vamos) a ver
seem   parecer
select   escoger
sell   vender
semester   el semestre
send   enviar, mandar
  send for   enviar (mandar) por
sentence   la frase, la oración (*pl.* oraciones)
September   septiembre
series   la serie
serious   grave
  if it is something serious   si es algo grave
  it is nothing serious   no es nada grave
serve   servir (i, i)
set   el aparato
  television set   el televisor
seven   siete
several   varios, -as
she   ella
shellfish   los mariscos
shirt   la camisa
shoe   el zapato
shopping: go —,   ir de compras
short: after a — time   al poco rato (tiempo)
short story   el cuento
shot   el tiro
should   *sign of cond. and imp. subj.*; deber, (*softened statement*) debiera
shout   gritar
  shout at each other   gritarse
show   enseñar (a + *inf.*), mostrar (ue)
since   como
  it is fifteen minutes since (it) began to play   hace quince minutos que empezó a tocar *or* empezó . . . hace . . .
sing   cantar
sir   señor
  dear sir   muy señor mío, estimado señor
sister   la hermana

sit down   sentarse (ie)

   let's sit down   vamos a sentarnos, sentémonos

site   el sitio

six   seis

skate   el patín (*pl.* patines); patinar

ski   el esquí (*pl.* esquíes); esquiar

skier   el esquiador

sky   el cielo

sleep   dormir (ue, u)

sleepy: be (very) —,   tener (mucho) sueño

slide   la transparencia

slope   la ladera

slowly   despacio

small   pequeño, -a

   the small one (*m.*)   el pequeño

   the smallest one (*f.*)   la más pequeña

   this very small one (*m.*)   este pequeñito

snow   la nieve

so (*with adj. or adv.*)   tan

   believe so   creer que sí

   so + *adj. or adv.* + **as**   tan . . . como

   so much *adv.*   tanto

   so that *conj.*   de modo (manera) que

social   social

solve   resolver (ue)

some *adj. and pron.*   alguno, -a, (*before m. sing. nouns*) algún; *pl.* algunos, -as, unos, -as; (*before numerals*) unos, -as; *often not translated*

someone   alguien

   someone (of them)   alguno, -a (de ellos, -as)

song   la canción (*pl.* canciones)

soon   pronto

   as soon as *conj.*   en cuanto, así que, luego que

   the soonest possible   lo más pronto posible

sorry: be (very) —,   sentir (ie, i) (mucho)

soup   la sopa

source   la fuente

south   el sur

   South America   la América del Sur

southwest   el suroeste

space   el espacio

Spain   España

Spanish *adj.*   español, -ola; (*language*) el español

in Spanish   en español

Spanish America   la América española, Hispanoamérica

Spanish-American *adj.*   hispanoamericano, -a

Spanish (Department)   (departamento) de español

speak   hablar

   speak up   hablar más alto

special: nothing —,   nada de particular

speed   la velocidad

   at full speed   a toda velocidad

spend (*time*)   pasar

sport   el deporte

   sports section   la sección de deportes

   winter sports   los deportes de invierno

sportswoman   la deportista

square   la plaza

start (to)   comenzar (ie) (a + *inf.*), empezar (ie) (a + *inf.*)

state   el estado

   United States   los Estados Unidos

stay   quedarse

steep   macerar

still   todavía

stimulate   estimular

stop   la parada

store   la tienda

story: short —,   el cuento

strange   extraño, -a

street   la calle

strong   fuerte

student   el (la) estudiante, el alumno

   art student   estudiante de arte

   Student Center   Centro de Estudiantes

   student dormitory   residencia de estudiantes

study   estudiar

stuffed   relleno, -a

such (a)   tal; tan

   such as   tal(es) como

   such definite rhythms   ritmos tan definidos

sufficiently   suficientemente

suit   el traje

suitcase   la maleta

summer   el verano

   all summer   todo el verano

Sunday   el domingo

on Sunday(s) el (los) domingo(s)

sunny: it is not —, no hace (hay) sol

supper: eat —, cenar

suppose suponer, *for conjecture use future or cond.*

supposed: be — to haber de + *inf.*

sure seguro, -a

  be sure that estar seguro, -a de que

surprise la sorpresa; sorprender

symphony *adj.* sinfónico, -a

  symphony concert concierto de música sinfónica

system el sistema

T

table la mesa

taco el taco

take tomar, (*carry*) llevar, (*photos*) sacar

  take a nap dormir (ue, u) la siesta

  take a trip hacer un viaje (una excursión)

  take a walk dar un paseo (una vuelta)

  take lunch almorzar (ue), tomar el almuerzo

  take off (*from someone*) quitar

  take off (*from oneself*) quitarse

  take (two hours) to tardar (dos horas) en + *inf.*

talk hablar

  talk louder hablar más alto

  talk on the telephone hablar por teléfono

tall alto, -a

tamale el tamal

tape la cinta; grabar

  tape recorder la grabadora (de cinta)

tea el té

teach enseñar

teacher el profesor, la profesora

team el equipo

  Chilean women's (basketball) team el (básquet) femenino chileno

telephone el teléfono

  talk on the telephone hablar por teléfono

television set el televisor

tell decir

  I shall tell her (it) se lo diré

temperature la temperatura

ten diez

territory el territorio

textbook el libro de texto

than que, (*before numeral*) de, (*before clause*) del (de la, de los, de las) que, de lo que

thank (one for) dar las gracias (a uno por)

that *adj.* (*near person addressed*) ese, esa (-os, -as), (*distant*) aquel, aquella (-os, -as); *pron.* ése, ésa (-os, -as), aquél, aquélla (-os, -as), (*neuter*) eso, aquello; *relative pron.* que

  that of el (la) de

the el, la, los, las

  the (best thing) lo (mejor)

theater el teatro

  at the theater en el teatro

their *adj.* su(s), de ellos, -as

theirs *pron.* (el) suyo, (la) suya, (los) suyos, (las) suyas, *or* (el, la, los, las) de ellos, -as

  of theirs *adj.* suyo(s), -a(s), de ellos, -as

them *dir. obj.* los, las; *indir. obj.* les, se; *after prep.* ellos, -as

theme el tema

then luego, después

there (*near person addressed*) ahí, (*distant*) allí

  that there is (may be) que haya

  there is (are) hay

  there would be habría

therefore por eso, por lo tanto

these *adj.* estos, estas; *pron.* éstos, éstas

they ellos, ellas

thing la cosa

  the best thing lo mejor

think pensar (ie), creer

  I think it (*f.*) is wonderful! ¡me parece magnífica!

third el tercio

thirsty: be —, tener sed

this *adj.* este, esta; *pron.* this (one) éste, ésta, (*neuter*) esto

Thomas Tomás

those *adj.* (*near person addressed*) esos (-as), (*distant*) aquellos (-as); *pron.* ésos (-as), aquéllos (-as)

  those which los (las) que

  those who los (las) que, quienes

though: even —, aunque
thought el pensamiento
three tres
thrill entusiasmar
throat la garganta
  does your throat hurt? ¿le duele a Ud. la garganta?
  his throat hurts le duele la garganta
through por
throw (into) echar (en, a)
throw: women's javelin —, el lanzamiento de jabalina femenino
ticket el billete
time (*in general sense*) el tiempo; (*of day*) la hora; (*series*) la vez (*pl.* veces)
  after a short time al poco rato (tiempo)
  at times a veces
  at what time? ¿a qué hora?
  have a (very) good time divertirse (ie, i) (mucho)
  have time to tener tiempo para + *inf.*
  in our time de nuestros días
  on time a tiempo
  (she has not seen him) for a long time hace (mucho) tiempo (que ella no le ve)
  we had been waiting for a long time hacía mucho tiempo que esperábamos
tired cansado, -a
to a, de, con, para, que
  (at a quarter) to (seven) (a las siete) menos (cuarto)
  have to tener que + *inf.*
  in order to *prep.* para
  to (Philip's) a casa de (Felipe)
today hoy
  today's game el partido de hoy
together juntos, -as
Tom Tomás
tomato el tomate
tomorrow mañana
  tomorrow (night) mañana (por la noche)
  tomorrow's newspaper el periódico de mañana
tone el tono
tonight esta noche
Tony Antonio

too también
  too much *adv.* demasiado
tostada la tostada
tournament el torneo
towards hacia
Track and Field Games Juegos Atléticos
trade el comercio
  foreign trade comercio exterior
traditional tradicional
travel viajar
trial la prueba
trip el viaje, la excursión (*pl.* excursiones)
  make *or* take the (a) trip hacer el (un) viaje (la *and* una excursión)
trouble: don't go to so much —, no se moleste Ud. tanto
true: be —, ser verdad
try (out) probar (ue)
  try to tratar de + *inf.*
tube el tubo
turn in entregar
turn off apagar
turn on (*radio, television*) poner
twenty veinte
two dos
  the two los (las) dos
type el tipo
typical típico, -a

U

uncle el tío
understand comprender, entender (ie)
understanding el entendimiento
unfortunately desgraciadamente, por desgracia
unification la unificación
United States los Estados Unidos
university *adj.* universitario, -a
university la universidad
  university newspaper periódico de la universidad
unjust injusto, -a
unless *conj.* a menos que
until *prep.* hasta; *conj.* hasta que
up: get —, levantarse

wake up (*oneself*) despertarse (ie)

upon + *pres. part.* al + *inf.*

urgent urgente

us *dir. and indir. obj.* nos; *after prep.* nosotros, -as

use emplear, usar

useful útil

V

vacation las vacaciones

very *adv.* muy, mucho

  very much mucho, muchísimo

vinegar el vinagre

visit visitar

W

wait (for) esperar

  wait longer (for) esperar más

  we had been waiting for a long time hacía mucho tiempo que esperábamos

wake up (*oneself*) despertarse (ie)

walk el paseo, la vuelta; andar

  take a walk dar un paseo (una vuelta)

want querer, desear

wash lavar, (*oneself*) lavarse

watch (wristwatch) el reloj (*de pulsera*)

  gold watch reloj de oro

water el agua (*f.*)

way: by the —, a propósito

  come this way venir (pasar) por aquí

we nosotros, -as

weakness la debilidad

wealth la riqueza

wear llevar

weather el tiempo

  be (bad) weather hacer (mal) tiempo

Wednesday el miércoles

week la semana

  all week toda la semana

  every week todas las semanas

  next week la semana próxima (que viene)

welcome: you are —, de nada

well *adv.* bien

  as well as así como

  (students) as well as (educators) tanto (los estudiantes) como (los educadores)

what *pron.* lo que

what? ¿qué?

what a . . . ! ¡qué . . . !

  what a fast game! ¡qué partido más (tan) rápido!

whatever lo que

when cuando

when? ¿cuándo?

where? ¿dónde? (*with verbs of motion*) ¿adónde?

whether si

which *relative pron.* que, el (la) cual, los (las) cuales, el (la, los, las) que

  that which lo que

  the one(s) which el (la) cual, los (las) cuales, el (la, los, las) que

  those which los (las) que

  which (fact) lo cual, lo que

which? ¿qué? ¿cuál?

  which one(s)? ¿cuál(es)?

while *conj.* mientras (que); *noun* el rato

white blanco, -a

  the white one el blanco, la blanca

who *relative pron.* que, quien(es), el (la) cual, los (las) cuales, el (la, los, las) que

  he (the one) who quien, el (la) que

  those (the ones) who quienes, los (las) que

who? ¿quién(es)?

whom que, a quien(es)

whom? ¿quién(es)? ¿a quién(es)?

whose *relative adj.* cuyo(s), -a(s)

whose? ¿de quién(es)?

why? (*reason*) ¿por qué?

will querer; *sign of future tense*

win ganar, vencer

window la ventana

winter el invierno

  winter sports los deportes de invierno

wish querer, desear

with con, de, en

without *prep.* sin; *conj.* sin que

woman la mujer

women's javelin throw lanzamiento de jabalina femenino

women's teams equipos de muchachas (mujeres)

wonder *for conjecture use future or cond.*

wonderful magnífico, -a

word la palabra

work trabajar

by working trabajando

worry (about) preocuparse (con, por)

would *sign of imp. or cond. tense*

(he) would not (lend) no quiso (prestar)

would that . . . ! ¡ojalá (que) + *subj.*!

wrap (with) envolver (ue) (de)

wristwatch el reloj de pulsera

write escribir

written escrito, -a

Y

year el año

next year el año próximo (que viene)

of the last few years de los últimos años

yellow amarillo, -a

the yellow one (*f.*) la amarilla

yes sí

yesterday ayer

yesterday (afternoon) ayer (por la tarde)

yet todavía

not yet todavía no

you (*fam. sing.*) tú, (*pl.*) vosotros, -as

with you contigo

you (*formal*) *subject pron. and after prep.* usted (Ud.), ustedes (Uds.)

young joven (*pl.* jóvenes)

young lady la señorita, la joven

young people los jóvenes

younger más joven, menor

your *adj.* (*fam.*) tu(s), vuestro(s), -a(s); (*formal*) su(s), de Ud. (Uds.)

yours *pron.* (*fam.*) (el) tuyo, (la) tuya, (los) tuyos, (las) tuyas, (el) vuestro, (la) vuestra, (los) vuestros, (las) vuestras; (*formal*) (el) suyo, (la) suya, (los) suyos, (las) suyas *or* el (la, los, las) de Ud. (Uds.)

of yours *adj.* (*fam.*) tuyo(s), -a(s), vuestro(s), -a(s); (*formal*) suyo(s), suya(s), de Ud. (Uds.)

INDEX

a: + el, 96; omission of personal a, 44, 183; personal a, 44, 102, 179, 183; preposition, 144; verbs which take a before an infinitive, 144, 332; verbs which take a before an object, 332

abbreviations and signs, 8 note, 59, 279 note, 309

absolute: superlative, 239; use of the past participle, 259–260

address: forms of, 8, 11, 59–60, 64

adjective clauses, 178–180; subjunctive in, 182–183

adjectives: agreement of, 38, 40, 117–118, 180, 217, 223, 237, 259, 310–312; comparison of, 237–239; demonstrative, 214–215; feminine of, 117–118; forms of, 117–118; past participle used as, 38, 40–41, 259; position of, 35 note, 37 note, 118–120, 237, 239; possessive (short forms), 217–218, (long forms), 217–218; shortened forms of, 93 note, 102–104, 119–120, 310–311; used as adverbs, 265; used as nouns, 223; with estar, 37–38, 40–41, 123, 259; with ser, 39–41, 123

adverbial clauses: subjunctive in, 200–202, 213 note

adverbs: adjectives used as, 265; algo and nada used as, 104; comparison of, 238–239; formation of, 4 note, 12 note, 265

agreement: of adjectives, 38, 40, 117–118, 180, 217, 223, 237, 259, 310–312; of cardinal numerals, 310–311; of ordinal numerals, 311–312

al: + infinitive, 142

alphabet: Spanish, 292

andar: with present participle, 261

"any," 97, 102–104

aquél, "the former," 216

article, definite: contraction of el with a, de, 96; el with feminine nouns, 96; for the possessive, 95, 184; forms, 94; in comparison of adjectives, 237–238; in dates, 312; lo, see neuter lo; omission of, 95–96, 219; omission with names of rulers and popes, 312; omission with seasons, 156 note; summary of uses, 94–96; to form possessive pronouns, 219; used as a demonstrative, 216; used to form compound relative pronouns, 180; used with adjectives to form nouns, 223; with name of a language, 95–96, 96 note

article, indefinite: forms of, 97; omission of, 97–98, 311; summary of uses, 97–98

"become," 64–65

breath-group, 16, 26–27, 57–58, 156–157, 176–177, 299–302

"by," translated by para, 257; translated by por, 257; with passive, 39–40, 257, 259–260; with present participle, 261

caer: forms of, 19–20, 30, 320

"can," 265–266

capitalization, 303

-car verbs, 8–9, 19, 324

cardinal numerals, 310–311; in dates, 312; used to express time of day, 313

-cer and -cir verbs, 325

cien(to), 120, 310–311

classroom expressions, 304–305

commands: familiar plural, 246; familiar singular, 11; formal direct, 8–9, 158; indirect, 165; irregular familiar command forms, 11, 158, 246; object pronouns with, 60, 165

commands and requests: intonation patterns in, 27

comparison: of adjectives, 237–239; of adverbs, 238–239; of equality, 241

compound nouns, 120–121

compound tenses, 29–30, 177–178, 316–317, 319

con: conmigo, contigo, consigo, 62; verbs which take con before an infinitive or an object, 332

conditional: for probability, 141; imperfect indicative of ir a for, 138; irregular forms of, 28, 319; perfect for probability, 141; sentences, 138, 203–204; regular forms of, 315; uses of, 78 note, 139

conocer: uses of, 45, 79, 79 note

continuar: forms of, 326; with present participle, 261

contractions: a + el, 96; de + el, 96

contrary-to-fact sentences, 203–204, 221, 267

"could," 266

creer: forms of, 19–20, 326

¿cuál? 125

cualquiera, 104

¡cuánto! 126

cuyo, 180

quizá(s), acaso, 220-221; future, 316 note; imperfect, 196-198, 316, 319; in adjective clauses, 182-183; in adverbial clauses, 200-202; in familiar commands, 11, 246; in indirect commands, 165; in noun clauses, 158, 159-164; in formal commands, 8-9; in si-clauses, 138, 203-204; in softened statement, 221; pluperfect, 198; present, 158, 315, 319; present perfect, 177-178, 317; theory of, 157-158; use of subjunctive tenses, 157-158, 198-199

superlative: absolute, 239; comparative, 237-239

suyo, -a: clarification of, 218; clarification of el suyo, la suya, etc., 219

"take," 82-83

tener: idioms with, 122-123; omission of personal a after, 44; special meanings in preterit of, 18, 79-80

tenses, *see* present, etc.

"than," 102, 237-238

time: of day, 39, 79, 95, 313

tomar, 82

triphthongs, 299

tú: use of, 11, 59-60

u, "or," 262

-uar verbs, 326

-uir verbs: forms of, 20, 326

uno: used as indefinite subject, 42

usted(es): use of, 8, 59-60, 246, 278 note

venir: with present participle, 261

ver: followed by infinitive, 143

verbs: *see* each separately and tables in Appendix D; followed by infinitive without a preposition, 45, 143-144, 331; governing prepositions, 144-145, 331-333; requiring the indirect object of a person, 82, 143, 159-160, 184; stem-changing, 6-7, 21, 31, 197-198, 327-330; whose meanings change when used reflexively, 64-65, 333-334; with changes in spelling, 323-325; with special endings, 325-327; with special meanings in the preterit, 18, 79-80, 139

verse: for estar, 38

vosotros, -as: use of, 59-60, 64, 246

weather: expression of, 122

"will," 138

word order, 8, 35 note, 37 note, 43, 44, 60, 61, 83-84, 102, 143

word stress, 295

words and expressions for the classroom, 304-305; for the laboratory, 305-306

"would," 78, 78 note, 139

—zar verbs, 8-9, 19, 324

PHOTOGRAPH CREDITS

408

COLOR SECTION

(Between pages 290 and 291)

"Jaguar's head" (detail), feather mosaic made in Peru 900 years ago *Courtesy The Brooklyn Museum, The A. Augustus Healy Fund. Photo by Andreas Feininger*

Aztec painting *Courtesy Museo Nacional de Antropologia, Mexico City. Photo by Bradley Smith*

"Christ in the Garden" by B. de Echave *Courtesy Museo de San Carlos Collection, Instituto Nacional de Bellas Artes, Mexico City*

"Virgin and Child Crowned" by Miguel Cabrera *Courtesy Philadelphia Museum of Art Dr. Robert H. Lamborn Collection. Photo by Alfred J. Wyatt*

"The Birth of Christ," anonymous *Courtesy Instituto Nacional de Bellas Artes, Mexico City*

"Composition with Clock" by Diego Rivera *Courtesy Museo Nacional de Bellas Artes, Buenos Aires, Argentina*

"Revolution, Germination" (mural) by Diego Rivera *Courtesy Escuela Nacional de Agricultura, Chapingo, Mexico. Photo by Bradley Smith*

"Revolutionists" by J. C. Orozco *Courtesy Museo Nacional de Arte Moderno, Mexico City. Photo by Bradley Smith*

"Echo of a Scream" by D. A. Siqueiros *Courtesy The Museum of Modern Art, New York, gift of Edward M. M. Warburg*

"The Fruit Vendors" by R. Tamayo *Courtesy Albright-Knox Art Gallery, Buffalo, New York, gift of Seymour H. Knox*

"The Call of the Revolution" by R. Tamayo *Courtesy Collection of Pascual Gutierrez Roldan. Photo by Bradley Smith*

"Water Bearers (Aguadoras)" by Jose Sabogal *Courtesy San Francisco Museum of Art, gift of Mr. and Mrs. Garfield Warner*

"The Young King" by C. Merida *Courtesy Carlos Merida, from the collection of Mr. and Mrs. Stanley Markus*

"The Eternal Present" by Wilfredo Lam *Courtesy Museum of Art, Rhode Island School of Design, Providence, R.I.*

Lithograph from the *Popol-Vuh*, Edition illustrated by Carlos Merida *Courtesy Carlos Merida*

"Constructive Art" by J. Torres Garcia *Courtesy Museo Nacional de Bellas Artes, Buenos Aires, Argentina*

"1943 America" by J. Torres Garcia *Courtesy Museum of Art, Rhode Island School of Design, Providence, R.I.*

"The Sun in the Moon" by R. Vergara Grez *Courtesy R. Vergara Grez and Antonio R. Romera, Santiago, Chile*

"Dynamic Symmetry" by R. Vergara Grez *Courtesy R. Vergara Grez and Antonio R. Romera, Santiago, Chile*

"Green and Black Immaterial Curves" (wood and metal construction) by J. Soto *Courtesy Museum of Art, Rhode Island School of Design, Providence, R.I.*

"In Violet" by E. Mac Entyre *Courtesy Museum of Art, Rhode Island School of Design, Providence, R.I.*

"Confession of an Iconoclastic Sea Urchin" by P. Friedeberg *Courtesy Mexican Nacional Tourist Council, and Galería Antonio Souza, Mexico City*

"Self-portrait" by J. L. Cuevas *Courtesy José Luis Cuevas, and Galería de Arte Mexicano*